MW01026954

Communication, Conflict, and the Management of Difference

Stephen Littlejohn
Kathy Domenici

Domenici Littlejohn, Inc.

WAVELAND
PRESS, INC.
Long Grove, Illinois

For information about this book, contact:
Waveland Press, Inc.
4180 IL Route 83, Suite 101
Long Grove, IL 60047-9580
(847) 634-0081
info@waveland.com
www.waveland.com

About the Cover

One of the authors, Stephen Littlejohn, photographed the café scene in Copenhagen. We selected this image because it communicates a common feeling experienced in conflict while also expressing change and challenge. The café was just minutes before a bustling, busy, and happy place and later will return to this. The sun will shine there again. The scene, like conflict, is a temporal state and constantly changing. The surrounding graphics and font were designed to put a constructive frame on the photo that opens up how the picture might be understood. We hope you find this contrast intriguing and provocative. The piece has lots to say and will be limited only by the imagination of the viewer.

10-digit ISBN 1-57766-503-1
13-digit ISBN 978-1-57766-503-8

Printed in the United States of America

7   6   5   4   3

Contents

Contents

Preface

People tend to think of conflict as an uncomfortable state that they should resolve or escape as soon as possible. Yet conflict is really a manifestation of the inevitable and ongoing process of managing difference. Once we understand that the human condition is constructed through a process of making distinctions, we come to see that conflict management is a continuous task of social life. The world of difference becomes the larger context in which conflict can be understood and managed.

Conflict exists when differences are challenging, when they require work to make them livable. Conflict, then, is not an objective state, but a way of experiencing a difference that requires some effort on the part of those who must live through it. The work of conflict involves making decisions about how to act within the situation and how to respond to the actions of others. It also means engaging in the potentially hard work of interpreting, thinking in new ways, and creating effective resources for change. The actions, responses, and interpretive schemes that emerge among the parties in a conflict determine whether the management of difference moves toward harm or toward value.

This book is based on the beliefs that human beings are characterized by difference, that difference is not trivial, and that it can be a source of great benefit to individuals, relationships, and communities. At the same time, human differences can lead to crippling harm if handled inappropriately. People understand and manage difference through social interaction, which makes communication the key process in situations where misunderstood differences could lead to conflict. We can respond to difference, then, in ways that enhance or damage our lives. This book invites you to engage in a thoughtful dialogue about human difference, conflict, and communication and to join us in finding pathways from harm to value.

Having been communication professors for many years, we understand the constraints and opportunities in college teaching. Most important to us over the years has been a desire, in classroom teaching and writing, to help students make useful connections that build both cognitive understanding and communication skill. We feel it important for students to connect ideas learned in one setting to contexts encountered in other settings, to relate concepts from one course to those of another, and to integrate communication practices across settings from relational to global.

One of the constraints of our field is the division of ideas into segments or levels of practice, which has dominated textbooks and curricula for generations. We hope that in its broad approach, this book accomplishes several things.

- We want readers to understand conflict within an integrated conceptual frame.

- We want readers to understand that conflict processes will permeate all aspects of their lives, not just the relationships that are most central to them at this point in their development.

- We want readers to see the applicability of communication theory across contexts, and

- We want them to develop awareness and reflexivity as they connect theory and practice within a principled life.

Our work in the world of communication and conflict has brought us many stories to tell, some practical tools to use, a variety of complex methods with which to experiment, and an abundance of hope for our personal and collective plight. We offer this book as an invitation to you to join us in this process. As you begin to explore *Communication, Conflict, and the Management of Difference,* you may feel this invitation is somewhat pointed. You may be asked to change or adapt your perspective on the nature and impact of conflict. You may be asked to undertake a new skills orientation, where your communication behaviors will be focused on the nuances of the human condition and how those differences can be managed. You may be asked to look deeper inside yourself, your family, your community, or your world. From whichever vantage point you may be entering this course and this book, we emphasize a common thread. Human beings are amazingly intricate and wonderfully diverse. The elements of this diversity are resources that can equip us to make it through each day. These resources are most effective if we use constructive communication to help us maneuver through the maze of surprises, challenges, struggles, and experiences that are a part of the package of human life.

PART ONE

UNDERSTANDING
CONFLICT

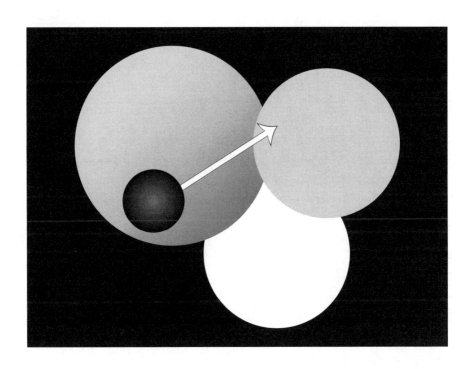

1

Conflict

When Differences Challenge Us

Human life is paradoxical. Our ability to create categories and to make distinctions is both a tremendous resource and a substantial challenge. If you were asked to describe yourself, you probably would not say, "I am a bipedal, social omnivore with an opposable thumb." Instead, your description would report qualities that distinguish you from other human beings. You might describe your personality, role, nationality, personal experiences, religion, or ethnic identity. If asked to say more, you might talk about your values, your interests and goals, your family, your work, and your beliefs. This combination of characteristics makes you unique among all human beings. Yet your identity is determined in large measure by the communities of which you are a part.

Humans need a set of social arrangements, meanings, and symbols—shared within a group—to provide the wherewithal to survive and thrive. Anthropologist Clifford Geertz puts the matter clearly: "There is no such thing as a human nature independent of culture." Without culture, human beings would be "mental basket cases," or "unworkable monstrosities with very few useful instincts, fewer recognizable sentiments, and no intellect."[1]

Instead of being born with what we need to thrive, we must make the tools of life. Our greatest tools consist of templates for understanding and acting in complex situations. We use language in interaction with other people to create perspectives—ways of seeing complete with value and meaning—and to create forms of action appropriate for these definitions. The interesting thing about these symbolic tools is that they are specific constructions, arising often from very local social groups, which enable survival in whatever situations we negotiate. The heart of human difference is that we have particular ways of understanding and acting on experience that may be different from those of others.

This aspect of the human condition is a blessing and a curse. It is a blessing because it provides the potential for an infinite variety of ways of framing and responding to the experiences we face in our lives. It is a curse because in situations other than the most simple, others may disagree with our opinions about what course of action is best. Disagreement is uncomfortable if we don't know how to address it; we must work with others in establishing appropriate meaning and action. It is a blessing because the numerous perspectives with which we can view any situation provide a rich kit of resources for creative solutions. It is a curse because we often cannot agree on what something should mean or what we should do about it. Society has established a wealth of methods for resolving matters of dispute—a blessing—but human history is replete with the great suffering caused by our inability to see things the same way—a curse.

Differences are to be expected, accepted, even embraced, but they sometimes spill over into a realm of discomfort, challenge, obstacle, and even harm—the world of conflict. Conflict is one manifestation of the inevitable differences that define the human condition. In this introductory chapter, we build a foundation for understanding how human difference is both created and managed through communication. By the end of the chapter, you should have a good general overview of the world of conflict and conflict resolution.

BEGINNING TO THINK ABOUT CONFLICT

Conflict exists when people experience their differences as a problem that needs special action. In other words, differences create an obstacle of some kind that requires some effort to manage. Consider these situations:

Tim is in a quandary. At 40, he wants to start building a nest egg for his retirement, but he also wants a new boat. Should he go for fun now or security later?

Sarah is taking care of her three-year old child, Molly. Molly wants a piece of candy, but Sarah says no, and Molly has a tantrum.

Bill has worked hard for a promotion and thinks he should get it, but his boss, Melinda, chooses someone else for the job. Bill is angry about this and complains bitterly to Melinda.

Kim, a Korean shopkeeper, has trouble with the predominantly Black neighbors around his store. He perceives them as loud and threatening, and they think he is cold and greedy.

Al Qaeda thinks that the United States is imperialistic and destructive to traditional culture. They launch an attack on the U.S. The U.S. views the attack as a vicious threat to its way of life, and a war ensues.

We would clearly identify each of these scenarios as a conflict. In the case of Tim, the conflict is internal, between two competing values, like differing voices in his head pleading their cases. Sarah and Molly are experiencing a difference in goals, and Bill and Melinda have clashing judgments. Kim and his neighbors are experiencing cultural conflict, and the Al Qaeda example illustrates a difference in perception of global threat and responsibility. In each case, many differences may be at play, including, for example, values, interests, power, perception, personality, style, use of language, and many others.

Is Conflict Really a Problem?

Because it involves some combination of obstacles that require special attention, people tend to define conflict as a problem. But let's reconsider this for a moment. Although you may find conflict difficult, it is not necessarily negative. Indeed, the "work" required in conflict situations can lead to very positive outcomes. If we had no conflict and never had to exert any effort to manage difficult differences, we would . . .

• Never be challenged to think critically about our ideas.

• Be very limited in our creativity.

- Be ineffective problem solvers.
- Limit the intellectual and emotional resources available to us.
- Miss interesting and important new experiences in life.
- Learn very little about other people.
- Have no basis for understanding what is important to us.
- Find no reason to build community with others.

Whether we experience conflict as good or bad depends on how we come to understand and respond to it. Jay Rothman wrote, "Conflict begs to be viewed not merely as a problem waiting to be solved but as an opportunity for growth, cooperation, and development waiting to be fulfilled."[2]

Why do people so frequently misunderstand the benefits of conflict? Why is it so tough for us? Uncertainty is often an uncomfortable state of affairs, and we tend to want to reduce it.[3] We resist conflict in part because it may mean the need to change, and change is something that is difficult for us at certain points in our lives; yet, change is always part of every relationship, whether at home, in the workplace, or among friends.

Box 1.1

On a sheet of paper, make a quick list of words that come to mind when you think of conflict. Don't think too hard; just use your stream of consciousness. You can increase the effectiveness of this exercise if you have a group brainstorm words together.

Now count the number of words that are (1) positive, (2) negative, or (3) neutral in connotation. What do you notice?

We have done this exercise many times in our classes, and the result is always a preponderance of words in the negative category. Why are most of our associations with conflict negative?

Now think only of positive terms that you could associate with conflict. See if you can come up with as many positive terms as negative. When you do this, what do you learn about conflict?

Definitions of Conflict

To begin to deepen our understanding of conflict, we have selected various definitions for discussion. These definitions illustrate something important about language. Language does not capture or mirror reality. In other words, a definition does not tell us what a thing really is. Conflict, as an example, is many things and largely constructed socially through the ways in which people talk about it. Definitions, then, are tools that enable us to identify what is important and not important to us in our world of experience. We are well advised, then, not to question whether a definition is true or accurate, but whether it is useful in helping us orient to our world of experience.

Conflict as Social Opposition. The first definition was written by James Schellenberg:

> *We may define social conflict as the opposition between individuals and groups on the basis of competing interests, different identities, and/or differing attitudes.*[4]

Notice several distinguishing features in this definition. First, Schellenberg concentrates on *social* conflict, not intrapersonal conflict. This qualification is useful because it helps us focus on conflict between people and eliminates the vast realm of psychiatry, personality, and human development that, if included, would make the subject so large as to be unmanageable. At the same time, this focus comes with a certain loss, as the struggles we experience inside our heads in many ways mirror the struggles we have with others. In general, we think that social interaction and self have an impact on one another, making both relevant. We want to recognize this fact in this book, even though, like Schellenberg, we emphasize social conflict here.

You will also notice that Schellenberg's definition characterizes conflict as an opposition—not just any opposition, but one involving competing factors. In other words, there is a sense that one party is opposing another. Again, this definition comes with a certain gain and a certain loss. The gain is that it captures the feeling we usually have about conflict—the sense of being frustrated by another person or group in some way. The downside is that many of the best forms of communication used in conflict are not always oppositional; they can be collaborative, a point that this definition does not highlight.

Finally, we see in Schellenberg's definition the identification of three important sources of difference—interests, identities, and attitudes. We will explore each of these factors in this book.

Conflict as a Clash of Goals. To show a somewhat different approach to conflict, we have selected a definition by Gay Lumsden and Donald Lumsden:

> *Conflict occurs when two or more people perceive their individual goals as being mutually exclusive—that is, if they perceive that accomplishing one person's goal keeps another's goal from being achieved.*[5]

This statement calls our attention to the frustration that occurs when we think that our goals are being blocked by other people. In this definition, perception plays an important role in conflict, in particular the perception that goals are "mutually exclusive." In other words, if we believe that when one person gains what he or she wants, the other person automatically loses.

The advantage of this definition is that it captures the competitive cultural belief commonly held by people embroiled in conflict—that both cannot win. However, this definition also simplifies conflict to goal achievement, which belies the complexity of many conflicts that may go well beyond conflicting interests.

Conflict as Antagonism.   As a final definition, we want to share the classic treatment of Clinton Fink, who argued after an extensive survey and analysis of literature on conflict that we should define the term very broadly to cast a wide net:

> *Conflict is any social situation or process in which two or more social entities are linked by at least one form of antagonistic psychological relation or at least one form of antagonistic interaction.*[6]

This rather academic definition is difficult to read, but the words are carefully selected to call our attention to a number of variables involved in conflict. The term *social entities* includes persons, groups, institutions, or even nations. We like it because it is broad enough to cover all levels of conflict. The next term, *linked*, conveys the idea that parties to a conflict are connected in some way. The problem is that this term does not specify very well what linkage means. We prefer to use the term *communication link*, to capture the idea that the parties are involved in a symbolic exchange through word or deed.

This definition also places antagonism as a feature of conflict. This characteristic is not unlike *opposition*, used by Schellenberg. It connotes one being *against* the other. Antagonism does not necessarily mean mutual exclusion or even competition, which opens a variety of possible types of opposition. The one specification that Fink does include is that the interaction between the parties must be antagonistic in some way. In other words, the parties' interaction is adversarial, a dimension not captured by either of the other two definitions. Antagonistic interaction could be angry and hostile, but it could also be calm and collected. Antagonism, then, does not necessarily involve emotionality, but it does involve something the parties themselves "feel," namely that opposition is occurring in the communication. We think that is a valuable addition.

Finally, Fink included the somewhat odd phrase "psychological relation," meaning something of importance to the individuals such as feelings, personality, or perception. The use of the term *psychological* does tend to eliminate larger social or cultural antagonisms that may also play a role.

OUR DEFINITION AND MODEL:
THE MANAGEMENT OF DIFFERENCE

As people find themselves making distinctions, conflict may appear. The distinctions we make bring differences to the fore that can be felt or seen as a moment of challenge involving resistance or struggle. In extreme cases, these differences may be experienced as harmful, destructive to relationships, damaging to ego or face, or hurtful to physical or emotional presence. Yet problematic differences often turn out to have positive consequences. Conflict has the potential to be a force for constructive positive change if it is addressed with an ongoing process focusing on the management of difference.

For us, then, *conflict is the state of being challenged by human differences.* We experience conflict when differences matter and are potentially problematic to us (see figure 1.1). This is not necessarily a negative state. Indeed, it affords the opportunity to move from harm to value in our communication about those differences.

Figure 1.1   Living in a World of Difference

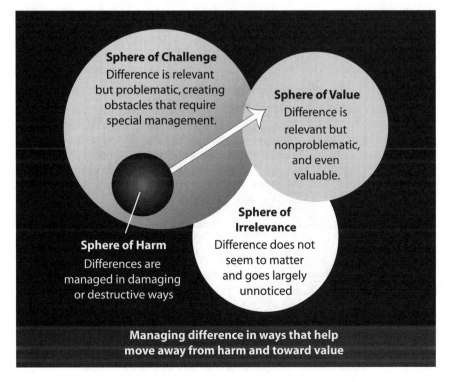

Sphere of Challenge
Difference is relevant but problematic, creating obstacles that require special management.

Sphere of Value
Difference is relevant but nonproblematic, and even valuable.

Sphere of Harm
Differences are managed in damaging or destructive ways

Sphere of Irrelevance
Difference does not seem to matter and goes largely unnoticed

Managing difference in ways that help move away from harm and toward value

Differences can be perceived as inconsequential, valuable, challenging, or even harmful. The way in which we manage our differences determines whether the outcome is valuable or harmful. As we emphasize throughout this book, you should respond to conflict in ways that help to move the outcome from harm to value.

Think of the world of difference as a universe of situations with which we must constantly cope. What differences stand out, what differences fade into the background, and what do salient differences mean to us?

We can think of the world of human differences in terms of four spheres, areas of life commonly encountered and managed. The first of these is the *sphere of irrelevance*. Because voices in this sphere are unified, difference does not matter. This is a cultural area in which we celebrate similarity and build on what we have in common.

In the *sphere of value*, we are very much aware of difference, and we appreciate it. We see differences as a positive resource. It is a world of diversity, and we build on the many different resources available to us. While the sphere of irrelevance is usually pretty easy, the sphere of value takes work. Because we are faced with new perspectives and ways of doing things within this sphere, we must be willing to explore and work with ideas different from our own. At some point, the work

of difference begins to become a challenge. It creates problems and obstacles that are not easily overcome. At this point, we cross over from the sphere of value to the sphere of challenge.

The *sphere of challenge* is not necessarily negative. Differences can still be viewed as valuable, and the hard work of managing those differences can itself be salutary. At the same time, however, the sphere of challenge often brings frustration, even exasperation, and we can begin to act in ways that are harmful to all or some of the parties involved. At this point, we enter the *sphere of harm*.

Conflict spans the spheres of harm, challenge, and value. Conflicts can be valued; they can be challenging; and they can be harmful. Our chief proposition in this book is that *we should manage differences in a way that avoids moving toward harm and encourages moving toward value.* In other words, we should manage differences in ways that increase dignity and honor, make creative problem solving possible, make use of diversity as a positive resource, acknowledge a multi-vocal world, minimize both confusion and destruction, provide opportunities for coherence and meaning in life, and continue the rich texture of difference that characterizes the human condition.

We can make choices about how to act within social situations. We are not locked into patterns that can lead toward increasing harm. We can invite others into a kind of dialogue that has some potential to transform cacophony to melody and enables us to blend voices in ways that both distinguish ourselves as persons and communities and to honor those who are different from ourselves.

TYPES OF CONFLICT

Christopher Moore introduced one of the first comprehensive books on mediation.[7] Seeing increasing contention in the world and a need for strong support of methods and models of conflict management, Moore asserted that if people are going to be able to assess their conflicts and design interventions, they will need to have more information on how conflict occurs, what the barriers are to resolving it, and what actions could be taken to address the conflict. He noted that conflict is caused by a variety of differences, each leading to a different type of conflict. More specifically...

1. *Data conflicts* are caused by

   a. Lack of information

   b. Misinformation

     c. Different views on what is relevant

     d. Different interpretations of data

     e. Different assessments of procedures

2. *Interest conflicts* are caused by

     a. Perceived or actual competition over substantive (content) interests

     b. Procedural interests

     c. Psychological interests

3. *Relationship conflicts* are caused by

     a. Strong emotions

     b. Misperceptions or stereotypes

     c. Poor communication or miscommunication

     d. Repetitive negative behavior

4. *Value conflicts* are caused by

     a. Different criteria for evaluating ideas or behavior

     b. Exclusive intrinsically valuable goals

     c. Different ways of life, ideology, or religion

5. *Structural conflicts* are caused by

     a. Destructive patterns of behavior or interaction

     b. Unequal control, ownership, or distribution of resources

     c. Unequal power and authority

     d. Geographical, physical, or environmental factors that hinder cooperation

     e. Time constraints

Consider the example of John and Eva, two employees of a company sharing an office and performing similar tasks. Their differences as coworkers seem to be getting in the way, and both notice that they are unable to be as productive as they used to be. What could be the problem?

- Data Conflict: John thinks that the goal of their most recent assignment is to develop a marketing strategy, while Eva was under the impression that they were to create a logo. A miscommunication occurred somewhere, and it could be addressed easily.

- Interest conflict: Both Eva and John want to position themselves for the yearly promotion. John needs the extra money, while Eva is looking for career advancement. Only one employee from their division will be promoted, and the decision is based on production.

- Relational conflict: Eva repeatedly comes to work late due to challenging childcare arrangements. John is an early riser and is often in the office early. Tardiness has always been a pet peeve of his, and in this case, he sees it as "typical of employing a single mother."

- Value conflict: Eva has always believed that it is imperative to take as much time as you need to get the job done well, rather than hurrying through a task to seem productive. She values quality over quantity. John knows the importance of high quality products but also understands the competitive market in which they exist. He pushes for production and efficiency at the expense of quality in some cases. His years of experience have shown him the benefit of high yield in their market.

- Structural conflict: John has a weekly meeting with the boss and continues to get special information that Eva does not have. This makes Eva feel disempowered.

We would like to add one additional type of conflict to Moore's list: *moral conflict*.[8] Characterized by differences of worldview or ideology, such conflict involves deep philosophical differences in which the parties' understandings of reality do not fit together.[9] We will address moral conflict in more detail later in the book. Important here is that such conflicts involve significant differences that lie much deeper than mere disagreement. Value differences are often part, but only part, of such conflicts. Moral conflicts tend to be persistent and difficult to manage.

Remember that metaphors are implied comparisons. Often we don't even recognize that the words we choose convey a specific

---

Box 1.2

Think of a conflict important to you. It might be a personal conflict you have had or are having with another person. It might be a conflict in your community or even an international conflict.

Now think of a metaphor that helps describe what this conflict is like. For example, your conflict may be like a crashing airplane or a barbed wire fence.

In a group, share your conflicts and metaphors with one another and discuss what you learn about these conflicts from the respective metaphors. In your groups, explore "solutions" to the conflict staying in the metaphor. If the conflict is like a barbed wire fence, for example, the solution may be to cut the wire or to climb over it with leather pants. What would these metaphorical solutions entail in real life?

Which of the adversarial or alternative methods of conflict management addressed in this chapter does your metaphorical solution best match?

meaning. For example, we commonly hear or say "he attacked me" or "they shot down my ideas," without necessarily recognizing that the phrases are metaphors for war.

APPROACHES TO CONFLICT

John (Sam) Keltner, a pioneer in the world of mediation, wrote about the struggle involved in conflict as:

> the act of striving against some form of resistance much like push-ing against a door that is sticking, as well as trying to overcome social or political patterns that inhibit us, as in trying to breach a police line or trying to push the military enemy back. It represents the fundamental effort to move away from or change the status quo or to sustain one's immediate position against efforts to alter it.[10]

In some cases, the elimination of struggle seems paramount to hinder further destruction. In other cases, the attempts to manage differences demand versatile problem-solving strategies. Most damage results from addressing struggle with violence or overpowering force of some kind. What approaches to the manifestation of difference pro-duce conditions that are productive and useful? Keltner sees that we need to make a place in our society for managed struggle. In this sec-tion, we introduce the choices and models humans have when con-fronted with conflict.

At the time of this writing, struggle in the world seems to be at a fever pitch. In an era marked by the 9/11 tragedy, the Iraq war, world polarization, backed-up court systems, and a high divorce rate, it is difficult to encourage methods of conflict management that offer hope. Yet society does sometimes manage to work through potentially devastating conflicts.

Various political systems address conflict in different ways. The founders of the United States, for example, anticipated that their new country would need a set of procedures, framed in law, that enable peaceful conflict resolution. Like that of most countries of the world, our jurisprudence system was established for this purpose. Addition-ally, the First Amendment of the U.S. Constitution allows us the free-dom to try to influence others and the ability to petition the government for redress. Nations use international diplomacy, sanctions, and armed force to settle international disputes. Families, organizations, and com-munities also work out ways to "make it through" conflict.

Approaches to conflict vary in the degree of confrontation and antagonism they employ. Let's look at two broad genres of conflict management—adversarial methods that tend to be confrontational and alternative methods that tend to be more cooperative.

If you are a communication major in college, you will probably have at least one course in persuasion or argumentation, in which you learn how to influence other people through communication. Persuasive influence is so deeply rooted in history and tradition that it has assumed tremendous importance in personal and community affairs of all types. Especially in Western societies, persons are encouraged to bring their individual intelligence to bear in creating a case for what they believe to be true. In conflict situations, this means that adversaries compete to produce the best argument and the most effective message. In theory at least, the democratic ideal is that everyone brings the best arguments forth, and truth will have a way of prevailing.

This ideal is based on the philosophies of liberal democracy, individual rationality, and pragmatism. In real life, we know that persuasion is only partly based on the power of rationality. In fact, persuasion also involves many nonrational appeals that use power to provide or withhold what others want and need, such as access to public forums including the media, authority to make decisions, and membership in powerful groups.

Persuasion, then, consists of a plethora of forms that, at least on the face, share nonviolence as a characteristic. In persuasion, we use words, rather than force, to influence. We may try to influence others directly, or we may appeal to a decision maker—a parent, boss, policy maker, judge, or jury—to take actions favorable to our point of view. Persuasion, of course, is not limited to individuals. Groups create whole campaigns and lobby to influence the outcome of legislation. A complicating factor is that conflicting parties do not always have a common logic of rationality, a shared sense of how to settle disputes, or a collective idea of what constitutes appropriate persuasion. Often the dispute not only involves the issues at hand but also the appropriateness of the forms of persuasion employed.

People do influence one another, and decision makers do listen to arguments, but persuasion commonly fails when conflicting parties are not willing to acquiesce to the others' proposals. Rhetorical strategies may be effective in some disputes, especially where communication competence brings clarity to the issues at hand. Debate, however, does not always work when the standards of argument of the two sides do not match up. In these circumstances, persuasion and argumentation may only "harden the categories" as disputants become frustrated, dig in their heels, and remain steadfast in their perspective.[11]

Adversarial Methods

Litigation.   When conflicts are not settled in the normal course of events, redress is possible in the courts. Here persuasion goes "formal," as attorneys follow strict rules to bring their respective cases to a hearing. The court "finds for" one party or the other, essentially settling the matter if appeals and other lawsuits do not follow. Parties are usually represented by an attorney and are often faced with consequences that they had no hand in crafting. These processes are open to public scrutiny and have little concern for upholding the relationship of the parties. As a "win/lose" process, litigation normally assumes fixed resources and pits one party's interests against the other's. Litigation is a zero-sum game in which the more one side gets, the less the other side gains.

Although litigation is supposed to be an orderly and peaceful method for settling disputes, it is often anything but peaceful, as those who have been sued will tell you. In litigation, the costs to emotions, time, and finances can be tremendous and take a heavy toll on those involved. Parties to litigation usually have little control over what happens once the process begins. For this reason, the threat of litigation is itself a powerful form of influence, and cases often settle out of court.

The former Chief Judge of the Family Court in Albuquerque, Anne Kass, had a banner in her office that read, "Do you want to win or be happy?" If communication and normal discourse do not satisfy people struggling with their differences, many of them turn to methods of legal assistance and litigation to attempt a remedy. Judge Kass often remarked that parties usually leave a courtroom with less money, less choices, and more unhappiness than when they arrived.

Diatribe.   You probably think of persuasion and litigation as civil discourse. Persuasion, whether in or out of court, does at least reflect a certain amount of eloquence and reason. Indeed, persuasive messages are often studied aesthetically in terms of their exemplary logic and use of language. Of course, you would not think of all persuasive messages as eloquent, but you would probably at least give the speaker the benefit of the doubt in trying to live up to some kind of standard of quality.

Too often in conflict situations—and we have seen this in public demonstrations, government hearings, and private mediations—the parties get so frustrated by the inability of the other side to see their point of view, that they slide (or jump!) into diatribe—name calling, yelling, chanting, demanding, and venting. In very hot conflict situations—whether at home or in public settings—the attempt to influence degrades to a shouting match, or *reciprocated diatribe*. This kind of communication never resolves the issue and often migrates from language to force.

Force. We live in a world in which force or the threat of force is common. At home, a parent may take a small child firmly by the hand and "force" her to comply. Managers essentially "force" employees to do things they may not want to do by applying any number of organizational sanctions, and governments force citizens to comply with laws. So force is both expected and necessary.

However, force can become sinister and violent in conflict situations. Necessary discipline of a child is one thing; child abuse is another. Normal organizational compliance is one thing; enforcement of inhumane working conditions is another. Law enforcement is required for an orderly society, but civil abuses comprise an entirely different order of influence. We only have to watch two minutes of the nightly news or glance at the front page of any newspaper to see the use of force for handling difference in our world. Once force is set in action, people can forget the underlying disagreement as the use of force brings conflict to the boiling stage.

Force as a form of conflict resolution, then, can reveal the worst of human behavior. At the time of this writing, insurgents in Iraq are capturing foreign nationals and beheading them publicly as a way of forcing corporations and governments to withdraw. This follows on the heels of extensive news coverage of prisoner abuse in the same country. Such incidents are public examples of the kinds of brutality possible even in the family and community, as the frustration of conflict accelerates to the level of violence.

Although common, violent force is not an inevitable extension of adversarial forms of conflict resolution. The adversarial assumptions about how conflict should be managed do, however, make violence possible in times of extreme frustration. One way of rethinking our whole approach to conflict is to look at a variety of methods that do not assume an adversarial relationship among the parties to the dispute. The following forms of communication take a turn from the customary view.

Alternative Dispute Resolution

Roger Fisher and William Ury tell a story to illustrate the win/lose mentality commonly assumed in conflict resolution:

> In 1964, an American father and his twelve-year-old son were enjoying a beautiful Sunday in Hyde Park, London, playing catch with a Frisbee. Few in England had seen a Frisbee at that time and a small group of strollers gathered to watch this strange sport.

> Finally, one Homburg-clad Britisher came over to the father, "Sorry to bother you. Been watching you a quarter of an hour. Who's *winning*?"[12]

The use of litigation or force to address many of the world's problems is just about as appropriate as asking "Who's winning?" at Frisbee. What game should we be encouraging people to play? Is it the game to win and to gain more of the pie than anyone else? Or is it the game to build a better process for dealing with our differences?

Communication is the centerpiece of working through any type of conflict. While most interpersonal conflict situations involve only the parties who are central to the disagreement, some situations benefit from the presence of other parties trained to facilitate communication in the management of differences. Even if you decide to navigate through conflict without enlisting trained communicators, the principles and practices described briefly below provide valuable insights into how to communicate effectively in situations with the potential for conflict.

The last twenty years have introduced a promising number of offerings to address differences in ways that maximize relationship building and effective outcomes. Alternative Dispute Resolution (ADR) refers to a set of alternatives to litigation, increasingly common methods of enlisting third-party participation in a conflict. ADR refers broadly to all the methods that resolve conflict in a nonadversarial way. Because ADR is the umbrella reference for so many methods, we follow the field in using the term *resolution* here, although a more descriptive phrase would be methods of *conflict management*. Resolution is temporary at best and is nearly always elusive. We will emphasize throughout this book that differences are *managed*.

Negotiation. Each day contains many opportunities to negotiate: determining what to have for dinner; deciding which projects get the first attention at work; establishing who will pay for a mistake; or choosing between attending a movie in the evening or relaxing in the city park. These situations invite back-and-forth communication intended to reach an agreement. Negotiation can be formal or informal; it can occur in private or public; it can be direct or conducted through representatives such as attorneys. It can develop anywhere at any time, with the parties having control over the private or public setting and the ability to have complete concurrence with the outcome.

Successful negotiation requires people to be able to identify their issues and interests, to communicate them clearly, to listen and understand the position of the other, and to work through possible options to reach an agreement.

Mediation. Mediation is facilitated negotiation in which interested parties meet to work together to find solutions to differences with the help of a neutral third party.[13] Though similar processes have been used for centuries in various cultures, mediation was popularized in the United States during the labor movement. Mediation is an extension of the negotiation process. It can be informal or formal, depending on the wishes of the parties. Ultimate control over the process and the outcomes depends on the parties and their efforts to generate options and evaluate those options. In some ways, a marriage counselor serves as a mediator; the presence of a third-party helps spouses work through their problems. Although many forms of mediation exist, mediators usually share the following characteristics.

1. *Mediators are impartial concerning the outcome of the process.* Their approach communicates no preference for any participant or any of the potential options for agreement generated by the participants. The mediator puts aside any personal bias.

2. *Mediators open communication channels.* By creating an atmosphere for problem solving, mediators can channel the communication so it is framed in a palatable way and opens up productive exchanges. By summarizing, framing, asking open-ended questions, acknowledging, and reality testing, mediators can assist the parties in building workable and reasonable paths forward.

3. *Mediators model dignity, respect, and compassion.* Beginning with the way the co-mediators communicate with each other, and continuing with the dialogue with the participants, mediators listen with care, express interest and concern for the issues at hand, and set an example for how the parties can treat each other. Mediators assume that parties are competent and intelligent enough to handle their own problems.

4. *Mediators recognize the need for humans to address emotions as well as facts and issues.* The mediation process is a safe place to share sorrows, anger, uncertainty, frustration, as well as a myriad of other emotions. Often these feelings can be expressed and acknowledged, creating a sense of relief, which facilitates the ability to move forward.

5. *Mediators believe in the strength of voluntary settlements.* Knowing that involvement in creating one's future brings ownership and commitment, mediators encourage the belief that cooperative attempts to settle differences bring the most satisfying results. Litigious processes contain tension and mystery about "what will happen next." In contrast, mediators reassure all parties

that the next steps are always in the hands of the participants, the most logical people to manage their issues.

Arbitration. Another third-party process, often mistakenly equated to mediation, is arbitration. Unlike mediation in which the parties craft an agreement, an arbitrator hears all sides of a dispute, reviews the evidence, and issues a decision, offering a kind of private judging in specific cases. A parent, for example, might be asked to arbitrate a quarrel between two siblings. After listening to both sides, the parent can issue a ruling. These processes can be court annexed or private; they are more formal than mediation, although less formal than litigation. Arbitration processes are usually ordered or determined by court rule, by contract, or by request. Binding decisions are legally enforceable decisions or agreements. Arbitration may occur in such cases as collective bargaining situations or in medical malpractice claims.

Notice that the move from direct negotiation to litigation changes the amount of formality and control in the process. Table 1.1 summarizes these differences.

Table 1.1   Continuum of Dispute Resolution Choices

	Personal Control over Process	Personal Control over Outcome	Formality	Public or Private
Negotiation	High	High	Informal	Private
Mediation	High	High	Either	Private
Arbitration	Low	Low	More Formal	Either
Litigation	Very Low	Very Low	Formal	Public

The number of alternative methods for managing differences has increased exponentially since 1980. The appendix outlines several methods that have attracted a number of adherents. Individuals can learn valuable communication skills to manage most of their differences. If the differences do become unmanageable, there are a variety of ways to work together without turning to adversarial methods.

How You Can Use This Chapter

We hope you will find this book useful in your life. We all face conflict situations that range from disagreements about what movie to see to life-altering (or threatening) situations. As you think about your approach to major or minor differences, reflect on the type of communication that will help you frame a disagreement so that you can construct a satisfactory outcome for all parties.

1. Human life is characterized by difference. Learn to live with difference and use it as a positive resource for your life.

2. Conflict is inevitable as differences force us into challenging situations. Consider conflict as an opportunity to think critically and creatively, to understand other people and yourself better, and to work collaboratively on problems that require work.

3. When faced with a challenging difference, think about what lies at the heart of the matter. Is it information, interests, values, relational expectations, or some combination of these?

4. Don't shy away from using persuasion when you want to influence others. If arguments do not settle the matter, other constructive forms of collaboration may be necessary. Before you jump into suppression, verbal and physical violence, or force, consider the devastating effects that these can have on yourself and others in conflict situations.

5. Litigation is only one possibility; make every effort to settle hard conflicts through alternative forms if at all possible.

Interactive Case Study

BEING NEIGHBORLY

Context: Finally you have found a place to live! You and three of your friends are college students about to enter your sophomore year. You lived in the dormitory last year and are looking forward to more freedom this year in renting the downstairs of a duplex. The duplex is walking distance to campus and is on a beautiful, tree-lined street. The only problem is lack of parking, which you all hope to compromise on as the semester continues.

Opening exercise(s): As the semester progresses, you begin to feel some friction with your upstairs neighbors. They are graduate students in biology specializing in bats and have lived in the duplex for two years. They often travel to bat habitat sites for research and host meetings at their apartment for those with similar interests. An elderly couple owns the duplex and lives about 15 minutes away. They are proud of the building in which they raised their three children; they remodeled it into the duplex five years ago for rental income to supplement their retirement income.

Divide the class into groups of eight students. Each group will contain the four undergraduates, the two graduates, and the elderly landlord couple. Role-play the first meeting between all the parties. The landlords have set up this meeting, outside on the front sidewalk, for the four new renters to meet the upstairs neighbors. Have a conversation for about five to ten minutes, getting to know each other and sharing some of your interests and perspectives. Close down the role-play and answer the following questions (about your role's experience in the first conversation) individually:

1. As you begin to get to know your neighbors and your landlord, what intrigues you?
2. Are you beginning to get a feeling for issues that will enable you all to get along well? Are there any issues that ring a small warning bell about potential conflicts?
3. What was the most difficult thing about this first meeting?
4. What was easiest for you at this first meeting?
5. Did anyone in the group rub you the wrong way? Why?

Focus #1: Types of Conflict (Small Group Role-Play)

Meet in your group of eight to think about potential conflicts. Looking at the list of "Types of Conflict," compare these to the lists you made (1–5 above) and discuss possible differences among you that might lead to difficult relationships. Choose one of these situations, and demonstrate it as a role-play. Only a few of you may be the participants in this case. Look at the type(s) of conflict that are being manifested. Play out the situation for five minutes or so, and then discuss with the group the following: *What differences among you brought this conflict to life? What could have been done to prevent this conflict from becoming adversarial?*

Focus #2: Adversarial Methods (Large Group Role-Play)

All eight of you should now come back to the conflict that emerged. You will meet on the sidewalk in front of the house again. Let the tensions escalate. Try to feel the depth of the conflict and how easy it is to dig in and become entrenched with positions. Close down the role-play after ten minutes or so. As individuals, take out a sheet of paper and record:

- What is the most important component of the issue at hand? What is the position of each participant?
- What stories, life experiences, or background do the participants seem to have that enables them to feel so strongly about this position?
- What values lie behind these positions?
- For each position, are there any "cracks in the armor"? Are there segments of the strongly held position that participants seem ambivalent about? Any dilemmas or confusions?
- Did you hear anything among these positions that seem to be held in common?

Focus #3: Alternative Methods (Mediated Role-Play)

Find an issue from this situation that might be conducive to two of the parties sitting down to discuss their differences. One of the other participants can serve as a third party, a mediator, to help guide the discussion. The three of you have found a private place to talk, and the third party is going to assist by summarizing the conflict in fairly neutral terms, suggesting a time limit to the conversation and offering some basic suggestions about how to talk together. See if the presence of a third party, even though it is informal, has any impact on how the conflict plays out. Others from the group can be observers.

Note to the mediator: Be careful not to give advice, suggestions, or ideas for solving their problem. You are there to clarify communication, frame issues in a way that helps participants move forward, and ask questions to put more information on the table. Participants will choose their own solutions and steps forward.

Switch roles. Observers can step in for the mediator, as a tag-team. Just tap the mediator on the shoulder and step in, modeling another idea for communication guidance.

For a debriefing conversation, consider whether the session illuminated any of the characteristics listed as common to mediators. What impact did the third party have on the conflict management process?

Endnotes

[1] Clifford Geertz, *The Interpretation of Cultures* (New York: Basic Books, 1973), p. 49.

[2] Jay Rothman, *Resolving Identity-Based Conflict in Nations, Organizations, and Communities* (San Francisco: Jossey-Bass, 1997), p. xv.

[3] William Gudykunst, "The Uncertainty Reduction and Anxiety-Uncertainty Reduction Theories of Berger, Gudykunst, and Associates," in *Watershed Research Traditions in Human Communication Theory,* ed. Donald P. Cushman and Branislav Kovačić (Albany, NY: SUNY Press, 1995), pp. 67–100; Stephen W. Littlejohn and Karen A. Foss, *Theories of Human Communication,* 8th ed. (Belmont, CA: Wadsworth, 2005), pp. 144–147.

[4] James A. Schellenberg, *Conflict Resolution: Theory, Research, and Practice* (Albany, NY: SUNY Press, 1996), p. 8.

[5] Gay Lumsden and Donald Lumsden, *Communicating in Groups and Teams: Sharing Leadership* (Belmont, CA: Wadsworth, 2000), p. 296.

[6] Clinton F. Fink, "Some Conceptual Difficulties in the Theory of Social Conflict," *Conflict Resolution,* 12 (1968): 456.

[7] Christopher W. Moore, *The Mediation Process: Practical Strategies for Resolving Conflict* (San Francisco, CA: Jossey-Bass, 1996).

[8] Stephen W. Littlejohn, "Moral Conflict," in *The Sage Handbook of Conflict Communication: Integrating Theory, Research, and Practice,* eds. John G. Oetzel and Stella Ting-Toomey (Thousand Oaks, CA: Sage, 2006), pp. 395–418; W. Barnett Pearce and Stephen W. Littlejohn, *Moral Conflict: When Social Worlds Collide* (Thousand Oaks, CA: Sage, 1997).

[9] Oscar Nudler, "In Replace of a Theory for Conflict Resolution: Taking a New Look at World Views Analysis," *Institute for Conflict Analysis and Resolution Newsletter* (summer), 1 (1993): 4–5; Jayne Seminare Docherty, *Learning Lessons from Waco: When the Parties Bring their Gods to the Negotiation Table* (Syracuse, NY: Syracuse University Press, 2001); Daniel Druckman and Kathleen Zechmeister, "Conflict of Interest and Value Disensus: Propositions in the Sociology of Conflict," *Human Relations,* 26 (1973): 449–466.

[10] John W. Keltner, *The Management of Struggle: Elements of Dispute Resolution through Negotiation, Mediation, and Arbitration* (Cresskill, NJ: Hampton Press, 1994).

[11] Pearce and Littlejohn, *Moral Conflict*.

[12] Roger Fisher and William Ury, *Getting to Yes: Negotiating Agreement without Giving In* (New York: Penguin Books, 1991), p. 148.

[13] Kathy Domenici and Stephen Littlejohn, *Mediation: Empowerment in Conflict Management*, 2nd ed. (Long Grove, IL: Waveland Press, 2001), p. 32. For a comprehensive discussion of mediation, see Margaret S. Herrman, ed., *Handbook of Mediation: Bridging Theory, Research, and Practice* (Malden, MA: Blackwell, 2006).

2

The World of Difference

Difference can be a positive resource for human enlightenment and problem solving, indeed, for life and growth. Most people would agree with this truism in the abstract, but the realities of conflict can be challenging and problematic. We want variety in our lives, but we also want unity and cohesion. We want diversity of perspective and engaging relationships, but we also want stability and predictability. We want fascinating communities and a heterogeneous society, but we also want to have a base of clear values that we can count on. How do we manage these tensions? This is the chief problem caused by human differences on an everyday basis.

When our personal, relational, and community lives feel stable and coherent, we experience the order of life. When differences create a problem, we may lose that sense of order and act to restore it.

A WAY OF THINKING ABOUT COMMUNICATION

Communication is usually considered a process for transmitting information and for influencing people. In a public speaking course, for example, you may learn to deliver an effective message to an audience. In a persuasion class, you will emphasize methods for influencing attitudes, and in advertising, the goal is to sell products, services, and ideas. This transmission model is useful, but it restricts our understanding of the power of communication in human life. For this reason, we would like to introduce a broader concept of communication: and show how communication is the inescapable medium in which human beings live.

More than a device, communication creates meaning and shapes the very realities in which we exist. The symbols and meanings that form human experience are built through communication, and our orientation to every aspect of life is determined by symbolic meanings emerging from social interaction. In short, our worlds are *made in communication.*

For many people, this is a radical idea. It is hard to grasp the point that nothing can exist outside of communication, so let us explain just a little more. We are not claiming that objects don't exist, but we can only know and relate to objects through socially derived meanings. The "things" we experience in our lives are conceptualized into categories, and we construct relationships through interaction within social groups. We orient not only "objects" in this way but also all forms of experience.

The Communication Perspective

When we look at how meanings are constructed, how human beings orient to the world through symbols, and how different people think about life, we are taking the *communication perspective.*[1] This perspective draws our attention to the distinctions people make that help them organize the flux and flow of their experiences and to talk about these things with other people. The communication perspective helps us see how any aspect of experience is created through communication.

In this chapter, we introduce the thesis—carried throughout the rest of the book—that *humans construct and manage their differences through communication.* Sometimes these differences are seen as valuable, sometimes as problematic, and sometimes as harmful. As we explore this thesis, we will look at the ways in which differences are constructed and how conflict is made.

How Worlds Are Made

Challenged by intriguing puzzles and problems, scientists formulate fascinating questions and answer them through observation. What do scientists need to do this kind of work? Clearly, they require technology, tools, and methods. They also need some way to control events so that they can see what happens when one thing impacts another, and they need knowledge and skill to do this. But this is not enough. Science cannot proceed without colleagues, assistants, students, reviewers, grants, universities, research institutions, courses, trainings, textbooks, lectures, demonstrations, papers and publications, theories, conferences, meetings, critiques, debates—all part of the social side of science and all intimately tied to language. Scientists need a set of concepts—categories and distinctions—that classify things in a useable form. They need scientific terms and mathematical expressions to symbolize these concepts and relations.

All of this is worked out socially through communication within the scientific community and beyond. From a communication perspective, then, science is a social endeavor in which language is used to create categories of understanding and explanation. The world must be symbolized, categorized, and organized into useful forms that enable us to think and talk about it.

All worlds are made through this process. What we know always comes in one way or another from experience, and our experience is inextricably social.[2] A useful question is what is made when we communicate. When you think about the communication you have had with your parents, for example, what do you think was made? A feeling of enmity? A close relationship? An ethic of mutual help? Probably many things were made at different points in your relationship with your parents.

We can think of what is made through communication as a set of *resources* on which we can rely. These resources are meanings, or ways of understanding, which could include values, attitudes, beliefs, moral principles, emotions, perceptions, and theories. Your identity as a person at any point in your life is comprised in part of the resources available to you, the accomplishments of communication. If you tell a friend something very private, and this person keeps the secret, you are constructing a relationship of trust. If your study group is very effective in raising everyone's grade on an exam, the group constructs a feeling of effectiveness. If your boss sets you up for training and your participation increases your professional performance, a relationship of confidence and loyalty emerge. Over the life course, your symbolic resources are made, remade, expanded, and changed through communication.

Your resources are not just material things—like money—that sit there and wait to be used. Instead, your symbolic meanings constantly guide your actions. You will confide again in your friend because you think you can trust this person. You will enthusiastically attend study-group meetings because of your belief that the group is effective, and you will perform well at work because of the confidence and loyalty you have developed there. Resources are always tied to practices, as shown in figure 2.1.[3]

So in addition to asking *what* is made, we need to ask *how* it is made. To answer the "how" ques-

Figure 2.1   Resource-Practice Loop

tion, we look at the sequence of actions in an interaction. If you respect your parents, what interaction sequence led to this accomplishment? If you trust your friend, what communication led to this accomplishment? If you are loyal to your company, how was this loyalty made in social interaction? The "how" does matter, and different patterns of interaction will lead to different outcomes.

Meanings can and do change, as communication introduces new perspectives. As people react differently to what we do, our existing resources are altered. We not only learn new expressions and meanings, but we also see others respond to our actions in new ways that can shift our understandings of what an action can mean and do. The more diverse our conversation partners, the more expansive our resources can become.

When our resources and practices are consistent and self-reinforcing, we experience *coherence*, a feeling of clarity and consistency. Coherence is experienced when our resources are clear and unambiguous, our actions seem appropriate to what we think should be going on, we understand and feel understood, and everyone responds in a way that feels appropriate. Coherence, then, is an achievement. In very tight communities in which resources are closely guarded and shared, coherence is both expected and common. The group uses a predictable set of practices that continually reinforce their resources, and not much changes. Contemporary life, however, is not so simple, as the lack of coherence challenges what we think we know, feel, and should do.

Conflicts can be coherent and confusing at the same time. They are coherent when the parties are acting in a way that feels consistent with their view of what a conflict should be and how it should be done. They lack coherence when they are unpredictable or inconsistent with what either party might want to be doing. Because of their potential for challenging our resources, then, conflicts can produce change. The most important question is what we want to make in an episode of conflict and how we should communicate in order to achieve the social world we seek. Out of confusion can come a new level of coherence that helps us manage our differences in a constructive and positive way.

Because we do have control over how we communicate, we can and should address the question: "What kind of social world do we *want* to make, and what new resources do we need to create such a world?" Another way of approaching this question is to look at what would be gained or lost if we had a certain kind of conversation. This is another manifestation of the *how* question, which we pose many times in this book.

The Social Construction of Difference

The meanings we construct in communication are rife with distinctions. We draw lines and make borders. We "see" differences—between things, ideas, values, people, and groups. Linguist Ferdinand de Saussure wrote that nothing has meaning in and of itself, but always arises in difference.[4] We understand things by how they differ from other things. If you are whining about the rain, that must mean that you like fair weather. If you think someone is talking too much, you must prefer more interaction (or silence). If you are a Republican, you have made a choice to favor some ideas over others. If you did not distinguish between what you want and what you don't want, there would be no basis for complaint. Distinctions matter.

The number of distinctions we could make is limitless, so we must somehow create a useful and manageable set of categories. Unless we are very confused, these categories will come to feel natural and real. It makes sense to distinguish different weather conditions, talkativeness, and political parties. Still, one person's boundary is another person's bridge. Many distinctions are widely shared across society, while others are rather local.

Box 2.1

For several days, keep a running record of all the conversations in which you participate. Use one index card per conversation; record the date, time, note the duration of the conversation, the participants, and the topic. What were you doing with whom? Think of verbs, not nouns. For example, you may write "having lunch with Bill" or "doing physics homework with Elise." Add a few descriptive words about each conversation. Think of adverbs and adjectives: "dull," "useful," "painful," or "vacuous."

If you compare these conversations, you will find that some of them seem more similar than others. Put those that are pretty much alike in a stack and make a series of stacks—at least two, perhaps as many as five or six—in which the conversations in each stack resemble each other in ways that those in different stacks do not.

The number of stacks gives you a rough description of the complexity of your social worlds. How many stacks do you have? Do these translate into the different worlds in which you participate in a normal day?

Now compare the stacks. What is the characteristic that all of the conversations in one stack possess that differentiate them from those in the other stacks? This is a way of answering for yourself how you structure your social worlds. Perhaps the difference is by persons; one stack includes all the conversations with a specific person. Perhaps you differentiate on the basis of purpose: some stacks have to do with your job, some with your schooling, some with your family, and some with your best friend. Perhaps you have several different criteria on which you base these distinctions.

Finally, look at the adverbs and adjectives you provided as descriptions of each conversation. Do they cluster? That is, do all the positive descriptions fall into a particular stack and all the negative ones in another? If so, what does this tell you about your social worlds? Or do you have more complex structures, in that a single stack contains both the most positive and most negatively described conversations? If so, what does this tell you about your social worlds?

Adapted from W. Barnett Pearce, *Interpersonal Communication: Making Social Worlds* (New York: Harper Collins, 1994), pp. 88–89.

THE COMMUNICATION ECOSYSTEM

Change, variability, and connection comprise our social worlds. We use the metaphor of the ecosystem to capture this idea. Ecosystems are dynamic; the forces among parts of the system create constant change and variability, and diversity is a positive force for life and health. In this section, we want to explore this metaphor, first by noticing how social worlds connect with one another and then by examining the "strata" or realms of our communication ecosystems.

If we were to ask you to describe yourself, you might say something like, "I am a hard working Baptist father." This clear description lists three dimensions of your identity—the *personal* (hard working), the *relational* (father), and the *community* (Baptist). Being a Baptist, father, and hardworking person connect to one another as part of a whole identity. Suppose you told us: "I love basketball." This simple description could be unpacked by asking a few more questions. We might discover that you play on the college basketball team, that you have important relationships with other members of the team, that you spend most of your spare time with the team, and that you consider yourself a good player. Notice again that your description is a slice from a larger ecosystem in which your sense of self, relationships, and community affect one another.

Now let's take a third example: "I am smart and creative but overweight." We can easily see how you view yourself, but where are the relationship and community components? Just a few questions would reveal them: "Who most often sees you as smart, and how do they show that they think you are smart?" "Who benefits from your creativity?" "By whose standards are you overweight? Where did you learn that this weight is too much?" After just a few minutes of reflecting on questions like these, the connections among your personal, relational, and community identities would soon become clear.

As these examples show, a useful way of organizing our place within the ecosystem of communication is to look at how we see ourselves as persons, how we define our relationships, and how we characterize the communities in which we live.[5] If you want to know more about yourself as a person, ask, "Who am I?" If you want to know more about your relationship with another person, ask, "Who are we?" If you want to know more about the community, ask, "Who are we all?"

Persons, Relationships, and Communities

We think of persons, relationships, and communities as realms of the ecosystem. Each realm is defined and shaped in large measure by the others. Two models illustrate this idea. The first, in figure 2.2, is a cluster model, designed to illustrate how the three realms overlap. This model features the composite worlds of many persons, many relationships, and many communities—all engaged with one another. Figure 2.3 is an "atomic" model that illustrates the worlds of a single individual.[6] Here, we see that the personal realm is embedded in relationships and communities.[7] These models show that the parts of the communication ecosystem cannot in reality be separated, as each entails the others. We will review some of the ways each realm penetrates the others.[8] First, personal

Figure 2.2   Communication Ecosystem Cluster Model

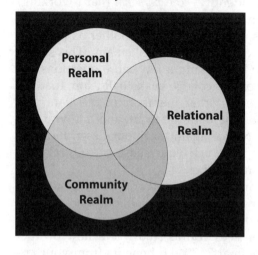

communication depends on standards of communication taught within the community and the various roles assumed in particular relationships. Religion, culture, and age-related communities also determine the patterns of communication that one adopts in different situations.

The same is true of communication styles within particular relationships. You will not communicate the same way with your best friend, son or daughter, coworker, or professor. People are amazingly adaptable in how they express themselves within particular relationships. Your manner of speaking will be influenced by both community and relationship, as the community may have expectations for how you should interact in particular kinds of relationships such as marriage. A Mormon marriage will probably be quite different from a Unitarian one. A Marine sergeant will have a thor-

Figure 2.3   Communication Ecosystem Atomic Model

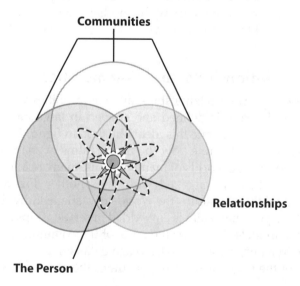

oughly different relationship with subordinates than the director of a nonprofit organization.

Second, self-understanding will be determined in part by the communities that are most powerful in one's life. Certain cultures, for example, teach that persons are independent and should be judged in terms of how well they achieve their personal goals apart from the group. Other cultures, in contrast, think of persons as part of collectives, judging them in terms of how well they reflect and support the common good.

Third, the kinds of relationships that we negotiate with others in particular situations depend in large measure on how we see ourselves within the relationship and how the community defines this particular relationship. For example, husbands and wives who view themselves as very independent will have a different kind of marriage than those who see themselves as highly dependent.

These ideas show that you need to take a systemic perspective when looking at difference and conflict. Consider two families as a case in point. One family defines itself as "religious," meaning that everything they do is determined by these teachings. Over time, the family members judge themselves and other members of the family in accordance with the teachings of the religion. Here we see a strong connection among the contexts of *religion, family,* and *person,* with religion being the dominant force. Being a good person and being a good family means following certain standards of piety.

The other family, in contrast, comes to value independence and encourages its members to pursue their own beliefs. Here, the family becomes a guardian of individuality and independent thinking. The connection of *family* and *person* is very strong, and the personal context becomes dominant. Being a good person means showing independent thinking, and being a good family means supporting everyone's individuality. We understand our differences, then, always in terms of the *reflexive relationship among contexts.*

Contexts and their connections are very important in conflict. When you say to another person, "I see where you are coming from," you probably mean that you have some idea of the contextual connections guiding their opinions and actions. Too often, however, we assume we know the contexts that drive other's actions and do not take the time to learn if our assumptions about the contexts that shape their meanings are correct.

Contradiction and Congruity

As persons, most of us are really a bundle of contradictions. Everyone experiences conflict from time to time because we all have a diverse world of voices in our heads, and sometimes they clash. Much of the time, we are largely successful in bringing the different aspects of our personal lives into congruence. Our values, attitudes, behaviors, and perceptions seem to line up. We tell stories that illustrate a consistent pattern of being in the world. At moments like these, we experience life coherently.

This feeling of congruity can also exist within relationships. Despite the fact that relationships are often conflicted or challenged, we do experience moments—many, really—in which relationships feel coherent and not problematic. We are getting along fine with our coworkers, everything is clicking along nicely in the team, and we enjoy going to work. Family life is great, and we feel together as a unit. No problems there. Moments of relational congruity happen when our expectations for one another feel coordinated, consistent, and appropriate. We understand one another and feel understood by others. R. D. Laing writes that such moments can build into *positive mutual spirals*, in which understanding continues to build between two people.[9]

In the above examples, diversity feels irrelevant, but it never really is. We face and manage difference on a daily basis. Sometimes difference is welcome and valuable; other times, it is challenging, difficult, and even problematic. When that happens, conflict can occur. Conflict can be personal, relational, or community-based. Personal conflict occurs when we become aware of inconsistent perceptions, attitudes, behaviors, or goals and feel the need to resolve these in some way. A whole tradition in psychology claims that we struggle with inconsistencies in our lives and work hard to resolve these.[10] Relational conflicts occur when individuals define a relationship differently, have different expectations, or pursue differing goals. Communities are rife with conflicts on the local, regional, national, and international levels.

Experiencing diversity as a problem is not necessarily bad. It only means that we need to give special attention to how we manage differences. Although conflict may be uncomfortable, it can be a positive force in our personal, relational, and community lives. How we manage conflict makes all the difference. If managed well, conflict can be a positive force; if managed poorly, it can lead to harm. The aim of good conflict management is to move from the sphere of harm toward the sphere of value.

Playing the Game of Life

Think of work, child discipline, romance, friendship, or television news as games, each with a set of rules. The analogy of the game is not meant to imply frivolity; rather, it is a useful metaphor for seeing the patterns and rule-like structure of everyday life.[11] Life games can be widely shared across diverse segments of the population or limited to a smaller group of players. Relationships can be viewed as games, with special rules worked out between two people. Rules help us understand what an action means, and they help us decide how to respond.[12] When the rules are clear, diversity is no problem; when the rules are ambiguous, diversity presents itself as something that requires special attention.

If we know how to play the game—for example, supervising employees at work—then we are qualified as *game players* in that form of communication. You not only have to know what the rules are, but you must also have the skills and experience to employ those rules effectively. When you can do this, you are a competent game player. A good broadcast news reporter is not necessarily a good husband, and an effective rapper is not necessarily a competent classroom teacher. We are all competent game players in certain types of communication but not in others.

It is one thing to be a good *game player* but quite another to be a *game master*. A game master not only knows how to play the game but also understands why and when such a game should be played, what would be gained and lost by doing so, when it is necessary to change

the rules of the game, and when it makes sense to create an entirely different game. A kindergarten teacher who talks to everyone as if they were five years old may be a good player of the kindergarten-teaching game, but not a very effective game master. A counselor who uses "therapy speak" in all settings can be irritating, as this person fails to switch from language appropriate in the therapy room to communication appropriate in other types of situations. The same is true of an urban youth who uses street talk in a job interview. There is nothing wrong with street talk; it just does not fit the rules for the communication game of employment interviewing.

When we are playing a communication game competently with others who are also good at this game, the situation feels stable. It is so stable sometimes that it can even feel scripted. Even when the game is unpleasant, as in a fight, reprimand, or punishment, we know that the form of the conversation is mostly predictable, and we have a set of guidelines for how to respond. When we encounter a situation for which we have no rules, we don't know the game, the other player does not know the game, the rules are inconsistent, or the rules have not been worked out very well, the situation feels unstable—unpredictable, unclear, and chaotic. These unstable situations occur when we try to do something for the first time (sing karaoke?), begin a new relationship, travel to exotic lands, start a new job, or conduct business in a foreign country. It is also the case in many conflicts.

Game players are good in stable situations, but they are usually lost and confused in unstable ones. *Game masters*, in contrast, can be competent in both kinds of situations. In fact, game masters can create clarity and establish order in otherwise unstable situations because they adapt, understand the need for rules, develop creative ways of working or methods, and invite others into new forms of communication. Game masters are not particularly afraid of ambiguity, as they realize that it is a natural part of life. They can live with uncertainty for a period while new rules and forms emerge.

The other evening our 16-year-old grandson called to ask if he "could live with us for a while." We had no rules for responding to this surprising and unstable moment. We said that we would need to think a little bit about how to talk about this issue and would call him back. After "strategizing" for a few minutes, we returned the call and explored the situation in more detail. We turned the unstable game into a stable one by employing rules we knew for a game called "interviewing." As we asked him questions about the situation, we quickly realized that he was trying to get out of being punished by his mother for something he claimed he did not do. We then "invited" him into a new kind of conversation in which we could together explore his options, ways that he could interact with his mother and brother in order to change the pattern of blame and recrimination that seemed to be going on there. We helped our grandson make a list of things he could do that would be different and indicate appreciation for his family. We identified concrete next steps for him. We asked him to call us back the next day, and he did not. The conflict evaporated in a matter of hours, at least temporarily.

As we move through this book, you will see that people who manage conflict well are game masters. They (1) know the powers and limits of normal ways of responding to difference, (2) understand when new patterns of communication are necessary, (3) respond to conflict in new ways and have the tools to do so, and (4) transcend patterns in which participants are entrenched in old games that do not work in new situations.

MANAGING CONFLICT

Personal Conflict

The personal realm consists of your ideas about yourself, who you are, what you are like, and what you do. What distinguishes you from others? How do you view yourself? In Western society, which tends to be individualistic in orientation, the personal context is very powerful in framing human differences. In fact, people often assume that their differences are just "personality conflicts."

The personal realm comes to the fore when we experience differing goals, values, and styles. It operates when issues of independence and freedom are at stake. When two neighbors have a conflict over whether or not to remove a tree, they will inevitably—at least in the United States—understand their difference of opinion within the context of personal freedom and responsibility.

Personal Identity. Personal identity is paradoxical: You know that you are not the same person at all times in all situations, but you nonetheless see yourself as unified—a single person separate from others. While you make distinctions about yourself, you also organize this cluster of identities into a coherent whole. Although you know that you do change over time, you also see yourself as relatively stable—at least most of the time. There are, of course, moments of rapid change—adolescence, graduation, marriage, and retirement—when you may be uncertain about personal identity, and there are times of dissatisfaction. During these periods, you might say that you are "trying to find yourself."

Your personal identity consists of perceived attitudes, certain behaviors and styles, personality, interests, abilities, character, and so forth. These characteristics populate the personal realm, but they are never "things" that can somehow be "found." Instead, aspects of personal identity arise in communication. Although a growing body of research and theory suggests that biological inheritance influences thoughts, feelings, and behaviors,[13] these have meaning only within the larger context of interactions.

Personal identity, then, is a cluster of organized meanings we give to our feelings, thoughts, memories, and behaviors. These are always products of communication and, hence, an important part of the communication ecosystem.[14] Although personal identity is very real for each of us, we are in fact somewhat different people within different relationships and in different communities.

The Moral Context.   The moral context consists of assumptions about what is right and true. It is a guiding light that helps us make fundamental decisions about how to think and act. Whenever you behave according to a general idea of right or wrong, you are acting within the moral context. Whenever you criticize behavior on the basis of moral violation, you are acting within the moral context. When someone makes a blanket judgment about how things are or should be for the world, they are operating within the moral context.

Here are some examples of assumptions that could be part of your moral context.

1. Mothers must protect their children.
2. God alone has the power to give or take life.
3. People should be allowed to do whatever they want, so long as they do not prevent others from exercising the same right.
4. All cultures are legitimate and worthy of respect.
5. All human beings have certain rights.
6. Good people know their place in society and fulfill their role without question.
7. Humans have dominion over the earth.
8. Mother Earth is sacred and must never be violated.
9. Only through science can we know the truth.

Each of these statements would be part of an elaborate belief system, or set of axioms about what it means to be a person, the place of humanity in the universe, what is valuable, and what constitutes moral action. A coherent and organized set of beliefs about "how things are" constitutes a *moral order*.

An important part of a social reality, your moral order is built up over time through interaction in groups, communities, and cultures. We live in a world of numerous, often clashing, moral orders, with confusion and conflict as two potential outcomes. Because we live in multiple social worlds and participate in the construction of many moral orders, confusion is common. What is right and what is wrong? What can we rely on? Is anything certain, or is everything relative? If everything is relative, then how can we ever know what is right and wrong? Some people respond to this confusion by indecision, even insanity; some respond by embracing relativism; some respond by retreating to a rigid moral order that gives them a feeling of certainty and clarity; and others respond by creating overarching moral orders that enable them to move successfully from one to another. The second eventuality of moral clash is conflict—conflict over basic assumptions about life and, hence, about right and wrong. Moral conflicts can be very difficult, and we return to this subject later in the book.

Intrapersonal Conflict. Intrapersonal conflict is part of the normal dilemmas of everyday life. Although downplayed in the conflict literature, this subject cannot be ignored altogether, as intrapersonal conflict reflects and affects our social worlds. Such conflict expresses personal doubts, uncertainties, and the inevitable tug of conflicting voices within our own heads. One scholar wrote that multiple selves battle for control over one's behavior.[15]

Despite all of the posturing and bravado common in conflicts with other people, we usually have personal gray areas that we will admit in moments of calm and safety. Frequently, too, our internal conflicts make us want to appear publicly solid and thereby exacerbate interpersonal struggles. Likewise, the many conflicts we have had with others during our lives can bring alternative voices into the conversations we have mentally with ourselves. We are diverse individuals because of the variety of perspectives we have encountered in others. Intrapersonal conflict can be experienced in many ways.

Intrapersonal conflict can stem from the normal diversity within yourself and differences between how you see yourself and how others see you. Although you may have certain recognizable characteristics, you are not entirely consistent. In fact, you have many characteristics and styles that come out in different situations. People usually think of personality tests as indicators of "how they really are," yet we could ask, "When are you like this, and when are you not?" "Who sees you that way, and who does not?" The same is true of emotions, moods, attitudes, beliefs, and even values.

The research literature in social psychology shows that no human being is consistent; everyone is diverse.[16] Diversity within oneself is the seat of constant development and change. It can provide different ways of looking at situations in your life and make you more creative. It can help you be adaptive to the various situations you face. In fact, if you could imagine someone without diversity within the self, the only likely candidate would be a robot—boring, ineffective, and amazingly uncreative. Although personal inconsistency can sometimes be a problem, diversity is more often a positive resource.

We sometimes experience conflict between how we see ourselves and how others see us. This type of conflict is difficult for most of us because it is disconfirming. We think we have talent; someone else thinks we are amateurish. We think we are smart; someone else thinks we are naive. We think we are inexperienced; others feel we are confident and self-assured. How can we think of these varying perceptions as positive resources? They can be positive if we allow them to prompt self-reflection: (1) to assess the impressions we are making on other people, (2) to analyze the relationship in which the difference is expressed, (3) to examine our own behavior and to think of how we might change, or (4) to set personal boundaries between what is important to us and what is desired or wanted by others. You can reach a certain point in life when the perceptions of other people really don't matter much. You can acknowledge them but feel self-assured in knowing who you are, what is important to you, and what you want. Here we discuss three of the most common sources of intrapersonal conflict—cognitive inconsistency, goal conflict, and value conflict.

Cognitive Inconsistency. Our thoughts, feelings, and behaviors are part of a complex cognitive system consisting of a network of conceptual connections constructed over a lifetime of interaction in social worlds.[17] These connections create a set of perceptions, meanings, beliefs, attitudes, emotions, and values that affect behavior. Cognitive systems are like pools of resources that help us navigate the situations we encounter on a daily basis. We act in accordance with these resources, and our actions in turn influence the cognitive system.

Many struggles in life result from trying to align cognitive resources with actions. Conflict can occur when inconsistent resources lead to confusion about how to act. We face a dilemma when two courses of action feel equally valuable, and we don't know which one to choose. We face a double bind when we feel punished no matter what course of action we take, and we face paradoxes when it is necessary to take an undesirable action in order to achieve a desirable one.

The alcoholic's paradox is a good example: In order to show that they are in control, they must not drink; but when they abstain, they demonstrate their ability to control their drinking and believe they can drink. But starting to drink again makes them feel they are now out of control and must stop drinking. Many alcoholics go back and forth between being on or off "the wagon" depending on where they are in this paradoxical loop. Notice that the problem here is that the meaning of drinking shifts from "being in control" to "being out of control," which leads to confusion and conflict over time.[18]

Seventy years of research and theory in social psychology show that people have a powerful tendency to want consistency in their thoughts and actions.[19] We want our behaviors to be consistent with our values and attitudes. We want our perceptions to be consistent with our beliefs, and we make considerable effort to align inconsistencies. Cognitive inconsistency—or dissonance, as it is sometimes called—is one form of intrapersonal conflict, which can lead to change.[20]

In his theory of *problematic integration*, Austin Babrow explains some of the ways in which this kind of conflict influences how we think and act.[21] Babrow has found that we have a tendency to line up our expectations with desires, but integrating what we think is likely with what we want to happen is often hard. Problematic integration can happen in several ways.

The first, *divergence*, occurs when a desire and an expectation do not match. You want to lose 50 pounds but seriously doubt that you can do it. The second, *ambiguity,* results from being unclear about what to expect. You have just had your first baby and don't know what to expect from parenting. The third form is *ambivalence*, or contradictory values. You like your roommate's personality but dislike his obsessive tidiness. Finally, problematic integration can happen under conditions of *impossibility,* as might be the case when you are in love with a movie star. Problematic integration happens to us on a small scale all of the time, but it is more significant when it involves a strong network of thoughts and feelings that are central to your belief system. The more you have at stake, the harder the internal conflict.

You manage these kinds of internal conflicts in a variety of ways. You may try to persuade other people to make changes that will increase the likelihood of getting what you want. You might reframe the situation so that eventualities seem less unpleasant. You might seek information to get greater clarity about what is going on. This kind of conflict can be a potent force for change. People stop smoking because they believe it will kill them; they change their political attitudes because of how the issue affects them personally; and they even change their religious beliefs when faced with life crises.

Goal Conflict. Kurt Lewin imagined life as a field of forces that push and pull us from point to point. His famous field theory depicts human beings as living within a lifespace of many, sometimes unseen, factors that work together in an interdependent way to influence one's behavior.[22] Field theory is very helpful in capturing the often conflicted nature of human life. Although our actions are goal-directed, goals are not always consistent, and there may be personal and social forces that pull us in different directions.

Goal conflict occurs when we are unsure what we want to do. In field theory, this means being pulled and/or pushed in different directions based on a combination of factors that include demands, constraints, needs, and values. For example, individuals commonly experience conflict between what they want to do and what they feel they should do. This is like a struggle between a "want self" and a "should self."[23]

Lewin identified four types of goal conflict commonly encountered in the lifespace. The first is an *approach-approach conflict*, in which two goals are equally attractive, but we can't achieve both. This is a classic dilemma of not being able to choose. You could major in accounting or management, both of which seem equally valuable to you. The second is an *approach-avoidance conflict*, in which a goal has both positive and negative consequences. You want to major in accounting, which would result in a high-paying job, but it would take an extra year of college, so you can't decide. The third kind of conflict from field theory is *avoidance-avoidance*, two goals are equally unattractive, as would be the case in which your parents expect you to major in business, either accounting or management, but you find both fields boring. The fourth is a *double approach-avoidance conflict*, in which two goals each have advantages and disadvantages. So, for example, accounting is maybe not so interesting (a disadvantage), but will be lucrative (an advantage), and management will be a fun major (an advantage), but may require that you go on for an MBA degree (a disadvantage).

Resolving goal conflict is a process of weighing options, or stewing about what we think will happen if we take a certain course of action. We resolve these conflicts regularly, although some are more difficult than others. We also can live with goal conflicts for considerable periods of time, hoping that the problem will eventually solve itself, which it often does because our lifespace changes. New goals appear, old forces die out, and our needs, wants, and values change.

Value Conflict. When our identities are strongly attached to a certain tightly knit community, our values seem quite solid, as they reflect a consistent set of priorities established by the community. However, most of us identify with several communities—religious, political, professional, and cultural—which may present us with conflicting values. When you add the values negotiated within our relationships, the matter becomes even more complex. Because of the tendency to want consistency, most people will work to bring values into alignment. This is why it is hard to find fundamentalist Christian liberals and why few hunters are vegetarians. Still, value conflict does occur. For example, you may come from a family that values nonviolence. Perhaps you went into the diplomatic corps to work toward peaceful solutions to world conflict. There you learned that it is sometimes necessary to take a police action or, paradoxically, even go to war to prevent violence.

You can see that the forms of intrapersonal conflict identified in this section are related to one another. Goal conflict can arise from value conflict, which is part of cognitive inconsistency. Shifting beliefs lead to dilemmas that are essentially goal-related. These kinds of personal conflict are problematic and challenging, and they require special action and energy. In the following chapters, we will discuss ways in which individuals can manage the inevitable conflicts of their personal lives, and we will see how communication provides the pathway to meaningful change in life.

Relational Conflict

The relational realm consists of a set of expectations that guide our interpretations and actions vis-à-vis another individual. We have many relationships, and each has its own set of expectations. The meaning of a particular behavior will change drastically from one relationship to the next. The way in which we are supposed to respond within a relationship shifts.

Negotiating Relationships. We will return to the topic of relational conflict in chapter 6, where we will see that expectations are negotiated and renegotiated across the life of the relationship. Many kinds of conflict result from this relational negotiation process, including, for example, roles within the relationship, levels of dependence or independence expected, permissible interactions with individuals outside the relationship, privacy issues, and use of space.

Relationships become an important context for difference when a behavior that is considered appropriate in one relationship is causing problems in another. For example, it is entirely appropriate for romantic partners to "come on" to one another, but such behavior in the workplace is not only inappropriate, but illegal. Here the relationship—personal versus coworker—defines how differing actions should be interpreted and how people should respond to one another. Different relationships come with differing expectations.

Relationships seem to be fertile ground for conflict. Whether romantic, family, workplace, neighborhood, or other types of relationships, differences of opinion are expected at some time or other. Relationships, consisting of mutual expectations for self and other—are negotiated. In other words, we establish together the nature of the relationship, including norms, roles, and behavior. In some cases, especially with employers and employees, this kind of negotiation is explicit, as in negotiating a job contract; but most of the time it is implicit, continual, and dynamic. Families are an excellent case in point. The family can never stay the same: New members come into the family, and former members depart; family members each have their own life course, and they establish new relationships with others. All of this means that the patterns of communication within the family will shift over time.

Much of the time, we achieve consensus and a feeling of cohesiveness within the relationship. Other times, however, expectations will differ, causing conflict. Partners might not respond the way they used to; they come to hold different meanings for what actions mean; and they adjust and move to a new level, live in the tension, or end the relationship.

We often think that individuals adopt a more or less standard way of responding to difference. A style is the predominant approach that a person takes in conflict situations. In our experience, however, these so-called styles are really response modes that you will assume at different times in different relationships. Stella Ting-Toomey and her colleagues identify eight such modes—dominating (competing to win), avoiding (escaping), obliging (accommodating), compromising (meeting in the middle), integrating (collaborating), emoting (using emotions), involving a third party (mediating), and neglecting (being passive-aggressive).[24] Although you may find yourself using one of these modes more frequently than you use the others, everyone employs all of them from time to time.

The patterns that develop as people respond to one another are fascinating. For example, if one person dominates and the other obliges, a complementary interaction occurs. Although this pattern of interaction could get stultifying over time, it at least feels orderly. On other hand, if two people each try to dominate one another, the ensuing power struggle could be disastrous over time. Look at some of the other interesting ways in which partners in a relationship might respond to one another. What would happen when one person tried to compromise, but the other person used neglecting, or avoiding? How about the combination of integrating and emoting? These are examples of a loss of order, confusion, and lack of consensus on how we should interact to manage difference.

It is also interesting and informative to analyze when and with whom you use various styles. In what relationships do you most often dominate? Oblige? Avoid? With whom are you most often emotional? On what occasions do you tend to collaborate or compromise?

Think about a close relationship that is important to you. When in this relationship are you expected to dominate, avoid, oblige, compromise, or neglect? How has this pattern been established with the other person over time, and what does the pattern of interaction make possible? What does it restrict or negate? We will explore these questions, as we look for constructive solutions in the following chapter.

Two people create a relational identity through interaction. How would you characterize the interaction patterns within your relationships? How is power distributed? Is the relationship intimate, supportive, collaborative, hostile? Most of the time, you can answer these questions in regard to a particular relationship, but there are moments in the development of a relationship (e.g., breaking up or moving away) in which you are less certain about it. We know too that relationships do shift and change over time. They can develop along a variety of trajectories, so that we can characterize a particular relationship in terms of where it has been and where we think it is going.[25]

Relational Dimensions. Carol Werner and Leslie Baxter outlined the changing qualities that characterize a relationship: (1) the strength of feelings and behavior apparent within the relationship—how active the relationship seems to be; (2) focus on past, present, or future—whether the partners concentrate on things that have already happened, are happening now, or may happen in the future; (3) durability of communication patterns—how long the relational partners stick with certain forms of communication within the relationship; (4) the organization and sequence of events in the relationship—the activities that occur within it and the order in which these activities occur; and (5) the pace and rhythm of activity—the speed and interval between happenings.[26] You can plot the development of a relationship over time using these qualities.

Think about how a marriage changes from being newlyweds, to raising children, to the empty nest, and beyond. The couple would answer the question, "Who are we?" quite differently at each stage, and the relationship changes as the interactions reflect the answers to that question.

Relational Tensions. Relationships are constantly defined by tensions among potentially opposing forces that must be managed by the partners in the relationship. The tension that most people feel in relationships is not only common but also is a natural part of the development and maintenance of relationships.[27] Such tensions are important because they are the impetus for communication; we manage differences through talk.

In a paradoxical way, relational diversity actually binds us together because we must communicate to manage such differences and in the process discover similarities that actually counteract the differences. Russian philosopher Mikhail Bakhtin uses the analogy of centripetal and centrifugal forces to express this idea.[28] Centrifugal force pushes objects apart, as in the case of spinning; centripetal force draws things together, as in the case of gravity. (In some ways of thinking, the universe is organized around motions that are both centripetal and centrifugal.) In our relationships, some forces pull us together, while other forces push us apart. Just when we are feeling centered, something happens that injects a bit of uncertainty or disorder that we must manage somehow. During the moment when we experience the tension or struggle in a conflict, we feel that we are being pulled apart. As we collaborate to create a temporary solution, we feel as if a centripetal force pulled us back together again. You have probably heard couples say that they hate to fight, but love to make up.

There are many potential sources of tension in a relationship. Barbara Montgomery and Leslie Baxter classify these roughly into three clusters.[29] The first is *integration* and *separation*. This is a tension between coming together and going apart. You might, for example, work closely with a coworker while you are learning a new job but at some point may feel that you need to establish yourself as a separate worker by pushing away a little bit. This dilemma is especially strong during the teenage years when adolescents run back and forth between dependence and independence. Parents experience the same tension when they have to make decisions about how much freedom to give a teen, when it is more appropriate for the adolescent to be involved in family activities, and when it is best to allow them to strike out on their own.

The second cluster of tensions involve *expression* and *nonexpression*, the conflict between being open and being closed, revealing information or keeping it private, disclosing more or disclosing less. This tension is largely one of boundary management, or establishing a division between what is shared and what is private. We set boundaries differently within different relationships—as between coworkers and spouses—but even in a single relationship, there is a tension between these two tendencies.

The third cluster of tensions that often appear in relationships is *stability* versus *change*. Sometimes we feel that we want things to be nice and consistent, while other times, we want opportunities for variety and movement. It is natural to feel that a relationship should provide stability to one's life, yet it is also natural to want relationships to provide variety. Both are essential. Imagine a workplace that is constantly chaotic because everyone wants to change how they work together. In contrast, imagine a workplace that never changed because no one wanted to rock the boat. Neither is very desirable. Sometimes we long for stability and sometimes for change, and we are always working to manage this tension, as we manage other tensions as well.

An important source of conflict within a relationship is that the partners are often at different points in these tensions. For example, a parent may want more integration with his or her teenager, while the child wants less. A husband may be at the point of wanting more openness in a relationship, while the wife wants more privacy. Or one friend wants stability, while the other wants the relationship to move and change.

Montgomery and Baxter advise that we use dialogue, or talk, as a way of managing the natural tensions of a relationship, and the dialogue shapes the nature of an evolving relationship over time. Excellent dialogue about differences can have an aesthetic quality that gives at least momentary form and coherence to our sense of relationship with another person. We use communication to construct a sense of order in an otherwise potentially disorganized system.

Community Conflict

When we ask the question, "Who are we all?" we are focusing on some important larger group. It can be huge, as in the case of "Who are we as women?" or rather small, "Who are we as a family?" We might ask, "Who are we as African Americans?" or "Who are we as residents in the Historic Downtown Neighborhood?" Community diversity is apparent when you draw a line between "people like us" and "people like them." In other words, when you make distinctions along the lines of ethnicity, gender, religion, sexuality, class, age, family origin, nationality, and regional background, the community realm stands out.

Michael Hecht and his colleagues refer to the community realm as *communal identities*, which transcend individuals and relationships but also have great impact on each.[30] When these identities stay with us for a long time, they are *master identities*, which can take the form of gender identity, race, class, sexual orientation, religion, and other communities that strongly affect our sense of identity.[31]

The Values of Diversity. The diversity movement in the United States centers on values of diversity in schools, universities, and workplaces. Although individuals have different opinions about this issue, diversity, at least in the public realm, is viewed as a positive value. This is actually a rather modern idea.[32] Modernity is character-

ized by the felt need for variety and change, and diversity provides
the variety of resources society needs to progress. Whatever is old is
thought of as outdated, even quaint, while the new is celebrated.
Pearce calls this particular version of modernity "happy modernism,"
precisely because it sees diversity as a positive experience. The complement of this state of affairs is "disillusioned modernity," where
diversity is more challenging and problematic—though not necessarily bad. We will explore such cases in following chapters. For now, we
will focus on the positive aspects of community diversity.

When community diversity is valued, difference is celebrated.[33]
Every summer our city sponsors a series of weekly ethnic and cultural
festivals, where cultural groups showcase their music, dance, and
food. Sojourners seek change by traveling to foreign lands as a form of
personal growth and education. When diversity is valued, we seek
change rather than resist it.

Fern Johnson refers to the diverse community as a *cultural complex*, in which many traditions overlap and influence one another.[34] In
a cultural complex, most cultures are both distinct and interrelated.
You may identify yourself as Chinese American, but this identity
relates to many other cultures. Johnson shows that certain cultures
within the complex will come to dominate others, a problem we will
address in upcoming chapters.

The cultural context consists of a set of beliefs and practices of a
community of people who share certain characteristics. It is the basis
for defining who we are as a group, what we should think as a group,
what we should do as members of the group, and what distinguishes
us from other groups. The cultural context is relatively stable over
time, although as individuals we may be members of several cultural
communities that subscribe to different values and practices.

Historical developments make certain groups very important to a
society, depending on the region or nation in which you live. Within
the United States, for example, Chinese-American, Japanese-American,
and Indian-American cultures contribute to the Asian cultural context.
The large, diffuse Hispanic culture, consisting of Mexican, Puerto
Rican, Cuban, and others, is also historically important in the United
States, as are African Americans and the many European immigrant
groups. All of these overlap with other important cultural communities, such as those related to gender, religion, and sexual orientation.[35]

When managed well, diversity can be valuable in many areas of
society. In her book on workplace diversity, Marlene Fine defines a
truly multicultural organization as one that values diversity, honors
all cultural perspectives, and encourages the full participation of all
cultural voices in organizational decision making. Fine writes that

such organizations are necessary in the twenty-first century because the workforce is inherently multicultural. Diversity will provide new and important perspectives for approaching organizational problems.[36] Diversity within cities and regions provides similar values. Imperative in democracies is the representation of all significant cultural groups in the political system at local, regional, and national levels. Democracy requires an ongoing dialogue among cultural groups at the local level to increase cross-cultural understanding, to define shared concerns, and to establish collaborative problem solving.

We encountered some of the values of diversity in our work in Cupertino, California.[37] By the 1990s, this suburb located south of San Francisco had experienced significant demographic change as a result of Asian immigration into the area. The once homogeneous community found itself divided along racial lines; citizens did not know how to talk about this issue. In a series of meetings, the Public Dialogue Consortium, working with local groups, created opportunities to explore the cultural richness of the community, which led to a stronger, more vibrant community in which race was a positive resource rather than a problem.

The Challenge of Diversity. We were once asked to mediate a dispute between business owners and residents of a suburban town over the issue of highway improvements. The city stood to receive several million dollars in federal money if they could agree on a plan to improve the main street of the town. The two sides had been locked in a struggle over this issue for a number of years and had fought it out both in the city council chambers and the courts. The business owners wanted a solution that would maintain good traffic flow through the town with lots of business access. The residents wanted a solution that would be both beautiful and safe for their community. The business owners felt that their livelihoods were at stake, and the residents felt that the safety and quality of their lives were threatened. In the end we failed to bring the parties to the table. The conflict had grown so that the community was divided. Hateful speech had hardened the boundaries between residents and businesspeople. Connections had been severed, and it was now impossible for the city to proceed. In like manner, we have seen a church in conflict over whether to spend funds on a stained glass window or to support mission work.

Community conflict, though disconcerting, is not surprising, as managing community differences has always been a significant challenge. It must be done in ways that permit cultural identity but encourage productive dialogue across groups. Our colleague Roxanne Leppington has developed a fascinating format for such dialogue.[38] Concerned about Jewish–Black conflict in her own community, Lep-

pington engaged members of these two groups in a staged set of discussions using video. She first had each group talk about the other
group while being videotaped. In the next stage, each group viewed
the video of the other group and talked about the stereotypes that
they heard portrayed there. Then, in a final stage, the two groups met
together to share their perceptions of one another's images of the
other group. Leppington found that this dialogue format had great
promise for bridging cultures, dispelling stereotypes, and building
intergroup understanding.

Communities exist because we make distinctions between "people
like us" and "people like them." Whenever we draw a boundary, a
community is formed; there is no end to where and when we do so.
Some communities draw few boundaries; others draw many. We knew
a graduate student who wanted to study a deaf lesbian community.
They would not allow her to interview them because, even though she
was proficient in American Sign Language and was herself a lesbian,
she was considered an outsider because she was not deaf. We also met
a female-to-male transsexual who told us that he had nothing to talk
about with anyone who was a male-to-female transsexual. As human
beings, we have a tendency to draw boundaries separating ourselves
from others, whether as individuals, communities, or nations.

Earlier we mentioned the problems that can result from assuming
the contexts and connections driving the behavior of others. A snap
judgment is frequently a stereotypical judgment. For example, the
Vietnam War (or the American War, as the Vietnamese called it)
resulted from drastically different contextual connections.[39] U.S. leaders interpreted the situation from the broad context of the world geopolitical order, which they defined in terms of two clashing powers:
democracy and capitalism versus communism. Within this context,
U.S. leaders saw their country as the guardian of freedom and North
Vietnam as a puppet of international communism. If South Vietnam
fell to communism, the rest of Southeast Asia would fall like domi-
noes. North Vietnamese leaders, in contrast, were working from a
very different set of contexts. They understood the events in terms of
nationalism, driven by the desire to reunify a divided nation. The
entry of the United States into Vietnam was understood as a brute act
of imperialism in which South Vietnam served as a puppet of the
United States. The war, from the North Vietnamese perspective, was
one of national defense and reunification.

Community conflict results from differing goals, values, and
belief systems. Communities can and do, however, manage their differences humanely and constructively. We will see some of the ways
they do this as the book unfolds. Living coherently in a world of dif-

ference means understanding difference as a manifestation of the social construction of contextual connections.

HOW YOU CAN USE THIS CHAPTER

Once you get past the idea that communication is a simple tool for transmitting information and influence to other people, whole worlds of possibility open up to you. Now you can begin to imagine the kinds of worlds you want to make and think about how to do so.

1. You construct differences that can create value, challenge, and harm. If you want to move toward value and away from harm, ask yourself how your communication practices can contribute to this.

2. You live in a complex world of personal characteristics, relationships, and communities. Which of these matters the most and when? Ask yourself, "When I communicate in certain ways, am I contributing to building the kind of communities, relationships, and personal ways of being that I want to make or am I contributing to something I don't want for myself and others who are important to me?" When you don't like what you see, change how you act in these situations and invite others to do the same.

3. In order to do the first two things in this list, what "games" do you have to know how to play well, and when do you need to move beyond them and become a game master? Build the capacity in yourself to play the games most necessary in your life and know when to play or not play these games, how to modify these games, and how to create new ones.

4. Understand that you will never be a unified, consistent person. You will always experience differences within yourself. Don't fight against this, but use these internal differences as positive resources for contributing constructively to the creation of social worlds.

5. Do not despair over the tensions and contradictions within relationships. These are natural and normal. As a game master, learn to manage these. If you try to eliminate them, you are wasting your time and maybe even creating a boring, unproductive, and uncreative life.

6. Embrace the differences within your communities. In helping to manage these, remember to try to move from harm toward value.

Interactive Case Study

PERSONAL IDENTITY

Context: It is your twenty-fifth birthday. You are planning to do a variety of things to celebrate this benchmark. An interesting surprise gift arrives from your parents. They gave you a weekend at a mountain resort, to be enjoyed by yourself! This resort has hikes, spas, comfortable rooms, and delicious food. You will have two days of solitude to relax, consider your future, and engage in some introspection about who you are and who you are becoming.

Opening exercise(s): You are going to be focusing on yourself in a variety of ways. Prepare yourself for some introspection. Brainstorm answers to the following questions. Try to get as many responses as you can. Fill the paper!

1. Who are you?
2. What are some of your characteristics, values, attitudes, and beliefs?
3. Who are the most significant persons in your life?

Focus #1: Congruence

Begin this intrapersonal discussion by thinking about what is coherent in your life. What is feeling organized, logical, and consistent in your world? List these as your "Coherent Moments." Now think of these moments as episodes, as actual examples of times when this coherency was exhibited in your life as *consistent patterns of being* in the world. When do your values, attitudes, behaviors, and perceptions align with each other? List these as your "Congruent Episodes."

Focus #2: Incongruence

Look at these lists again. Now, shift your thinking to times when you are aware of inconsistent perceptions, attitudes, behaviors, or goals. If these are in conflict with each other, they may need attention. List these instances of incongruence, and in a corresponding column, list the effects of each.

Focus #3: Personal Diversity

We attempt to manage intra- and interpersonal differences, our personal diversity, in a variety of ways. Look at the three forms of diversity and consider how they are manifested in your life. When do you experience diversity within yourself, diversity between yourself and others, and diversity between how you see yourself and how others see you? Try to recall some concrete examples of each.

Focus #4: Relational Diversity

You have a relational identity and it is sometimes characterized by differences. Focus on the differences that are revealed through your relationships and the identity created by your interactions. List five of your most significant relationships. Make a chart that lists the five of them as rows on the left side and three columns listing clusters of tensions (*integration* and *separation*, *expression* and *nonexpression*, *stability* versus *change*) at the top of the page. In each corresponding square, record how (and if) you are experiencing these tensions with the other person in that relationship. What is the result?

Focus #5: Community Diversity

Finally, spend some time considering yourself in relation to the communities of which you are a part, possibilities include your neighborhood, your school, your town, your church, your ethnicity, your club, or distinguishing personal characteristics (the left-handers association). In each of these communities, where do you experience diversity? In any of these communities, is diversity explicitly valued?

1. List three examples of interactions within a community when diversity provided a challenge or a conflict.

2. Record some of the impacts of these interactions.

3. Recall times when these differences were valued, bringing a variety of values, attitudes, behaviors, and perceptions together to produce productive dialogue.

4. What was created (or already in place) to foster this dialogue?

5. How did each of these situations affect your personal identity?

Endnotes

[1] The communication perspective was introduced by W. Barnett Pearce, *Communication and the Human Condition* (Carbondale: Southern Illinois University Press, 1989).

[2] For more detail on the social approach to communication, see Wendy Leeds-Hurwitz, ed., *Social Approaches to Communication* (New York: Guilford Press, 1995).

[3] Adapted from Pearce, *Communication and the Human Condition*, p. 24.

[4] Ferdinand de Saussure, *Course in General Linguistics* (London: Peter Owen, 1960).

[5] Kathy Domenici and Stephen Littlejohn, *Communication and the Management of Face: Theory to Practice* (Thousand Oaks, CA: Sage, 2006).

[6] Adapted from W. Barnett Pearce, *Interpersonal Communication: Making Social Worlds* (New York: Harper Collins, 1994), pp. 34–35.

[7] Adapted from the analysis by Karen Tracy, *Everyday Talk: Building and Reflecting Identities* (New York: Guilford, 2002), pp. 17–20.

[8] Adapted from the analysis by Tracy, pp. 17–20.

[9] Ronald D. Laing, H. Phillipson, and A. Russell Lee, *Interpersonal Perception: A Theory and Method of Research* (New York: Harper and Row, 1972).

[10] See Stephen W. Littlejohn and Karen A. Foss, *Theories of Human Communication, 8th ed.* (Belmont, CA: Wadsworth, 2005), pp. 77–81.

[11] This analysis adapted from Pearce, *Interpersonal Communication*.

[12] For a summary of rules theory, see Susan Shimanoff, *Communication Rules: Theory and Research* (Newbury Park, CA: Sage, 1980).

[13] Michael J. Beatty and James C. McCroskey, *The Biology of Communication: A Communibiological Perspective* (Cresskill, NJ: Hampton Press, 2001).

[14] For a summary of work bearing on this issue, see Eura Jung and Michael L. Hecht, "Elaborating the Communication Theory of Identity: Identity Gaps and Communication Outcomes," *Communication Quarterly*, 52 (2004): 265–283.

[15] Thomas C. Schelling, *Choice and Consequence* (Cambridge, MA: Harvard University Press, 1984).

[16] Littlejohn and Foss, pp. 77–81.

[17] See, for example, Patricia G. Devine, David L. Hamilton, and Thomas M. Ostrom, *Social Cognition: Impact on Social Psychology* (San Diego: Academic, 1994).

[18] Robert J. Branham and W. Barnett Pearce, *Quarterly Journal of Speech*, 71 (1985), p. 26. See also, Vernon E. Cronen, Kenneth M. Johnson, and John W. Lannamann, "Paradoxes, Double Binds, and Reflexive Loops: An Alternative Theoretical Perspective," *Family Process*, 20 (1982): 91–112.

[19] Littlejohn and Foss, pp. 77–81.

[20] Leon Festinger, *A Theory of Cognitive Dissonance* (Stanford, CA: Stanford University Press, 1957).

[21] Austin Babrow, "Uncertainty Value, Communication, and Problematic Integration," *Journal of Communication*, 51 (2001): 553–573.

[22] Kurt Lewin, *A Dynamic Theory of Personality* (New York: McGraw-Hill, 1935).

[23] M. H. Brazerman, A. E. Tenbrunsel, and K. A. Wade-Benzoni, "Negotiating with Yourself and Losing: Making Decisions with Competing Internal Preferences," *Academic of Management Review*, 23 (1998): 225–241.

[24] Stella Ting-Toomey, K. Yee-Jung, R. Shapiro, W. Garcia, T. Wright, and John G. Oetzel, "Cultural/Ethnic Identity Salience and Conflict Styles in Four U.S. Ethnic Groups," *International Journal of Intercultural Relations*, 24 (2000): 47–81.

[25] Carol M. Werner and Leslie A. Baxter, "Temporal Qualities of Relationships: Organismic, Transactional, and Dialectical Views," in *Handbook of Interpersonal Communication*, ed. Mark L. Knapp and Gerald R. Miller (Thousand Oaks, CA: Sage, 1994), pp. 323–379.

[26] Werner and Baxter, "Temporal Qualities."

[27] Barbara M. Montgomery and Leslie A. Baxter, eds., *Dialectical Approaches to Studying Personal Relationship Processes* (Mahwah, NJ: Erlbaum, 1998).

[28] Gary Saul Morson and Caryl Emerson, *Mikhail Bakhtin: Creation of a Prosaics* (Stanford, CA: Stanford University Press, 1990).

[29] Barbara M. Montgomery and Leslie A. Baxter, "Dialogism and Relational Dialectics," in *Dialectical Approaches to Studying Personal Relationships*, ed. Barbara Montgomery and Leslie Baxter (Mahwah, NJ: Erlbaum, 1998), p. 160.

[30] Jung and Hecht, "Elaborating the Communication Theory of Identity."

[31] Tracy, p. 18.

[32] Pearce, *Communication and the Human Condition*.

[33] W. Barnett Pearce and Stephen W. Littlejohn, *Moral Conflict: When Social Worlds Collide* (Thousand Oaks, CA: Sage, 1997), pp. 111–113.

[34] Fern L. Johnson, *Speaking Culturally: Language Diversity in the United States* (Thousand Oaks, CA: Sage, 2000), p. 61.

[35] Marlene G. Fine, *Building Successful Multicultural Organizations: Challenges and Opportunities* (Westport, CT: Quorum Books, 1995).

[36] Fine.

[37] Shawn Spano, *Public Dialogue and Participatory Democracy: The Cupertino Community Project* (Cresskill, NJ: Hampton Press, 2001).

[38] Personal communication.

[39] This analysis is based on Robert S. McNamara, James Blight, Robert Brigham, Thomas Biersteker, and Herbert Schandler, *Argument without End: In Search of Answers to the Vietnam Tragedy* (New York: Public Affairs, 1999).

3

Taking a Systems View

Conflicts are often viewed as something that *happens to a person*, or perhaps something that *happens to two people*. Yet we know that conflicts are more complex than this. There is a dynamic that lies between or among individuals that creates the character of a conflict. In this chapter, we look more broadly at conflicts as systems.

Systems arise not from the characteristics of individual parts but in the interaction among the parts.[1] In a system, the whole is more than the sum of pieces. If you and I work together to push a boulder off a cliff, the collective force of the two of us may provide enough energy to move the object, but this is not a system. A system has vibrancy, an energy that is not apparent by adding up the individual forces. In systems, there is an interaction, sometimes called "assembly effect," leading to a synergistic outcome. From a systems perspective, we might find that as each of us exerts force on the boulder, an interaction effect actually creates more overall force. This is certainly true in team sports. The skills of individual players are leveraged by an interaction dynamic that occurs when they are playing together.

A LITTLE SYSTEM THEORY

If you observe a system in action, you notice that it moves in concert. The interaction patterns within the system create a certain state. Much of the time, this is *homeostatic*, meaning that it exerts energy to stay in balance (like a heater and thermostat). Sometimes, a system will exert energy to change or move to a new state, a condition called *morphogenesis*. Any complex system will go through both balance and change, with emphasis sometimes on the former and sometimes on the latter. Often change in one part of the system is counteracted by change in another. Frequently a period of change in the system is followed by a period of stability. These processes of change and balance are *cybernetic*, meaning that the system exerts energy to organize itself.

Conflict can be a force for balance or change. Old conflicts are probably sustained because of a tendency of the system to maintain a steady state. The conflict may even function in some way to help maintain stability. This is not necessarily a bad thing, although when the conflict maintains an unwanted state or creates an obstacle to constructive relationships within the system, it probably needs to be changed, and one way of doing that is to shift the responses typical of the cybernetic patterns within the organization. New conflicts may actually spark change. Again, these conflicts might be positive because they create needed change within the system.

Children commonly begin to show independence when they experience puberty, often in ways that worry parents. They may become disobedient, insolent, and in extreme cases even self-destructive. New conflicts that arise in adolescence rock the previously steady boat requiring a change in navigation and attention to sea conditions. This is a time when a family may undergo considerable movement, as new patterns of interaction are required. Parents may set new rules, permit more independence, or shift forms of discipline. Such conflict is not necessarily bad, as it brings about necessary changes in the family system that enable children to move from the dependency of childhood into the self-responsibility of adulthood and to allow parents to change their own roles accordingly. At the same time, parent-adolescent conflicts may become homeostatic and destructive when they develop a persistent life of their own. How can this happen?

In system terms, figure 3.1 illustrates the positive relationship between parental pressure and teenage rebellion. The more the teenager rebels, the less control the parents have, and the less control they have, the more pressure they exert. This simplified system shows how the conflict can sustain itself in a balanced state. How could this be changed? The parents could imagine ways of exerting control other than pressure, they could define control differently, or they could disconnect their sense of control from the child's behavior. Perhaps one

Figure 3.1   A Simple Parent-Child Feedback Loop

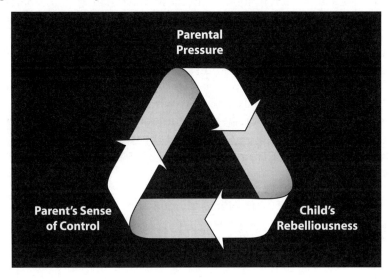

of the most common ways of handling the situation is to stop trying to control altogether.

This example is overly simple because it leaves out the larger system of other siblings, friends, ex-spouses, and the behaviors related to interactions with each. Conflicts may be sustained by rather complex cybernetic feedback loops throughout the family system. We sometimes conduct mediation sessions between family members, coworkers, or even neighbors. In this kind of mediation, we know that what happens between the two parties in conflict is rarely isolated from what is happening in the larger system of which the conflict is a part. In workplace and family conflicts especially, we notice that there are others who are always affected by the conflict and its resolution. Although mediators prefer to have all the stakeholders present, there is a practical limit, and all of the stakeholders are rarely present. As a result, in mediations we ask questions designed to raise the parties' consciousness of larger systemic interactions and to encourage thinking about implications for others in the system and indeed the system as a whole. For example, an increase in arguments at home may result from deteriorating relationships at work.

Systems are complicated because they too have relationships to other systems in the environment. Indeed, where we draw the line, or boundary, of a system is actually rather arbitrary and related to what we want to observe at a given time. When we look at small systems, then, we need to remain conscious of the larger environment. A

mother and her two children constitute a small system, but their interactions are very much influenced by how they relate to grandparents,
neighbors, friends, and so forth. If a system is highly homeostatic, it
will have internal mechanisms that counteract influences from outside the system. If it is more adaptive, it will have mechanisms that
integrate with influences from outside.

System thinking helps us see that many forces interact with one
another in a complex network that works more in circles than in
straight lines. When we pushed the boulder off the cliff, we observed
the effect of linear causation—a force causing movement of an
object—but causation is mutual in systems so that elements impact
one another in a network of influences.

We are interested in the network of influences of which conflict is a
part. Our discussion of this topic is divided into three parts: (1) *How system theory changes what we see in conflicts*; (2) how conflict involves *connections across time*; and (3) the implications of *intervening in a conflict*.

HOW SYSTEM THEORY CHANGES WHAT WE SEE

The system perspective allows us to look beyond the obvious and
to see a number of things happening in conflict situations.

Connections

Once we adopt a systemic view, we begin to see actions affecting
other actions, the way in which our statements and behaviors are connected, and we become interested in what lies between actions. Furthermore, we begin to notice that interactions affect other interactions.
In a family, for example, a conflict between mother and father impacts
the interactions between parents and children and between the siblings themselves, and, further, those other interactions feed back to
influence what mother and father are doing together. Moreover, the
children's interactions in school and in the community are affected by
the dynamics at home.

Connections can be described as *correlations*, in which things vary
together. For example, when mother gets mad, father also gets mad.
The more angry one gets, the more angry the other becomes. From a
systems point of view, we would be interested in the mutual spiral in
which anger breeds more anger. As another example, we might notice
that the more father nags, the more mother withdraws. Father says
that when mother becomes more distant, he must become more insis-
tent. Mother says that when father becomes more demanding, she

must be more protective. They have different explanations, but the pattern is clear.

In systems, things rarely connect one-on-one, as other individuals and variables are usually involved. The feeling, direction, and impact of a conflict are established in these kinds of system connections. We can extend the family example above to a connection between family/school systems. "A father's dominance could cause the mother to withdraw, which causes the child to get depressed, which prevents her from going to school, which creates problems with the teacher. The teacher calls the parents, and the father gets mad. In his domineering style, he tells the mother to get the kid to school, and the mother withdraws."[2] We could assume all kinds of other connections within this family/school system.

The Environment of a Conflict

Systems are never isolated; they always connect to other systems, just like the family and school in the above example. Where does one system end and the other begin? The answer depends on where you want to draw the line. When you take a systems view, you make a decision about what system to look at, while also recognizing that other systems constitute the environment. This is important, because systems both influence and are influenced by their environments. The family affects the school, but the school affects the family. There are similar interactions between a family and its extended family, the workplace, church, neighborhood, and community.

Box 3.1

Starting with a blank piece of paper, write in the middle a brief description of a community or current event conflict that you have read or heard about. On the rest of the page, list the individuals, organizations, agencies, communities, or other entities that influence this conflict or may have an interest in its outcome. Connect these entities with lines where other relationships occur or where they interact with each other to affect this conflict. Look carefully at those connecting lines (not the entities themselves). For each line, ask the following questions:

1. How does this set of interactions affect another set of interactions?

2. What patterns of interaction are occurring?

3. How does this pattern affect the conflict?

Looking at the whole map, ask:

1. How do multiple interactions affect the entire system?

2. How do multiple interactions affect the conflict?

3. What other systems (larger or smaller) could this system connect to?

In our practice, we often mediate disputes between coworkers. During the mediation session, we are concentrating mostly on the interaction between the two parties involved. A systems view, however, leads us to understand that their conflict is not isolated from the larger workplace in which it occurred. Other things happening there affect it, and the conflict certainly has an impact on this environment as well. One of the goals of this kind of mediation is to help the disputants themselves see this larger picture and to make these important connections. You can carry this same kind of analysis into every conflict situation. The war in Iraq originated in a geopolitical system, including many political, economic, and social forces both within the United States and Iraq and beyond their borders as well.

Self-Organization

Conflicts seem to have a life of their own. Like any system, a conflict is *cybernetic*, exerting energy to organize itself. This is why conflicts are often self-perpetuating. The participants seem powerless to change the state of affairs in which they are engaged. A systems perspective, then, helps us see how the interaction patterns in the system work to maintain some balance. Expectations that arise in conflicts are strongly cybernetic. If I expect you to be mad at me, I may act in ways that provoke your anger. If you perceive that I withdraw into inaction, you become even more persistent in trying to make me assume responsibility, which keeps the pattern going.

Sometimes conflict patterns are so strong that only a new set of forces can change them. In a family, for example, patterns may change with the birth of a child, the death of a parent, the departure of a teenager to college or the service, or a divorce. Managers in organizations sometimes find it necessary to reassign certain employees in order to break a pattern that poisons the workplace. Elections may serve the same function in political systems.

A common way of "jolting" the system in order to bring about a new, more constructive organizational pattern among the disputants is third-party intervention. The involvement of a counselor or mediator is a good example. Because of its potential impact and importance, we write more about systemic intervention later in the chapter and return to it again at various points in the book.[3]

MAKING CONNECTIONS ACROSS TIME

Among the different kinds of systemic connections are those that occur across time. What I do and say now is connected to what I said and did in the past and what I will say and do in the future. What I say and do now is connected to what you have said and done in the past and will do in the future. These relationships over time are very important from a systemic point of view.

We like to think of communication as an ongoing conversation. We take turns at talk, but each turn stems from what was said before. The history we construct forms part of the context. History is made through interaction, which is held in memory and which at any given moment we construct or frame in certain ways. Conflicts are rife with disagreements and varying interpretations of the history of interaction between the parties and with others. How one party responds in the moment is very much connected to his or her view of what happened before, and the other party makes connections based on his or her perspective of the history of the interaction. Another way of thinking about this is that communicators—whether in a conflict situation or not—bring their stories of the past to bear on the current situation. Their stories may be the same, overlap, or be quite different. The narratives of our stories influence and reflect our sense of reality.

The time continuum, of course, reaches beyond the current moment and anticipates a future. We act in a situation not only as a response to our view of the past but also in anticipation of what might come next plus eventualities well beyond the current episode. We not only construct stories of the past but also stories of the future.[4] When differences are managed, we want to hear a variety of scenarios of where we might go and what could happen if we did make those futures a reality. When differences are not managed very well, then we may get stuck in narrow views of what the future holds, or we may struggle with others to prevail in creating the kind of future to which we are committed. In the best collaborations, we work together to develop a shared vision to create future possibilities.

INTERVENING IN A CONFLICT

So far, we have spoken as if systems were something you can understand by observing from outside. This is not really a very accurate portrayal, however. Whenever we look at a system, we bring our own interaction histories and socially constructed realities to the task. The mere act of looking affects the system we are looking at. Once you engage a system, the system expands to include you. This is true whether you are looking as a mere observer or whether you take a more active role to intervene.

Conflict intervention can take many forms. The systems perspective gives us a particularly useful way of understanding what happens when third parties intervene. An approach called *second-order cybernetics* shows that the intervention agent—a diplomat, mediator, arbitrator, attorney, counselor, or friend—both influences and is influenced by the interactions within the system.[5] At the very least, the third party will perturb or disturb the system, in a way that can bring about change within it. Just by asking questions, a third party can help disputants think about things in new ways. We were recently brought in to facilitate meetings in a highly conflicted department and began with a series of interviews to gather information and assess the situation. The interviews themselves brought about change before we ever had a meeting. People began to think and act differently because we were there and asking questions.

Any kind of third-party action has the potential of perturbing the system. Even if the third party—a parent observing two siblings in a fight, for example—decides to "stay out of it," that is a form of action that will, in some way, affect the interaction between the children. Notice that this influence is two-way. The siblings' interaction affects the parent's action, and the parent's action affects that of the children.

Conflicts are "owned" by others as well. Divorces, for example, occur in a larger network of relationships with family, friends, and even coworkers. A civil war affects and is affected by neighboring nations and, indeed, the entire international community. When we take a larger system view, we orient to conflicts differently. Such a view brings three principles into focus.[6]

1. *The principle of concern*: In ideal conflict management, we are guided by concern for everyone who may be affected. How we respond to the conflict will have consequences; we should be guided by a deep concern for the well-being of all involved.

2. *The principle of shared responsibility:* In ideal conflict management, the parties should share the responsibility for managing the conflict humanely and constructively. Good conflict management is participative and collaborative.

3. *The principle of the third side*: In ideal conflict management, we engage all relevant parts of the system. We think beyond the confines of the disputing parties and look for positive resources in the system to help us manage the conflict in a way that moves from harm to value.

Conflict theorist William Ury offers an invitation to transcend "yes" and "no" and move to what he calls the "third side."[7] He challenges us to move beyond individual communication transactions and to create a culture of coexistence. *The Third Side* discusses preventing the escalation of destructive conflict; addressing latent tensions, which can sometimes prevent the emergence of conflict; resolving overt conflicts that do develop; and containing escalating power struggles.

Preventing the Conflict

Ury advises analyzing latent tensions as one means to prevent differences from developing into conflict. "Prevention means addressing the root causes of conflict and laying the foundation for the cooperative management of difference."[8] Conflict can arise from frustrated *needs*, lack of *skills* or attitudes to defuse the conflicting needs, and the lack of good *relationships* to prevent conflict in the first place. Three main preventive roles address these needs—the provider, the teacher, and the bridge builder.

The Provider. Our basic human needs can often put us at odds with one another. People want to feel safe, respected, and free. If we can help people address these needs, we act as a provider and ward off some of the destructive conflict. The water shortage in the Southwest has threatened many basic needs. Farmers see their livelihood being threatened; manufacturers imagine a loss of water will stop operations; native communities wonder about the availability of water for their traditions and ceremonies; and community members speculate about their own water consumption and the effect on future lifestyles. Providers share resources, give knowledge, and open doors to resources that others can use to help themselves.

The nineteen Pueblo Indian Tribes in New Mexico are an excellent example of working together despite difference. The All Indian Pueblo Council (AIPC) is a consortium that acts as provider by encouraging the common welfare, fostering the social and economic advancement of all the Pueblo Indians, and preserving and protecting their common interests.

The Teacher. Teachers can give people the skills to handle conflict. We have had the opportunity to teach conflict management in university and other settings for more than fifteen years. Some of the most meaningful classes have occurred in high schools and with younger children. We remember a school training where one of the participants, an 18-year-old male, reacted strongly. We had just spent a day "teaching" the young adults some methods to handle conflict, and this young man broke down crying. He said furiously, "This is not fair. I have gone my whole life acting out violently in conflict situations, and NO ONE has told me that there is another way."

There are countless ways that we can act as teachers to help prevent the escalation of conflict. Teachers do more than pass on theoretical knowledge about conflict; they offer a starting point for the significant task of managing conflict in your own world. There are thousands of school conflict management programs across the United States and around the world, where children and youth are learning about joint problem solving, mediation, violence prevention, and effective communication. However, teachers are not limited to schools. Parents, friends, coworkers, and coaches can be teachers as well, teaching by example as well as by precept.

The Bridge Builder. The bridge builder forges relationships across lines of difference to work toward third-side prevention of conflict. Ury suggests three ways that bridge builders work by creating cross-cutting ties, developing joint projects, and fostering genuine dialogue. The Southwest Strategy (SWS) is an excellent example of such a bridge builder. A collaborative group of leaders from federal, state, and tribal natural resources and environmental agencies, SWS tackles the big issues in the Southwest, such as water, fire, and border issues. The organization establishes working groups to carry out the recommendations of the executive committee. One such working group deals with rangeland management.

This collaborative group, which includes agency employees, ranchers, farmers, and environmentalists, met weekly for about two years to address the growing problems with rangeland issues and to discover and create ways of working together. They shared a meal during each meeting and invited each other to their "neck of the woods" to attend a community gathering. Under the auspices of Southwest Strategy, this group forged relationships that crossed boundaries. It was not always the most constructive communication. After all, how do you talk about endangered species to parties whose primary concern is increasing acreage for cattle to graze? The most difficult task was to find common values and goals among the diverse group. Exploratory questions included: What is the most important aspect of the rangeland in New Mexico and Arizona? What are you willing to give up to make sure that your primary goals are included? What resources need to be in place to ensure that all issues are addressed? What are you willing to contribute to make sure those resources are guaranteed?

When they got stuck in talking about principles, the group was able to move forward by making a decision to do something concrete. Their idea was to create a "Rangeland Monitoring Handbook and Training Guide" for local ranchers and land use agencies in New Mexico and Arizona. The process of developing this training and the accompanying materials took about a year. It was in the process of developing the project together that differences were minimized and forward movement was maximized.

In our own conflict management practice, we often use similar methods of transcending a "stuck spot." Create a project or a goal together, and do something! A common activity for groups where their differences seem to paralyze them is to undertake a planning exercise. Differences can be confronted in a safer and more comfortable manner during a planning session.

Resolving the Conflict

Ury believes that the way we deal with conflict matters more than the conflict itself, and third parties can help make a better process. The escalation of conflict can be attributed to three factors—interests, rights, and power—each of which can be mitigated by the third side. *Mediators* work with interests, *arbiters* work with rights, and *equalizers* work with power.

The Mediator.   We have been active mediators for many years now and have found immense satisfaction in both the process and the results. As introduced in chapter 1, mediation is a process where parties get together to address their issues with the assistance of a third party who facilitates the conversation. The presenting focus at the mediation session is on an issue for which the parties are experiencing differences in perspective, opinions, positions, and needs. Mediators help parties identify and integrate their interests and help them explore mutually satisfactory solutions. Although mediators work in different ways, the primary focus is to help disputants talk to one another about what is important to them, to share their versions of the situation, to frame the problem, and to identify possible options for solutions. Mediators can also help parties evaluate the options, test possible solutions, and come to agreement.

The goal of mediation is a mutually satisfactory solution—not necessarily a spectacular big finish but something that both sides can accept. Formal mediation programs abound. You can find mediation offerings in schools, courts, workplaces, universities, hospitals, communities, companies, and government agencies.[9] For example, the U.S Equal Employment Opportunity Commission (EEOC) was established in 1965 to eliminate illegal discrimination from the workplace. To accomplish that goal, various approaches (some dictated by statutory requirements and some by philosophical and managerial considerations) have been employed. A major shift occurred in the early 1980s when the Commission began offering "alternative dispute resolution" or mediation as an innovative way of addressing the disputes brought to them. Today, mediation is a significant force in managing EEOC cases. From 1999 through 2003, over 52,400 mediations were held and more than 69% of the charges were successfully resolved.[10]

Many schools have implemented peer mediation programs, in which children are trained to mediate disputes with their peers. In a typical program, students involved in conflicts are referred to a mediation center, where they can have a third party help resolve the dispute. A recent evaluation of school peer mediation programs found overwhelming evidence that (1) student-trained mediation programs can be successfully implemented in both elementary and secondary schools, (2) such programs are effective in resolving disputes, and (3) that student satisfaction with the results of peer mediations tend to be positive. Mediation helped improve school climate, academic achievement, and self-esteem while reducing conflict levels.[11]

Mediation need not be formal. Any "third-sider" can communicate like a mediator by modeling constructive communication as well as helping others develop their own solutions through their communication. Involvement leads to commitment: people support what they create. It's as simple as saying to your young child, "What outfit would you like to wear today?" or as profound as "What type of leadership would you like for this organization?" Get the people who will be impacted by the future state involved in the creation of that state.

The Arbiter. If mediation is a process in which the parties have ultimate control over the outcome, arbitration is a form of adjudication in which parties give the decision-making power to a third party. Arbitration-type processes occur in work settings, with judges in courtroom settings, by teachers in classrooms when dealing with discipline, or with a parent deciding on a sibling rivalry dispute. Sometimes it is necessary to hand over the decision-making control. When rights are in dispute, it is important to determine who is at fault and to repair the harm done to the victim and the community. The EEOC keeps mediations confidential. If the parties do not reach agreement, a formal investigation ensues. The investigators are arbiters. They determine if rights were violated and order restitution.

The Equalizer. Picture two children on a seesaw attempting to adjust themselves until they feel balanced. If someone talked with them and facilitated their movement, without giving suggestions or advice, by asking them, *"How could you move so the seesaw is balanced?"* this person would be acting as a mediator. If the children cannot find equilibrium and begin arguing or fighting about their imbalance, a parent or teacher (arbiter) could come and order each one to move slightly to achieve equal balance. The equalizer comes in and actually moves the fulcrum, making a judgment about where the imbalance is occurring and who seems heavier.

Ury sees an equalizer as one who democratizes power and promotes the fair sharing of power. Acting as an equalizer assists the weaker party by publicizing their concerns. Equalizing can range from nonviolent public protest to more divided efforts to bring opponents to the negotiation table or even support for an industrial strike, lockout, or boycott.

Since April 1977, the Madres de Plaza de Mayo in Argentina, mothers of children who have disappeared, have marched in the main Buenos Aires city plaza to protest their children being taken and presumably executed by the oppressive government.[12] Most of the mothers were housewives who did not work outside the home and had not previously been engaged in political struggle. As far as we know, they still protest every Thursday, many of them now grandmothers (Abuelas de Plaza de Mayo). We were able to walk with them in 1999 and experienced what equalizing power might feel like.

The Healer. A pastor from a local church was asked to leave the position he dearly loved and had planned on enjoying until retirement. The claims against him were: "He is getting boring in his sermons; he is not relevant to this modern age; he is stuck on a theology that is too closed minded." The pastor and his family were very hurt and sorrowfully moved to a new state. As we travel through this world of human difference, we will find countless examples of grief, hurt feelings, damaged reputations and egos, and frustration. As a healer, we can work to repair those feelings and the injured relationships that accompany them. How do we act as a healer?

- Create the right climate; pay attention to the communication environment. Have we made sure all parties are comfortable? Are we committed to using communication that is respectful? Have we built trust in a way that opens communication rather than engaging in behavior that creates an environment of defensiveness, hostility, or suspicion?

- Listen and acknowledge. If we are really listening, we acknowledge other people fully, both verbally and nonverbally. We let them know that we have heard them, without indicating our own judgment, experience, or opinion on the topic. It is amazing how much healing can occur by offering active and respectful listening to the other.

- Encourage apology. When sincerely offered, apologies can affect both the individuals and the injured relationships. This type of healing can be longer lasting than most monetary awards or court judgments. The full healing then can occur when reconciliation is the goal. Apology is offered from one side, but reconciliation and forgiveness are gifts that involve all parties.

The alienated pastor wished that he would have known what was coming. He looks back and sees that he could have structured staff meetings in a way that respected sincere concerns and offered dialogue about how to address those concerns. He wishes he had created venues to hear and to acknowledge the congregation's perceptions and to engage them in honest discussions about meeting their needs and moving their church forward in the rapidly changing world. He desires to turn back the hand of time and apologize to those who felt "left out" and to listen to the apologies of those who had said the most hurtful things to him. That communication environment did not exist at that time, but this pastor has moved to a place of reconciliation. He wishes the best for his previous church family. He strives to create a place of healing and wholeness in his new church family.

Containing the Conflict

The final challenge for those of us who are interested in managing differences—or answering the question, "Why can't we get along?"—comes when we attempt to contain the conflict. A full-blown conflict erupts. Who is paying attention to the conflict? If you do, you can act as a *witness*. Who is setting limits on the fighting? If you do, you are acting as a *referee*. Who is intervening to providing protection? If you do, you are acting as a *peacekeeper*.

The Witness. A large organization with 400 people was embroiled in a conflict over organizational principles and values. The leader told a few people that trouble was brewing, but no one really paid attention to it until it became a battle that erupted in public. Many of the people involved asked later, "Why didn't we notice that this was escalating?" We can pay attention to escalation by watching for early warning signs. These signs can be physical (depression, irritability, erosion of infrastructure, increased conflict) or more subtle (dwindling resources, loss of accountability, water fountain gossip, or decreased camaraderie). If those signs are noticed, Ury says to *go on patrol! Speak out! Get help fast!* We cannot afford to use avoidance as our conflict management tool, as avoiding the issue gets us nowhere.

The Referee. If and when people get embroiled in conflict, it is important to set limits. The referee can reduce the harm by establishing rules for fair fighting. While in the midst of conflict, the most effective interpersonal interactions occur when strong guidelines for communication—ground rules—are firmly established at an early date. We recently facilitated a staff meeting where distrust and animosity existed. In fact, the staff members had resorted to communicating only by e-mail and memo. When they gathered, we had them first develop a set of group rules for their communication. They were not allowed to address the issues that divided them until they had created a set of communication rules that they all agreed to use and support. Their mutually established rules were:

1. Each person is allowed uninterrupted speaking time;
2. Make comments brief so all persons can be heard and acknowledged;
3. Turn off all cell phones, pagers, and PDAs;
4. Use common courtesy and talk to each other in a respectful manner;
5. If the conversation gets uncomfortable, ask for a break or a new type of communication;
6. Decisions will be made by consensus, in which everyone agrees to live with the result (even if they do not favor that decision);
7. If someone disagrees, we will continue the discussion;
8. All participants will help keep us on the agenda;
9. If the group is straying off on a tangent, anyone can do a process check and inquire if the group is comfortable with the direction of the discussion.

The Peacekeeper.   The situation globally today warrants various peacekeeper entities in hot spots. Peacekeepers provide protection, intervene in conflicts, enforce the peace, and preempt violence before it starts. The contradictory image of peacekeepers carrying guns is a stark reminder that this complex world requires complex answers. What is at the heart of peacekeeping? What is the goal? Can we be peacekeepers as parents, employees and employers, and as citizens? The hope is that if we act as peacekeepers, we will never be called on to fight. Instead, we can model the attitudes and methods that prevent, resolve, and contain conflict.

TRENDS IN CONFLICT MANAGEMENT

If conflict is inevitable, given the human differences at play in our world, the strategies and procedures for addressing those differences must adapt to human challenges. As conflict managers and communicators become more adept at noting the early indicators of conflict and find ways to minimize, divert, or resolve these differences, development of new techniques and methods will follow. Here are some general observations about the current trends in conflict management.

Conflict management processes are becoming more system focused. The system view of conflict says that there are many interrelated pieces of the puzzle, and some aspect of each of these pieces is needed to construct an appropriate and successful path forward. As organizations look for ways to address their most significant challenges, they are asking for methods that convene all the interested parties in some manner. In some cases, the process may merely convene the interests by gathering the information by survey, online query, or brief interviews. In other cases, the actual parties may assemble to clarify the issues at hand, explore viewpoints and perspectives, negotiate options for agreement, and evaluate decisions and commitments.

An example of this system-focused trend is the City of Albuquerque Facilitated Land Use Meetings. When a land use proposal is sent to the city to be approved, neutral facilitators convene all those with an interest or a stake in the proposed development (the developer, consultants who performed traffic, air quality, and other environmental impact studies, neighborhood association leaders, interested community members, local businesses and schools, etc.). Facilitators guide a process where the plans are shared, clarifications are made, and questions are answered. Public comments are considered and recorded, to be taken under consideration by the city when deciding about the use of land in the city boundaries.

Strategic system planning processes are becoming more commonplace as a means of managing conflict. Early in our practice, it was common to wait until conflict broke out and then try to find some method for "resolving" it. Today, organizations and agencies are beginning to realize that difference must be managed before conflict breaks out. Process consultants are frequently hired to facilitate processes of planning that enable a common vision to be established so that consensus can be built on actions for the future.

The Southwestern United States is experiencing a severe drought; conflict over how to manage this scarce resource has been continual for many years. There has been litigation, arbitration, mediation, force, persuasion, and lots of frustration. We are happy to report that many communities are now shifting to future-looking planning initiatives to address the conflict. Multiyear water planning projects are in place, where the people in conflict are setting aside their differences and collaborating on planning, rather than fighting over scarce resources.

We are seeing an increasing emphasis on communication, as opposed to methods of intervention, in conflict management. There seems to be

increasing attention to what constructive communication looks like or how people should communicate in managing their differences. An important distinction within this trend is between *dialogue* and *debate*. Whereas debate is designed to pit one idea or position against others in a competitive environment, dialogue is designed to explore complexity by sharing personal experience and multiple perspectives. Facilitated dialogue is a choice for people and organizations grappling with conflict paralysis and polarization over difference. Carefully constructed agendas that privilege listening and understanding help parties discuss tough issues while feeling safe and empowered. We return to this subject in part 3 of this book.

Besides these general trends, a variety of programs are gaining momentum in the world of conflict management. One of the most amazing is the development of a whole new field, *Online Dispute Resolution* (ODR).[13] The conflict management world quickly took advantage of the benefits of the Internet. New ODR companies and new processes showcase the contribution of technology to the resolution of disputes. Ethan Katsh and Janet Rifkin saw the rapid growth of online commerce, growth of nontraditional marketplaces, and a heightened interest by governmental bodies and ADR organizations as proof that ODR has broad implications.[14] As the field develops and the possibilities are amassed, ODR raises a number of questions:

1. Can online processes take the place of face-to-face meetings? Alternatively, is there a way to merge the two processes?

2. Can mediators and interveners who work in face-to-face settings gain the skills necessary to use electronic tools with efficiency and effectiveness?

3. Does ODR use the same policies, precedent, and standards as
other ADR processes?

4. What types of cases are most (and least) appropriate for use
with ODR?

5. What type of technology is most effective: synchronous (chat
rooms or places where all are present at the same time) or asyn-
chronous (e-mail-type exchanges where people have a choice as
to when to communicate)?

Sometimes called cybermediation or digital dispute resolution, ODR
usually addresses two types of cases: Internet disputes (those that
arise in cyberspace) and offline disputes (those that have traditionally
been dealt with face-to-face).

As the ADR world ponders this rapidly expanding field, many
feel that the disadvantages of ODR will be addressed with the
advancement of technology. As videoconferencing becomes more
commonplace, and Internet connections are fast enough for lengthy
video and audio sessions, the impersonal nature of ODR processes
may fade. The powerful future of ODR is more than just experimental.
The field of conflict management looks forward to the contribution of
technology as a tool for managing human difference.

We are seeing emphasis on new forms of communication, as
opposed to methods of intervention, in conflict management. There
seems to be increasing attention to identifying just what constructive

Box 3.2

Do a Web search of Online Dispute Resolution sites on the Internet. You
will find numerous pages. List the sites, and compare their offerings using
the following questions as guidelines:

1. What type of cases do the sites offer to address?

2. How do the processes work? What are some examples of types of processes (for example, mediation, negotiation, arbitration)?

3. How much does the process cost?

4. How automated is the process? Does a "real person" monitor or facilitate the negotiations?

5. Do any of the processes offer encouragement for face-to-face negotiations combined with the online focus?

6. What most surprised you about these sites?

communication looks like and how people should communicate when managing their differences.

HOW YOU CAN USE THIS CHAPTER

System thinking not only broadens our understanding of what happens in conflict situations but also opens many avenues for action and effective management of difference. Here are a few ways you can think systemically about conflict and the management of difference.

1. Never boil a conflict down to the traits of the people involved. Look instead to the interaction pattern between them. How do they act toward one another?

2. Look at broader system influences on communication patterns. How are the individuals most entrenched in conflict affected by their environments? How does their behavior, in turn, affect the larger system?

3. Look at how conflicts perpetuate themselves in a balanced system, where changing the interaction pattern is scary because it would require new behaviors that the parties are not ready, able, or willing to accept. You can get out of a repetitive conflict by deliberately (1) changing the way you respond, (2) concentrating on other interactions in the system, or (3) involving third parties.

4. Realize that conflicts can be positive and can lead to constructive change, especially when they break a homeostatic pattern than is no longer benefiting the system. Realize, too, that system change itself can be painful because of the conflicts that it may spark. In times of change, concentrate on constructive, humane methods for managing salient differences.

5. Third parties can help. Think about the roles you could take in helping others in conflict and think about the kinds of help you need when you yourself are involved. As you interact with individuals and groups, you create links that will influence the system; you, in turn, will be influenced by the system. Your participation may only be temporary, but it is real nonetheless. What you say and do will perturb the system in some way that could be important; following constructive guidelines can result in a positive disturbance.

Interactive Case Study

AT THE BORDER

Context: You are living in a Southern border town where the issue of illegal immigration has become a hotly contested topic. During the summer, many people have died of heat and thirst while trying to cross the border. Law enforcement, social service groups, religious organizations, federal, state, and local governments, and citizens from both sides of the border occasionally find themselves confronting each other, usually resulting in flared tempers and deepened polarization.

Opening exercise(s): The past month has resulted in an increased number of deaths and deportations, due to the high desert temperatures and lure of new jobs in the United States. Since tensions are at a crescendo, the community knows that something has to be done. This is an opportunity for a third-side perspective. Before exploring the possible intervening roles, it will be important to get a grasp of the immigration issue and its dimensions.

Hold a class discussion about the issue. Some research may be needed to illuminate the dimensions of the conflict. As the class discusses, someone should record highlights of the conversation on a board or easel.

1. List the stakeholders as they emerge, and record some of their interests.
2. List possible competing values and goals that could be at play.
3. Assuming this conflict resides in the sphere of challenge or harm, list some of the examples of harm that may result.
4. Finally, list any opportunities that may be inherent in the conflict that may allow this system to enter the sphere of value.

Focus: The Third Side

The class will be divided into three groups. Each group will focus on one of the categories of third-side intervention. Then divide each of the three groups into further subgroups:

Group 1: Prevention
   Subgroup: Provider
   Subgroup: Teacher
   Subgroup: Bridge builder
Group 2: Resolution
   Subgroup: Mediator
   Subgroup: Arbiter
   Subgroup: Equalizer
   Subgroup: Healer
Group 3: Containment
   Subgroup: Witness
   Subgroup: Referee
   Subgroup: Peacekeeper

Each subgroup will discuss and decide on their approach to intervention for the immigration issue. Make a plan to work with the system in addressing this border issue and then present this plan to the larger group. Each of the three groups will then coordinate their information in a format that will be presented to the whole class.

Three group presentations will occur: Prevention, Resolution, and Containment. After each presentation, the class will discuss:

1. Does this perspective engage all the relevant parts of the system?

2. Does this perspective find resources in the system to help the conflict move from the sphere of harm to value?

3. How is each of these interventions creating connections that influence individuals as well as the system?

4. Could this intervention create a culture of coexistence?

Endnotes

[1] For an overview of system theory, see Stephen W. Littlejohn and Karen A. Foss, *Theories of Human Communication, 8th ed.* (Belmont, CA: Wadsworth, 2005), pp. 40–42; Armand Mattelart and Michele Mattelart, *Theories of Communication: A Short Introduction* (London: Sage, 1998), pp. 43–45; and Stephen W. Littlejohn and Kathy Domenici, *Engaging Communication in Conflict: Systemic Practice* (Thousand Oaks, CA: Sage, 2001), pp. 218–221.

[2] Littlejohn and Foss, *Theories of Human Communication*, p. 38.

[3] See also, Littlejohn and Domenici.

[4] Littlejohn and Domenici, pp. 68–70.

[5] See, for example, Heinz von Foerster, *Observing Systems: Selected Papers of Heinz von Foerster* (Seaside, CA: Intersystems Publications, 1981).

[6] Adapted from David M. Jabusch and Stephen W. Littlejohn, *Elements of Speech Communication* (San Diego: Collegiate Press, 1995), pp. 7–12.

[7] William Ury, *The Third Side: Why We Fight and How We Can Stop* (New York: Penguin Books, 1999). See also, *Getting to Yes: Negotiating Agreement without Giving In*, with Roger Fisher and Bruce Patton (New York: Penguin Books, 1981), *Getting Past No* (New York: Penguin Books, 2000), and *Must We Fight?: From the Battlefield to the Schoolyard—A New Perspective on Violent Conflict and Its Prevention*, William L. Ury, ed. (San Francisco: Jossey-Bass, 2001).

[8] Ury, *The Third Side*, p. 114.

[9] Nancy A. Burrell, Cindy S. Zirbel, and Mike Allen, "Evaluating Peer Mediation Outcomes in Educational Settings: A Meta-Analytic Review," *Conflict Resolution Quarterly*, 21 (2003): 7–26.

[10] 5 February 2007, www.eeoc.gov/mediate/history.html

[11] Burrell, Zirbel, and Allen, pp. 7–26.

[12] Karen A. Foss and Kathy L. Domenici, "Haunting Argentina: Synecdoche in the Protests of the Mothers of the Plaza de Mayo," *Quarterly Journal of Speech*, 87 (2001): 237–258.

[13] Janet Rifkin, "Online Dispute Resolution: Theory and Practice of the Fourth Party," *Conflict Resolution Quarterly*, 19 (2001): 117–124.

[14] Ethan Katsh and Janet Rifkin, *Online Dispute Resolution: Resolving Conflicts in Cyberspace* (San Francisco: Jossey-Bass, 2001).

4

A Closer Look
at the Conflict System

Chapter 3 discussed the synergy of the system and its significance in conflict situations. While the system is greater than the sum of its parts, it is useful to look at some aspects of the system in a little more detail. Without trying to be comprehensive, we have written this chapter to outline some elements that you should think about in conflict situations. Specifically, we want to encourage you to think about (1) conflict styles, (2) message strategies, (3) emotions, (4) the social environment, and (5) culture.

CONFLICT STYLES

If you look at behaviors that a person tends to repeat—how the person is predictable—you will begin to identify traits. If a person is frequently outgoing, for example, you would say that he or she is high in the *trait* of extroversion and is friendly in *style*. We have to be careful here because traits and styles only identify observed patterns over time. Even a person who is very precise in some situations may be quite inexact in other ones.

Some psychologists view traits as caused by genetic make-up, which assumes predictability. In this view, you don't have much control over your style; it will be determined by the neurochemistry of your brain.[1] Yet, we know that people make plans, create strategies, act voluntarily, and adapt and shift their behavior according to their goals. In other words, the style of communication can depend on personal comfort zones, situational factors, objectives, and choices. Although some individuals stay mostly within a narrow range of styles, other individuals move widely among many styles. For these reasons, we prefer not to ask *what* characteristic or style you *have*, but *when* you display various styles and *what happens* when you use these styles.

J. R. Davitz found that people in general respond to others in one of three ways—*moving toward, moving against,* and *moving away.*[2] These three categories are (1) cooperating and building a relationship, (2) aggressing or competing, and (3) withdrawing or avoiding. Ralph Kilmann and Kenneth Thomas provide more detail.[3] These authors note that you will tend to respond cooperatively if you have high concern for the other person but aggressively if you have only high concern for yourself. If you don't care one way or the other, then you will tend to avoid the conflict altogether. These tendencies result in five styles:

1. *accommodation* (giving in);
2. *avoidance* (ignoring or diverting attention from the conflict);
3. *competition* (trying to win);
4. *compromise* (give and take); and
5. *collaboration* (working together to find a mutually beneficial solution).

Avoiding and Accommodating

If you do not care very much about outcomes for yourself or for the other person, you will probably *avoid* the conflict. There is no sense having a conflict over something that does not matter to you. At the same time, we can think of all kinds of reasons we might want to avoid a conflict even when we do care. It may not be the right time. We may care more about the potential emotional wear and tear than immediate gains, or we may be "picking our battles" and saving energy for more important fights.

If you care a lot about the other person but your own potential gains are inconsequential, you will probably *accommodate*. Accommodation is common in conflict situations. We may accommodate because we care greatly for the other person (as in the case of a child or someone greatly in need); the relationship is most important to us, and we are willing to give up a lot for it; or some harm could come to us if we tried to get our way.

Competing and Compromising

Competition is both realistic and common in conflicts. When you compete, you are trying to win, meaning that you care more about your own gains than any concern for the other party. *Compromise* means a give-and-take negotiation where each party gets something of what they want, but must give up something as well. Sometimes we think of compromise as positive, because it settles the matter and you gain something out of it. Other times, however, compromise has a negative feeling, meaning that everybody gave up important things just to get the dispute resolved. In everyday life, compromise turns out to be an expedient and convenient way of settling a dispute, and most of us frequently use this form. On matters that are very important to us, however, collaboration is preferred.

Collaboration

Collaboration means that you want success for everyone. This is a classic win-win position. How does it work? Later in the book—and in the appendix as well—we talk in some depth about collaboration. Sometimes called *integrative problem solving* or *principled negotiation*, the parties try to create solutions that help everyone achieve as many of their goals as possible.

In accommodation, compromise, and competition, the goal is to distribute or divide a fixed set of assets among the disputing parties. In competition and accommodation, one side gets more than the other. In compromise, both sides split the goods. Collaboration is different; the outcome is not a division of resources but a mutually created solution that integrates gains for everyone.

Suppose that you are arguing with your neighbor about a broken fence on the property line. If you are competitive, you will try to get your neighbor to pay for the kind of fence you want. If you are accommodating, you will share the expense, and your neighbor will get to decide on the kind of fence. If you compromise, you will split the bill and find some type of fence that neither one of you likes very much.

Collaboration works differently. Rather than focusing on dollars, you will work together to identify what each of you wants and try to come up with a solution that provides this. For example, you may want an attractive "natural" fence like a hedge, and your neighbor wants a secure boundary to keep his dog in. In addition, each of you wants an inexpensive solution. You agree to work together to install a wire-mesh fence that will keep the dog in and put in planting beds on each side with attractive vines that will fill in the mesh and hide them from view. Aside from a small investment in fencing and bedding plants and some sweat equity, there is little out-of-pocket expense, and both neighbors are delighted. This is what we mean by collaboration.

Collaboration is not always possible, nor efficient. There is really nothing wrong with any of the approaches to conflict; each has its advantages and disadvantages. The problem is that we too often fall into whatever pattern is familiar, when collaboration would indeed be the best approach.

Box 4.1

Assemble the class into groups of three. These triads will be exploring the five modes of communication available to us in conflict situations. Two students will be negotiating, and one will be observing. For each of the following scenarios:

1. Two students will negotiate for what they want.

2. Each negotiator will privately choose one of the modes of communication and use that style throughout the negotiation (accommodation, avoidance, compromise, competition, collaboration).

3. The observer will attempt to note the style being used and observe the results of that style both individually and in conjunction with the style of the other negotiator. What was gained by the use of those styles? What was lost?

4. After each scenario, switch roles and switch styles.

Scenarios:

• One of two roommates wants to order cable TV services; the other does not.

• Two employees disagree about the time line for the report they are working on. One wants to finish it quickly and impress the boss with efficiency. The other wants to take a longer time and do higher quality work.

• South Side and North Side are discussing putting up a fence along the border between the two areas. One wants a fence for easier logistics and organization of cross border traffic. The other does not want a fence, citing the loss of neighborly relations and impression of distrust.

MESSAGE STRATEGIES

When we ask our students to talk about cases in which they used one (or more) of the five modes of communication, the conversation inevitably leads to a richer set of ideas about how, when, and why people communicate in certain ways. The communication in extended conflict situations requires a certain amount of planning.[4] In matters of marriage, work, and state, communicators usually think carefully about their goals and how they want to achieve them. In most important cases of conflict, three related sets of goals will operate—identity goals, relationship goals, and instrumental goals.

Communication Goals in Conflict

Identity goals relate to how we wish to present ourselves—the image we want to create. Frequently we are interested in sustaining or changing a relationship in some way, leading to *relationship goals*. Our *instrumental goals* are the substantive outcomes we wish to achieve relative to the issues at hand. Each of these goals supports and provides a foundation for the others, and communicators integrate them.[5] Figure 4.1 illustrates that we rarely have just one goal in conflict communication.

Figure 4.1   Conflict Goals

For example, a wife in a divorce may want to show that she is competent and in command of the situation (identity goal), to influence her husband (relationship goal), and to get full custody of the children (instrumental goal). She will probably not achieve her instrumental goal without success in the other goals as well. Parties in a dispute will constantly adjust the content and style of their communication—and sometimes modify their goals as well—to the responses of others. When our differences really matter—when we are required to work through a difference—we think about strategy.

Using Power to Achieve Goals

A strategy is a general approach to meeting your goals—the question of how you want to deal with the challenge of a difference that has become a problem. One of the most common goals in such situations is to seek the compliance of the other parties involved. Here we try to get others to see things our way, to do what we want them to do.[6]

Lawrence Wheeless, Robert Barraclough, and Robert Stewart found that compliance-gaining strategies are based largely on power.[7] You assess the power you have and approach the conflict in a way that makes use of this. Three sources of power are common—the ability to *manipulate consequences*, the ability to *set certain aspects of the relationship*, and the ability to *define values and obligations*.

Controlling Outcomes.   When you *manipulate consequences*, you are able to control the outcomes of another person's choices. Parenting is a good example. Parents frequently use this source of power to gain children's compliance. Parents give and use rewards and punishment. Nations and international organizations try to manipulate consequences to gain the compliance of other nations. At the time of this writing, Iran and Korea are moving rapidly ahead to develop nuclear capability. This has the international community worried, because it could mean the development of nuclear weapons. We don't know what will happen, but the United Nations, Russia, the United States, China, and Europe are all working on sanctions that will deter these countries from following through on their nuclear plans.

Controlling the Relationship.   The second kind of power is *relationship power*, which means that you make use of your position in the relationship to be able to "call the shots," or to establish how others should behave. The principle of least interest is a perfect example.[8] It has long been established that the party with the least interest in the conflict has the power. If you don't really care what happens, you can walk away at any time; if you care a lot, you will be willing to do much more to keep the relationship going. Have you ever had a boyfriend or girlfriend who didn't care as much about the relationship as you did? Who had the power? Children often gain power over parents in this way. They are not aware of the dangers and problems associated with their behavior and are willing to risk a lot. Parents on the other hand want the best for their children and often have a much greater interest in the outcome of a conflict situation. There are other dynamics that can lead to relational power as well, as is the case when one's established role—e.g., manager, elected official, teacher, or judge—grants them the power to determine what happens.

Controlling Values and Obligations.   The third source of power that many people rely on in compliance-gaining situations is the perceived ability to *define values and obligations*. This can happen because of cultural factors that grant certain individuals credibility, leadership, or authority. In most Native American cultures, for example, elders are held in high esteem and often establish the norms of the society. Often we defer to others because of their education, perceived intelligence, life experience, or other factors that demand deference. This is a true source of power to influence others, and when you use this to gain compliance—as a captain in the Army does in giving orders—then you are relying on your ability to define values and obligations.

We often use two or three sources of power. In the divorce example above, the wife is interested in getting full custody of the children. How might she approach this? What strategies might she use? If she believes that she has the power to manipulate consequences, she might tell her husband that she will go to court to prevent him from having visitation rights. Here she reasons that since he wants to see the children, he will give her custody in order to have visitation. Perhaps she thinks that she can control the relationship between herself and her soon-to-be ex-husband. Here she might suggest, for example, that if she has full custody, she will be a lot more pleasant and easy to communicate with in the future; otherwise, she'll make his life miserable. Finally, the divorcing wife might feel that she can define values and obligations, taking the general approach of saying that mothers are better parents and that the children will not benefit emotionally by living with their father.

From Power to Perspective

The communication literature generally supports the idea that sophisticated strategies are generally more effective than simplistic ones.[9] One reason for this is that more sophisticated strategies are usually *person-centered*, meaning that they acknowledge and adapt to the feelings, positions, and interests of other people. To use such strategies, you must learn to take the perspective of others, a skill commonly called *perspective taking*. This requires that you have the cognitive ability to make many distinctions and to see things in a variety of useful ways. A five-year-old child will say, "I wanna trike." At age ten, the child could say, "I want a bike so I can ride to my friend's house." A teenager might say, "If I had a car, you would not have to drive me all over the place." Notice how these messages move increasingly from being self-centered to being other-centered. It is clear that in most adult situations, taking the perspective of the other is more effective than staying in a self-serving mode.

Message design is based on a certain logic that we employ within the communication situation. Barbara O'Keefe identifies three common *message design logics*—expressive, conventional, and rhetorical.[10] The *expressive logic* sees messages as a form of self-expression, designed to tell another person how we feel or what we think. Such messages tend to be open, transparent, and simple, with little regard for the feelings of others. For example, the statement "I am unhappy in this relationship and don't want to see you anymore" allows the speaker to get a burden off his or her chest, but it may be very hurtful to others.

The *conventional logic* follows established rules and norms. Polite and appropriate, such messages appeal to an individual's rights and responsibilities. Using this logic, the speaker might say, "You have been such a good friend to me, and I want to keep a close relationship. However, we did agree that we could see other people, so maybe it would be better if we stopped dating for a while."

The *rhetorical logic*, in contrast to the other two, attempts to negotiate new rules that achieve complex goals, both for the other person and for oneself. Here, the speaker might say, "How are you feeling about our relationship lately? I just want to make sure that we are both able to do what we want. How could we talk about this in a way that would allow us to maintain a friendship and yet permit each of us to grow as people? Let's talk."

Notice that as these strategies increase in complexity and person-centeredness, they open up more possibilities for collaborative solutions. The expressive logic is simple, direct, and not very person-centered. The conventional logic is a bit more complex, because it must appeal to social rules, etiquette, and show respect and politeness, while also asserting a point of view. The rhetorical logic can be complex and may take a while to develop. It is very person-centered and very much directed at both self and other in a way that permits numerous goals to be achieved.

Directness and Politeness

Daniel Canary and Andy Gustafson created a model called DINN to illustrate approaches to conflict.[11] DINN stands for "direct, indirect, nice, nasty." A message can be direct and nice, direct and nasty, indirect and nice, and indirect and nasty. *Direct and nice messages* show a willingness to manage the problem along with support for the other person. Such messages also offer to share information and show a desire to get information from the other party as well. These messages would use a conventional or rhetorical logic. *Indirect, nice messages* minimize personal responsibility, but use humor, teasing, and distraction. Very much within conventional logic, such messages are friendly in tone but do not acknowledge responsibility for the problem.

Direct and nasty messages are filled with accusation, demands, hostility, and put-downs, while *indirect and nasty messages* minimize personal responsibility through evasion, minimizing, noncommitment, and stonewalling. Such messages may attempt to manipulate the conversation by such tactics as distraction, topic avoidance, and interruption. They tend to be condescending and negative in tone. In general, nasty messages rely on an expressive logic, although indirect nasty messages may be cloaked in certain conventions.

The Role of Attribution

The way in which we frame our messages in conflict situations, then, depends largely on what we see happening or what we think is going on—as well as our ability to take the perspective of the other and the logic we use to design the message. A lot of research addresses the question of how our understanding of the situation affects our responses. Let's look at an example.

If your teenage son slams his bedroom door in your face, you will certainly try to figure out why he did it, creating an explanation in your mind. You might think, "He is so irresponsible and never thinks of anyone else," implying that he is to blame for what happened. On the other hand, you might think, "Oh, gosh, I haven't given him much attention lately," taking the blame yourself. On another occasion, you might consider, "Hm, maybe he's sick," attributing the behavior to circumstances. You can see that you would respond quite differently,

depending on which of these explanations you chose to believe. This is the process of *attribution*. Attribution theory looks at how individuals perceive the causes of behavior, or, more broadly, how they explain their own and others' actions.[12]

Alan Sillars and his colleagues found that when you blame the other person, you are more likely to react in a competitive way, using criticism, rejection, hostility, and denial of responsibility. On the other hand, when you blame yourself, you tend to be more cooperative.[13] The problem is that people fall prey to a *fundamental attribution error* of overattributing another person's actions to personal motives and ignoring circumstances. When someone does something bad, you will tend to blame that person rather than look at other possible reasons. On the other hand, when you do something bad, you tend to blame circumstances. If you do something good, what attribution do you think you would make? You would almost certainly take responsibility for the good action.

Many conflicts, we believe, stem from this fundamental attribution error. Instead of pausing to look at the whole situation, people are quick to blame others, while rationalizing their own behavior. This is why they may jump to quick, expressive, and nonperson-centered responses rather than more thoughtful rhetorical ones.

EMOTIONS

Strong emotion is common during intense conflict. You may feel remorse, sadness, regret, tension, frustration, guilt, shame, and even some positive emotions such as relief, satisfaction, humor, caring, interest, and curiosity.[14] Because emotions are so strongly connected to conflict, we bring the subject up at several points in this book.

Your responses in a conflict situation will be shaped by (1) your understanding—and consequent attribution—for what is happening, (2) the resultant emotion you feel about this, and (3) your level of arousal.[15] If, for example, you believe that someone intentionally did something to spite you (attribution of blame), you might feel a lot of anger, and your tendency might be to strike out or be aggressive. If, on the other hand, you believe that you caused someone else to be hurt (attribution of self-blame), you might feel guilty and tend to run, escape, or avoid.

Anger

Because it is so commonly associated with conflict, let's look at the first example of anger. G. L. Clore and colleagues found that there are a variety of types of anger, depending on your explanation of what is happening (your attribution).[16] *Pure anger* results from your perception that another person's behavior hurts you in some way. You have asked your son to help you get ready for a dinner party, but he refused, slamming the door in your face. *Reproach* as a type of anger happens when you perceive that another person has done something wrong and you want to let them know. You are upset that your son slammed the door in your face. *Frustration* occurs when you are unable to achieve a goal, but you can't really blame another person for it. You have a lot of work to prepare for the dinner party, but you issued the invitation and can't expect your son to help. Finally, *resentment* happens when something good happens to another person that this person does not deserve. Unaware that your son has been rude, your spouse comes home from work and gives him $20 for a date. You would probably respond differently to each emotional characterization.

The Social Construction of Emotion

We typically think of emotions as raw physiological states that just spring from our bodies. While we can feel strong emotions physiologically, we can also develop a set of beliefs or concepts with which to understand and make decisions about how to respond when we feel angry. Emotions, then, are just as much socially constructed as anything else.[17] We learn what an emotion is, what to call it, and how to respond to those feelings and labels from a lifetime of interaction with significant other people in our lives. Further, different cultures handle emotions in different ways. For example, the Eskimo tend to "feel" emotion not as an individual thing but as a collective experience. As a result, emotions are displayed publicly as a group.

Because people understand situations and behaviors differently, define appropriate emotional responses in a variety of ways, and learn to react differently, we really cannot predict how people might feel or respond in different situations. Something that could make one person very mad and lead to direct, nasty messages could lead to another person being a bit surprised and perhaps curious. Don't think of emotions as set in stone, and certainly do not feel that you are obligated to respond in certain ways when you feel particular kinds of emotions. This is a vital point in developing the skill to manage differences in ways that will lead from harm toward value. We will return to this issue later in the book.

THE SOCIAL ENVIRONMENT

One of us has a five-year-old daughter, and we delight in watching her run up to hug a friend as a way of saying, "Hi, I'm glad to see you." This gesture existed long before she was born and will survive long after her lifetime. Yet, as she grows up, goes to school, enters a career, and moves through life, she will participate in creating new gestures, expanding the meaning of old ones, and constructing whole worlds of meaning that we cannot now anticipate. After all, this is a world in which *cool* has come to mean *good*, *hot* means *attractive*, and *bling bling* is expensive, flashy jewelry. From a social perspective, then, nothing is just contained within you. Your words, gestures, thoughts, perceptions, feelings, and actions are always understood through a filter of meanings created through social interaction. This is why conflict is never a raw form; like a dance, it is always created or constructed through coordination with others.

Taking a social perspective enables us to see that conflict is created and determined by how we communicate about our differences. A person cannot make a conflict individually; it takes at least one other person to respond in a way that makes something they would call "conflict." Consider:

> Joe: There you go again. How many times have I told you not to do that?
>
> Bill: Right, I never listen. Sorry.
>
> Joe: But, Bill, you are such an idiot!
>
> Bill: I didn't realize you knew me so well. Yeah, I am kinda dumb.
>
> Joe: You're hopeless. Get out of here.
>
> Bill: Right, I have a lot to do anyway.

Poor Joe, he keeps trying to have a conflict with Bill; but Bill just won't cooperate. Watching Joe and Bill is like seeing one dancer doing the fox trot with a partner who is trying to waltz.

Unintended Consequences: The Process of Structuration

When issues are important, the question is not whether to avoid a conflict but how to respond and what kind of conflict to make. The social environment that we create through communication consists of a micro side (the back-and-forth interaction of everyday conversations) and a macro side (enduring social structures that have been built up through interaction across time). An ordinary conversation, then, constitutes a *microenvironment* that occurs within a larger social frame such as the family, church, workplace, government, school, or nation, all of which is the *macroenvironment*.

Of course, there's a lot going on between micro and macro, and this middle ground is really where the social environment gets made. Anthony Giddens uses the term *structuration* to describe the connection between micro and macro.[18] When you do something to reach a goal, certain unintended consequences occur. These are important because they build up over time in larger structures that shape and limit what you can do in the future. A good example of this process is role development. Your roles at home, at work, among friends, and in the community are not assigned; they develop through a process of interaction. You don't start out to be the "social secretary," "money manager," or "taxi driver" of your family, but you develop these roles by taking certain actions that the family comes to expect. Notice how these roles confine your future action, as it becomes difficult to break the pattern of expectations.

In essence, this same process shapes organizations, political systems, cultures, and institutions of all kinds. The social environment gets constructed and reproduced—solidified over time—by repeated interactions of a certain type. The good news here is that patterns of structuration give us something we can count on. The bad news is that they can also lock us into sometimes negative patterns we would like to overcome, but cannot. The school bully does have a reputation to live down to, for example.

Structuration creates three elements of the social environment that are resources for human action. These are (1) a way of *understanding* or interpreting what is going on; (2) a sense of *morality*, or the proper way to act; and (3) a source of *power* to influence events. How people understand conflict, how they believe they should act in conflicts, and how they proceed to influence the outcome of a conflict are determined in large measure by what they have learned from previous interactions. Your family experiences may have taught you that conflict is uncomfortable and harmful, and that you can prevent strife by withdrawing and distracting. Alternatively, you may have learned that conflict shows concern, people who really care about an issue should speak up, or the one who yells the loudest cares the most.

These dimensions of the social environment affect our behavior at all levels. In apartheid South Africa, for example, the dominant society came to believe—through a century of structuration—that they lived in a land of racial division, and they interpreted all manner of events as divided by color. Dominant society believed that the proper and moral way of maintaining social order was through separation, and they used their power to maintain this state of affairs. Only when large groups of citizens decided—sometimes at great personal sacrifice—to act differently, could new forms of interpretation, morality, and power be established.

The social environment does affect what we understand as conflict, how we act in conflicts, and how we try to influence conflicts; but this is not a one-way process. Our actions also shape the social environment, which means that we can reproduce the pattern or break it.

Patterns of Conflict Interaction

The social perspective shows that a conflict is never the result of one person's actions alone. The outcome is always the product of interaction among various parties. What would happen if one person used a competitive style and the other an accommodating one? How would the outcome be different if a competition-minded communicator were interacting with an avoider? How would it work if one person wanted to collaborate, but the other responded as an accommodator? In other words, what a conflict "looks like" depends on how the participants respond to one another.

As noted in chapter 2, the game metaphor is useful for describing this process.[19] The moves, or turns, in a conversation follow gamelike patterns that help us understand what is happening by calling our attention to the rules that define the event. We use different rules for, say, "chastising" than we do for "comforting." We use different rules for "giving comfort to our best friend" than we do for "giving comfort to an acquaintance." Interaction, then, is governed by *meaning rules* that tell you what actions "count as," and *action rules* that tell you how to respond.[20] You know that when a stranger says, "Hi, how are you," this is a greeting and not an inquiry into your health; and you know that the proper way to respond is, "Fine. How are you?" The rules are different when you are talking to your child, the doctor, or your mate.

An *unwanted repetitive pattern*, or URP, can be especially disconcerting because it feels impossible to break.[21] You know the game, you play it well, but you wish you did not have to play this game and do not seem to have the resources to change the pattern of interaction. Many husbands and wives, parents and children, and coworkers live with unwanted patterns of conflict for a very long time. The same can be true of neighboring countries, as the Israeli–Palestinian conflict illustrates.

Patterns of interaction are easy to see on the interpersonal level. They are perhaps harder to perceive in larger social structures, in organizations, institutions, nations, and society at large. Yet, all interaction—even at the macro level—is based on rules that emerge through communication over time, have meaning, are more or less stable, and may be wanted or not wanted. In the next section, we look at some of these larger structures.

Conflict and Social Institutions

Social institutions are large-scale arrangements that have withstood the test of time and serve important societal functions. Families, religions, education, politics, economy, and government are all examples of social institutions. A social institution is a set of widely shared beliefs, norms, or procedures necessary for meeting the basic needs of society. If we are to be a member of a community or society, we live within a set of social institutions.

Whether simple or complex, we hear about many of these social institutions every day. The family has standards of behavior that are transferred from one generation to the next. We produce and raise children, equipping them to take over from the older generation the task of keeping society going. Educational institutions teach people to become effective contributors to the order and stability of society. Economic institutions provide food, shelter, employment, banking, and the services we need to live. Political institutions make and enforce laws to allow citizens the freedom to live their lives in an orderly society.[22]

While these institutions are the basis of much of our satisfaction and prosperity, they are also resistant to change and tend to support the status quo. They overlap one another and require an integrated means to address change. If an aspect of an institution needs attention or faces conflict, it is difficult to tweak the section that needs attention without moving the whole elephant.

Churches are usually well-established religious institutions with a formalized structure of belief, ritual, and authority. As our world undergoes massive changes due to the technology revolution, churches are challenged by televangelism, by global issues in our living room, by busier-than-ever lives, and by a frustrating pace of life. How can church leaders adapt to the changes? Do they develop flashy contemporary worship services with all types of music, quick theological sound bites, and deliberate efforts at diversity and inclusion? Alternatively, do church leaders remain true to the centuries old beliefs and traditions that many members rely on and remember, such as liturgy, hymns, strong creeds, and fervent prayers? Do churches interact with political institutions and get involved by supporting candidates? Do churches interact with educational institutions and recommend curricula (creationism versus evolution)? Do churches interact with the institution of family and try to influence birth control options? Conflict management in these instances requires complex

and determined efforts that acknowledge the balance between emergence of change and being the architects of change.[23]

Institutional Power

Power is not a bad thing. It gets things done. It provides a basis for
influence. It is, in fact, a necessary part of the communication structure of society. Empowerment is generally considered a source of
strength and self-determination. Yet, institutional power almost inevitably leads to conflict as those with power try to retain their advantage and those without power seek to gain more control. You read a
little bit about power earlier in the chapter, but to really understand
power, we need to take a more societal view, because power is constructed in social interaction.

Like all aspects of human life, institutional power is constructed
over time by certain patterns of interaction. If someone tells you to do
something and you comply, the result is consistent with what the
other person wanted. If every time that person asks you to do what
they want and you comply, then a larger frame of dominance is estab-

lished. This may be okay, but it may also lead to disempowerment, or an inability to hold your ground and achieve what is important to you. Notice here how power is a pattern of communication rather than some intrinsic or stable quality.

Notice also that this kind of power is very much established by how groups respond to one another. Power itself is rarely contained strictly within the relationship of two people; it is fueled by arrangements in the larger social network. For example, if we come to value money, then wealth grants power. When a society comes to define men as the authority, then power is largely a matter of gender. When the values and actions of certain ethnic or racial groups get defined as "normal," then all others are put into a marginal, or disempowered, position. This process becomes insidious when certain stakeholder groups repress and sometimes oppress (or even try to eliminate) other stakeholder groups in order to maintain their social power.

For many years in the southeast region of the United States, Blacks could not drink from the same fountains, eat in the same restaurants, or sit in the same part of the bus as Whites. This pattern was reproduced every time a Black person went to the back of the bus or drank from a fountain labeled "Negro." On a more violent level, it was reproduced every time a Black person was lynched, and those in power did little or nothing to change the injustice.

The patterns of power between Black and White began to change when civil rights workers refused to go to the back of the bus, had sit-ins in restaurants, and deliberately violated the existing order of power. In other words, they acted in ways that over many years of struggle in the movement established new, egalitarian rules of shared power. The prolonged conflict created a realignment that eventually achieved needed social reform. The macrostructure had to change, which meant, in turn, that interaction patterns and social relationships had to be altered. People had to respond in new ways.

One of the changes that can occur in a realignment of power is that one group gains power they did not formerly have. Another kind of change is a movement from competition for power to a state that more or less achieves ongoing shared power. Here stakeholder groups can work creatively to define their problems in a mutually acceptable way and together construct creative solutions in what is commonly referred to as a win-win situation. At the macro level, a purely win-win state is probably unrealistic most of the time, but recent history shows that we can approach or approximate it. We will return to how to engage multiple stakeholders in collaborative processes later in the book.

CULTURE

What do you first think of as your culture? You might focus on national origin, such as Swedish. You might consider religious affiliation, such as Muslim. Or you might consider race, such as Black, or race and nation, such as African American. Cultural forms stem from ethnic, national, regional, linguistic, religious, gender-based, sexual-preference, or organizational identities. The many cultures that have affected our lives provide resources in the form of symbols, meaning, and practices that shape our ways of understanding and acting in the situations of life.

Culture is "a set of fundamental ideas, practices, and experiences of a group of people that are symbolically transmitted generation to generation through a learning process." It consists of a set of "beliefs, norms, and attitudes that are used to guide our behaviors and to solve human problems," and "a system of expressive practices and mutual meanings associated with our behaviors."[24] In short, a culture consists of a relatively enduring way of thinking and acting common to a group of people that provides coherence to their lives.

In this section, we look at two large cultural concerns. First, we examine the ways in which cultural differences matter. Second, we address the always-challenging issue of managing conflict across cultures.

Cultural Differences that Matter

Fern Johnson provides a useful model to characterize cultures.[25] Every culture can be described in terms of three systems of related factors. The first is the system of *cultural abstractions*, or ways of thinking. These are a culture's concepts, values, morals, and ideas about how things fit together logically. The second is the system of *cultural artifacts*, or products of the culture, including, for example, art, music, dance, architecture, and tools. The third is the system of *language and communication*, or ways of speaking. Each culture has a discourse, a way of using words, grammar, and nonverbals, to communicate both within the culture and in the larger community. Communication is the central system of a culture, as it is the way that a culture's meanings are developed and expressed in interaction with others.

When we refer to the language of a culture, we are discussing languages like German, English, Spanish, Swahili, Diné, and Japanese; but the system of language and communication includes much more. A culture's discourse entails ways of speaking common to the group, including dialects and accents, vocabulary, expressions, nonverbal gestures and nuances, common metaphors, rituals, ways of telling stories, and many other forms that distinguish a particular community. All of these add up to a cultural code, or shared set of symbols and meanings.[26] As members of several cultures, we have at our disposal many ways of speaking that serve as a rich set of resources for our lives.

These different systems of abstraction, artifacts, and language make this a very diverse world, indeed. We really can't talk about conflict, then, without noting the importance of cultural communication. Sometimes conflict results from a clash of cultural ideas—different ways of thinking that don't match up. Sometimes, too, these cultural differences lead us to disagree on particular issues such as women's rights, abortion, or prayer in the schools. Other times, people in conflict find that their cultural differences, especially language, can get in the way of managing already difficult differences. To help us understand the ways in which cultural differences can affect conflict, we'll look at three variables that can help us organize our thinking on this subject.

Cultural Contexts. Back in the 1970s, anthropologist Edward Hall began to write about the role of context in a culture's system of meanings.[27] Some cultures, thought of as *high context*, assume that communicators already know a lot about what is going on from the relationship and situation. If they do not, they will take the time to build a relationship and a context for mutual understanding. High-context communicators rely on often-subtle cues for meaning. Their discourse will tend to be indirect and not necessarily clear and to the point. Other cultures, *low context*, rely less on the situation and relationship and more on directness in the use of words: Don't make people guess; say what you mean. Cultural context is a variable, and groups fall at various points on the spectrum between high and low context.

In a high-context environment—as might be experienced, for example, in China, France, or Ghana—communicators would tend to get meaning from the social situation, get a feeling of the group, take more time to establish a relationship, speak indirectly, use more feeling words, and speak around rather than directly to issues. In low-context situations—as in Germany, Israel, or the United States—communication is more direct and individualistic, gets to the point faster, relies more on words and less on nonverbals, and includes detail and specifics.

You can immediately see how these cultural differences could create or exacerbate conflict. Conflicts in low-context cultures arise from differences of opinion or a clash of goals. In high-context cultures, they arise more from differences in expression or violation of norms or cultural forms. In low-context cultures, conflicts tend to be worked out directly through confrontation, but in high-context cultures, they are dealt with indirectly. Members of low-context cultures tend to argue their points of view, while high-context counterparts speak more intuitively and use feeling-oriented messages. When members of different cultures attempt to work through a potential conflict situation, the interaction may seem uncoordinated, disjointed, and frustrating, as the behavior of each participant seems rude, irrelevant, and/or offensive to the other.

Individualism-Collectivism. A second variable that helps us organize the world of cultural difference is the degree to which a culture most values the group or individual.[28] *Individualistic cultures* tend to honor the person over the group, while *collectivist cultures* think more in terms of the group than the individual. For the former, individual rights are very important; for the latter, community values prevail. Self-expression and the assertion of what an individual wants or needs dominate conflicts, while group differences matter more in collectivist conflicts. Conflict could look quite different in North America, Australia, and northern Europe, where individualistic cultures predominate than in the more collectivist cultures in much of South America and Asia. In general, individualists tend to use more self-defense, domination, and competition in conflicts, while collectivists are more integrative and compromising in their approach.[29] Conflict often is created in individualistic cultures when persons feel that their interests, goals, and rights have been violated. Conflict in collectivist cultures arises more often when the sense of community is threatened or violated.

Power Distance. Another distinction that can be helpful in understanding cultural differences in conflict is power distance, or the degree to which a culture relies on relatively equal versus hierarchical power.[30] Some cultures are *high-power-distance*—the Philippines, Mexico, and India, for example. Certain individuals have more authority based on age, sex, generation, or status. Other cultures (Scandinavian countries, for example) distribute power more evenly across society and, hence, are classified as *low-power-distance* cultures. In conflict situations, individuals from low-power-distance cultures will negotiate more and assert their needs and goals. Individuals from high-distance cultures will ask those in authority to assert influence and make decisions.

Within a cultural group, a conflict will have a certain look and feel based on the systems of abstraction and communication within the culture. The conflict will be coherent, as participants share a set of rules for how to negotiate it. Conflicts across cultural groups are a different matter, as the parties may have divergent ideas about reality and rather diverse approaches. Let's take a closer look now at this challenging prospect.

Box 4.2

Gather in small groups of 4–5 students. Each group brainstorms a list of cultural practices that are common in the university setting. These examples may reflect a form of culture based on national, regional, linguistic, religious, gender-based, or organizational identities. For each of the examples, discuss the possible conflict that may result from this cultural practice being exhibited. Each group should choose one of these cultural examples and create a short skit or role-play illustrating this practice and the potential conflict that may occur as the culture is displayed. For example, you might imagine what conflicts could occur between a professor, who is an immigrant expecting to be treated with extreme respect and deference, and an American student, who believes everyone should be treated the same way. For each skit, relate the conflict to one or more of the seven assumptions about intercultural conflict by Ting-Toomey and Oetzel in the following section.

Conflict across Cultures

After considerable research on intercultural conflict, Stella Ting-Toomey and John Oetzel identified seven aspects of intercultural conflict:[31]

1. *Intercultural conflict involves emotional frustrations or mismatched expectations that stem, in part, from cultural group membership differences.* Cultural expectations are palpable in conflict situations and can be very frustrating. With a northern European heritage, for example, you may get downright angry when a Southeast Asian person refuses to acknowledge your personal rights. From the perspective of Chinese heritage, you may feel very uncomfortable when a person of Canadian descent confronts you directly in a way that feels embarrassing. Such conflicts can be emotionally draining.

2. *Intercultural conflict involves varying degrees of biased intergroup perceptions and attributions in assessing what transpires in an ongoing conflict episode.* Too often, we fail to acknowledge that another person's behavior reflects a cultural difference. Instead, we may blame the other person for acting insensitively, inappropriately, or negligently. You might accuse a Southeast Asian person of being oblivious, or you might conclude that a northern European is rude. Neither would define themselves that way.

3. *Intercultural conflict involves different face needs.* Face is the universal desire to be treated with honor and respect in whatever way your culture teaches honor and respect. In individualist

cultures, for example, people often want to be seen as competent and in control. In collectivist cultures, people are more
likely to want to be seen as fulfilling their social role in a way
expected in their society. You can see, then, why people from
Canada and China might feel very unsatisfied in a conflict episode as neither honors the other as they expect or want to be
honored. Face is a very important issue in conflict, and we will
discuss it further in chapter 5.[32]

4. *Intercultural conflict involves multiple goals, and the goals people
   have largely depend on how they define the conflict episode.* People
   from different cultures often emphasize different types of goals.
   For example, individualists may emphasize instrumental, or
   content, goals—what they personally want to achieve. Collectivists, on the other hand, may emphasize relational or community goals. In intercultural conflicts, then, the parties may be
   fighting essentially different battles. A northern European
   might aim to get a salary raise, while his or her Southeast Asian
   counterpart aims to build a feeling of mutual support.

5. *Intercultural conflict involves divergent procedures and styles in
   approaching the various developmental phases of the conflict.* This
   assumption seems clear from the cultural differences described
   in the previous section. Indeed, when cultures possess different
   communication styles—direct versus indirect, for example—
   then they will approach conflict management very differently.
   The northern European, for example, may see individual negotiation as the way to resolve a conflict, while the Southeast
   Asian may prefer to build a common vision.

6. *Intercultural conflict is a situationally dependent phenomenon.* Conflicts never happen in the abstract. They happen in a physical
   place (or virtual one), with certain artifacts, where individuals
   have particular roles, where certain goals are important, and
   where different skills are required. Disputes between participants from different cultures will depend in part on whether
   they are a married couple, coworkers, international negotiators,
   or fellow travelers on a train. Situations matter.

7. *Competent intercultural conflict management demands systems
   thinking.* To manage intercultural differences effectively
   requires that we move out of a restricted cultural view and that
   we consider numerous interrelated factors. We must look at the
   whole system, not just our own restricted perspective.

How You Can Use This Chapter

Conflict theory covers a lot of territory. Exploring individual aspects of conflict helps build a more solid foundation for understanding conflict in a wider context.

1. No conflict style is best, but getting stuck in one way of "doing" conflict will not help move from harm to value. Be adaptive, and select the style of communication that will best serve the situation at hand.

2. Be deliberate about your conflict goals. What do you want to achieve, and how can you reach your goals in a way that does minimal damage to yourself and other people?

3. Avoid simplistic, nonperson-centered strategies. Take the perspective of others in your approach to a conflict, and aim for mutual gain.

4. Emotional reactions do not need to be automatic and preprogrammed. You can control both how you understand a situation and the most appropriate emotional response. From your interactions with many others over the course of your lifetime, you have learned many appropriate ways to define, label, and respond to feelings. Make use of these to help move from harm toward value in conflicts.

5. Understand the many ways in which you can be empowered, not only to achieve your own goals but also to create mutually beneficial outcomes for others and, indeed, for the community at large.

6. Although rights, roles, and responsibilities embedded in our social and cultural heritage do constrain what we can do, we also have choices and can move to change the very social institutions that keep us in the sphere of harm. History is full of examples of ways in which well-meaning people were able to change the system and move from harm to value.

7. Never let your culture become invisible to you. Everyone is cultural, and we need to understand the cultural basis of our behavior and the ways in which we respond to conflict. As we will emphasize throughout this book, be culturally aware.

Interactive Case Study

AT THE GROCERY STORE

Context: New Millennium Groceries has three stores in town and has 100 employees. The company makes a nice profit. The executive management team meets weekly for an hour in the CEO's office conference room. One of the major dilemmas facing the team today is the "dashboard dining" phenomenon. The grocery industry is being challenged to offer innovative food-on-the-go: soup that heats in the cup, yogurt in squeeze tubes, and products that fit in cup-holder friendly containers (for use in vehicles), all with kid- and car-friendly packaging.

The CEO has been with the company 15 years and models responsive, collaborative leadership. The marketing director is eager to reach the 20+ crowd and wants a long-range plan to "contemporize." The R & D director is interested in the trend but wants to consider all the implications carefully. The HR director is very traditional and is not too happy with a flat management style.

Opening exercise(s): The executive management team has gathered for its weekly meeting. The CEO asks each member of the team what they have been working on, and each gives a brief report followed by a few minutes of discussion on each activity. The purpose of this exercise is for the role-players to internalize their roles. The class will divide into groups of six students, four for the role-play team and two observers. (Pronouns are assigned arbitrarily here. Please assign roles as you see fit.)

- **The CEO** started the company 15 years ago, following the same career path as his father. He sees the value of food as an equalizer, a means for bringing community together. He has successfully added two more stores to his original store. The CEO uses a facilitative leadership style and is dedicated to empowering his employees to make decisions. He models responsive leadership, balancing his own perspectives with being open to the perspectives of others. He wants to focus on and model healthy living. At the weekly executive team meetings, the CEO tries to address both internal issues and external trends and opportunities.

- The **Marketing Director** recently got an MBA from the University of Minnesota. Her graduate program stressed the importance of "contemporizing" to keep competitive. She is always researching ways to reach the 20+ crowd, and knows the value of shorter sound bites, sexy packaging, and upbeat music. She is very interested in having a segment of the company's long-range plan focus on how to contemporize. She has worked with the company for five years, but was part-time during her graduate program and is thankful that the company waited for her to finish her degree and then offered the marketing director position. She has an eager, sometimes pushy personality.

- The **R & D Director** has been with the company since its inception. She has a degree in nutrition and is very interested in the health food trend. She has always wanted to segment an area of Millennium Groceries into a small health food center. The R & D Director also sees the value in the trend for more modern packaging and foods for the active lifestyle. She wants to go a step further and make sure they offer foods that are enriched with vitamins and minerals. She enjoys herb-infused drinks and feels much better when she drinks orange juice that has been fortified with calcium. Research shows that the typical diet in our society is lacking in the necessary nutrients. She is interested in the unveiling of the new food pyramid from the FDA, as she hears it will offer new insights on low carbs and a nutrient-packed menu. She is a careful negotiator and is willing to work with the team. She is hesitant to move too quickly in decision making and wants to think through every decision carefully. She is quiet and shy.

- The **HR Director** is a traditional human resource professional and is the president of the State Human Resource Association. He has not seen much benefit from flat management styles, but he respects this executive team immensely. With 100 employees, and all of their individual interests and needs, he knows that there is an appropriate time and place to solicit employee input. He also wants management to "tell them what to do" when it is appropriate. He wants his employees to work efficiently and be satisfied. The satisfaction comes from a job well done (as well as the company's profit!). He has been with the company 10 years and has hired most of the current employees. He has a great memory and prides himself on knowing lots of personal information about each one (family, hobbies, strengths). He is forceful and dominating.

Focus #1: Styles of Communication

The group (role-players and observers) will discuss the styles of communication and the styles of the executive management team. Which modes are most prevalent? Which styles seem to combine well? Which combination of modes might lead to challenging (or even harmful) conversations? Role-players can address which of the styles they felt most comfortable with in this team meeting.

Focus #2: Structuration

Convene a role-play to address a specific issue brought up at the weekly staff meeting. The marketing director wants to start a "food-on-the-go" campaign and to make some major changes to what the store offers. The R & D Director is hesitantly supportive, and the CEO is much more hesitant to make changes. The HR Director is adamant that they cannot and should not make changes to the current offerings. The CEO will convene the meeting and tell them he wants a decision about this new focus for the company. Hold this meeting for fifteen minutes or so, trying to come to a decision about this new campaign.

The observers will watch for structuration. What is the macroenvironment? What is the microenvironment? How do the three elements of the social environment show up in this conversation? Do you see (1) a way of *understanding* or interpreting what is going on; (2) a sense of *morality*, or the proper way to act; or (3) a source of *power* to influence events? How did these elements affect the behavior of the participants in the conversation? Observers will share what they found with the whole group.

Focus #3: Patterns

Either refer to the previous role-play for this exercise or hold a short role-play of the next weekly team meeting.

Look as a group at the three systems of cultures. Have a discussion about the culture exhibited in these role-plays. First look at the three systems in terms of the grocery store world, then in terms of the executive management team of this store, and then in terms of each of the team members. How is this culture manifested by each of the system dynamics?

Focus #4: Cultural Contexts

Either refer to the previous role-play for this exercise, or hold a short role-play of the next weekly team meeting. Look as a group at the three variables for addressing cultural dimensions. Do you see any high-context communicators? Low-context? Give examples of each. Do you see any examples of individualistic or collectivist cultures? Give examples of each. Do you see any examples of power distance distinctions? Give examples.

Focus #5: Systemic Implications

Hold one final executive management team meeting. The CEO convened the meeting to bring a final dimension to the decision about the new campaign. He wants to ask the employees what they think and to give recommendations about next steps. The HR Director is not in favor of this decision. He thinks that management has the responsibility to make such decisions. Play out this conflict for ten minutes or so.

Taking a systems perspective, describe the communication in the role-play according to systemic dimensions. Observers will look carefully to see what is occurring as far as systems connections, boundaries, and self-organization. Observers will share thoughts with the full group and all will then discuss the findings.

Endnotes

[1] See, for example, Hans J. Eysenck, "Biological Dimensions of Personality," in *Handbook of Personality*, ed. Lawrence A. Pervin (New York: Guilford, 1991), pp. 244–276; Michael J. Beatty and James C. McCroskey, *The Biology of Communication: A Communibiological Perspective* (Cresskill, NJ: Hampton Press, 2001).

[2] Joel R. Davitz, *The Language of Emotion* (New York: Academic Press, 1969).

[3] Ralph Kilmann and Kenneth Thomas, "Interpersonal Conflict-Handling Behavior as Reflections of Jungian Personality Dimensions," *Psychological Reports*, 37 (1975): 971–

980; we have used the adapted version of William W. Wilmot and Joyce L. Hocker, *Interpersonal Conflict* (New York: McGraw-Hill, 2000).

[4] See, for example, Charles R. Berger, *Planning Strategic Interaction: Attaining Goals through Communicative Action* (Mahwah, NJ: Lawrence Erlbaum, 1997).

[5] Daniel J. Canary, "Managing Interpersonal Conflict: A Model of Events Related to Strategic Choices," in *Handbook of Communication and Social Interaction Skills*, eds. John O. Greene and Brant R. Burleson (Mahwah, NJ: Lawrence Erlbaum, 2003), pp. 515–550.

[6] For an overview of research on compliance gaining, see James B. Stiff, *Persuasive Communication* (New York: Guilford, 1994), pp. 199–211.

[7] Lawrence R. Wheeless, Robert Barraclough, and Robert Stewart, "Compliance-Gaining and Power in Persuasion," in *Communication Yearbook 7*, ed. Robert N. Bostrom (Beverly Hills, CA: Sage, 1983), pp. 105–145.

[8] See, for example, William W. Waller and Reuben Hill, *The Family: A Dynamic Interpretation* (New York: Warner Books, 1951).

[9] This idea has been explored extensively by Jesse Delia and his colleagues. See, for example, Anne Maydan Nicotera, "The Constructivist Theory of Delia, Clark, and Associates," in *Watershed Research Traditions in Human Communication Theory*, ed. Donald P. Cushman and Branislav Kovačić (Albany, NY: SUNY Press, 1995), pp. 45–66.

[10] Barbara J. O'Keefe, "The Logic of Message Design: Individual Differences in Reasoning about Communication," *Communication Monographs*, 55 (1988): 80–103.

[11] Canary.

[12] See, for example, Eliot R. Smith, "Social Cognition Contributions to Attribution Theory and Research," in *Social Cognition: Impact on Social Psychology*, ed. Patricia G. Devine, David L. Hamilton, and Thomas M. Ostrom (San Diego: Academic Press, 1994), pp. 77–108.

[13] Alan L. Sillars, "Attributions and Communication in Roommate Conflicts," *Communication Monographs*, 47 (1980): 180–200; Alan L. Sillars, "The Sequential and Distributional Structure of Conflict Interaction as a Function of Attributions Concerning the Locus of Responsibility and Stability of Conflict," in *Communication Yearbook 4*, ed. Dan Nimmo (New Brunswick, NJ: Transaction, 1980), pp. 217–236; Alan L. Sillars, Gary R. Pike, Tricia S. Jones, and Kathleen Redmon, "Communication and Conflict in Marriage," in *Communication Yearbook 7*, ed. Robert Bostrom (Beverly Hills, CA: Sage 1983), pp. 414–429.

[14] For a detailed exploration of various emotions, see Laura K. Guerrero and Angela G. La Valley, "Conflict, Emotion, and Communication," in *The Sage Handbook of Conflict Communication: Integrating Theory, Research, and Practice*, eds. John G. Oetzel and Stella Ting-Toomey (Thousand Oaks, CA: Sage, 2006), pp. 69–96.

[15] Guerrero and LaValley.

[16] Gerald L. Clore, Andrew Ortony, Bruce Dienes, and Frank Fujita, "Where Does Anger Dwell?" in *Perspectives on Anger and Emotion: Advances in Social Cognition*, ed. Robert S. Wyer, Jr. and Thomas K. Srull (Hillsdale, NJ: Lawrence Erlbaum, 1993), pp. 57–87.

[17] See, for example, Rom Harré, "An Outline of the Social Constructionist Viewpoint," in *The Social Construction of Emotions*, ed. R. Harré (New York: Blackwell, 1986), pp. 2–14; James Averill, "A Constructivist View of Emotion," in *Theories of Emotion*, ed. K. Plutchik and H. Kellerman (New York: Academic, 1980), pp. 305–339.

[18] Anthony Giddens, *Profiles and Critiques in Social Theory* (Berkeley: University of California Press, 1982), pp. 8–11. See also, Stephen P. Banks and Patricia Riley, "Structuration Theory as an Ontology for Communication Research," *Communication Yearbook 16*, ed. Stanley Deetz (Newbury Park, CA: Sage, 1993), pp. 167–196.

[19] W. Barnett Pearce, *Interpersonal Communication: Making Social Worlds* (New York: Harper Collins, 1994), pp. 31–86.

[20] The metaphor of rules stems from speech act theory, or ordinary language philosophy. For a summary, see Stephen W. Littlejohn and Karen A. Foss, *Theories of Human Communication*, 8th ed. (Belmont, CA: Wadsworth, 2005), pp. 46, 108–112, 170.

[21] Vernon E. Cronen, W. Barnett Pearce, and Lonna Snavely, "A Theory of Rule-Structure and Types of Episodes, and a Study of Perceived Enmeshment in Undesired Repetitive Patterns (URPs)," in *Communication Yearbook 3*, ed. Dan Nimmo (New Brunswick, NJ: Transaction Press, 1979), pp. 225–240.

[22] Jack Knight, *Institutions and Social Conflict* (Cambridge, England: Cambridge University Press, 1993).

[23] Alex Thio, *Sociology* (Needham Heights, MA: Allyn & Bacon, 2000).

[24] Guo-Ming Chen and William J. Starosta, *Foundations of Intercultural Communication* (Boston: Allyn & Bacon, 1998), pp. 25–26.

[25] Fern L. Johnson, *Speaking Culturally: Language Diversity in the United States* (Thousand Oaks, CA: Sage, 2000), pp. 53–68.

[26] Dell Hymes, *Foundations in Sociolinguistics: An Ethnographic Approach* (Philadelphia: University of Pennsylvania Press, 1974).

[27] Edward T. Hall, *Beyond Culture* (Garden City, NY: Anchor, 1976).

[28] Geert Hofstede, *Culture's Consequences* (Beverly Hills, CA: Sage, 1984).

[29] Stella Ting-Toomey and John G. Oetzel, *Managing Intercultural Conflict Effectively* (Thousand Oaks, CA: Sage, 2001), pp. 48–50.

[30] Hofstede.

[31] Ting-Toomey and Oetzel, pp. 17–26.

[32] See also, Kathy Domenici and Stephen W. Littlejohn, *Facework at the Center* (Thousand Oaks, CA: Sage, 2006).

5

Communication and the Challenge of Conflict Management

BEGINNING WITH A METAPHOR

If you were to enter the student center at any university about midday, you would encounter a buzz of voices—hundreds of people engaged in conversations around the spaces of the building. Russian literary scholar Mikhail Bakhtin writes that social life is like this—a jumble of voices.[1] This drone begins to make sense only when you start to pay attention to particular conversations in the room. If you try to hear all the voices at once, you end up with a mumble, a generalized sound without focus. But even a mumble does have some meaning, as it reveals the state of many voices, or *heteroglossia*, as Bakhtin called it. It tells you many things are happening all at once, a realization we do not always keep in our consciousness.

Sit in an active public place, away from any one conversation, close your eyes, and listen. You will hear many different voice types, various rhythms and tones. Occasional laughter will peal out, a slap on the table, the jingle of metal, the brush of cloth. If you do this little exercise, you will also discover that you cannot stay in the mumble for long, as your brain inevitably begins to focus on certain voices and particular conversations, even if you can't fully understand what is being said. It is a natural tendency to find some area of coherence in an otherwise fuzzy field.

We think that the *metaphor of voice* is powerful in helping us understand the nature of human difference from a communication perspective. We commonly say that people "voice" their opinions. Ideas and feelings are "voiced," and the "tone of voice" tells us much about what is going on with the speaker. At different moments in your daily life, you experience voice in a variety of ways that can be taken to symbolize various states of similarity and difference in society.[2] Here we will talk about four experiences of voice—the solo, the choral reading, the choir, and the cacophony.

One of the ways we achieve coherence is to focus on one particular voice. In music, the solo is the use of a single voice as the centerpiece of a performance. Occasionally, we hear a solo with no accompaniment, a pure a cappella voice. More commonly, however, the solo voice is supported by other singers, instruments, even rhythmic clapping. Whether alone or accompanied, the solo is a privileged voice, a center voice, a featured voice. The one clear voice stands out, much like listening to one person stating a point of view. It is like listening to a sermon, a political speech, or a lecture. At least in the moment, we are focusing on a single source.

In choral reading, several people speak in unison. Each person's tone is different, but they come together and are integrated into a pleasing common voice. Analogues include a political rally, a worship service, a family celebration, or a romantic dinner. Differences are essentially irrelevant or out of awareness.

In a choir, many different voices are integrated into a complex whole. The different voices fit together, they complement one another, and they create a fascinating performance that no single voice can duplicate. Unlike the solo and the choral reading, difference is not irrelevant. It is very much present and valued. Blended voices are like

a conversation in which many points of view and forms of expression are brought together into a coordinated interaction. Each expressed point of view is enhanced or elaborated by others. Everyone learns from the conversation, and the whole is definitely more than the sum of the parts. Sometimes the voices are discordant, but this is not considered a problem. The dissonance creates a fascinating interplay.

Finally, there is a state in which voices clash in an uncoordinated, noisy way. The differences among the voices are neither unified nor blended. The lack of coherence is jarring and creates a feeling of harm.

The metaphor of voice helps us imagine the states of difference we encounter in society and in our lives. Sometimes difference is out of our awareness and is irrelevant, sometimes it is unified, sometimes blended, and sometimes problematic.

PATTERNS OF COMMUNICATION IN THE WORLD OF DIFFERENCE

We have seen that people respond to differences with various reactions. Sometimes they ignore them; sometimes they embrace them; other times they resist them; and often they fight differences. There is another possibility as well—to transform differences, which we explore later in the chapter.[3] Each of these involves different patterns of communication, and each constructs a different reality around difference.[4]

Ignoring Difference

Some of the time, difference seems irrelevant and even lies out of awareness. Our focus is on similarity rather than difference. Your family may be different from other families, but on holidays, you celebrate family togetherness without questioning differences. On the Fourth of July, citizens of the United States celebrate what they have in common and don't think much about their differences. After finishing a major project, a team of technicians celebrates the accomplishment, and they don't want to spoil it by arguing about the conflicts they had along the way.

Barnett Pearce calls such moments *monocultural*; they are truly of "one" culture.[5] These are times when the way we are doing things seems very natural and unchallenged. Monocultural communication happens without conflict. These are moments when we can just be ourselves within a family, organization, community of faith, or other setting without struggling over different identities. This pattern is self-sustaining. It reproduces the very resources that make it possible.

No resources are put at risk, as our meanings and actions go unchanged, at least for a while.

It is very important for us to ignore differences some of the time. What gets made when we communicate in this way? We build important connections with others; we find common ground and places where we can relax and be ourselves without threat of criticism. Ignoring difference increases the identity of a group or community, clarifies values, and allows us to internalize what is most important. It provides the opportunity to build ideas about what it means to be a person, have a relationship, or establish a community.

Ignoring difference, however, can only be momentary. If a group ignores differences for very long, it will seal off its resources into a tight box, which is hard to maintain in today's world. If we stay too long in this pattern, we will construct a social reality that is narrow-minded, inflexible, and unstimulating. For this reason, we must regularly adopt different patterns of communication.

Embracing Difference

A second pattern of communication seeks out and celebrates difference. We use this pattern because difference feels exciting, provides a learning opportunity, or expands our resources in some desired way. This is a pattern commonly seen among sojourners and explorers. It is a pattern common in modernity, where growth and change are highly valued. When we embrace difference, we want to expand our resources. We are unsatisfied with the limitations on our meanings, values, perceptions, and ways of doing things, and we welcome a challenge. Embracing difference, then, is very much a pattern in which we deliberately put our resources at risk.

Although the search for change can be stimulating, it also can be limiting. Over time this pattern can create a feeling of being lost in a maze of constant change, uncertain identity, elusive community, and the inability to find a place to stand. If you step back and look at the pattern over a long period of time, you see a circle of repetition: *Seek change, celebrate the new, the new becomes old, seek change, celebrate the new, the new becomes old, seek change.* Often the pattern of embracing difference in youth gives way to a search for solid identity, a return to one's roots, and a redefinition of values. The desire to try everything shifts to a desire to know who you are. Living for years in this pattern can turn you into a neotraditional, a person who goes back in time to a more reliable way of life, someone who returns to a religion abandoned in youth, who takes lessons in the language spoken in a parent's native community, and who moves family relics from the basement to the mantel.

What, then, is made in this pattern of interaction? Embracing difference builds creativity, curiosity, and social change. It creates the value of multiculturalism, positive intercultural communication, and honor and dignity for all groups. Embracing difference is an important and powerful pattern of communication. At the same time, however, embracing difference can lead to confusion, loss of identity, erosion of values and standards, and, in a paradoxical way, the demise of community. Embracing difference can cause the loss of important distinctions that give meaning to our lives.

Resisting Difference

Embracing difference involves putting one's resources at risk, but most people are not always willing to do this. When we resist difference, we are aware of alternatives but are not willing to change. We become protective about our beliefs, values, and actions. Our own way of being is taken as normal, while others are viewed as aberrant or unacceptable in some way. Patterns of resistance can take many forms. For purposes of discussion, let's talk about soft resistance and hard resistance.

Soft resistance acknowledges that differences are probably valuable but holds that people should debate their respective points of view. We argue, use persuasion, and try to change others in a more-or-less civil way. We recognize that although we may think of our ideas as superior, other people feel the same way about their own ideas, and society must have a respectful way of working through these conflicts. In rhetorically eloquent communication, we use our best argumentation and reasoning to demonstrate the validity of our own point of view. If this fails, we trust legislatures, agencies, and courts of law to settle matters democratically. Soft resistance, then, exists within an atmosphere of pluralism and tolerance.

Hard resistance is different. Sometimes called *ethnocentrism,* resistance means building a hardened wall around our way of thinking and doing. We judge all others as inferior, and we do what is necessary to protect and preserve what we think is right. We work to keep the infidels at bay. Hard resistance is common throughout the world in certain political, religious, and ethnic groups. It is an extreme identification with the resources of one's own identity group. This pattern can be characterized by separatism, defamation, oppression, and sometimes even harsher methods.

What do we make when we resist difference? Communities are certainly made in this form of communication. Clarity is bred here as well. Solidarity is another product of resistance, and resistance can lead to positive social change, especially where one group is able to overcome the oppression of another group through resistance. But resistance can also be a social reality of right-and-wrong and good-and-bad. It can construct demons and enemies. Rarely is resistance creative; it is usually defensive.

Fighting Difference

The need to protect our resources sometimes moves from resistance to aggression. Here the pattern is one of moving to repress a group whose beliefs, attitudes, values, and actions endanger one's own. It often results from the frustration that occurs when softer forms of resistance fail, and we feel that our way of life is truly threatened by others. When we fight difference, persuasion becomes diatribe, display becomes violence, influence becomes force, and tolerance becomes persecution.

Although stakeholders may fight for land, natural resources, or material advantage, this form of communication most often has a moral base. We believe so strongly that we are threatened that we "take to the streets." William Ascher found that violent organizations in the United States and abroad tend to have three characteristics: a strong identity with the in-group; a shared sense of moral indignation about the actions of the out-group; and a belief that the other group hates them.[6] Extreme groups justify violence not merely to repress but also to achieve important moral goals.

Transforming Difference

Each of the four patterns of communication discussed above aim to preserve, protect, or change a group's resources—their ways of thinking and forms of action. The fifth pattern approaches difference in a new way. The new pattern attempts to coordinate the resources of different groups and to achieve a level of communication that allows all stories to be told and to be heard without asking anyone to give up what is important to them. This pattern acknowledges difference, but it also acknowledges what is shared—that we all use language and other expressive forms to construct the realities that impact our lives, that we all have resources formed in our unique social histories, that we all make distinctions and note the ways that we are different from others, that we all have communities with which we identify, that we are all cultural beings, and that everyone has experiences that provide a moral basis for their actions.

This pattern of communication acknowledges both similarity and difference. When we work to transform difference, we do not place this story at risk, because it serves us well in moving into new patterns of interaction in which our differences can be expressed, understood, and new forms of relationships established.

What does this pattern look like? It is a pattern in which individuals say what is important to them without trying to change others. It is a pattern in which individuals listen deeply to what others are saying in an attempt to understand their social worlds. It is a pattern in which participants tell stories from their experience to help others get a glimpse of their social world. It is a pattern in which communicators attempt to build respect, to come to some understanding of both the powers and limits of their respective social worlds, and to learn significant new things. It is a pattern in which change is possible, but not the primary objective.

This fifth pattern of communication is idealistic, yet it can be and often is experienced. It is usually difficult, however, because we are unaccustomed to this form of communication, and our social realities frequently do not include the possibility of talking and listening in these ways. In this pattern we walk the narrow ridge between being who we are and being profoundly open to the other.[7]

We like to think of the fifth pattern as a search for a set of second-order resources, a set of categories that can be used to transcend our differences, to allow us to talk in ways that bring about learning, reflection, and respect—a place where diversity is seen as a positive resource that can benefit everyone. In later chapters of this book, we will explore a number of ways in which this might be done.

FACEWORK AND THE MANAGEMENT OF DIFFERENCE

The human face provides a fascinating metaphor for the presentation of self. Because it is normally the first thing we observe about people and because we attribute such value and meaning to the face, it has come to stand for the very identity we wish others to see in us.[8] We want to be seen as competent, honorable, and respected. We want to be treated with dignity, and we put work into achieving this both on individual levels and by coordinating with others in communication. *Facework*, then, is "a set of coordinated practices in which communicators build, maintain, protect, or threaten personal dignity, honor, and respect."[9]

Most of the time, we put effort into building our own sense of identity and worthiness, and we often work to bolster that of others as well. In conflict situations, however, face is often threatened, especially when we demean, put down, or attack another person or group. At the same time, some people choose not to confront but rather to accommodate, avoid, or even compromise in conflict situations because they don't want to damage the identity of the other person. We want to "save" their face.

When differences are challenging, facework itself is challenged. Destructive facework can move us from challenge to harm, and constructive facework can mitigate this and bring us back toward value. Facework is a complex process and involves a set of goals related to how we treat ourselves, other persons, relationships, and even larger systems. Table 5.1 describes the levels of facework that people do.[10]

If you think about your own sense of identity, you will probably be able to identify three significant needs—(1) a certain amount of freedom and latitude to make decisions, (2) inclusion and acceptance by others, and (3) belief in your own abilities and effectiveness. Tae-Sop Lim and John Waite Bowers refer to these as autonomy face, fellowship face, and competence face.[11] *Autonomy face* is a sense of independence and choice. It may mean being left alone and being free from interference. It may mean having authority and responsibility, and it may mean feeling that others trust you to do the right thing. *Fellowship face* is a feeling of being included and accepted. It may mean that other people want to be with you, support you, and involve you

Table 5.1   Levels of Facework

| Focus of Attention | Scope of Action | | | |
	Act	**Conversation**	**Episode**	**Lifescript**
Person	An act that affects face of self or other.	A conversation affecting face of self or other.	Multiple conversations affecting face of self or other.	A long-term series of episodes creating an orientation to self and to other.
Relationship	An act of facework aiming to help define the relationship.	A conversation of facework shaping the relationship.	Multiple conversations on a topic defining the relationship.	A long-term series of episodes defining relationships.
System	An act of facework aiming to help define the system.	A conversation of facework shaping the system.	Sequential conversations on a subject shaping the system.	A long-term series of episodes shaping larger systems.

in their activities and lives. Finally, *competence face* is the perception that you know what you are doing, that you are effective and can make a mark. In many social situations, we act in ways that build a sense in self and in others of autonomy, inclusion, and competence; but in other social situations—especially conflict—we attack or threaten the same elements of identity. When moving from harm to value in the management of difference, maintaining face becomes vital. One of the quickest ways for conflicts to move into harm is destructive facework.

Face goals are an important part of every conflict situation.[12] When communicators are being especially competitive with one another, they will tend to build themselves up and tear down the other person. Both verbally and nonverbally, combatants may reproach, criticize, blame, and demean their opponents. We occasionally see mediations in which one party is delighted to have the opportunity to tear the other down in a kind of "degradation ceremony." Disputants may also give all kinds of reasons why their own behavior is laudable.

When attacked, communicators usually attempt to recover from a negative impression or to rebuild a positive image. They may do this through excuses, explanations, apologies, and denials. Ironically, of course, in their attempt to rebuild esteem, they may return to degrading the other person, which maintains the attack-attack pattern. Parties sometimes try to prevent attack in a way that protects their own integrity. They will actually anticipate attacks and counter these in advance by providing disclaimers, advanced excuses, and justifications. Also common are attempts to control the process or topics of conversation to minimize or prevent face threat. One reason for the common expression, "Let's not even go there," is that the participants really don't want to suffer the consequences of talking about a subject they know will be mutually destructive.

In contrast to some of these negative patterns, communicators are sometimes very polite in conflict situations. This may be a way to show general social competence and be viewed in a positive light. The reasoning is: *if I am polite and nice, I will look good.* This approach is especially common when third parties are present, and is, in fact, one of the advantages of mediation. Although disputants are not always polite in mediation, there is a tendency to "show off" a kind of "strategic politeness" when other parties could judge you badly for behaving boorishly.

What makes constructive facework possible in conflict situations? We think there are four keys to the creation of a positive facework environment. To enable an atmosphere where people feel they can uphold their preferred identity, it is important to address collaboration, power management, process management, and a safe environment. Because these are especially important in professional situations, we elaborate on them in more detail in chapter 8. As a preview, *collaboration* is a spirit of working with rather than against the other person. *Power management* means allowing everyone to express and work toward what is most important to them in a manner that benefits everyone. *Process management* means paying close attention to the way in which differences are expressed and worked through, and a *safe environment* is one in which communicators are free to explore, try out new ideas, and be innovative without fear of threat.

COMMUNICATION PROCESSES IN CONFLICT MANAGEMENT

When difference becomes a problem, we use communication to co-construct a semblance of order in our lives. Sometimes we do this through influence and domination and sometimes by negotiating solutions. A third alternative is available, and that is to transform the conflict from a theatre of struggle to a place of dialogue. Let's take a closer look at these three genres of conflict communication.

Processes of Gaining Compliance

One of the most common responses to difference is competition, or the desire to prevail and win. When faced with opposing ideas, values, and actions, we often use communication to influence others in such a way that we are able to gain the higher ground.

Advocates for particular positions on an issue apply their best arguments to persuade others of the validity of their respective ideas. The rhetorical arts have a long and esteemed history in the West. When we believe in our point of view, we formulate appeals that lead others to see the power of our ideas. Persuasion employs a variety of logical and emotional proofs, bolstered by the credibility of the communicator, to make the case for a position. Good persuasion can employ effective word play, storytelling, and other cultural forms of eloquence. There are entire literatures and curricula on persuasion, argumentation, and debate designed to teach students the fine arts of influence.[13]

For centuries persuasion has been considered the *normal discourse* of society marked by reasoning and the observation of cultural rules that define civility in social exchanges. Persuasion also acknowledges the right of stakeholders and decision makers to deliberate and choose, which is why it is considered a vital tool of democracy and jurisprudence. Effective argument, however, is almost always judged in terms of whether it wins adherents.

Unfortunately, as we will see below, civil discourse that embodies the ideal of careful consideration does not always settle conflict. Conflict can sometimes accelerate to more extreme and damaging levels, moving from the sphere of value to that of harm. When domination becomes the goal and the discourse degrades to blame and defamation, we run into the limits of persuasion as a way of managing conflict.

Hegemony.   Hegemony is the encroachment of one group on others through established authority.[14] Usually used in a political sense, the term refers to a process of one group asserting its ideas and practices over those of others. One nation can assert authority over other nations; one community can assert authority over other communities; and one culture can assert authority over other cultures. In hegemony there is an assumed superiority on the part of one group that subsumes or subverts the interests of a less powerful group. Hegemony may employ force, but it is usually more subtle—to the point that marginalized groups sometimes unconsciously accept the authority of the other. Hegemony is a response to difference and a way of establishing a sense of order, but it can lead to conflict on a large scale.

A common characteristic of hegemony is that the dominant group co-opts the interests of the subordinate one. For example, a male-dominated corporation might use a women's liberation theme in its advertising in order to gain the support of women. The question is whose interests are really being promoted, as the interests of profit subsume the interests of individuals. Of course, co-opted groups may resist, and the situation can become very dynamic as influence flows back and forth in a field of many stakeholders.

Notice the difference between persuasion and hegemony. In persuasion we try to influence other people deliberately through reasoned arguments. In hegemony, the struggle to prevail is more subtle and involves a host of conscious and subconscious processes that feel normal and right to both the dominant and marginalized group. Hegemony may include persuasion, but, by definition, it is really the use of authority to assert what should be accepted as the right way of doing things.

Cultural hegemony can be especially insidious, as it establishes one cultural way as normal and others as "different." Rather than think of cultures as different from one another, cultural hegemony puts one culture at the center and measures all others against this norm. Dividing cultures into "majority" and "minority" simply reinforces this view.

Diatribe and Violence. When we are frustrated that our best arguments do not prevail, we too often resort to personal blame, angry epithets, and degrading slogans. If we get frustrated enough, we move to force and violence. These patterns are especially common in *moral conflicts*, in which parties do not share a common set of values for what constitutes normal discourse.[15]

Moral Conflict. Moral conflict is a clash based on deep philosophical differences. Although it surfaces in disputes about what the parties say they want and need, the division lies at a much deeper level—involving assumptions about what is real, what is right, and how we can know what is real and right. The problem with moral conflict is that normal discourses of persuasion and hegemony cannot resolve it, as the parties disagree fundamentally not only on how to measure truth but also on what constitutes the normal order of things.[16]

The abortion conflict is a perfect example: Pro-life advocates believe fundamentally that only God can give and take life, that life begins at conception, and that every fetus has a right to live. Pro-choice advocates believe that the quality of life is supremely important, that individuals have the right to make decisions about their bodies, and that personhood begins at birth not at conception. Notice that this is not an interest-based conflict. The difference lies at a very deep level about what it means to be a person, what establishes truth, and how human beings should live their lives. This is why the conflict cannot be reasoned or legislated away.

The devastating conflict between the Branch Davidians and the U.S. government near Waco, Texas, in 1993 is another example of deep philosophical difference. Believing this religious sect to be an extremist group preparing for armed conflict, the FBI and Bureau of Alcohol, Tobacco, and Firearms surrounded the group's compound. The 51-day standoff led to a violent confrontation in which several people were killed or wounded on both sides. In the end, the government gassed and burned the complex, and all of the Davidians inside, including 21 children, perished.

In her analysis of this case, Jayne Docherty showed why the negotiations between these two sides were unsuccessful.[17] The government divided the world into two groups—the "good guys" trying to enforce the law and maintain order and the "bad guys" who were planning unspeakable harm. The Davidians also divided the world into good and evil. For them, the good people were believers, who would be saved; the bad people were nonbelievers who would be condemned. The government relied on psychological knowledge, while the Davidians relied on scripture. They did not accept the government and the established order as right and normal; rather, they viewed them as materialistic and anti-godly. When the government tried to negotiate a nonviolent solution, the Davidians responded by inviting the negotiators into a Bible study. Both sides became extremely frustrated when their respective "civil" attempts to settle the issue failed. This kind of interaction is frustrating because the worldviews are incommensurate, logically inconsistent. Neither side had any basis for understanding the world of the other, leading to an inevitable collision.

The clash between the government and the Branch Davidians is an extreme example of how violence results from frustration and the inability to settle conflict through normal attempts. The Davidians would not be co-opted through normal processes of hegemony, which caused the FBI to be suspicious of them; attempts to persuade in a barricade situation were doomed to failure.

As these stories remind us, we live in a world confronted by immense challenge. One of our friends, a respected psychology teacher and conflict management researcher, Steve Alley, says, "When I look at the world's problems, I just don't know what to do. But I do know one thing for sure—we don't know how to talk to each other." Persuasion, hegemony, diatribe, and violence are processes that enable one group to prevail over another. Whether applied in the courtroom, the boardroom, the kitchen, or the war room, we engage in these processes—deliberately or as a matter of course—to win our way. This is not the only mode of managing conflict; compromise and collaboration offer alternatives to winning.

Processes of Negotiation

Negotiation has always been an honored form of conflict resolution. It is a standard approach to managing business and organizing the potentially conflicting affairs of society. It is so powerful in settling conflicts that it is prevalent in all walks of life, from international conflict to roommate disputes. There are two approaches to negotiation—positional bargaining and collaborative negotiation.[18]

Positional Bargaining. Sometimes called *distributive bargaining*, positional bargaining is a form of compromise in which the parties state opening positions and move toward a compromise somewhere in the middle. This form of negotiation aims to *distribute* a limited set of resources, like money, land, goods, benefits, or even love and attention. In distributive bargaining, good negotiators are individuals who "win" as much as possible for themselves, or at least gain a fair share. This form of negotiation is common in situations where people perceive that options are limited and one side's gains will always result in losses on the other side.

Collaborative Negotiation.   The last two decades have produced insight into a new form of negotiation that addresses conflict more creatively and constructively.[19] In general, this form of negotiation is called *integrative problem solving*, because the parties *integrate* their interests into a unified whole. Various names are used for this style of conflict resolution, including *win-win*, *interest-based*, *principled*, or *collaborative* negotiation.[20] By *win-win*, we mean that the people negotiating no longer try to prevail over one another; instead, they conduct their negotiations intending for everyone's interests to be met. Everyone wins. By *interest-based*, we mean that the negotiators concentrate not on their competing positions but on the goals and interests they are trying to achieve. If negotiators are creative, they can come up with solutions that meet everyone's needs. By *principled*, we mean that the negotiation honors principles higher than any one party's goals. And by *collaborative*, we mean that the negotiators see themselves as working together to create mutually satisfactory solutions rather than competing for gains.

Successful integrative negotiation involves several characteristics:[21] (1) The bar is set high so that negotiators must be both careful and thorough in analyzing the situation and exploring options for mutual gain; (2) compromise is used only as a last resort; (3) negotiators are open with one another about their goals, values, and information; (4) negotiators are able to minimize their biases and evaluate options objectively; (5) the parties stand their ground, but remain open to the needs of all parties; and (6) stakeholders in integrative negotiations show genuine concern for one another.

Negotiation in the Relational Frame.   Occasionally, as in establishing the price of a car, negotiation is a one-time thing. In the most significant situations, however, negotiation is a process between participants who have an ongoing relationship. Not only must they negotiate solutions in the present moment but they must also pay attention to how this will affect their relationship and make possible continual negotiations on many issues into the future. This is true in negotiations between communities, nations, politicians, businesses, marriages, and labor and management. Negotiators, then, must think of two things at once: (1) How do we solve the immediate problem between us, and (2) how do we build a positive relationship for the future? Research shows that successful negotiation requires that the parties communicate in a way that will not harm the relationship and that all parties make sacrifices along the way.[22]

Successful negotiation—whether distributive, integrative, or relational—requires the parties to have some shared sense of what is at stake, a common idea of how to negotiate, and a similar understanding of the relationship itself. When these factors are missing, negotiation will probably fail. When negotiation on important issues fails, parties will tend to fall back on the most destructive responses, including interminable litigation, reciprocal diatribe, force, and violence. This is the case in the most intractable conflicts where matters are never resolved or settled except by escape or destruction—divorced couples who cannot attend the same social functions with their adult children, employees who finally quit their jobs rather than live with certain other employees and managers, and residents who sell their homes and move rather than live near a big-box store that they tried to keep out of the neighborhood. Failed persuasion and negotiation is why armed conflicts in Sri Lanka, Indonesia, and elsewhere continue for centuries. There is another way. Instead of trying to resolve the conflict, we can communicate in ways that transform it.

Transformation and Dialogue

Processes of domination and negotiation typically aim for *first-order change*. People are trying to change the immediate resources, practices, and attitudes of self or other. Processes of transformation, in contrast, create conditions for *second-order change*, or a shift in how we define the relationships among the parties or the system in which the conflict is occurring.[23] Participants may not change their opinions on the issues they face, but they do change how they view themselves, others, and the community itself. Transformative processes make it possible for groups and individuals to accept the values of diversity, acknowledge the legitimacy of positions other than their own, respect people who hold very different ideas, and continue a constructive conversation that permits multiplicity and harvests the benefits of diversity.[24]

Collaborative negotiation itself can be transformative, as it enables parties to redefine their challenge from a conflict to be resolved competitively to a problem to be solved together. This is especially the case when people undertake negotiation with the full intention of building a relationship of respect. However, negotiation in any form cannot overcome the most serious, intractable, moral conflicts. Instead, new processes of dialogue may be necessary to transform the relationship so that negotiations might proceed in the future.

Dialogue has several characteristics.[25] First, it creates categories that transcend differences among the parties by encouraging participants to find joining places, shared concerns, and mutual goals. Second, it shifts the discussion from persuasion, influence, and bargaining to listening, understanding, and respect. Third, it creates a forum in which all participants can learn significant new things about themselves and other people and develop fresh ways of understanding the situation itself. Fourth, it encourages participants to learn how each participant is a complex, fully formed individual with a history, values, and good intentions. Fifth, transformative processes allow difference to stand without resolution. Intelligent, well-meaning people can and should disagree, and that's okay. Finally, these forms of communication set the stage for collaborative work in the future.

Increasingly in recently years, drought and forest fires have driven wild animals into residential areas in the western United States. As housing developments have moved more and more into wildlands, they have created what is called an urban interface. Several years ago a jogger in the San Diego area was attacked and killed by a mountain lion. Near Tucson, mountain lions were seen in schoolyards, and the popular Sabino Canyon in that area had to be closed to the public for a while. As a result of the Tucson encounters, the Arizona Department of Game and Fish realized that it needed a welldesigned plan to determine how to respond to various human–lion encounters. The issue was contentious among hunters, homeowners, and animal rights groups, and we were called on to design and facilitate a process in which stakeholders could transform this conflict into a productive exploration of options.

In two stakeholder engagement events, members of the public gathered to consider the issue. Knowing that a typical public hearing would lead to contentious debate, the department wanted a transformative process. We knew that the clash among the 150 participants could turn out ugly and solve nothing, so we structured a process in which participants were put in small groups where they could first get to know one another as persons, explore their common values, and then express their views of the problem. We explicitly set up the daylong meetings to allow good deliberation—not to resolve or settle the issue—while agency policy makers would listen in. When disagreements arose, we reminded participants just to listen and try to understand multiple perspectives. Using this kind of format, several common values were clear. These included good science, public involvement, public safety, effective natural resource management, appreciation for the animal and its habitat, and effective use of public resources.

These six values became transcendent categories that participants could discuss comfortably. Although they disagreed about specific solutions, these values enabled participants to come together on several issues. They recognized that the problem was multidimensional and could not be handled in just one way. They agreed that the old

Box 5.1

In a group, create a difference you might encounter in a family, between roommates, or in the workplace. Assign roles and play this situation out three ways in front of the class. In the first role-play, participants should try to dominate the others. In the second, they should try to negotiate, and in the third they should try to transform the conflict.

How did each role-play feel? What were the consequences?

protocol needed to be revised. They also agreed that encounters needed to be carefully documented and that public safety was a priority. Discussed in this more nuanced way, participants were able to see that they agreed that euthanasia is sometimes necessary, even if they disagreed about when, and they also agreed that interactions between humans and mountain lions provide an opportunity for public education. The diversity of thought among participants was used as a valuable resource, and participants were able to communicate about their differences in a way that moved from a sphere of potential harm to one of value. Such processes are becoming increasingly common throughout the world. Another lens through which to explore the possibilities for bringing human differences into the sphere of value is by attending to the dimension of facework.

HOW YOU CAN USE THIS CHAPTER

As we will see in the following chapter, people tend to respond to conflict in certain patterned ways. This happens because many of us are not very reflective about how to act in conflict situations. We just do what comes naturally, behavior that will tend to be somewhat different for various individuals and groups. Yet, we do have choices, and our choices have consequences. We encourage you to use this chapter as a reminder of these choices and potential impacts.

1. Differences are not necessarily bad. It's okay to ignore them when in-group solidarity and cohesion are at stake. You can even embrace differences and use them to build a stimulating, creative, and productive life. By deliberately encountering differences, you can build the resources available to solve problems, cope with adversity, build cultural sensitivity, and develop conflict-management tools.

2. Resisting and even fighting difference are sometimes necessary. History shows that vital social change has occurred because

courageous leaders "went to battle." Just know that this is a choice. There are other choices, and the decisions to resist or to fight have consequences and can lead to "collateral damage" you may not want to live with in the future. Be deliberate and careful when deciding to respond in these ways.

3. The tendency to "camp up and strike out" is strong in society. Never do this without reflecting on alternatives. As Gandhi and King taught us, there are other ways.

4. Think about the advantages of second-order change and the move to transform. This requires awareness, self-reflection, and a willingness to innovate. Too often we choose direct confrontation and lose the values of dialogue.

5. If you choose to confront, be open and clear about your aims and constructive in your methods. Be wary of insidious and hidden, even unconscious, forms of hegemony that presume the superiority of one way of being over others.

Interactive Case Study

WORKING WITH HUMAN DIFFERENCE

Context: You will be working with some of your own personal experiences and stories, choosing one to illustrate to the class. You will work first as individuals and then in various subgroups (dyads, triads, and in larger groups). The cases you will be exploring will have one common feature: they will offer a glimpse of a personal relationship (or a set of relationships) that is marked by human difference.

Opening exercise(s): Spend some time alone carefully considering your personal relationships. These relationships can be either one-on-one interactions or groups of people that interact around a compelling issue. Choose one of these relationships, especially one where the differences among or between you cause concern and create challenging communication. Write an outline so that a specific instance can be told as a story. Gather in groups of three and tell each other your stories. Highlight the differences between or among the people in the story. Choose one of these stories and decide how to illustrate this story for another group (role-plays, murals, computer presentation, metaphor, video).

Focus #1: Orienting toward Difference

Two groups of three will now get together. One group will illustrate their story, followed by a full group (of six) discussion. Then the second group will illustrate their story, followed by a full group discussion. Focus the full group discussions on the orientations to difference: ignoring it, embracing it, resisting it, or fighting it. Did you see or hear any indications of these orientations? If so, what type of social world is being created?

After the discussions, choose one of the stories to portray for another group of six. Decide on roles and a method of depiction.

Focus #2: Facework

Two groups of six will now meet, and each will depict their story to the other in some manner. After each presentation, discuss the "face" implications. For the human interactions depicted in each story, how is face affected?

Focus #3: The World of Difference

Each group of six will now meet and focus on the same story they have been depicting and have a group discussion. Referring to the world of difference model on page 9 in chapter 1, in which sphere are the differences residing? Are there any signs that the relationship is moving from one sphere to another? What choices are available that could enable these differences to reside in the sphere of value?

Focus #4: The World of Difference

Each student will now return to his or her original personal story and work alone. According to the world of difference model, in which sphere are the differences residing? Are there any signs that the relationship is moving from one sphere to another? What choices are available that could enable these differences to reside in the sphere of value?

Endnotes

[1] For a summary of Bakhtin's work and a list of his writings, see Stephen W. Littlejohn and Karen A. Foss, *Theories of Human Communication*, 8th ed. (Belmont, CA: Wadsworth, 2005), pp. 196–202.

[2] This analysis is adapted from J. Kevin Barge and Martin Little, "Dialogical Wisdom, Communicative Practice, and Organizational Life," *Communication Theory*, 12 (2002): 375–397.

[3] Adapted from W. Barnett Pearce and Stephen W. Littlejohn, *Moral Conflict: When Social Worlds Collide* (Thousand Oaks, CA: Sage, 1997), pp. 110–125.

[4] This analysis is adapted and extended from Pearce and Littlejohn, pp. 107–125.

[5] W. Barnett Pearce, *Communication and the Human Condition* (Carbondale: Southern Illinois University Press, 1989), pp. 96–117.

[6] Willliam Ascher, "The Moralism of Attitudes Supporting Intergroup Violence," *Political Psychology*, 7 (1986): 403–425.

[7] W. Barnett Pearce and Kimberly A. Pearce, "Combining Passions and Abilities: Toward Dialogic Virtuosity," *Southern Communication Journal*, 65 (1999): 161–175.

[8] This analysis is based on Kathy Domenici and Stephen W. Littlejohn, *Facework: Bridging Theory and Practice* (Thousand Oaks, CA: Sage, 2006). See also, Stephen Littlejohn and Kathy Domenici, "A Facework Frame for Mediation," in *The Blackwell Handbook of Mediation: Bridging Theory, Research, and Practice*, ed. M. S. Herrman (Malden, MA: Blackwell, 2006), pp. 228–246.

[9] Domenici and Littlejohn, pp. 10–11.

[10] Domenici and Littlejohn, p. 18.

[11] Tae-Sop Lim and John Waite Bowers, "Facework: Solidarity, Approbation, and Tact," *Human Communication Research*, 17 (1991): 415–450.

[12] Adapted from Sandra Metts and Erica Grohskopf, "Impression Management: Goals, Strategies, and Skills," in *Handbook of Communication and Social Interaction Skills*, eds. J. O. Greene and B. R. Burleson (Mahwah, NJ: Lawrence Erlbaum, 2003), pp. 357–402.

[13] See, for example, Timothy C. Brock and Melanie C. Green, eds., *Persuasion: Psychological Insights and Perspectives* (Thousand Oaks, CA: Sage, 2005).

[14] Littlejohn and Foss, pp. 318–319.

[15] Pearce and Littlejohn, *Moral Conflict*; Stephen W. Littlejohn, "Transcendent Communication and the Problem of Moral Conflict," in *The Sage Handbook of Conflict Communication: Integrating Theory, Research, and Practice*, eds. John G. Oetzel and Stella Ting-Toomey (Thousand Oaks, CA: Sage, 2006).

[16] See Littlejohn, "Transcendent Communication and the Problem of Moral Conflict," pp. 395–418.

[17] Jayne S. Docherty, *Learning Lessons from Waco: When the Parties Bring their Gods to the Negotiation Table* (Syracuse, NY: Syracuse University Press, 2001).

[18] For a summary of literature on these forms, see Michael E. Roloff, Linda L. Putnam, and Lefki Anastasiou, "Negotiation Skills," in *Handbook of Communication and Social Interaction Skills*, eds. John O. Greene and Brant R. Burleson (Mahwah, NJ: Lawrence Erlbaum, 2003), pp. 801–834.

[19] See, for example, Roxanne Lulofs, *Conflict: From Theory to Action* (Scottsdale, AZ: Gorsuch Scarisbrick, 1994); Stella Ting-Toomey and John G. Oetzel, *Managing Intercultural Conflict Effectively* (Thousand Oaks, CA: Sage, 2001); Phyllis Beck Kriteck,

Negotiating at an Uneven Table (San Francisco: Jossey-Bass, 1994); Stephen W. Little-john and Kathy Domenici, *Engaging Communication in Conflict: Systemic Practice* (Thousand Oaks, CA: Sage, 2001).

[20] This approach is most often attributed to Roger Fisher and William Ury, *Getting to Yes: Negotiating Agreement without Giving In* (New York: Penguin Books, 1991).

[21] Adapted from Roloff, Putnam, and Anastasiou, pp. 801–834.

[22] Roloff, Putnam, and Anastasiou.

[23] Paul Watzlawick, Janet Beavin, and Don Jackson, *Pragmatics of Human Communication: A Study of Interactional Patterns, Pathologies, and Paradoxes* (New York: Norton, 1967).

[24] Stephen W. Littlejohn, "The Transcendent Communication Project," *Conflict Resolution Quarterly*, 21 (2004): 337–360; Littlejohn, "Transcendent Communication and the Problem of Moral Conflict."

[25] Littlejohn, "Transcendent Communication and the Problem of Moral Conflict."

PART TWO

MANAGING CONFLICT
FROM HARM TO VALUE

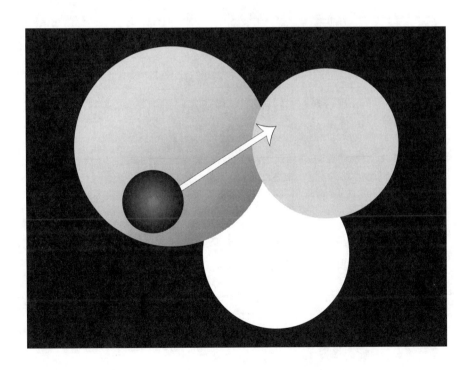

6

Moving toward Value in Relational Conflicts

This chapter is based on the belief that life is always relational. We make our social worlds in relationships, and the people who matter to us most are particularly important in helping us construct a sense of reality. Yet relationships are rife with difference, and some of the most difficult challenges we face occur within relationships.

MANAGING CONTRADICTIONS

As we saw in chapter 2, diversity is normal within a relationship. Normal diversity arises not only from the differences between partners but also from the dynamics of the relationship itself, requiring us to manage the natural flux and flow of interaction. Some forces within a relationship—like centripetal force—tie partners together; other forces—like centrifugal force—push them apart. Such forces sometimes feel like a "knot of contradiction."[1]

In chapter 2, we outlined three contradictions that seem to be especially powerful in relational conflict—tensions between integration and separation, expression and nonexpression, and stability and change. Should a relationship bring two people together into a close bond, or should it allow partners to be individuals and have self-expression? Should a relationship be disclosing, open, and sharing or allow individuality and privacy? And should relationships be stable and predictable or innovative and changing?

These tensions manifest themselves differently at different points in the history of a relationship, and couples handle them in a variety of ways. Some partners are quite good at integrating two apparently contradictory values. For example, if you and your partner both value individuality, then a certain amount of separation would probably bring you closer together. Expression and nonexpression can also be managed in a way that does not create tension. For example, you might think of silence as a kind of statement ("I want to be left alone right now.") that is valued as a clear message to the other person.

Not everyone is able to integrate opposing values in this way. Some partners will waver back and forth between one side and the other, or argue relentlessly. Regardless of the strategy, these tensions create moments of change, and the tensions themselves are experienced in different ways at different points in a relationship. If you are in a new romantic relationship, you probably have a strong need for integration, expression, and stability. After a period of time, you may come to long for a bit of individuality, privacy, and even some change. We do know that relationships go through cycles of this nature.[2] It is through activities that address and manage these kinds of differences that relationships are formed and move in various directions over the course of the time.

In any relationship, some periods seem more conflicted than other periods. During times of relative stability, a couple may feel free of conflict, only to find new sources of conflict arising unexpectedly at other times. The key for successful integration in times of change seems to be synchronizing efforts to manage contradictions.[3] If one party is into high self-disclosure at times when his or her partner feels more private, conflict will ensue. In contrast, if both parties are at the same place on openness and privacy, the relationship will feel more coordinated. Think of relational development as a dance, where the parties sometimes move apart, turn in different directions, and then move together. Even if the dancing partners are facing different directions, they can still feel coordinated as long as it is part of the aesthetic of the dance. The partners have danced together for a long time, and the various turns and movements are orchestrated or choreographed in a way that feels natural, even beautiful at times. Of course, some dancers are better than others.

RELATIONAL PATTERNS OF INTERACTION

A relationship consists of a set of expectations that two people have for their separate and mutual behavior. When our mutual expectations are matched or coordinated, life can be fairly conflict free. For example, a husband may assume responsibility for cooking dinner each day, and his wife—a working spouse—comes to rely on this. If he enjoys cooking and presents a wonderful meal every evening, the couple will come to understand this act as a pleasurable way of showing support. The relationship itself is defined, in part, by this pattern and its associated meanings. If all of their expectations matched this well, the couple would be quite stable and probably very happy. Relational struggles occur when one partner's expectations do not coordinate with those of the other.

Coordination

Over time, a set of meanings and patterns come to define the relationship itself. There is a "logic" of interaction that determines what makes sense and what forms the expectations that have been negotiated over time in that particular relationship. This is why a pattern that feels quite normal in one relationship would seem odd, even abrasive, in another one. Couples are not always together in their logics of meaning and action. One person may be operating by one set of rules, while his or her partner has an entirely different set. When this happens, something has to give.

Relational negotiations are not usually explicit and conscious, but they do occur every time one person acts, tests the other person's response, and adjusts to what happens.[4] In everyday interaction, we "read" or interpret others' actions and make decisions about how to respond. Sometimes our responses reinforce expectations; at other times, they move toward new ones. This is how relationships change. The idea of interpretation and action within a relationship is expressed in the serpentine model in figure 6.1. Shaped like a serpent, this model shows the back-and-forth process of human interaction.[5]

Notice how interaction is a process of coordination. If two people are responding to one another in a way that feels logical or appropriate, we can say that the interaction is coordinated. In contrast, if the interaction feels out of

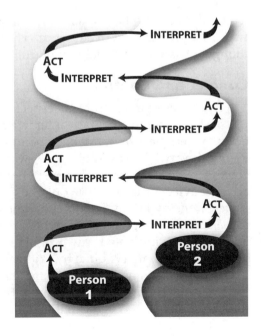

Figure 6.1   Serpentine Model of Communication

sync, inappropriate, confusing, or unexpected, we may feel uncoordinated, like one person is playing chess while the other checkers on the same board.[6]

When we say that a relationship consists of a set of expectations about self and other, we mean that our actions and meanings are organized or that they mesh. This does not mean that life is a happy state of affairs. For example, an alcoholic relationship may be one in which the drinker abuses others, and his or her partner unwittingly supports and enables this behavior. This perfectly coordinated pattern defines the relationship, but it is not a very happy state of affairs.

Coordination also does not mean that the parties to a relationship have the same meanings. You can have a well-coordinated interaction, but each participant could understand what is happening in quite different ways. For example, a young woman may take her boyfriend's behavior to be "loving," while the boyfriend thinks of it as "protective." He thinks she is "vulnerable," but she interprets her own behavior as "close and intimate." It may not really matter that they have different understandings of what is happening because they both find the pattern satisfying and coordinated.

Just because the partners do not understand their relationship the same way does not mean that they will experience conflict. If the interaction is coordinated and both parties are happy with it, conflict will probably not arise. However, if one or both parties are unhappy with the pattern of interaction, then conflict is a distinct possibility. Conflict can happen, too, when one party is surprised or even offended after learning that the other person did not see the relationship the same way. Many tears have resulted after discovering that someone you thought of as a lover actually thinks of you as "just a friend."

Conflict and Control

Two types of interaction are especially interesting. These are symmetrical and complementary interactions. A *symmetrical* interaction occurs when the two partners respond to one another in a similar or identical way. For example, one worker may offer advice to a coworker, and the coworker responds with advice of his own—advice-advice. Example: "It would be a good idea for you to get your project done by Friday." "Forget it, and stop being so bossy!" A *complementary* interaction occurs when two partners respond to one another in a coordinated way. Example: "It would be a good idea for you to get your project done by Friday." "You're right; I will." Single interactions—symmetrical and complementary—are not particularly important or significant, but when patterns repeat consistently over time, they do become significant.

Symmetrical or complementary patterns are most often associated with *control*.[7] When you say something that directs or suggests a particular outcome, you are asserting control of the relationship at that moment. Just to say, "Let's go out to dinner," is a control move, but it does not by itself result in control, as your partner might say, "No, I'm too tired." This is a classic example of a symmetrical interaction in which both parties assert an attempt to control at that moment. One wants to go out to dinner, and the other does not. It might end with that, or it might accelerate into an argument, as each participant tries to "win."

Of course, there is another way in which we can respond to a suggestion, direction, demand, or command. We don't have to respond by agreeing or disagreeing, but by neutralizing the control move, at least in the moment. For example, if one worker tells his or her coworker to finish a project by the end of the week, the other person might respond in a variety of neutralizing ways:

"Thanks, I'll think about it."

"I can see that getting this thing done is really important to you."

"Let's see how my work shapes up this week, and then I can decide."

"Will you help me?"

These are statements than neither assert nor accept the control of the other party.

We don't want to leave the impression that there is something wrong with asserting control. Control helps to organize action and can even bring a sense of coordination. Imagine two friends standing in the rain looking at a map on a street corner in a foreign city. One says, "What should we do?" Not wanting to look pushy, the friend replies, "Whatever you want," whereupon the first person replies, "I don't care. You decide." This is another kind of symmetrical interaction in which each side wants to defer to the other. We have all experienced this sometimes humorous and often aggravating kind of situation, in which neither person wants to say what to do. It does illustrate the importance of control, because when no one provides direction, we end up confused and exasperated (and possibly wet). After a round or two of these, they may just laugh it off, as one of them makes a quick decision about which way to turn.

Isolated interactions like this usually don't matter very much. More important are the patterns that can develop over time. Let's discuss three possibilities.

Complementary Patterns in Conflict.   A dominance-submission relationship commonly leads to conflict. A complementary pattern

can be perfectly coordinated and sometimes happily so. However, dominance can also lead to resentment, power inequity, and even downright oppression. Whether a pattern of dominance leads to conflict depends on relational expectations, which can be colored by cultural and personal considerations as well. In some cultures, dominance is both expected and accepted. In many organizations, for example, managers are expected to be dominant most of the time. In certain religions, husbands are labeled decision makers, and wives are to be supportive. In other religious traditions, this kind of pattern would be anathema.

Many couples expect their complementary patterns to be flexible. For example, one partner may dominant at some moments, while being submissive on other occasions. Sometimes, too, we divide things up, so that one person is dominant on some issues, while the other person is dominant on other ones.

Although complementary patterns do not usually lead to conflict, there are three situations in which they can do so. The first is when one of the parties comes to reject or resent the dominance of the other, and it becomes an issue between them. The second happens when the parties feel the need to realign certain areas of control. For example, a wife wants to start cooking, but the husband does not want to give it up. When conflict results from a complementary pattern in either of these ways, the interaction—and hence the relationship—may shift to one in which control is up for grabs. The third problematic pattern, known as *demand/withdraw*, happens when one partner nags, complains, or criticizes, and the other avoids, or withdraws consistently over time. The results of this pattern can be mixed. It often predicts relational dissatisfaction, but it can be a transitional state into decline or in some cases improvement.[8]

Symmetrical Patterns in Conflict. *Submissive symmetry* happens when no on wants to assert leadership. This is the unfortunate state of affairs in which neither party asserts control. Everyone wants to abrogate it. More than one person has returned unhappy from traveling with friends abroad because no one was willing to take leadership in making decisions about what to do. The whole trip became a struggle of deference. The malaise that can result from this pattern makes you long for a little conflict. It is not very coordinated, and submissively symmetrical relationships tend not to last very long.

Competitive symmetry, in contrast, is the classic pattern of power struggles. Each person wants to assert control, and neither is willing to accept the control of the other. Over time in a competitively symmetrical relationship, a pattern of mutual domination emerges. Neither side wishes to accept the control of the other, and no real dominance-submission arrangement emerges. A particularly insidious form of competitive symmetry happens in *negative reciprocity*, in which partners continue to exchange negative responses such as complaints, defensiveness, anger, etc.[9]

This kind of relationship is not very fun, especially when it gets destructive. When you watch this kind of argument, you probably feel that the climate is highly defensive. Here is what you see:[10]

- Strategy—The communicators are "plotting" or thinking consciously about how to win.
- Lack of empathy—They are unable or unwilling to see the other's point of view.
- Superiority—Each claims the privilege of knowing what is best.
- Evaluation—Each makes clear negative judgments about the other.
- Pressure—Both sides exert pressure to conform.
- Certainty—No one admits doubts or areas where they might be wrong.

We have to be careful in making these attributions, however. This pattern is not necessarily a sign of conflict if it is taken by the parties themselves as a display of caring, engagement, or fun. Although constant fighting may look bad from the outside, you never know how the parties themselves define it from within their system.

Unwanted Repetitive Patterns.   This kind of communication can become an *unwanted repetitive pattern*—aptly nicknamed URP—which neither partner wants nor seems able to change.[11] The main reason this pattern of communication is frustrating is that people often do not know how to respond any other way to one another. They feel stuck in a habitual pattern of communicating. Unwanted patterns can hinder communicators from moving away from the sphere of harm and toward the sphere of value. We usually talk about movement toward value as "forward movement." Forward movement begins to happen when stuck relationships realize that they have the means to communicate differently.

The problem with URPs, such as those apparent in power struggles, is that they reflect a lack of imagination about how to respond to unwanted actions of others. Later in the chapter, we talk about some ways to change the conversation from a defensive to a constructive climate—one in which the partners come to feel (1) more spontaneous and less strategic, (2) more empathic, (3) equal, (4) descriptive rather than judgmental, (5) oriented to mutual problem solving rather than control, and (6) provisional rather than certain.

Blame and the Punctuation of Interaction Sequences

Disputants in mediation often begin by listing the terrible things the other person has done to them. Commonly in conflicts, anger and hurt associated with blame can make conflict resolution challenging, to say the least. When you are in a conflict, it may feel like the other person is out to get you, but when you view it analytically from outside, a different perspective may come into focus. We are convinced that blame is not usually the result of some true or objective thing that one person actually did to someone else; instead, it stems from the *punctuation of interaction sequences.*[12] Let us explain what we mean.

When you write, you divide paragraphs up into smaller pieces with punctuation marks. As you speak, you also punctuate nonverbally by pausing, changing tone of voice, using facial expressions, and gestures. In communication, then, punctuation is vital to help get across what you are trying to say. How you parse, or divide up, a sentence influences the meaning you convey.

If you read something written by a child, a nonnative writer of English, or someone who simply never learned the conventions of English punctuation, you might have to struggle a little bit to place the punctuation marks mentally so that the discourse makes sense. Metaphorically, this is what happens in interaction. As people take turns talking in a conversation, they place unconscious mental markers that organize the conversation into some meaningful whole.

The punctuation of an interaction, then, can be complex, and what one person thinks is happening may not match what others see. When two people punctuate differently—even when they don't realize they are doing so—conflict and blame may result.

Let's look at an example: An engaged couple goes to counseling to resolve some issues before getting married. In their first counseling session, the soon-to-be groom tells the following story:

> Well, I think we argue too much. Yes, that's something we need to change. She gets mad so easily, and when I suggest something, she sometimes just yells at me, and that makes me feel bad, then I can't talk to her. I would like to talk rationally about things, but she just gets so emotional and attacks me, and that makes me get upset.

Here is what the bride has to say:

> Yes, we do argue. That's because he keeps bugging me about stuff, and then he gets mad and lashes out. When he gets like that, I just don't know what to do, and then I get upset, and we argue. I just wish he could be more rational.

Notice that each partner here is blaming the other for the arguments. They don't realize that they are punctuating their conversations in opposite ways. The man places his fiancé's anger first, which he said causes him to get mad. The woman brackets the sequence differently, viewing her anger as a response to his "bugging" and "being emotional." To him, the problem is her fault, but to her, it is his. Both of them think they start off being rational, but the other's emotionality upsets them. The groom punctuates like this: *When I'm rational, she gets emotional, and that makes me mad, and we argue.* She punctuates it like this: *He bugs me and is angry, which makes me mad, and we argue.* It's the same sequence, just punctuated differently by the two parties. Over time, this subtle difference can lead to resentment.

This is an example of the classic case of misplaced blame caused by the fact that the partners assign different meanings to the sequence. A good counselor will help them learn to describe the pattern without attributing blame and to explore the different ways in which it might be punctuated or understood and then to talk about how to change it without assuming that one person "caused" the other to respond a certain way.

We are not surprised that people punctuate interaction sequences differently. A person's meaning of a sequence of action depends on the context, and much of the time this is a frame of self-interest. When you look at an interaction from inside your own eyeballs, you see that you are responding to others; they, in contrast, see that they are responding to you.

If we can get out of rigid punctuations and explore interaction sequences more creatively, we will begin to find new ways to respond to one another in conflict situations.

When Logics Clash: Conflict of Meaning and Action

You will always evaluate a situation in terms of a *logic of meaning and action*, or a set of connections used to make sense of the situation.[13] This logic tells us what something means and how we should respond to it. For example, as mentioned in chapter 4, in the United States we follow a very powerful "greeting logic," where the question, "How are you?" is taken as friendliness, and you are obligated to reply by saying, "Fine," no matter how you feel. In another situation, however, you might use a different logic such as "caring and concern." Here you would take the question, "How are you?" as a genuine inquiry into the state of your health, and would reply something like this: "Well, the surgery went well, but I had some complications that made me pretty sick for a few days, but now I'm home from the hospital and doing much better. Thanks for asking." The context is different, and the logic of meaning and action differ also.

Things usually go pretty well when we share the same logic of meaning and action, but when we have different logics, conflict can result. Sometimes what feels like a personality or style conflict results from this state of affairs: You just want to be friendly with a coworker and make the mistake of asking how they are, whereupon you get a dissertation on the state of their health. Not what you wanted. More serious disputes can also arise from exactly the same situation— divergent logics of meaning and action.

Conflict and Differing Contexts.   You can think of logic as a set of rules that guide how you interpret what you see and how you act within a given situation. These rules operate within particular contexts that seem important to the situation you are facing. Often, for example, your culture provides a logic that guides your behavior. This might be the case when you take off your shoes upon entering a mosque. Sometimes you operate from a logic that comes from your sense of self. For example, if you think you are a "problem solver," then you would tend to define what you see as "problems" and respond by presenting "solutions." Other times, you may operate out of the logic of a relationship, or the expectations negotiated between you and another person. An example would be inviting your neighbor to a party at your house to reciprocate an earlier invitation on his part. On other occasions, your logic might stem from the episode or type of conversation you are having, so that you behave certain ways at business meetings, other ways at weddings, and still other ways at worship.

Obviously, these contexts—culture, self, relationship, or episode—are connected to one another. The logics of meaning and action in one context may affect and be affected by others. Because no two people share exactly the same contexts at any given moment, they may differ in the logics that inform their interpretations and actions. Imagine one partner, for example, driven by a strong sense of personal duty and another motivated by cultural standards of appropriateness. The first partner might want to rush in to "manage" every situation, while the other would prefer to be watchful and nonintrusive.

Conflict and Differing Logics. The rules within a logic guide how we interpret and respond. Sometimes, for example, we operate from a *causal logic,* in which we consider one thing determining another. We act in certain ways because we believe we have little choice. Our behaviors are determined. For example, you might justify an angry response to a friend by saying you couldn't help it because the friend did something that caused you to "get mad." Notice that you interpret the situation as one in which one action gives rise to or causes another action. In this example, anger is seen as a reaction that is out of control and determined by something else.

Another common logic is called *practical* because it comes from a sense of acting to accomplish something in the future. You might, for example, react angrily because you believe from previous experience that anger will motivate your friends to do something you want them to do. Notice the difference between a causal and practical logic. In one case, the behavior is caused; in the other, it is strategic. The causal logic says, if A happens, B will result. The practical logic says, if I want to get Y, I should do X. The causal logic is past-oriented, while the practical logic is goal-oriented.

A third logic is *contextual,* in which the situation demands certain interpretations and actions: "This situation demands that I take a stand and show my feelings. The most appropriate thing that someone like me in this situation can do is get mad!" You are not saying that any specific antecedent caused your anger, nor are you suggesting that you are trying to meet some goal by this behavior. Instead, it is based on a strong sense of appropriateness within a context. You pray in church because that's just what you are supposed to do in church. You may go to college because that's just what everyone in your family is supposed to do. You may race cars because "people like you" just need excitement in their lives.

The logics that shape our understanding and actions within situations guide how we interpret what is happening and how we react to this. A fascinating study of grievances in an ombuds office in a university illustrates this very well.[14] An ombudsperson is an individual in an organization who hears complaints and disputes and tries to resolve them, much like a mediator. An interview of 50 people involved in disputes revealed that some people are *information seekers*. These individuals thought of their cases as a matter of circumstances and did not place blame on others for what happened to them. They came to the ombuds office to seek information to help clarify the situation and to find a solution. Others were *exception seekers*, seeing their situation as a policy objection. These clients made the case that they should be treated as an exception. *Victims* took a harsher view. These individuals blamed the system for treating them badly. They felt they were being punished by events beyond their control. Everyone was to blame, and they were seeking personal redress through corrective action.

Another group were *enforcers*, and these disputants placed blame firmly on specific other people, although they acknowledged that the other person might not have intended to be hurtful. The motivation of enforcers was to make sure that a high standard of justice was upheld. The next group, *protectors*, held the same interpretation as the enforcers—blaming someone for doing something wrong—but the motivation for action was different. Protectors aimed to have corrective action taken to prevent harm to other people in the future. Finally, there were a few individuals who could be described as *destroyers*. In every case, these disputants believed that another person had intentionally harmed them. Interpreting the other person as evil, they aimed for vindication in the form of extreme punishment—for example, destroying the other person's career.

As you can imagine, many of the disputes heard at the ombuds office at a university relate to grades or conflicts with professors. Notice how a person's logic of meaning and action influences their understanding and reaction to an adverse grade. An information seeker might say that the bad grade is the kind of mistake that just happens sometimes in a large system and wants to know what he or she can do about it. An exception seeker might understand that the grade was given in accordance with the syllabus, but that the instructor just didn't understand the personal problems that the student was having. A victim might say that the grading system is unfair and insensitive to individual needs. An enforcer might claim that the professor was capricious and should be held to a higher standard of fairness. A protector might want someone to make the professor more accountable so that other students are not hurt in the future, and a destroyer may attribute the grade to personal vendetta and seek to have the professor fired. Each of these types of disputants has a set of rules about how to interpret the grading situation and how to respond to it.

We are never limited to just one logic. Over time, and in different situations, we may employ a variety of logics, depending on cultural norms, sense of self, relational expectations, and sense of appropriateness. In daily life, however, we are not normally conscious of the logics we employ. In conflict situations, we rarely consider that what looks like a difference of opinion or a conflict of goals could actually be a clash of logic. Two people are simply interpreting and acting on the basis of different rules. One of the things that distinguishes sports and politics is that they are guided by a common purpose and an agreed-upon set of rules (most of the time!). We cannot say this for many interpersonal conflicts. A key for working through a conflict is to negotiate a common logic or method for resolving it. If different logics led us to have this conflict, can we agree on a set of rules by which we will manage it in the future? Mediators work with this idea by bringing parties into a common logic of meaning and action within the conflict-resolution episode. If the parties are so entrenched in their respective rule sets, the resulting conflict may become intractable and very difficult to manage—a topic we address later in this book.

Box 6.1

With one or two friends, see a movie that features the relationship between two individuals. Watch it twice, once just to enjoy it and get a sense of the plot and a second time to analyze the relationship in detail. The second time you view the film, you should take notes and then discuss the following questions:

1. How did this relationship change over time, and what conflicts or differences led to these changes?

2. What forces tended to push the characters apart (centrifugal forces), and which ones tended to pull them together (centripetal forces)?

3. What contradictions did the characters have to manage in their relationship, and how did they do it?

4. To what extent and in what ways where the characters' interactions complementary and symmetrical? Which of these were salutary and which destructive?

5. Describe the control patterns in this relationship.

6. Did the characters punctuate their interactions the same way? Did any conflicts result from differing punctuations?

THE EMOTIONAL SIDE OF RELATIONAL CONFLICT

People typically think that emotions are reactions beyond their control. Yet feelings are never divorced from how we interpret and act in a situation. In other words, the meanings we ascribe to what is happening create the emotions we feel. Our logics of meaning and action include rules for how we should respond emotionally. If someone treats you disrespectfully or rudely, you interpret this act as an attack on your personal identity, making anger an appropriate response. If you do something that you think is wrong, your resulting feeling of guilt or shame, though painful, will seem appropriate.

Emotions as Rule-Governed

Emotions, then, are not simply neurochemical reactions; they are very much relational in orientation.[15] Emotional activity is an important aspect of the pattern of communication negotiated between two people. Suppose, for example, that your housemate is constantly picking up after you. Your appraisal of this situation will result in an idea of how relevant your housemate's behavior is to your identity.[16] Assuming that you take this act personally, then you are making a judgment about how to respond. Your primary appraisal—establishing the personal relevance of the act—will lead to certain emotions (anger, perhaps), while the secondary appraisal will establish a response that can mitigate or even exacerbate the emotions you are feeling.

Figure 6.2   Interaction Model of Emotion

Your logic of meaning and action gives you a set of rules for understanding behavior, how to feel about that behavior, and what to do about it. This is not a linear pattern of interpretation → feeling → action; as illustrated in figure 6.2, the pattern revolves and circulates.

This means that emotions are not strictly reactive, but in many cases, they are part of the rule-governed actions that you deem necessary at the moment. How you respond emotionally depends in turn on the contexts shaping your rule set in the situation. That context might be cultural, it might be relational, it might be episodic, or it might be personal.

Culture, for example, can be a powerful influence on feelings. Some cultures, like the Eskimo, use emotion to show connection to the group. Thus, they tend to laugh together or to cry together to show solidarity.[17] Emotions are very much tied to belief systems, including rules that guide how you should feel and how you should express those feelings.[18] If, for example, you are following a causal logic, you will see your expressed feeling as a consequence of some previous action or event. If, on the other hand, you are operating from a practical, goal-oriented logic, then your expressed feeling may be somewhat strategic and designed to achieve a certain result. This does not mean that you are faking your feelings in some kind of manipulative way; emotions are genuinely felt. It means that the feeling of the emotion—and its expression through action—is socially constructed in the back-and-forth interaction in a relationship and is governed by a set of rules established within the contextual logic of meaning and action.

Negotiating Emotions

Emotions, then, are actually negotiable, and they do change. When your housemate keeps picking up your stuff, you may react angrily at first; but over time, your feeling may actually shift to amusement, or even guilt. What feels like an appropriate response at first may not feel so appropriate later, as new rule sets emerge within the relationship.[19] It is entirely possible to discuss what certain patterns mean and how best to respond. "Why do you keep picking up my things?" The answer to this question and the subsequent discussion will result in a negotiation of emotion. If the answer is, "You are such a slob," then you will probably get angry. If it is, "I'm a neat freak. Sorry," it might shift to amusement or mild irritation. If it is, "I think we should try to keep our common areas neat and clean," you might come to feel a little guilty. If it is, "Sorry, I didn't mean to be intrusive. Maybe we should talk about how to divide up the cleaning chores," then you might feel some satisfaction.

Many times in mediations, we have seen the parties shift their understandings and emotional responses significantly during the session. What comes out at the beginning of the session as "righteous indignation" is not just an uncontrollable chemical reaction, but the result of a particular set of meanings and response rules, and those can and do change as a result of the mediation.

We knew a young couple who, despite being deeply in love, could not stop fighting. Emotional encounters quickly accelerated to rage. The couple recognized how destructive the pattern had become, but they

seemed powerless to change it because of a strong causal logic. In counseling this couple, we encouraged them to think of other ways to understand what was going on and to respond to situations based on new interpretations. We said that if the relationship was worth maintaining, they would have to decide to behave differently; and they did! Over time, their rule sets shifted to more practical, goal-oriented ones, which made rage an unacceptable response.

In thinking about emotion, then, we need to realize that feelings are relative, that we construct meanings for our feelings, and that we make decisions about how to react to feelings. This being said, however, strong emotions feel very real, and we often experience such emotions physiologically. Let's take a closer look at four of the most common emotions experienced in relationships: anger, jealousy, hurt, and guilt.[20]

Hard Feelings: Anger, Jealousy, Hurt, and Guilt

We don't need to cite research to prove that *anger* is common. Research studies affirm what we know intuitively; anger can be associated with rage, irritation, exasperation, disgust, and even envy. Anger is common in situations in which our goals or plans are thwarted. It can be especially challenging when our identity is attacked and/or we feel frustrated, treated unfairly, or as though we were incompetent. Anger can also result from a perceived threat to a valued relationship.[21] Naturally, many people tend to strike out or aggress when they get mad, and this can happen even in romantic relationships.[22] Yet, this is not always the case, and, as we saw above, people can chose to respond in more constructive ways that do not reproduce the anger-attack cycle.[23] One of the most positive responses when you get angry is to speak assertively and clearly without blame or attack. State what happened and how you feel about it. It's okay to reveal your anger, but do so in a spirit of dialogue to learn more about what is going on with the other person and how to remedy the situation.[24]

Jealousy is usually a horrible experience. It can come on us as a "jealousy flash" consisting of a palpable increase in heart rate along with a flushed feeling.[25] This response can be followed by associated feelings such as anger, fear, sadness, guilt, and even sexual arousal.[26] People handle jealousy in a variety of ways: (1) direct, aggressive communication; (2) distancing ("the silent treatment"); (3) counterjealousy, or attempts to get back; and (4) inducing guilt. Violence against people and even objects can occur.[27] As hard as it may be, you don't have to respond to jealousy in these ways. Relationship-maintaining strategies like talking the situation through or even just monitoring what is going on can be more productive and ultimately valuable.

When we perceive that we are being attacked—our identity is being challenged—we will usually feel *hurt*. This is usually experienced as an intense emotion, as if we had been physically injured in some way. It can be associated with anguish, anger, and suffering, but mostly we feel sad.[28] But what counts as a threat sufficient to cause hurt? There are several possibilities. We can feel accused, negatively evaluated, rejected, or threatened. Even jokes can be hurtful, as we all know.[29] One of the most common sources of hurt in close relationships is the *relational transgression*, or betrayals, which is why hurt and jealously go hand in hand.[30] There seem to be three common responses to hurt: (1) direct, emotional outbursts, such as anger or defensiveness; (2) acquiescence, conceding, or crying; and (3) showing invulnerability in the form of stoicism, laughing, and ignoring.[31] Usually these responses are not completely satisfactory, unless they shift the tone, allow partners to vent, or provide clarity on the harm that has been done. Eventually, *relational repair tactics* are more fruitful, and these involve trying to patch things up, disclosing feelings in a non-threatening manner, and opening up new avenues of conversation.[32]

The fourth common emotion experienced in relational conflict is *guilt*. Ironically, guilt seems to stem from many of the same things that can cause hurt. The difference is really in the attributions that you make. If you blame another person for what is happening, you will probably be inclined to feel anger or hurt; but if you blame yourself in some way, guilt is likely to result. Guilt, then, is very much self-reflective.[33] It is based on a sense of identity, how you think of yourself, and how you wish to behave. When you feel that you have violated your expectations for your own behavior, you will probably experience something you would call guilt.[34] This could, for example, be betraying or neglecting a significant other, failing to meet a relational obligation, not fulfilling an expected role, feeling that the other person made sacrifices for you, or comparing yourself to the other person in a negative way.[35] Although we will sometimes avoid, deny, or justify feelings of guilt, more often we are inclined to try to repair the damage in some way.[36] Indeed, a little guilt can actually help move a relationship in a positive direction.

There are a few generalizations we can make about the role of emotion in relational conflict. First, it is often hard to identify exactly what we are feeling because several emotions cluster together. We may feel a twinge of anger, hurt, and jealousy, for example. Second, strong emotions often result from having our expectations violated. We think one kind of thing should be happening, but the other person (sometimes oneself) behaves differently.[37] Third, conflict emotions are normally experienced as negative, and they can be destructive. However, if handled well, these difficult feelings can actually help stimulate necessary dialogue and change within a relationship. Fourth, one's first reaction is often not the most constructive response. Striking out, withdrawing, or denying may provide temporary relief, but subsequent constructive action can help repair and even improve the relationship.

HOW TO MANAGE RELATIONAL CONFLICTS

Managing difference in relationships means managing interaction patterns. What we talk about, how we talk about it, how we understand what we are doing together, and how we respond to one another are all negotiable and can be refined and improved in situations where difference seems to be a problem. There are three keys to effective conflict management—being reflexive, working to maintain the relationship, and negotiating patterns that work.

Being Reflexive

Reflexivity is the quality of something bending back on itself, like a snake. We use the term metaphorically here to capture the ability of people in relationships to be self-reflective, to look in a critical way at their interpretations and actions. When we are being reflexive, we (1) are aware of the ways in which our interpretations and actions both influence and are influenced by those of others; (2) become more conscious of the contexts that guide our rule sets; and (3) explore other possible contexts and rules for interpreting and acting within the situation.[38]

When you are being reflexive, you realize that you have choices; meanings are not fixed; you can move to new contexts; you can respond to the actions of others in a variety of ways; and how you respond will make a difference. In general, we would say that being reflexive means being aware that you are always engaged in a process of social construction and that you have some ability to shape the world being made by how you communicate. You can experiment with different ways of framing events and play with the pragmatic effects of these different approaches. We encouraged the young couple in the earlier example to do exactly this: Instead of feeling locked into rage, how else might they respond, and what would be different if they tried to understand the situation differently and to respond in new ways?

Managers, for example, sometimes engage in "invitational reflexivity," in which they actively invite others to talk freely about how they interpret events and how they feel they can and should respond to these.[39] If, for example, a coworker were to say, "I feel that this work environment is so oppressive sometimes," a manager might reply, "Really? Okay, gee, could we talk a little bit about what you mean by *oppressive*. I'm interested in learning more about when you feel oppressed and who else might feel like that." Partners in a relationship can explore their patterns of interaction together, what these might mean, and how they might be changed. True reflexivity involves a search for alternative ways of interpreting and acting and wondering aloud about how things would change if different rule sets were used.

Working to Maintain the Relationship

You don't always want to maintain every relationship. Indeed, the time occasionally comes when a relationship wanes and ends. This is true of friendships and romantic relationships as well. However, if you value the relationship and want to maintain it, effort must be put into managing differences in a way that leads from harm to value. At the minimum, this will mean four kinds of work.[40]

First is *maintaining interaction*. Over time, there is sometimes a tendency to reduce, even eliminate, significant interaction within a relationship. Challenging differences, including conflict, can exacerbate this tendency in some couples. Concerted effort may be required to spend time together, share activities, talk, and include the other person in what you are doing.[41] Many married couples, for example, ritualize time together. This could happen at the dinner table, golf course, before bedtime, or even in the car. The effort to maintain interaction must be deliberate and positive. A lot of conflict will fade into insignificance if the couple makes sure that joint time, inclusion, and interaction are frequent and positive.

Second, good relationships—especially with romantic partners, spouses, and friends—are fueled by *liking*. But liking does not necessarily reproduce itself without work on the part of the partners in the relationship, especially after difficult differences and conflicts surface. Deliberate expressions of affection, being positive, showing openness, assuring other people, sharing friends within a social network, and working together on tasks can breed and reinforce liking within the relationship.[42]

Third, *intimacy* must be maintained, especially within families and romantic relationships. Intimacy means openness and sharing. It can be maintained by self-disclosure and showing closeness, but these by themselves do not always influence feelings of intimacy.[43] Like the other factors of relational maintenance, each relationship has its own ways of continuing intimacy. The important thing is for partners to establish ways to stay close.

Finally, relational maintenance requires occasional *repair*. When things go south, partners have to deal with it, and if they don't, the relationship itself will be threatened. This may require taking time to talk the situation over and to assess and discuss how to move forward under threatening circumstances. In the research literature, this is called *metacommunication*, which means "talking about our interaction."[44] There is some question about whether it is better to deal with relational issues directly and openly or indirectly. The research literature on this question is mixed, in part because direct communication in times of difficulty requires a lot of skill, and many people are just not comfortable with it.[45] We think, too, that different relationships and different cultures have different ways of dealing with conflict, and directness may or may not feel appropriate.

Negotiating Patterns that Work

We often encounter negative and potentially damaging patterns in mediation. An effective way to intervene at such moments is simply to ask the parties: "Is this working for you? Is this how you want to be communicating right now?" More often than not, this question gives pause and helps the parties reflect on other patterns that might help to move them in a positive direction. When anyone is stuck in a difficult conflict, we encourage them to ask the same question of themselves: "Is this how we want to be communicating, or is there a better way?" Notice that these questions are reflexive in nature and ask the parties to look at how they are framing the dispute.

At some point, they can begin to negotiate a different pattern. They can begin to craft a new framework or context for the conversation.[46] What do we want to accomplish here, and how should we do it? In many cases, this means creating a "container" or "safe environment" in which hard issues can be discussed in constructive ways.

Using a construction metaphor, we see that conflicts are made by those who engage in them. We can also construct ways of working within conflict, or within the differences that make us human. Conflicts can be renovated, remodeled, or remade, in new ways. Conflicts can also be abandoned, rebuilt, occupied for a time, or deemed suitable for new uses. If we are going to construct a way of living, working, and communicating together in the midst of our differences, collaboration becomes a powerful design strategy and tool for the building project.

You will see references to collaboration in almost every interactive or team-based activity these days. It is a process where interested parties participate in a cooperative process to reach their shared goals. A common assumption about collaboration is that there are better outcomes for all parties involved, whether for two people or a large group. When we move past the "fixed pieces of the pie" metaphor, we realize the multitude of choices available for moving forward in relationships.

In summary, the key to effective conflict management is to take a step back, look carefully at the process, and build a more effective framework in which to manage the difference. This approach essentially acknowledges that we may have evolved a negative pattern that is not very effective; that we may be punctuating interaction differently; and that we may be operating with different logics, or rule sets. It also propels us to try to find a common form or logic within which we can move forward constructively and humanely. There are many ways in which we might do this, and we explore several in the appendix of this book.

Box 6.2

Think of a relationship that was or is important to you: for example, a relationship with a boyfriend or girlfriend, fiancé, spouse, friend, family member, or coworker. Consider the history of the relationship and what the two of you did or did not do to manage differences effectively. To what extent were you self-reflexive? Did you work to maintain the relationship, and if so what did you do? To what extent did you negotiate patterns that worked?

HOW YOU CAN USE THIS CHAPTER

Although large-system conflicts occurring in organizations and nations are a great concern, for most of us, the relational conflicts in our immediate presence consume the majority of our efforts to reach understanding. We hope this chapter has provided some insights that will help you manage such differences constructively.

1. Understand that even though you experience times of relative stability, long-term relationships always change. Conflict is normal, and contradiction must be managed effectively if the relationship is to survive and thrive.

2. Patterns that occur over time within a relationship will make a difference in the extent to which partners are able to make it through hard times. If you don't like what you see in a relationship, change the pattern.

3. Successful patterns are coordinated, appreciated, and lead to a constructive climate in which relational partners can talk about their relationship competently and make effective decisions about how to move forward.

4. People rarely do harm to others—especially those they love—intentionally. Before you level blame on another person, think about other ways to interpret what is going on. Better yet, have a dialogue about what is going on.

5. Expect to feel strong emotions in relational conflict. Don't be surprised if you are confused about what you are feeling. Remember, too, that your feelings can clarify and change, and you have some control over how you respond to your feelings.

6. When experiencing relational conflict be reflexive, work to maintain the relationship, and negotiate patterns that work.

Interactive Case Study

CUBICLE NEIGHBORS

Context: You work for a large car manufacturing company. The building where you reside consists of a large room full of cubicles, each consisting of a compact workstation and comfortable chair. The only opportunities for personalization allowed for each worker are some personal photos, decorations such as plastic flowers or trinkets, and maybe a colored rug on the floor. Your days are spent at the computer, with occasional departmental meetings and smaller workgroup project meetings, all held in the central conference room. Two of you have been "cubicle neighbors" for eight years now, focusing on similar tasks with similar degrees of success. You both have a two-year degree in business accounting and hope to rise to more skilled positions based on performance-based advancement opportunities offered in the company.

Opening exercise(s): The cubicle neighbors have begun experiencing some difficulties in their relationship. They have dropped hints to each other about their differences but have not directly communicated their concerns to each other yet.

Divide the class into groups of three. One role-player will portray Pat and one role-player will portray Chris, while the other will act as an observer. The Pat–Chris teams should read the following roles and be prepared to explore their relationship.

> Pat: You have been increasingly aggravated by the strong perfume/cologne your cubicle neighbor, Chris, is wearing. You also have noted new choices in attire, very modern and even outlandish. You have noticed it for many months now, but you don't want to rock the boat and bring it up. Chris also seems so short tempered lately, and you just can't afford the time for a confrontation. You wonder why he/she would do something as obnoxious as this, and are now questioning the positive regard you have held him/her in for so long.

> Chris: You have noticed a coldness coming from Pat lately. You are hesitant to bring it up, since you are feeling a bit self-conscious this past year, and don't want to seem paranoid. Your marriage is about to break up, after a year of counseling and struggles. Your partner does not seem attracted to you any more, and you have attempted to make yourself more interesting by taking more care about how you dress and groom yourself. In fact, you are only recently beginning to wonder about dating again. After this year of struggles, you are confused about most of your relationships.

Focus #1: Control in Relationships

Each Pat and Chris team should get together and plan a short skit (depiction) of their relationship to offer insights into conflict and control that create a type of social world for them. Half of the Pat–Chris dyads will portray a symmetrical relationship, and the other dyads will portray a complementary relationship. Be very explicit in showing the patterns that depict this control dimension for about five minutes or so. After each skit, the observers should discuss the following questions:

1. What communication pattern did you see emerging in this relationship?
2. What are the impacts on the relationship?
3. What world is being built by this pattern of communication?

Focus #2: Logic in the Interactions

One of the dyads will portray a longer (ten minutes or so) discussion, this time with increasing difficulty, accusations, defensiveness, and illumination of the irritations they each have about the other. The four observers will look carefully at the logic in this conversation. What set of rules seem to be guiding each other's interpretation of what they see and how they act within the situation? Whether causal, practical, or contextual, note how the logics arise as similar or different.

Focus #3: Reflexivity

The Chris and Pat dyads will now continue the conversation, which has turned into an argument, thoroughly residing in the sphere of harm. One dyad and an observer will enact the scene while the other dyad and observer does the same in another part of the room. The role-players can now bring their differences to a crescendo, followed by an invitation to movement toward the sphere of value by negotiating patterns that work. After a few minutes of destructive fighting, one of them can ask a question like:

> "Is this working for you? Is this how you want to be communicating right now?"

> "Is this how we want to be communicating, or is there a better way?"

Let this role-play end after the questions are asked. The goal of this exercise will be simply this: to experience the reflexive look back at themselves. Each role-player can comment on "How does it feel when asking this question?" "How does it feel when being asked this question?" The observer can comment on what this interaction looked like and how it felt to observe it.

Focus #4: Integrative Problem Solving

Use the same one-dyad plus one-observer groups. Go back to the previous arguments and restart them again, letting the tension go on for five minutes or so. Someone will once again ask the reflexive question as above, and this time, role-play some integrative problem solving. Use the following questions as a bridge from the reflexive question into a new conversation and a new way of communicating.

1. How have we been able to make positive decisions in the past? What do we have between us that can help us make decisions?
2. When thinking about the future, what do we see happening? What mutual vision do we have of our relationship, both personally and professionally?
3. What needs to happen to make our vision a reality?
4. How can we discuss this issue in a way that enables us to move forward?
5. What activities, attitudes, or behaviors are we willing to give up to achieve a mutual vision?

The observer can look carefully at the new type of communication and how the transition was invited.

Focus #5: Collaborative Outcomes

Group members can now discuss methods and skills for keeping relational difficulties, like the one experienced by these cubicle neighbors,

within the sphere of value. Consider the ingredients for successful collaboration. As a group, discuss what needs to happen to develop this ingredient.

Endnotes

[1] Leslie A. Baxter and Barbara M. Montgomery, "A Guide to Dialectical Approaches
to Studying Personal Relationships," in *Dialectical Approaches to Studying Personal
Relationships*, eds. B. Montgomery and L. Baxter (Mahwah, NJ: Lawrence Erlbaum,
1998), pp. 1–15.

[2] Irwin Altman, "Dialectics, Physical Environments, and Personal Relationships,"
Communication Monographs, 60 (1993): 26–34; Irwin Altman, Anne Vinsel, and Barbara Brown, "Dialectic Conceptions in Social Psychology: An Application to Social
Penetration and Privacy Regulation," in *Advances in Experimental Social Psychology*,
vol. 14, ed. Leonard Berkowitz (New York: Academic, 1981), pp. 76–100.

[3] C. Arthur VanLear, "Testing a Cyclical Model of Communicative Openness in Relationship Development: Two Longitudinal Studies," *Communication Monographs*, 58
(1991): 337–361.

[4] This notion is based on the now classic work of Paul Watzlawick, Janet Beavin, and
Don Jackson, *Pragmatics of Human Communication: A Study of Interactional Patterns,
Pathologies, and Paradoxes* (New York: Norton, 1967).

[5] Adapted from W. Barnett Pearce, *Interpersonal Communication: Making Social Worlds*
(New York: HarperCollins, 1994), p. 31.

[6] This analysis is based on the theory of the coordinated management of meaning, origi-
nally elaborated in W. Barnett Pearce and Vernon Cronen, *Communication, Action, and
Meaning* (New York: Praeger, 1980); see also, Stephen W. Littlejohn and Karen A. Foss,
Theories of Human Communication, 8th ed. (Belmont, CA: Wadsworth, 2005), pp. 170–174.

[7] This discussion is based on the work of Frank E. Millar and L. Edna Rogers, "Relational Dimensions of Interpersonal Dynamics," in *Interpersonal Processes: New Directions in Communication Research*, eds. Michael E. Roloff and Gerald R. Miller
(Newbury Park, CA: Sage, 1987), pp. 117–139; see also, L. Edna Rogers and Valentin
Escudero, *Relational Communication: An Interactional Perspective to the Study of Process
and Form* (Mahwah, NJ: Erlbaum, 2004).

[8] John P. Caughlin and Anita L. Vangelisti, "Conflict in Dating and Marital Relationships," in *The Sage Handbook of Conflict Communication: Integrating Theory, Research,
and Practice*, eds. John G. Oetzel and Stella Ting-Toomey (Thousand Oaks, CA: Sage,
2006), pp. 129–157.

[9] Caughlin and Vangelisti.

[10] Adapted from Jack Gibb, "Defensive Communication," *Journal of Communication*, 11
(1961): 141–148.

[11] Pearce and Cronen.

[12] Watzlawick, Bevin, and Jackson.

[13] Pearce and Cronen.

[14] Tyler R. Harrison, "Victims, Targets, Protectors, and Destroyers: Using Disputant
Accounts to Develop a Grounded Taxonomy of Disputant Orientations," *Conflict
Resolution Quarterly*, 20 (2003): 307–329.

[15] This analysis adapted from Daniel L. Shapiro, "Negotiating Emotions," *Conflict Resolution Quarterly*, 20 (2002): 67–82.

[16] Richard S. Lazarus, *Emotion and Adaptation* (New York: Oxford University Press, 1991).

[17] Rom Harré, *Personal Being: A Theory for Individual Psychology* (Cambridge, MA: Harvard University Press, 1984).

[18] James Averill, "A Constructivist View of Emotion," in *Theories of Emotion*, eds. Robert Plutchik and Henry Kellerman (New York: Academic, 1980), pp. 305–339.

[19] Barbara Parkinson, *Ideas and Realities of Emotion* (New York: Routledge, 1995).

[20] This analysis is from Laura K. Guerrero and Angela G. LaValley, "Conflict, Emotion, and Communication," in *The Sage Handbook of Conflict Communication: Integrating Theory, Research, and Practice*, eds. John G. Oetzel and Stella Ting-Toomey (Thousand Oaks, CA: Sage, 2006), pp. 69–96.

[21] Phillip R. Shaver, Judith Schwartz, Donald Kirson, and Cary O'Connor, "Emotion Knowledge: Further Explorations of a Prototype Approach," *Journal of Personality and Social Psychology*, 52 (1987): 1061–1086; Daniel J. Canary, Brian H. Spitzberg, and Beth A. Semic, "The Experience and Expression of Anger in Interpersonal Settings," in *Handbook of Communication and Emotion: Research, Theory, Applications, and Contexts*, eds. Peter A. Andersen and Laura K. Guerrero (San Diego: Academic Press, 1998), pp. 189–213.

[22] Richard S. Lazarus, *Emotion and Adaptation*; Ira J. Roseman, Cynthia Wiest, and Tamara S. Swartz, "Phenomenology, Behaviors, and Goals Differentiate Discrete Emotions," *Journal of Personality and Social Psychology*, 67 (1994): 206–221; David B. Sugarman and Gerald T. Hotaling, "Dating Violence: Prevalence, Context, and Risk Markers," in *Violence in Dating Relationships: Emerging Social Issues*, eds. Maureen A. Pirog-Good and Jan E. Stets (New York: Praeger, 1989), pp. 3–32.

[23] Canary, Spitzberg, and Semic.

[24] See, for example, Laura K. Guerrero, "'I'm So Mad I Could Scream'": The Effects of Anger Expression on Relational Satisfaction and Communication Competence," *Southern Communication Journal*, 59 (1994): 125–141.

[25] Carolyn Ellis and Eugene Weinstein, "Jealousy and the Social Psychology of Emotional Experience," *Journal of Social and Personal Relationships*, 3 (1986): 337–357.

[26] See, for example, Laura K. Guerrero, Melanie L. Trost, and Stephen M. Yoshimura, "Emotion and Communication in the Context of Romantic Jealousy," *Personal Relationships*, 12 (2005): 233–252.

[27] Laura K. Guerrero and Peter A. Anderson, "The Dark Side of Jealousy and Envy: Desire, Delusion, Desperation, and Destructive Communication," in *The Dark Side of Close Relationships*, eds. Brian H. Spitzberg and William R. Cupach (Mahwah, NJ: Lawrence Erlbaum, 1998), pp. 33–70.

[28] Shaver, Schwartz, Kirson, and O'Connor.

[29] Anita L. Vangelisti, "Messages that Hurt," in *The Dark Side of Interpersonal Communication*, eds. William R. Cupach and Brian H. Spitzberg (Hillsdale, NJ: Lawrence Erlbaum, 1994), pp. 53–82.

[30] Sandra Metts, "Relational Transgressions," in *The Dark Side of Interpersonal Communication*, eds. William R. Cupach and Brian H. Spitzberg (Hillsdale, NJ: Lawrence Erlbaum, 1994), pp. 217–239; Anita L. Vangelisti and Rhonda J. Sprague, "Guilt and Hurt: Similarities, Distinctions, and Conversational Strategies," in *Handbook of Communication and Emotion: Research, Theory, Applications, and Contexts*, eds. Peter A. Andersen and Laura K. Guerrero (San Diego: Academic Press, 1998), pp. 123–154.

[31] Anita L. Vangelisti and Linda P. Crumley, "Reactions to Messages that Hurt: The Influence of Relational Contexts," *Communication Monographs*, 65 (1998): 173–196.

[32] Guy F. Bachman and Laura K. Guerrero, "An Expectancy Violations Analysis of Factors Affecting Relational Outcomes and Communicative Responses to Hurtful Events in Dating Relationships," *Journal of Social and Personal Relationships*, in press; Alan L. Sillars, "Attributions and Communication in Roommate Conflicts," *Communication Monographs*, 47 (1980): 180–200.

[33] See, for example, Karen C. Barrett, "A Functionalist Approach to Shame and Guilt," in *Self-Conscious Emotions: The Psychology of Same, Guilt, Embarrassment, and Pride*, eds. June P. Tangney and Kurt W. Fischer (New York: Guilford, 1995), pp. 25–63.

[34] Lazarus, *Emotion and Adaptation*.

[35] See, for example, Anita L. Vangelisti, John A. Daly, and Janine R. Rudnick, "Making People Feel Guilty in Conversations: Techniques and Correlates," *Human Communication Research*, 18 (1991): 3–39.

[36] See, for example, Lazarus, *Emotion and Adaptation*.

[37] See, for example, Judee K. Burgoon and Jerold L. Hale, "Nonverbal Expectancy Violations: Model Elaboration and Application to Immediacy Behaviors," *Communication Monographs*, 55 (1988): 58–79.

[38] Karl Tomm, "Interventive Interviewing Part 3: Intending to Ask Lineal, Circular, Strategic, or Reflexive Questions," *Family Process*, 27 (1988): 1–15.

[39] J. Kevin Barge, "Reflexivity and Managerial Practice," *Communication Monographs*, 71 (2004): 70–96.

[40] Kathryn Dindia and Lindsay Timmerman, "Accomplishing Romantic Relationships," in *Handbook of Communication and Social Interaction Skills*, eds. John O. Greene and Brant R. Burleson (Mahwah, NJ: Lawrence Erlbaum, 2003), pp. 685–721.

[41] Kathryn Dindia and Leslie Baxter, "Strategies for Maintaining and Repairing Marital Relationships," *Journal of Social and Personal Relationships*, 4 (1987): 143–158.

[42] Dindia and Baxter, "Strategies"; Laura Stafford and Daniel J. Canary, "Maintenance Strategies and Romantic Relationship Type, Gender, and Relational Characteristics," *Journal of Social and Personal Relationships*, 8 (1991): 217–242.

[43] Robert A. Bell and John A. Daly, "The Affinity-Seeking Function in Communication," *Communication Monographs*, 51 (1984): 91–115; Robert A. Bell, John A. Daly, and Cristina Gonzalez, "Affinity-Maintenance in Marriage and Its Relationship to Women's Marital Satisfactions," *Journal of Marriage and the Family*, 49 (1987): 445–454.

[44] Dindia and Baxter, "Strategies."

[45] R. E. Kaplan, "Maintaining Interpersonal Relationships: A Bipolar Theory," *Interpersonal Development*, 6 (1975/1976): 106–119.

[46] Barge, "Reflexivity."

7

Moving toward Value in Family Conflicts

Families provide the closest, most important relationships in our lives; yet, family differences can be very challenging. Conflict is common in the nuclear family and extended family as well. Hopefully, everything you have read in this book so far will be helpful in understanding and managing family conflicts. This chapter provides additional depth and insight.

WHAT IS A FAMILY?

Ask several people to describe their family, and you will get a variety of responses:

1. My parents got married in 1941 and started a family. When my brother and I were kids in the 1950s, our family lived in a small house in La Habra, California. Dad worked, and mother stayed home to take care of us. We often got together with our grandparents, aunts and uncles, and cousins, especially at Christmas.

2. My family hails from North Dakota and Minnesota. We are Norwegians, and our ancestors first arrived in the U.S. in 1886. We can go back six generations on my mother's side and eight on my father's.

3. Our household is a real family. We do everything together, take care of one another's kids, and support each other just like brothers and sisters.

The first description references a *nuclear* family, identifying parents and their children as they are connected to an extended family of parents, children, and siblings. The second description is *lineal*, emphasizing generations of parents and children in a family tree. The third is *emotional* and based on emotional ties and familial feelings.

These descriptions differ in other ways as well. The first one emphasizes the family located in time and space, and its connection to a contemporaneous extended family. This family lives in the consciousness of the speaker, whether members are still living or now dead. Interpersonal relationships are important in this description. The second description emphasizes cultural and national ties. It emphasizes heredity and goes well beyond the immediate consciousness and memory of the person speaking. It is not a family of relationships, but of bloodlines that are distributed across time and space. The third description is based on function, or what is typically done in a family whether the members are related by blood or not. It is primarily a family of relationships located in the present.

Box 7.1

Define your family in nuclear, lineal, and emotional terms. How does your consciousness of family relationships change as you define your family in these ways?

In this chapter, we concentrate on *the family as a system of living relatives whose actions connect to and affect those of other members*. Even when they are not related by blood, certain groups are so family-like in this regard that they experience what may well be called family conflict.

The quality of conflict management impacts the effectiveness of the relationship. One indicator of the effectiveness of a marriage is the extent to which spouses feel confident in their ability to resolve a variety of marital issues.[1] The literature on marital communication is quite clear that poor conflict management is a sign of distress in a relationship, and children can be harmed by exposure to poorly managed conflict between parents.[2] This is true whether the couple eventually divorces or not. Children learn their parents' approaches to conflict and often carry these interaction styles into adulthood and marriage.[3] Clearly, it is not the fact of conflict that is damaging to families, but the manner in which conflict is managed. Indeed, conflict provides an opportunity for family members to communicate about important issues in order to renegotiate their roles and responsibilities.[4] It also provides a means for expressing important emotions in a potentially nurturing environment and to teach children how to express their feelings and to manage differences constructively.[5]

THE FAMILY SYSTEM

Because of the tendency of systems to sustain balance (see chapter 3), our feelings, attitudes, and actions are often coordinated with those of others. We never feel, think, or act in isolation from our perceptions of significant other people. This is a process of *co-orientation*.

Co-orientation in the Family

We orient to things and people together and are conscious of that fact. One of our mothers hated cauliflower and rarely cooked it. Every now and then, she would serve it, always saying, "Well, your father likes it." She had to manage a co-orientation toward the vegetable and her regard for her husband. Co-orientation can be quite complex, but is best understood by a simple triangle depicting two people and an object.[6] Figure 7.1 illustrates this idea.

Although our mother didn't like cauliflower, she wanted to please our father, and served it occasionally for that reason. If she had refused to serve it, she probably would have heard about it from him (Maybe she did!). Of course, this small example belies the complexity and associated conflict that can result when the object of mutual attention is very important. Several possibilities are apparent.

In families, conflicts over sex, money, space management, time, possessions, and many other issues can have significant implications for co-orientation. Consider ex-spouses who hate each other. The bad relationship between the parents will affect how they orient toward their children, unless they take conscious measures to avoid allowing it to do so. In contrast, a divorced couple on friendly terms may find that co-orientation toward their children is smoother and more congruent.

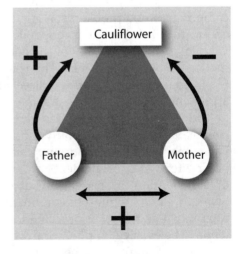

Figure 7.1   A Simple Example of Co-orientation

Co-parenting can be a significant source of conflict, but it can also be an area of cooperation, collaboration, and problem solving typical of excellent conflict management. How do parents co-orient to the job of parenting? This question extends our thinking from the single rela-tionship between mother (or father) and child to mother, father, and child—a triad.[7] This is a dynamic set of relationships, constantly formed and changed through interaction and negotiation, which always will involve the management of difference. If handled well, co-parenting offers the opportunity for excellent problem solving and adaptability. If handled poorly, the resulting conflict can harm every-one involved.

As family members co-orient to the important things in their lives, they develop certain patterns of interaction. Sustained over time through systemic influences, these patterns provide the key to under-standing how families manage conflict and how they might improve the management of difference.

Cooperation and Directness

Families manage their differences in many ways. Alan Sillars, Daniel Canary, and Melissa Tafoya codified these into a helpful scheme that classifies conflict-related behaviors as direct or indirect and coop-erative or uncooperative.[8] Four pattern types result from this scheme—negotiation, direct fighting, nonconfrontation, and indirect fighting.

Negotiation tends to be direct and cooperative. We acknowledge our differences and try to work them out through a process of persuasion, compromise, and problem solving. Negotiation involves a lot of back-and-forth talk. Because it is cooperative, it tends to be agreeable, friendly, validating, and sometimes even conciliatory. Even when negotiation is hard and a bit rough, it at least aims to find a solution somehow.

In contrast, *direct fighting* (direct and uncooperative) is marked by argument, debate, and disagreement. Direct fighting tends to be stri-dent, so it commonly includes blame, coercion, attack, and rejection. *Nonconfrontation* is cooperative, but indirect. Here friendliness pre-vails; any disagreement is typically expressed through joking and poking fun. Many statements are noncommittal, and people tend to divert attention or change the subject when it gets difficult. Finally, *indirect fighting*, while passive on the surface, is definitely not very cooperative in the sense of trying to deal with the situation at hand. It tends to be evasive, implicit, and whiney.

These patterns can be well coordinated and feel appropriate, depending on the rules of conflict in force. Some families, for example, seem to have a consistent pattern of trying to work things out, avoid-ing conflict, or of fighting. More problematic can be uncoordinated activity in which one person wants to negotiate while the other avoids, or one family member tries to fight while others refuse to con-front. When patterns are uncoordinated in this way, a double conflict develops in which there is difference about some issue and also difference about how to deal with that issue.

The literature on the effects of directness in family conflict is mixed, probably because these patterns mean different things in different families. In some families, direct engagement is a sign of mutual caring, a willingness to hammer things out, and a good thing. In other families, this kind of pattern would signal distress, lack of support, and hostility. In some families, indirectness is viewed as a sign of respect and nurturance, while in other families it is taken as latent hostility or avoidance.[9] Research on cooperation tends to be a little more consistent in showing that competitive patterns are more typical in unhappy families, while cooperative patterns are more common in well-adjusted ones.[10]

Patterns can also involve shifting behaviors. For example, some married couples begin talking about a conflict in a cooperative way but then shift to hostile comments as the conversation progresses, a pattern that seems to lead to considerable dissatisfaction in many couples. Indeed, when negative comments outweigh positive ones, dissatisfaction often results.[11]

Box 7.2

Think about how your family handles conflict. When and how frequently do you use negotiation, direct fighting, indirect fighting, and nonconfrontation? What does your family gain and lose when these forms are used? Are any used with sufficient frequency to call it a pattern? If so, what does this say about your family?

What type of family would you say you have? Do any of the family types discussed in this section fit your family?

Many people have more than one family. How do your families differ in terms of conflict patterns and family types?

Family Types

Every family has a flavor or feeling determined by interaction across time and the communication patterns that emerge from those interactions. Mary Anne Fitzpatrick and her colleagues have identified four types of families based on patterns of communication.[12]

Consensual families tend to value conversation, and they also conform easily to family standards, as articulated by the parents. Parents may listen well to their children, but in the end make the decisions, and the children are expected to obey. Parents in consensual families tend to be traditional and are conventional in their views of spousal roles. Parents will tend to be more interdependent, and, when functioning well, experience companionship. Such spouses will share time and space and have routine schedules. Consensual families do not experience very much conflict because they assign decision-making roles, and matters get settled pretty quickly.

Although people in a *pluralistic family* like to talk a lot, family members tend to make independent decisions. There is not a lot of parental control in these kinds of families, and everyone participates in family decision making. The husband and wife in a pluralistic family tend to be independent and often unconventional in their views of family life. They may spend quite a bit of time together, but they also value their autonomy and typically enjoy their own time and space. Eschewing traditional roles, pluralistic families tend to negotiate roles constantly, and conflict frequently surfaces. They tend to be expressive and active in their communication and understand one another well.

The third type is the *protective family.* Protective families do not value open communication very much and therefore tend to appear somewhat quiet. At the same time, they do display quite a bit of conformity and obedience. They do not spend time talking things through or explaining their actions to one another. The husband and wife are not very interdependent and do not share much. They may even be "emotionally divorced." Conflict is typically short-lived, as matters are settled quickly.

Finally, there is the *laissez-faire family.* This is a hands-off, low-involvement family, in which members do not care that much about what others do, and they are not apt to waste time talking about it. This family type shares much with the protective family, except that conformity is low. Conflict is low too, but for a different reason. While protective families may care, they settle their differences quickly and without much fanfare. Laissez-faire families have little conflict because they really don't care all that much and certainly do not demand conformity. Of all the family types, this is probably the least effective and satisfying.

RESPONDING TO DEMANDS

Conflict often arises when one member of the family makes a demand on others. There are many ways to respond to the demands of other family members, but two seem especially problematic. We do not want to imply that these are universally negative patterns, as some families may function just fine in ways that other families would find troublesome. In general, however, research and experience indicate that these patterns usually cause rather than solve problems in the management of difference.

The Demand-Demand Cycle

A common sign of distress in a marriage are repeated patterns of escalating negativity.[13] The pattern is exacerbated when blaming and aggressive statements are delivered in an angry or emotionally depressed tone. Most married couples experience negative escalation from time to time, but well-adjusted couples are able to shift the pattern quickly and repair the damage. ("Stop interrupting me!" "Sorry, go ahead and finish what you were saying.") Distressed couples don't seem to have the ability to change the pattern in this way. There is another difference as well. In highly conflicted relationships, partners tend not to interpret the situation the same way and have different views of what is going on. As the conflict escalates, the couple's perceptions become increasingly incongruent, which in turn feeds the conflict even more.[14] It seems clear that direct, cooperative communication is the answer to this problem. This is not always easy, however, as the extreme familiarity within the family frequently leads to making assumptions about things based on previous knowledge rather than listening for new information. In addition, it is difficult to process information when you are upset. In this pattern, aggressive behavior is reciprocated.

The Demand-Withdraw Cycle

Commonly noticed in research on marital conflict is the pattern in which one spouse pursues an issue of concern and finds that the other spouse avoids, retreats, or ignores. When encountered repeatedly in a marriage, the demand-withdraw cycle seems to be a considerable source of tension.[15] You can see how frustrating this would be if you wanted to talk about an issue important to you, but your partner avoids the subject. In many cases, this type of conflict occurs when one partner wants change, and the other resists. The person to whom change is important will be more frustrated and dissatisfied with this cycle of interaction than his or her spouse.

CONFLICT AND PRIVACY MANAGEMENT

Most people experience a tension between the need for privacy and the need for openness. This is certainly an issue in many relationships, especially in individualistic cultures (see chapter 4). There is a boundary around private matters that can be opened up or closed down, a process Sandra Petronio calls *boundary management*.[16] When you are more private, you will have greater autonomy and safety, but relationships may be guarded. At less private moments, you may develop greater intimacy and sharing, but you also risk personal vulnerability. The tension between protecting yourself and protecting the relationship has to be worked out, and the family is a setting in which this negotiation is constantly taking place. In some families, boundaries are quite permeable, while in others they are rather opaque. In your own family, you probably have some areas in which information is easily shared and other areas in which information is kept more or less secret.

Boundary tensions are a potential source of conflict. Parents want to know more about their children, but the children may actively hide things from their parents. Spouses may have areas of privacy that are contentious, and family members may stew over whether or not to reveal certain information. We all have heard, if not participated in, arguments that include statements like, "What is going on?" "Why don't you tell me?" "It is none of your business." "Get off my back." "Leave me alone." "Don't come into my room." "This is off limits." "When the door is closed, stay out."

There is another level of conflict related to privacy management as well. Once information is shared, a kind of "co-ownership" develops.

Here, family members feel a moral responsibility to keep private family information private. Families differ in terms of family secrets. For some, financial information is quite private, while for others, things like emotional problems, misbehavior, or even drug and alcohol issues are not to be discussed outside the family. Again, family boundaries vary. Some families are open about almost everything, while other families are extremely private.

One of the worst affronts to family members is to reveal private matters outside the family. The family develops its own set of boundary-management rules that dictate what can be discussed, who can discuss it, with whom it can be discussed, and when it can be discussed. Of course, these rules will change over time. For example, a family may have a very strong rule not to reveal financial information to people outside the family, but eventually, maybe in retirement, the risks and benefits change, and the family finds itself freely discussing these issues among friends.

PARENTING AND CONFLICT

One of us had a very interesting talk with his father a few days before his wedding after graduating from college. The father took his son for a drive to talk to him about the "facts of life"—no, not those facts of life, but different ones. The father told his son that as a new husband and future father, he would need to assert his authority right away. He would have a special responsibility to be the family decision maker and that he should make that clear from the beginning. Passing this cultural knowledge to his son was an important symbolic moment for this father.

The son suddenly realized that this was exactly how his family had functioned. His father had been the family decision maker and his mother was the chief consultant. He and his brother had been greatly loved, but they had had little voice in family matters. They knew the rules, and if they broke them, they would pay a steep price. His father would listen to his mother for a time, but he would also shut off the conversation at a certain point and "lay down the law." His mother became a lightning rod for the sons' objections and whining because she would listen, but this would enrage the father, who would always say, "Never argue with a child." If you asked the father why he wanted the boys to do something, his answer was a standard: "Because I said so." And that was that. This is a classic example of an *authoritarian parenting* relationship.

Authoritarian and Permissive Parenting

The authoritarian form of parenting described above affected the two brothers quite differently. It seemed ideal for one. Basically compliant by nature, this son responded well to authoritative parenting. He rarely had a conflict with his parents. He always knew his values and rarely experienced ambiguity about what to do. Except for a brief time of conflict with his father when he was a young adult, they came to have a very close relationship later in life.

The other son was constantly at loggerheads with the father. Unlike his brother, he was not very compliant and rebelled at every turn. He turned out to be a very different kind of adult—much more freewheeling, creative, and experimental than his brother ever would become. It was almost as if one brother used his father's authoritarianism as a standard, while the other used it as a foil.

Our cousins grew up in just the opposite kind of home. Their mother and father believed in giving the children maximum freedom to do whatever they wanted as long as they met the basic requirements of life and kept out of danger. They got to tear around the house, jump on the beds, skip meals, snack all day, stay out past bedtime, and all manner of things we would never have been allowed to do. Their family had a *permissive parenting* pattern. In our authoritarian home, there was really not much conflict because father settled everything. Conflict wasn't allowed; differences could not be expressed. In our cousins' home, there was little conflict, because parents made no issue of anything. In both cases, differences really were not managed in any sense.

It is interesting that our oldest cousin became a teacher and then a business manager, her middle brother became a hippie and then an organic farmer, and her youngest brother went on to become an accomplished concert violinist. They all have wonderful and very close families of their own. Makes you wonder.

Authoritative Parenting

Another form of parenting—neither authoritarian, nor permissive—is called *authoritative parenting*. There is a good deal of evidence to suggest that this includes a pattern that enables both the expression and management of difference in a way that is constructive and productive for family life and human development.[17] Authoritative parenting has three dimensions—connection, regulation, and autonomy.

Connection involves patterns of acceptance, attentiveness, nurturance, patience, and sensitivity. Communication tends to be companionable and playful much of the time. *Regulation* involves instructing, correcting, teaching, and disciplining. It involves setting limits, providing explanations, setting consequences, and reinforcing the positive. Prevention rather than correction is emphasized. *Autonomy* means that parents allow children to make decisions and choices. There is substantial collaborative problem solving rather than adherence to arbitrary rules. Children are not encouraged to do whatever they want but to engage in discussion and establish guidelines and principles by which good decisions will be made.

Authoritative parenting combines and balances all three values. It is adaptable because it engages children in talking through and making decisions about the situations they face and contrasts significantly from authoritarian and coercive forms of parenting. It also encourages collaborative approaches to conflict and teaches children the skills they need to move away from potentially harmful forms of conflict management toward forms that realize the values of inevitable differences yet coordinate and manage these in a way that leads to productive outcomes.

We are loath to recommend any one approach to parenting, as many forms can be right. The most appropriate forms of communication between parents and children are often highly cultural. Yet we think that the three dimensions of connection, regulation, and autonomy are potentially valuable as standards or principles by which parents can make decisions about communication with their own children. We also believe there are many ways to achieve these three values.

DIVORCE

We commonly associate divorce with conflict, but this is somewhat misleading for several reasons.[18] If conflict is handled well, it can be a source of family strength. Many families manage conflict just fine. Indeed, conflict is not the leading predictor of divorce, especially in couples who have been married over seven years.[19] There are many

potential sources of marital dissatisfaction. In some cases, the lack of conflict may signal underlying problems that eventually cause the marriage to fail. More accurate is the premise that divorce is the result of ineffective management of difference, whether it comes out as open, divisive conflict or other forms such as the inability to solve problems together, ineffective expression of emotion, lack of responsiveness, or loss of love. All of these things can lead to unsatisfying interaction and to divorce.

One thing is certain: Divorce will alter the family's patterns of interaction, and communication is usually worse after divorce.[20] Conflict will usually be higher after divorce than before, and sometimes it remains strident for years. Couples who experienced a lot of strife when they were married may experience even more severe conflict after the marriage ends. At the same time, conflict avoiders may avoid even more when they are divorced. If they were unable to solve problems effectively when they were married, they probably will not be able to do so any better afterwards. The exception seems to be divorced couples without children, where both contact and conflict just fade over time.[21] Several patterns of communication have been observed in divorced couples, including, for example, "cooperative colleagues," "the pursuer and the pursued," "mutual avoidance," "perfect pals," and "fiery foes."[22]

The report from the research literature is not very optimistic, but we know that divorced couples can change communication patterns in ways that allow them to manage difference effectively and constructively. Not only is this possible, but it is essential for the well-being of the children. Postdivorce collaboration and effective co-parenting are among the strongest positive influences on the children's adjustment following divorce.[23] The key seems to be a conscious renegotiation of the relationship away from old roles and patterns to new ones. Our friend, Ann Kass, the former Chief Judge of our local district family court, recommended that divorcing couples use mediation to change their relationship from that of feuding spouses to parenting copartners.

Too common is a different course—a devolution of the relationship from co-parenting to parallel parenting, in which the mother and father create two families where communication is either nonexistent or highly conflicted. Family life where children are shuttled from one communication pattern to another usually compromises the welfare of the children.[24]

Box 7.3

> How have you experienced divorce? As a spouse, child, friend? If you were to design the "perfect" divorce, what would communication look like within the family, and how would differences be handled?

FAMILY VIOLENCE

The most extreme case of poor conflict management is family abuse; 25% of women and 8% of men indicated in a U.S. survey that at least once in their lifetime a spouse, partner, or date had assaulted them. Children witness up to 30% of domestic adult assaults, and at least 10% of children in the United States are themselves battered by parents each year.[25]

You can conceptualize family violence in a number of ways. We see it as a communication pattern marked by particular kinds of interpretations and responses by various family members. Here are some of the factors associated with violent communication in various families.[26]

1. Narrow repertoire of communication strategies and conflict management skills, associated in part with a limited opportunity to observe and practice good communication.

2. Tendency to attribute hostile intent to the comments of a child or partner and to interpret critical comments as an attack that calls for escalation.

3. Frustration arising from an extreme demand-withdraw cycle (discussed above).

4. Belief that violence is an effective and appropriate means of conflict resolution.

5. Association of violence with a positive self-image, especially in men.

6. Tendency to minimize the violation or to interpret it as well motivated, sometimes even a manifestation of love and caring.

7. Perpetuation of violent patterns outside the home.

How does it happen that violence can last such a long time in a family? We think the answer lies in the cybernetic mechanisms of the family system. Something is going on that keeps the unwanted pattern going. Nalla Sundarajan and Shawn Spano found that some patterns of violence between husbands and wives seem to have a life of their own.[27] The husband places a high value on his own sense of self and acts to establish self-importance. The wife, in contrast, aims to protect the relationship, minimizing her own needs and tolerating his behaviors. Over time, a pattern is established in which the man's needs are primary, and he expresses his anger, while his wife, worried about the relationship, does not feel free to assert her own rights or to protect herself. She is expected to be tolerant, but he has no such restraint.

Typically, then, the husband gets mad when his wife acts in a way that he perceives to frustrate his needs, which at some point may escalate to the point of verbal and physical aggression. When this happens, the wife sees a threat to the relationship and responds by trying to placate his anger. Not wanting to see himself as an aggressive person, the husband apologizes; and his wife, thankful that he seems to care, quickly forgives him. In a self-protective mode, the husband next minimizes the importance of his aggression, and after a honeymoon period, the pattern starts over again.

The pattern will continue until one or both partners shift their interpretation of what is happening or their responses. This is the key to therapy in these situations. Usually this means helping the wife reframe the situation in a way that will enable her to get out of the abusive relationship. One possible reframing is to shift from seeing the situation as protecting the relationship to seeing it as a sign of danger. When the wife comes to see that she and her children are in danger and acts on this understanding, then she can begin to establish boundaries. In some cases, this may mean the dissolution of the relationship; in other cases, it may spark a change. There is no universal cybernetic mechanism behind all violent family patterns. The dynamic discussed above is one example, and there are probably many others. Having discussed two distinct negative patterns we now shift our attention to more positive ones.

MANAGING FAMILY CONFLICTS EFFECTIVELY

Every family must find a way to manage the inevitable differences that will occur. The following list of communication forms is not intended to be universally prescriptive or exhaustive, but it does suggest some approaches that often help move family differences away from harm and toward value.

Acceptance

One difference between families that manage difference effectively and those that do not is their relative focus on trying to change other family members. At one extreme is full acceptance of others, even though their feelings, thoughts, and behaviors differ from your own. Complete acceptance in the family is never fully realizable, and it probably should not be. If you accepted everyone's behavior, you would show no values, no moral sense. Indeed, most parenting philosophies acknowledge in one form or another that parents have a responsibility to shape their children's behavior. A marital relationship requires a certain amount of accommodation. Full acceptance would breed either extreme independence to the point of having no relationship at all or the opposite, complete accommodation. At the other extreme is no acceptance at all. In such cases, there is often an attempt to change the other person.

There is a significant distinction between trying to change the other person and trying to work out a reasonable set of relational expectations. The first mode is one of struggle; the second is one of negotiation. There is a fine art in knowing when and how to "let go" of the struggle and even to come to some level of appreciation for others' qualities even if you do not endorse them for yourself.[28]

What does acceptance actually look like as a communication behavior? One sign of acceptance is the expression of one's own feelings rather than attributions to the other person. Another is "soft" disclosure about one's own preferences, as opposed to "hard" disclosure of anger and resentment about something the other person said or did. Acceptance can also be seen when partners remove the person from the problem, focusing on solving a problem rather than correcting someone's behavior.[29]

Apology and Forgiveness

Forgiveness is often overlooked as an extremely restorative form of communication. In the flux and flow of family life, transgressions do occur. Children misbehave, spouses do not always treat one another with sensitivity, and extended family members say and do things that sometimes offend. A simple acknowledgment of one's misdeeds can be amazingly disarming in conflict situations. Being forgiven does honor to a relationship and can be a huge step in conflict resolution.[30]

Apology and forgiveness require skill and sensitivity to the family system. When viewed as phony, out of character, or manipulative, an apology can do more harm than good. When someone apologizes to get out of genuine problem solving, the apology may be perceived as an attempt to avoid the hard work of dealing with the situation. Forgiveness can also be hazardous if not done honestly and appropriately. Saying, "I forgive you," can be taken as an insult in situations where a person does not feel guilty about anything.

Adaptability

Effective communicators in families and elsewhere are able to clarify what they want, interpret what is going on, and adapt their actions to their goals and to the situation in which they find themselves. You can modulate, adjust, and adapt your thoughts, feelings, and behaviors to the problems at hand. Rather than react in a predictable and stylized way, effective family members make active decisions about what is the best approach, given the situation and goals at hand.[31]

Empowerment

Empowerment is a pattern in which family members allow one another to express what is important to them; they take each other's perspectives seriously. Even when one member is a decision maker, as in the case of a parent-child relationship or a traditional marriage, "one-down" persons feel that they have a chance to talk about the issue and are listened to. Empowered families do not allow extreme power imbalances to occur.[31] This might be done in a variety of ways. For example, a family member who is adept at arguing could refrain from doing so in order to empower a less fluent spouse or child to enter the conversation and to be taken seriously. A family member designated as a "decision maker" could defer to someone else when the other person's opinion seems to matter a lot. A family member who is easily annoyed and usually leaves the room when irritated decides to stay, calm down, and listen. All of these are acts in which someone who could have exerted power to sway a situation moderated this tendency and deliberately deferred to another family member in that situation.

HOW YOU CAN USE THIS CHAPTER

Don't expect to eliminate family conflict. As long as important differences are present, we will be challenged to manage these effectively. However, you can keep several things in mind in order to move from harm to value in family relationships.

1. Understand the patterns of communication within your family and realize that these will change over time. Reflect on which patterns are constructive and which are destructive, and move to new patterns as needed.

2. Watch for the demand-demand and demand-withdraw cycles. If you find that you are involved in either of these, look carefully at their appropriateness and understand that they can be destructive.

3. Avoid violence within the family. If you are the victim of violence, learn to frame what is happening so that you do not contribute to the perpetuation of the pattern and can escape the inevitable harm of violence over time.

4. Divorce means redefining the nature of the relationship from being spouses to being co-parenting partners. Negotiate new and constructive relational rules that enable you to communicate collaboratively for the benefit of your children.

5. Take seriously the four principles of acceptance; apology and forgiveness; adaptability; and empowerment. Use them appropriately.

Interactive Case Study

THE FAMILY DYNAMIC

Context: You will create family structures and use them to explore communication dimensions of small systems (larger than two people and smaller than an entire organization or community). Students will meet in groups of four or five to build a "family" group, which will stay together for a variety of exercises. One student will take leadership of the family group and will base roles and experiences on his or her own family experience and structure. Each group will assign family roles and create some stories and examples of actual interactions, interests, and demographics for each family member. These roles will be internalized, discussed, and played out in preparation for a variety of exercises.

Opening exercise(s): After exchanging initial information about the family structure, the family will role-play a meal together (preferably over a real meal!). Patterns of interaction will begin to emerge as players adapt to their roles. After the role-play, allocate some time for the participants to ask further questions about their roles to clarify the relationships.

Focus #1: A Discussion about Families in Balance and Change

In small groups, tell some actual stories from your families of origin.

1. Discuss a time when this family experienced a time of balance and stability. What was each of the family members experiencing at that time?

2. Discuss a time when this family was undergoing change. What was each of the family members experiencing at that time?

3. Were there any interaction patterns present that may have enabled the balance or the change?

Focus #2: Patterns of Interaction

Choose one of the challenging issues presented in the role-play or in the narratives from the focus above. Role-play in your new family groups a time when this issue blossomed into a conflict. Play out the scene where the issue is confronted, according to the conflict patterns on page 160. Now repeat the role-play four times using the patterns of negotiation, direct fighting, nonconfrontation, and indirect fighting. Finally, engage in one last role-play. This time, each family member will secretly pick a pattern and use it throughout the interaction. Debrief with the following questions:

1. Which patterns, when used in concert or in combination, seemed to move the challenging pattern of communication toward the sphere of value?

2. Which patterns, when used in concert or in combination, seemed to keep the conversation in the sphere of challenge or move it to the sphere of harm?

Focus #3: Family Types

Each group (family) will have a discussion, trying to define which of the family types this family most nearly resembles *(consensual, pluralistic, protective, and laissez-faire)*.

Focus #4: Managing Family Differences

Look at the communication forms that can lead to effective communication and interactions in families: acceptance, apology and forgiveness, adaptability, and empowerment. Each family member in this role-play group should look over the list and consider acquiring these skills. Which of these would be the most difficult to assume? What is it about that form that makes it hard to assume?

Each family member should then choose one of the forms and plan to improve on its use. Choose another challenging issue. Talk through ways these forms might be manifested. Demonstrate specific interactions that exhibit the new communication forms.

Focus #5: Responding to Difference

Your new "family" has looked at its patterns and ways to manage their differences. Using what you learned from the four focuses above, role-play a family discussion over a meal. Following the role-play, discuss the communication environment that was created by the interactional choices made.

Endnotes

[1] William J. Doherty, "Cognitive Processes in Intimate Conflict: II. Efficacy and Learned Helplessness," *American Journal of Family Therapy,* 9 (1981): 35–44; Clifford I. Notarius and Nelly A. Vanzetti, "The Marital Agendas Protocol," in *Marriage and Family Assessment: A Sourcebook for Family Therapy,* ed. Erik Filsinger (Beverly Hills, CA: Sage, 1983), pp. 209–227; Adrian B. Kelly, Frank D. Fincham, and Steven R. H. Beach, "Communication Skills in Couples: A Review and Discussion of Emerging Perspectives," in *Handbook of Communication and Social Interaction Skills,* eds. John O. Greene and Brant R. Burleson (Mahwah, NJ: Lawrence Erlbaum, 2003), pp. 723–752.

[2] E. Mavis Hetherington and Margaret M. Stanley-Hagan, "The Adjustment of Children with Divorced Parents: A Risk and Resiliency Perspective," *Journal of Child Psy-*

chology and Psychiatry, 40 (1999): 129–140; Paul R. Amato and Bruce Keith, "Parental Divorce and the Well-Being of Children: A Meta-Analysis," *Psychological Bulletin,* 110 (1991): 26–46; Julia M. Lewis, Judith S. Wallerstein, and Linda Johnson-Reitz, "Communication in Divorced and Single-Parent Families," in *Handbook of Family Communication,* ed. Anita L. Vangelisti (Mahwah, NJ: Lawrence Erlbaum, 2004), pp. 197–214.

3   Paul R. Amato, "Explaining the Intergenerational Transmission of Divorce," *Journal of Marriage and the Family,* 58 (1996): 628–640; Lewis, Wallerstein, and Johnson-Reitz, "Communication."

4   Brett Laursen and W. Andrew Collins, "Parent-Child Communication During Adolescence," in *Handbook of Family Communication,* ed. Anita L. Vangelisti (Mahwah, NJ: Lawrence Erlbaum, 2004), pp. 333–348.

5   Julie Fitness and Jill Duffield, "Emotion and Communication in Families," *in Handbook of Family Communication,* ed. Anita L. Vangelisti (Mahwah, NJ: Lawrence Erlbaum, 2004), pp. 473–494.

6   Theodore M. Newcomb, "An Approach to the Study of Communicative Acts," *Psychological Review,* 60 (1953): 393–404; Fritz Heider, *The Psychology of Interpersonal Relations* (New York: Wiley, 1958); Ascan F. Koerner and Mary Anne Fitzpatrick, "Communication in Intact Families," in *Handbook of Family Communication,* ed. Anita L. Vangelisti (Mahwah, NJ: Lawrence Erlbaum, 2004), pp. 177–195.

7   William J. Doherty and John M. Beaton, "Mothers and Fathers Parenting Together," in *Handbook of Family Communication,* ed. Anita L. Vangelisti (Mahwah, NJ: Lawrence Erlbaum, 2004), pp. 269–286.

8   Alan Sillars, Daniel J. Canary, and Melissa Tafoya, "Communication, Conflict, and the Quality of Family Relationships," in *Handbook of Family Communication,* ed. Anita L. Vangelisti (Mahwah, NJ: Lawrence Erlbaum, 2004), pp. 413–446; Evert van de Vliert and Martin C. Euwema, "Agreeableness and Activeness as Components of Conflict Behaviors," *Journal of Personality and Social Psychology,* 66 (1994): 674–687.

9   Sillars, Canary, and Tafoya, pp. 422–424.

10   Daniel J. Canary, William R. Cupach, and Susan J. Messman, *Relationship Conflict* (Thousand Oaks, CA: Sage, 1995); John M. Gottman, *What Predicts Divorce? The Relationship between Marital Processes and Marital Outcomes* (Hillsdale, NJ: Lawrence Erlbaum, 1994).

11   John M. Gottman and Robert W. Levenson, "Marital Processes Predictive of Later Dissolution: Behavior, Physiology, and Health," *Journal of Personality and Social Psychology,* 63 (1992): 221–233.

12   Ascan F. Koerner and Mary Anne Fitzpatrick, "Communication in Intact Families," in *Handbook of Family Communication,* ed. Anita L. Vangelisti (Mahwah, NJ: Lawrence Erlbaum, 2004), pp. 177–196; Ascan F. Koerner and Mary Anne Fitzpatrick, "Toward a Theory of Family Communication," *Communication Theory,* 12 (2002): 70–91; Ascan F. Koerner and Mary Anne Fitzpatrick, "Understanding Family Communication Patterns and Family Functioning: The Roles of Conversation Orientation and Conformity Orientation," in *Communication Yearbook,* 26, ed. William B. Gudykunst (Mahwah, NJ: Lawrence Erlbaum, 2002), pp. 36–68; Mary Anne Fitzpatrick, *Between Husbands and Wives: Communication in Marriage* (Newbury Park, CA: Sage, 1988).

13   B. Berman and Gayla Margolin, "Observed Patterns of Conflict in Violent, Non-violent, and Non-distressed Couples," *Behavioral Assessment,* 14 (1992): 15–37; Gottman, *What Predicts Divorce?;* Frank D. Fincham, "Communication in Marriage," in *Handbook of Family Communication,* ed. Anita L. Vangelisti (Mahwah, NJ: Lawrence Erlbaum, 2004), pp. 83–103.

14   Frank D. Fincham and Thomas N. Bradbury, "Cognition in Marriage: A Program of Research on Attributions," in *Advances in Personal Relationships,* eds. Warren H. Jones

and Daniel Perlman (London: Kingsley, 1991), vol. 2, pp. 159–203; Sillars, Canary, and Tafoya, pp. 427–428.

[15] Andrew Christensen, "Dysfunctional Interaction Patterns in Couples," in *Perspectives on Marital Interaction*, eds. Patricia Noller and Mary Anne Fitzpatrick (Clevedon, England: Multilingual Matters, 1988), pp. 31–52; Sara B. Berns, Neil S. Jacobson, and John M. Gottman, "Demand-withdraw Interaction Patterns between Different Types of Batterers and their Spouses," *Journal of Marital and Family Therapy,* 25 (1999): 337–348; Kristin L. Anderson, Debra Umberson, and Sinikka Elliott, "Violence and Abuse in Families," in *Handbook of Family Communication*, ed. Anita L. Vangelisti (Mahwah, NJ: Lawrence Erlbaum, 2004), p. 633; Fincham, "Communication in Marriage"; Kelly, Fincham, and Beach, "Communication Skills in Couples," pp. 731–732.

[16] Sandra Petronio, *Boundaries of Privacy: Dialectics of Disclosure* (Albany: State University of New York Press, 2002); Sandra Petronio, *Balancing the Secrets of Private Disclosures* (Mahwah, NJ: Lawrence Erlbaum, 2000).

[17] Brian K. Barber and Joseph A. Olsen, "Socialization in Context: Connection, Regulation, and Autonomy in the Family, School, and Neighborhood, and with Peers," *Journal of Adolescent Research*, 12 (1997): 286–315; Marjorie R. Gray and Laurence Steinberg, "Unpacking Authoritative Parenting: Reassessing a Multidimensional Construct," *Journal of Marriage and Family,* 61 (1999): 574–587; Craig H. Hart, Lloyd D. Newell, and Susanne Frost Olsen, "Parenting Skills and Social-Communicative Competence in Childhood," in *Handbook of Communication and Social Interaction Skills*, eds. John O. Greene and Brant R. Burleson (Mahwah, NJ: Lawrence Erlbaum, 2003), pp. 753–797.

[18] Lewis, Wallerstein, and Johnson-Reitz.

[19] Gottman, "A Theory of Marital Dissolution"; John M. Gottman, *What Predicts Divorce? The Relationship between Martial Processes and Marital Outcomes* (Hillsdale, NJ: Lawrence Erlbaum Associates, 1994).

[20] Alan Booth and Paul R. Amato, "Parental Predivorce Relations and Offspring Postdivorce Well-Being," *Journal of Marriage and Family,* 63 (2001): 197–212.

[21] Sandra Metts and William R. Cupach, "Postdivorce Relations," in *Explaining Family Interactions*, eds. M. A. Fitzpatrick and A. L. Vangelisti (Thousands Oaks, CA: Sage, 1995), pp. 232–251.

[22] Lewis, Wallerstein, and Johnson-Reitz, p. 203.

[23] Robert E. Emery, "Interparental Conflict and the Children of Discord and Divorce," *Psychological Bulletin*, 92 (1982): 310–330; Julie S. Linker, Arnold L. Stolberg, and Robert G. Green, "Family Communication as a Mediator of Child Adjustment to Divorce," *Journal of Divorce and Remarriage*, 30 (1999): 83–97; Lewis, Wallerstein, and Johnson-Reitz.

[24] Frank F. Furstenberg, "Divorce and the American Family," *Annual Review of Sociology,* 16 (1990): 379–403.

[25] Anderson, Umberson, and Elliott, p. 629.

[26] Anderson, Umberson, and Elliott.

[27] Nalla Sundarajan and Shawn Spano, "CMM and the Co-construction of Domestic Violence, 13 February 2007. http://pearceassociates.com/essays/documents/documents/84954_SundarajanandSpano.pdf.

[28] Neil S. Jacobson, "Behavioral Couple Therapy: A New Beginning," *Behavior Therapy,* 23 (1992): 493–506; Neil S. Jacobson and Andrew Christensen, *Integrative Couple Therapy: Promoting Acceptance and Change* (New York: Norton, 1996); Kelly, Fincham, and Beach, "Communication Skills in Couples."

[29] Jacobson and Christensen.

[30] Fincham, "Communication in Marriage."

[31] Paul Karoly, "Mechanisms of Self-Regulation: A Systems View," *Annual Review of Psychology*, 44 (1993): 23–52; W. Kim Halford, Mathew R. Sanders, and Brett C. Behrens, "Self-Regulation in Behavioral Couples Therapy," *Behavior Therapy*, 25 (1994): 431–452; Kelly, Fincham, and Beach, "Communication Skills in Couples."

[32] Howard J. Markman and Cliff I. Notarius, "Coding Marital and Family Interaction: Current Status," in *Family Interaction and Psychopathology: Theories, Methods, and Findings*, ed. Theodore Jacob (New York: Plenum, 1987), pp. 329–390; Mark A. Whisman and Neil S. Jacobson, "Power, Marital Satisfaction, and Response to Marital Therapy," *Journal of Family Psychology*, 4 (1990): 202–212; Fincham, "Communication in Marriage."

8

Moving toward Value in Organizational and Community Conflicts

When we think about "going to work," we usually imagine a paying job, but most of us work in other kinds of settings as well, including volunteer organizations, communities of faith, political organizations, and others. Some of the most profound conflicts are experienced within such settings, including neighborhoods, cities, and organizations. Large organizations and communities often struggle with conflicts. Where policy must be set, community members will have different opinions and ideas about what should be done. Conflict can be seen as strength rather than a weakness—an attitude that is essential for the movement to the sphere of value.

THE VALUE OF CONFLICT

We have argued from the beginning of this book that conflict, if well managed, enhances life on many levels. Diversity of thought and style is a reality and a positive resource. Some groups in which we work may be homogeneous, but most are not. Once a group starts working together, members will begin to show a spectrum of diversity in style, thought, feeling, perspective, ideas, knowledge, life commitments, relationships and connections, and a host of other differences that make most of our groups diverse indeed.[1]

Struggles are inevitable and potentially valuable if managed well. Anne Nicotera and Laura Dorsey focus on the constructive nature of conflict, aiming at understanding rather than prescribing. They see conflict as "an important vehicle through which the work of organizations gets accomplished."[2] Linda Putnam writes that conflict also "enhances adaptation, growth, and stability of organizations; it guards against groupthink; and it facilitates effective decision-making through challenging complacency and illusions of invincibility."[3]

You may wish you could work with individuals who are just like you, but you would face a stark reality if this were possible. Highly homogeneous groups are not very effective, simply because they do not have sufficient human resources to see all the angles, to come up with a variety of good ideas, and to challenge one another's thinking.[4] Diversity creates some obstacles that have to be dealt with, but if a group manages its differences well, a kind of "assembly effect" occurs in which the group decision or product is better than even the best individual member could have achieved alone.[5] Conflict over ideas and task directions can help a group perform better, so long as members are able to separate their content differences from their relationships.[6]

Synergy

When groups make a decision, solve a problem, or complete a project, they engage in a certain amount of group energy, or *synergy*. Some of a group's synergy helps manage the differences among members. This would include the effort that goes into understanding others' ideas, resolving conflicts, and creating an environment conducive to accomplishing the task. If this interpersonal synergy is too high, the group will not be able to accomplish the task very effectively. ("We are discussing our differences all the time and never have time to do the job!") On the other hand, if it is too low, the group will lack stimulation, fail to garner resources, and lack the critical thinking necessary to be productive. ("We never seem to know what to do and flounder around a lot.") So the key is balance—effective management of difference that makes excellent outcomes possible.[7]

Critical Thinking

The importance of managing conflict effectively is illustrated by the problem of *groupthink*.[8] Groupthink is the failure of a group to test its assumptions through critical thinking. This happens when disagreements are suppressed, especially when there is a strong, charismatic leader. Such groups emphasize cohesiveness (togetherness) instead of effectiveness, and they become overly confident in the result. Groups can clearly avoid groupthink by making sure they have sufficient diversity, taking time to explore a variety of ideas, and allowing members to challenge one another's assumptions and ideas. This has to be done in a supportive and productive climate, or the group will fall into contentiousness and fail to achieve consensus at all. The question for diverse workgroups is not whether such differences will or should surface, but *how* co-professionals choose to manage differences. The key then is to allow conflict but to manage it in a way that leads to productive rather than destructive outcomes.

A SYSTEM OF STAKEHOLDERS

If a difference matters to you, you become a *stakeholder* in managing that difference. Something important to you is at stake because you have an interest in the outcome. This is true in a relationship, family, or even a larger system such as an organization or community.

Although every conflict has stakeholders, we begin to think more seriously about stakeholders when the system becomes large and complex. In organizations and communities, the number of stakeholders is usually vast, and it makes sense not to think of a network of stakeholder groups rather than individual persons. Because a stakeholder group shares important interests, it is sometimes known as an *interest group*. In large systems, then, people typically think of conflicts as occurring among stakeholder groups rather than between individuals.

The system of stakeholders is never fixed; it is fluid and depends on the differences in play and the issues that arise. A department or neighborhood may be a stakeholder group for certain issues but not others. Therefore, stakeholder identification can be tricky. Indeed, a group that hangs together with shared interests in one conflict may actually fight among themselves in other conflicts. The engineering and manufacturing departments of an industrial corporation may band together as a single stakeholder group when competing with another company for a contract, but they could struggle mightily as separate stakeholder groups when vying for internal resources once the contract is secured.

Another complication in identifying the stakeholder system is that groups and individuals may relate in different ways to various stakeholder groups. You may find yourself a stakeholder in one way with one group and in another way with a different one. You may live in a neighborhood threatened by a new development but also be a member of the planning council that must approve development proposals. This is a classic case of a *conflict of interest*. In official policymaking processes, rules govern how officials must behave in conflict of interest situations such as this one. Judges, mediators, and agency personnel all have rules requiring that potential conflicts of interest be disclosed and avoided when possible.

Some groups are organized, have a clear identity, and establish leaders. These are the easy stakeholder groups to identify, because they make themselves known. Other groups are more amorphous. They may be aware of their stakes, but they do not have much identity as a group. Leaders may not be known, and it may be different to identify who is in and who is out of the group.

Some stakeholder groups are institutionally established. These include, for example, departments in an organization, bureaus and agencies, legislatures, boards, unions, political parties, and so forth. Other groups come together on an ad hoc, informal basis when a conflict affecting them emerges. Some stakeholder groups have a clear form of representation. Certain people stand out as leaders who can represent the interests of the group. Other stakeholder groups are hard to represent, as no leaders or spokespersons emerge. Where stakeholder groups are organized, they stand a greater chance of being heard in the organization or community; where they are diffuse and unorganized, their interests may fade out of the discussion.

Depicting the Stakeholder System

You can define a stakeholder system in a variety of ways. Here we will describe three—affinity groups, circles, and maps.

Affinity Groups. This is perhaps the most clear-cut method of depicting the system. It consists of a list of groups that are held together by an affinity among members sharing some set of interests. Any one person might be a member of several affinity groups. If you wanted to involve stakeholders in planning nuclear policy, for example, you might start with a list of affinity groupings something like the following:

- Department of Defense
- Department of Energy
- Environmental Protection Agency
- Nuclear Regulatory Commission
- State, local, and tribal governments
- Environmental advocacy groups
- Antinuclear advocacy groups
- Nuclear industry associations
- National Commission on Energy Policy
- Universities and research organizations
- Foundations and funding organizations

Stakeholder Circles. Some stakeholder groups are involved with more intensity than others. These are key stakeholder groups. Other groups may have less interest or be less involved in the conflict. You can distinguish levels of involvement by *stakeholder circles*.[9] The inner circle consists of the most highly involved stakeholder groups, and a second ring consists of less central groups. You can continue adding rings as useful. Figure 8.1 illustrates a two-ring circle on the issue of nuclear policy.

Stakeholder Maps. Although stakeholder circles are helpful when designing conflict-management processes and systems, they do not often reflect the complexity of the system. They also fail to recognize the connections among various groups and sectors. The map depicted in figure 8.2 on the following page begins to approximate the system of stakeholder affinity groups on the nuclear-policy issue.[10]

Whether simple, as in an affinity-group list, or complex, as in a stakeholder map, these depictions are designed to identify key points of difference and similarity among groups that have an interest in the issues at hand.

Figure 8.1   Stakeholder Circles

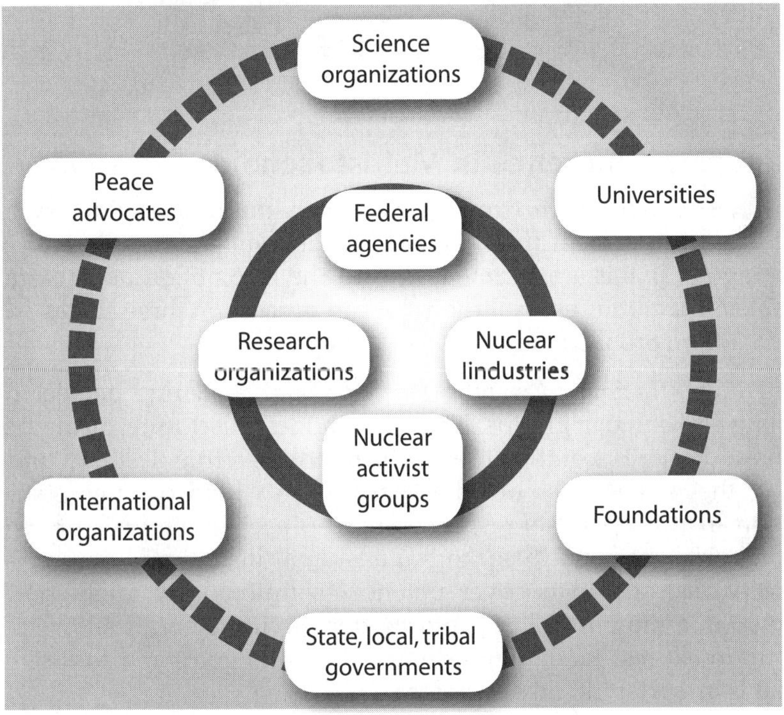

Figure 8.2   Stakeholder Map

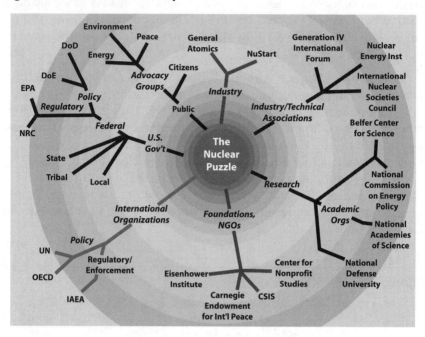

Managing Difference in Multistakeholder Systems

Constructive conflict management in a multistakeholder system involves a movement from the attitude of competition to one of collaboration. This is a movement toward the recognition of a common problem that requires a solution.[11] It can proceed in three stages—differentiation, problem definition, and integration.

Differentiation. An important first step is sharing perspectives among stakeholder groups. This is an honest disclosure of the positions and interests of the group, which reflects a true desire to understand the perspectives of other parties. This kind of open sharing within an atmosphere of respect empowers each group to clarify what is most important to them, to build mutual insight and accuracy of perceptions, and to uncover potential solutions that might not be known in a more restrictive information environment. It allows each group to express its distinguishing values and goals and to discover what is important to other groups.

Mutual Problem Description. Next, groups frame a set of issues or questions that enable them to bridge their separateness and begin to integrate positions and interests. This is a transition from a feeling of isolation to one of interdependence within the system. As an example, each of the following questions on nuclear policy could be used to create constructive communication across the nuclear stakeholder system:

1. What technical and policy-related actions are key to building public trust in nuclear policy?
2. What role must public stakeholders and others take in order for public trust to be established?
3. What should be the role of nuclear power in a portfolio of solutions designed to produce sufficient, safe, and environmentally sound energy?
4. What are the chief opportunities and threats in the development of nuclear energy? What trade-offs are we willing to make or not make?
5. What is an acceptable level of safety and how can it be achieved?
6. How should nuclear waste be managed?
7. What directions should reactor development take?
8. What approach to weapons development and stockpile management best assures global security?
9. How should nuclear nonproliferation be achieved?
10. What are the most effective measures to prevent nuclear terrorism?

Integration. This is the actual problem-solving stage. Here groups work together to propose potential solutions. They deliberate on these, weigh them, establish criteria, and reality-test potential solutions in terms of how well their respective interests will be met. This is never easy and may take considerable time and money. We offer several methods in this chapter and in the appendix.

Multistakeholder conflicts require both personal and institutional responses, which we explore in the remainder of the chapter.

INTERPERSONAL RESPONSES TO CONFLICT

In the previous section, we described stakeholder systems, but when you are actually involved in managing complex differences in an organization or community—or participating yourself in such a conflict—you must decide how to respond. We hope this section provides some guidance.

Reflexivity as the Key

Reflexivity, as discussed in chapter 6, denotes a reflection or aware-ness, but it is more than simple observation and attentiveness to detail. When people are reflexive, they are aware of their own role in interaction with others. Reflexivity also involves actively looking for the many possible ways to understand a conflict and one's own part in it. For example, if you are reflexive, you will understand that the way in which you frame a problem will encourage certain kinds of solutions and discourage others. You will actively experiment with various forms, knowing that each has certain powers and limits.[12] Reflexivity is a "critical awareness, description, and a way of being with others."[13] Because it deliberately plays with diverse meanings and interpretations, reflexivity is a habit especially appropriate for the management of difference.

When encountering a conflict, a reflexive manager (or any other member of the community) might (1) think of the conflict not as an obstacle, but as an opportunity for problem solving; (2) reframe the issue from emotional reaction to substantive issues; (3) turn the situa-tion into an opportunity for building respect; (4) present a variety of options for resolution such as negotiation, mediation, or adjudication;

and (5) shift attention from positions to interests and then to mutual interests.[14] Notice how each of these moves requires the manager to work toward a fresh way to understand, or frame, the situation. Notice too that reflexivity of this type involves a constant movement of the mind, an awareness of one's own involvement in the system, and a willingness to experiment with a variety of possible approaches.

In his study of the reflexive managerial practice, Kevin Barge identified a pattern he calls *invitational reflexivity*. This involves careful attention to the forms of communication needed to build effective outcomes that are based on a diversity of thinking while consciously exploring processes in which managers and others can act effectively together.[15] Invitational reflexivity means inviting others into a new kind of conversation where participants appreciate difference, while keeping an eye on productivity.[16]

Crafting Conversational Frameworks

Within organizations and communities, it is necessary to craft frameworks that set the context, purpose, and desired outcomes of various conversations. A *conversational framework* is like a container in which stakeholders can communicate. Whether a brief "floor" meeting at the beginning of the shift, a weekly staff meeting, an impromptu meeting between manager and staff, a performance evaluation, an Internet conversation space, or any number of other forums, the conversational framework will acknowledge the culture and rules of the community, stretching them into new realms in which beneficial outcomes might emerge.

In our practice as communication consultants, we frequently must help groups work to recognize their differences before they can move toward resolution of a specific conflict. In our experience, there are four qualities that characterize effective conversations: collaboration, power management, process management, and a safe environment.[17] In chapter 5, we introduced these characteristics as essential to creating a positive facework environment.

Collaboration.   Diversity in a group can be an opportunity for unleashing creative potential in the members through effective synergy. Ting-Toomey and Oetzel acknowledge that we have the ability to move beyond traditional either-or thinking, sometimes called "win-lose," and move toward the expansion of diverse options.[18] "Whether we are involved in solving multiethnic community problems, a school-based intergroup problem, or an international workplace problem, no single individual possesses the depth and breadth of knowledge to resolve an entangled conflict issue."[19]

The Tremaine Foundation found that collaborative processes are the key to creating solutions that meet the interests of all stakeholders. The following six ingredients were identified for successful collaboration:[20]

1. Participants must agree on a *shared goal* or a set of solutions to work toward from the outset. This does not mean that each party needs to be motivated by the same reason to work toward the goal.

2. *Trust* must exist among the participants. Trust can be earned through the collaborative process itself; it is an essential ingredient to moving toward shared goals.

3. Collaboration requires *commitment and patience.* Collaboration takes time and energy. Progress is often measured in inches at first, before the great strides occur.

4. A *leader* committed to collaboration is also necessary. He or she could be a process management leader or someone experienced and committed to the issue being addressed.

5. *Incentives* to keep the process going must be in place. Sometimes, this may be a mandate or condition; other times it may be the deeper interests of the individuals or parties motivate them.

6. The process must exhibit *inclusiveness and equality.* All participants must be treated as equals. When one person is seen as carrying more weight than another, mistrust builds and corrodes the process.

Collaboration is easier said than done. If we are to move out of ruts past our stuck spots, a good faith commitment to collaboration is essential. Answers to the following questions can guide the process.

1. Is collaboration appropriate? The answer to this question comes from a discussion and assessment about the conditions for collaboration. Are the above six elements in place? Is collaboration workable in our situation? If so, move forward!

2. Who has an interest in the process and the outcomes? In the early stages of collaboration, it is important to identify those who need to be involved in the process.

3. Do we know how to collaborate? It may be essential to build individual capacity by some type of training or introduction to process tools that can make the process as effective as possible.

4. What communication guidelines do we need to guide our process? Sometimes called ground rules, and sometimes called process agreements, it is often helpful to determine guidelines for the type of communication that would fit the styles and

experience of the participants, while assisting them in being efficient in meeting the goals.

5. What information is available to help us make the right decisions? The people involved will identify and explore the information and facts necessary for them to know the parameters of the issue they are facing.

6. What solutions or options for moving forward are there for addressing the issue we face? Often the solutions are negotiated by a process that separates the generation of options from the evaluation of options. When a workable set has been generated, narrow the choices by determining which options best meet the interests of all.

7. How do we want to state our agreements: a formal written document, a memo, a report, or an announcement? All members should participate in selecting the form of the agreement and in producing it.

A few years ago, we facilitated a process to engage educators in New Mexico in designing a new teacher licensure system. Although the legislation was controversial, the sponsors wisely arranged to involve teachers and other educators from around the state in the implementation. In a large one-day event, representatives from every level of education in the state (including union representatives, administrators, and legislators) gathered in Albuquerque to talk about how teachers should be evaluated to advance through the licensure system.

The group took the task very seriously, because everyone would be affected by the result. The group, which filled a large meeting room, did a wonderful job of collaborating on key components of the system. The size and diversity of the group and limited time precluded them from making refinements, but the participants prioritized the main components. A committee then refined the ideas. The sponsors hosted a follow-up meeting to address the question: Did we get it right? This was an opportunity for stakeholders to weigh the issue again. The sponsors then went around the state to meet with educators locally in several regions to continue the conversation. The final result now guides teacher licensure in the state and stakeholders are pleased with the collaborative efforts.

Power Management.   We briefly discussed empowerment at the end of chapter 7. Empowering people to communicate effectively assumes a goal where each group member contributes fully and confidently, using the skills available to them. How do you put a culture of empowerment in place in the organization? Groups can follow these guidelines to establish empowering interactions.[21]

1. Clarify priorities.

2. Explore why certain priorities are important to various group members.

3. Be aware of available options and control over those options.

4. Increase the use of conflict management skills: listening, communicating, organizing, generating options, and evaluating options.

5. Make clear and deliberate decisions.

6. Assess the strengths and weaknesses of personal and group interests and make decisions based on these assessments.

One aspect of empowerment is *constructive controversy*. Stakeholders openly and cooperatively debate ideas in a spirit of improvement rather than personal attack. Performance can be enhanced if groups are willing to confront issues and discuss ideas critically without taking it personally.[22] The spirit of the group enables everyone to test ideas from their various perspectives.

We recently worked with a team at a national defense laboratory to set up a self-assessment system for the entire organization. The idea was that every department should be involved in evaluating its own work, an example of empowerment. It was interesting to watch the stakeholders do their work. A diverse team of representatives worked for about five months to create the system. The group accomplished each of the six points above as it worked through various approaches and ideas. Empowerment was possible in this group because (1) management took the group's work very seriously, (2) team members cared about the issue and had a great deal of respect for one another, and (3) the team took time to create options and truly deliberate potential outcomes. Although we worried about possible conflict, the spirit of empowerment was so strong that the group was able to work out its differences as it went along without destructive arguments taking place.

Process Management. Stakeholders need to attend to *how* they work together, as well as *what* they do together. An important question to ask at the beginning of any initiative and throughout the process is, "How can we best communicate about this project in a way that works effectively?" Participants or leaders can ask pertinent process questions, such as: Where will we meet? How long will we meet? What goals do we have for this meeting? How much time do we have for this initiative? Who should be at the meeting? Which interests (goals, needs, people with a stake in the outcome) should be included? How should we create an agenda? How will meeting facilitation be provided? How will we make decisions? How should we capture information, discussion points, and decisions?

Empirical evidence and experience point to the importance of process management in effective group decision making; yet, people often resist discussions of process.[23] Many times we encounter groups that say, "Don't talk about *how* to do it; let's just do it!" Yet later in the discussion, they become lost, disorganized, frustrated, and unable to manage differences. One of the most helpful interventions mediators and facilitators can make at this point is to return to process: "How do you want to work through these issues?"

We were called in recently to mediate a conflict in a sixteen-person department of a local agency. The climate in the department had deteriorated to the point that employees dreaded going to work. Attitudes had become cynical and hateful; rumors and backbiting circulated freely. Several conflicts between individual members had broken out, and some of these had led to angry outbursts in front of other workers. We knew going in that process management would be very important, and we carefully worked with the employees to establish a process that could lead to constructive change. We interviewed every employee in the department privately to explore process possibilities. We then developed a planning process in which the members could collaborate on solving various workplace issues together. Over a period of weeks, we met for departmental dialogues in which the participants followed carefully crafted guidelines and a procedure that enabled them to explore their emotional issues in a safe environment. The results were remarkable. Misunderstandings were clarified; positive feelings were expressed; and promises were made for improved work relationships.

Safe Environment.   One of the biggest problems we faced with the department discussed above was helping the group establish a safe environment. We took several steps to help the participants move forward. First, we allowed individuals to vent privately about their frustrations. Second, we provided strong facilitation, which ensured that personal attacks could not occur. Third, we allowed time (up to four hours for each meeting) to explore issues deeply and to move beyond knee-jerk reactions. Fourth, we invited the group to collaborate on setting up communication guidelines that would encourage constructive, respectful interaction. We encouraged the group to model the kinds of professionalism they wanted for their workplace. Fifth, we spent time in the group designing a dialogue format that would feel safe. Although the group was hesitant at first, it quickly embraced the format and communication guidelines. Remarkably, they kept asking to meet over several months because they found that the process worked so well for them.

Participants want to be able to have constructive conversations in a comfortable atmosphere where they are not threatened or hindered. A safe environment assumes differences can be explored productively and creatively. This type of environment requires a commitment to diversity. One organization we worked with had the following foundational message for their team.

> We know that we all have differing perspectives, and invite those to stand in full view. We can explore the perspectives of others without necessarily changing our own views. In that process, we hope that we can become more self-aware of our own perspectives and the reasons we hold them, while realizing the good reasons others have for their views.

Valuing confidentiality is another way for stakeholders to feel safe. If the members can hold discussions with the knowledge that privacy is honored where appropriate, they can feel free to brainstorm and share potentially controversial ideas. It is often through these conversations that the most creative options emerge. The team members need to negotiate the safe environment internally—to create an atmosphere that values diversity and offers comfort and secure communication opportunities.

Box 8.1

Think about a conflict you have experienced in a group. How did each of the following factors enter into the management of this conflict?

- Collaborative communication
- Empowerment
- Process management
- Safe environment

In retrospect, how could the group have made better use of these characteristics?

Facework at the Center

In chapter 5, we introduced the concept of facework. We want to continue that discussion here because of its importance as a key to each of the four characteristics of constructive communication outlined above and illustrated in figure 8.3.[24] When stakeholders manage their differences effectively, they maintain a feeling of dignity and self-worth within the system. Groups "manage face" by upholding

Figure 8.3   The Conversational Framework

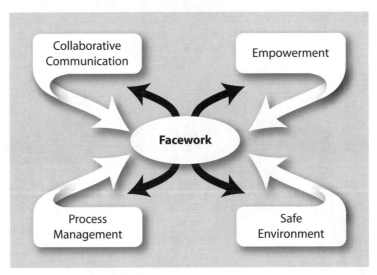

one another's self-image. People are not put on the spot, surprised, or made to feel embarrassed and defensive. They are not confronted or approached in ways that are disrespectful.

In chapter 5 of this book, we defined facework as a set of coordinated practices in which communicators build, maintain, protect, or threaten personal dignity, honor, and respect.[25] Constructive facework aims to build or maintain face, while destructive facework aims to tear it down. The kind of facework that people do often determines whether differences are managed in a helpful way or a harmful one. Too often in conflict, power struggles and disagreements are marked by face threats, and parties actively try to demean one another. Face threats are often motivated by the desire to prevail. Ironically, they can do just the opposite. They accelerate the struggle, which becomes increasing contentious and personal.

Constructive facework is designed to build or maintain the face of other people. More than making people feel good about themselves, this kind of communication requires constant vigilance and demands simultaneous and sometimes paradoxical effort on a number of levels. It is sometimes tough, and group members do not always "feel good" about what is happening in the immediate moment. Instead, they are conscious of the need to build honor and personal identity within the organization over time. Good facework, then, may mean working through hard places to achieve a better sense of purpose, worth, and dignity for everyone.

Each of the four dimensions outlined in the previous section—collaborative communication, empowerment, process management, and a safe environment—contribute to good facework.

> Act with intent, but understand that you are always co-constructing something larger than the objective you are trying to achieve in the moment. Notice what you are making in your ongoing social interactions and expand your goals as needed to create an atmosphere of positive facework. . . . Communicate with others in a way that honors the complex identities of each person. . . . Show respect even when the experience of the other person is not consistent with your own.[26]

INSTITUTIONAL RESPONSES TO CONFLICT

Poor conflict management can be costly in the world of business. So how do organizations move forward in ways that make conflict productive rather than destructive? Increasingly, organizations design whole systems for managing conflicts in ways that maximize the potential for value and minimize harm.

Conflict System Design

If our goal is to enable human voices to "sing together in the same choir" and produce pleasant, satisfying, even harmonious music, we can begin upstream, where the choir is being assembled. Can we design the system (the choir) in a way that accomplishes this goal? Sometimes called *dispute settlement design, conflict management design, conflict systems design,* or simply *system design,* the focus in these design opportunities is to draw conflict to the surface and channel it.[27] System design attempts to grasp a deeper understanding of the nature of conflict while offering alternative strategies to address it.

The pioneers of conflict systems design sought sustainable change in large systems. William Ury, Jeanne Brett, and Stephen Goldberg produced a dispute system design concept in the 1980s. Their work centered on troubled organizations, communities, and other large systems. The most famous example is their work in the Cavey Creek Coal Mine, a place that had been experiencing much conflict since the 1970s.[28] The power struggles at the mine resulted in numerous strikes and walkouts because the workers had found that the quickest way to get management's attention was a strike. Ury, Brett, and Goldberg advocated *negotiating interests* as a much more desirable focus than adjudicating rights or addressing the conflicting power dynamics. If negotiating interests doesn't work, the parties try a rights-based approach (such as a legal suit) or a power-based approach, such as a strike. Interest-based negotiations focus on what the parties *want* to do based on their interests, rather than what they *can* do based on their rights or power dynamics.

Design Principles. Ury, Brett, and Goldberg outlined six principles to follow when considering the creation of sustainable change.[29] First, *put the focus on interests.* Look first at the individual or group interests that lie beneath the strongly held positions. Next, *provide low-cost rights and power backups.* There are other low-cost options that come from the field of Alternative Dispute Resolution (ADR) that can address the requested focus on rights. These may include mediation or arbitration processes and can be offered as backups when the negotiation of interests is stalled or falls apart. Third, *build in "loop-backs" to negotiation.* The rights-based or power-based struggles may still arise and can benefit from a system that continually offers interest-based negotiation with opportunities to return to negotiation at any stage. Fourth, *build in consultation before, feedback after.* The struggling parties need to rely on dependable methods to share information. It is essential to determine methods for information sharing before any type of feedback or evaluation. Fifth, arrange *procedures in a low-to-high-cost sequence.* Assuming that this design will have a series of steps, it is important to keep the lowest cost means to address the differences early in the process. Low-cost options include face-to-face discussions, guided negotiations, or other informal mediation-type processes. The more formal the processes become, the more costly in terms of expenditure of resources, whether money, time, or logistical arrangements.

Finally, *provide the necessary motivation, skills, and resources.* The system activities need to be reinforced with the knowledge and behaviors necessary for it to function smoothly. If the system is to cooperate, it is important to involve the participants in all stages of the design and implementation, while offering the appropriate resources they may need to understand and show commitment to the process.

Designing Systems Collaboratively. Many have followed in the footsteps of Ury, Brett, and Goldberg to continue the exploration of conflict management systems design. Cathy Constantino and Christina Merchant expanded the systemic conflict management options by acknowledging the constant flux of systems, which never reach a state of equilibrium.[30] Conflict within these systems is inevitable and can best be addressed in system design. They emphasized designing systems *with* the stakeholders rather than *for* them. Beginning with an assessment of the system, the conveners invite participation, openness, and feedback at all stages of the design process. Constantino and Merchant recommend that the evaluation process be created at the beginning of the design stage, rather than at the end. The system needs the opportunity to change and clarify itself in response to the evaluation, at any stage in the process. If the system is to identify and address potential constraints and possible resistance, participants must be involved at the outset. Rather than imposing a framework without any internal cooperation, everyone works through concerns interactively. Constantino and Merchant call this "having tea with your demons."

The "Listening to the City" Online Dialogues held in New York City in 2002–2003 are an example of a system design where a process was created to address sharp differences in the community.[31] Eight hundred participants, consisting of survivors of the September 11, 2001 tragedy, relatives of victims, medical professionals, police, and residents of New York City and the surrounding area engaged in face-to-face discussions in small groups and online.

The dialogues focused on two things: the plans for redevelopment of the World Trade Center site and the creation of a permanent memorial for the victims and heroes of September 11. One compelling design component of the dialogues was the use of an intentional and explicit social agreement that helped relax skepticism and build trust. This agreement was negotiated within each small group, intending that the group would: work together as a group toward both individual and group goals; adhere to certain safety and group behavior guidelines as well as give and receive feedback, both positive and negative; and work toward changing behavior where it was appropriate.[32] The online nature of these discussions required an extra degree of safety for a successful outcome.

Human social systems can benefit from conflict management designs that can manage and prevent differences from entering the realm of harm. Eric Brahm and Julian Ouellet explain how inefficient dispute-resolution systems can be identified and how effective replacements can be designed.

> We can think of this process as the design of new, more efficient ways of agreeing not to agree. It does not imply eliminating dissent, or encouraging constant cooperation. Instead, it argues that when cooperation breaks down there are better and worse ways of resolving the resulting conflict. Third parties who work with intractable conflicts often focus on designing new dispute-settlement systems, tailored to the situation, using best practices of conflict resolution.[33]

Many processes of ADR used in organizational systems are outlined in the appendix.

Box 8.2

Make an appointment with a spokesperson for the human resources division of a large corporation or federal agency. Interview this individual to learn more about the organization's conflict management system.

Resolving Serious Organizational Conflicts

In large organizations and communities, conflict management takes on different textures and complexions as disputes deepen and become more intractable. For this reason, conflict systems need to address a spectrum of conflict. If differences are not managed well at lower levels, they have the potential to accelerate to more serious conflicts that will take significant time and money to resolve with increasingly negative impacts on the organization. David Lipsky and Ronald Seeber identify three levels of conflict that require different kinds of organizational intervention: workplace disagreements, disputes, and litigation.[34] As you move from one to the next, conflicts become more serious, more formal, and more complex. Table 8.1 outlines key differences in how organizations must respond.

Table 8.1   Managing Three Types of Workplace Conflict

	Managing Disagreements	Managing Disputes	Managing Litigation
Who is responsible?	First-line supervisors and managers	HR managers, middle managers, and attorneys	Corporate counsel, counsel's office, outside counsel
Type of conflict	Latent or expressed disagreements, differences of opinion, frictions	Complaints, grievances, charges (usually written)	Lawsuits, allegations of statutory infractions, formal charges
What techniques are used?	Exercise of supervisory authority, discussion, problem solving, negotiation	Discussion, negotiation, mediation, arbitration, other ADR techniques	Risk assessment, risk management, negotiation, advocacy in legal proceedings
Nature of outcome	Compliance with supervisory decision, mutual consent, informal agreement, no resolution	Negotiated or mediated agreement, complaint withdrawn or dismissed, arbitrated award, no resolution	Lawsuit or charge withdrawn or dismissed, negotiated agreement, jury trial and decision, bench trial and decision
Third-party involvement	Seldom but occasional use of consultants, facilitators, ombudspersons, etc.	Facilitators, mediators, ombudspersons, arbitrators, etc.	Court-appointed mediators, administrative law judges, magistrates, judges, etc.

COMMUNITY CONFLICT AND THE MANAGEMENT OF PUBLIC ISSUES

People tend to think of communities as messy, disorganized clusters of individuals and groups. A healthier way is to consider a community as an interlinked set of conversations that bring different groups together in a systemic network of connections and relationships. As always, the quality of communication that occurs within the community determines the social worlds that are made.

When Conflict Erupts

Communities are constantly faced with issues such as funding for education, siting of waste disposal plants, decisions about residential and urban priorities, and dilemmas about zoning that have the potential of breeding community conflict. Three factors lead to conflict in these kinds of situations.[35]

- The issue touches on an important aspect of stakeholders' lives—education of their children, their means of livelihood, religion, taxes, or something similar.
- The issue affects the lives of various community members differently. A tax proposal, for example, affects property owners one way and nonproperty owners another.
- The issue is one on which stakeholders can take action—not one that leaves the community helpless.

In the United States, environmental conflict offers an excellent illustration.[36] There are several reasons conflict exists around environmental issues. First, these issues have assumed enormous importance in society. Second, they impact the quality of life in communities, and people care deeply about these issues. Third, the federal government has mandated public participation in environmental policymaking. Fourth, the public itself has a strong ethic and social demand for confronting environmental issues.

In general, the public is demanding environmental quality, but they do not trust the government to manage natural resources effectively. In addition, there is no national consensus on what is the right way to manage our natural resources. Indeed, numerous stakeholders have very different ideas about how to manage a sustainable environment. Recognizing these factors, most government agencies are committed to improve public participation on these difficult and contentious issues.[37] While formerly relying mostly on the DAD (Decide-Announce-Defend) model of public policymaking, agencies now realize the importance of engaging stakeholders from the beginning.

Public Participation

Within a community at a given time, open conflict may or may not be present, but important differences always exist. If these potential conflicts are not handled well, open conflict will become destructive.

Agencies have a spectrum of ways in which to engage the stakeholders in important issues. In general, these are to (1) educate, (2) get input, (3) discuss, (4) engage, and (5) partner. The following is a useful set of guidelines for these kinds of involvement.[38]

- *Inform and educate* when (1) the decision is already made; (2) there is no time or opportunity for public input; or (3) there is an emergency or crisis that requires quick action.

- *Get input* when (1) the purpose is primarily information gathering; (2) policy options are unclear; or (3) there is not yet agency commitment to act.

- *Discuss* when (1) stakeholders will be affected by the outcome and need to talk among themselves; (2) community building is desired; or (3) the agency needs good ideas to help shape policy options.

- *Engage* when (1) issues are complex and value laden; (2) the community has the capacity to help shape policy; (3) there is plenty of opportunity and time available.

- *Partner* when (1) stakeholders must be empowered to help manage the process; (2) stakeholders are willing to do this; (3) agencies are willing to share control; and (4) process agreements can be reached.

Partnering: Stakeholder Consensus Building

Consensus building is a process of creating solutions that all participating stakeholders can support. Interest-based negotiations mean that participants agree that they have come up with the best solution possible under the circumstances, that they are willing to support it, and that if they have the power to block implementation of the solution, they will not do so. Consensus does not mean that the result is everyone's favorite option, and it does not mean that the ideal solution has been reached—rather, it means that the outcome is acceptable to everyone.

Consensus building is hard work and not always possible. It is most feasible when (1) issues are negotiable and high in priority; (2) stakeholder interests are well defined; (3) power is relatively balanced; (4) a unilateral decision on the part of the government agency would be met with contention, resistance, and political rancor; and (5) there are sufficient resources and time.[39] More information about consensus can be found in the appendix.[40]

Consider the case of Cupertino, California, in the 1990s. Cupertino, known in Silicon Valley as the home of Apple Computer, had developed from a small rural town south of San Francisco to a high-tech suburban city. Primarily because of immigration from Asia, Cupertino had become a multiracial community marked by a palpable set of differences the community did not know how to address.

Indeed, race had become an undiscussable issue within the community. City Manager Don Brown described the situation.

> As these changes accelerated into the 1990s, and became more and more evident to the "traditional" community, signs of discomfort and resistance were evident. The community was changing right before people's eyes and they were not sure what to make of it. As the "minority" cultures approached 40% of the total population of the community the sense of uncertainty increased.[41]

Cupertino was at a turning point, and the quality of communication about differences would determine whether the situation would become an opportunity for excellent public dialogue or a stimulus for open clashes.

In a multiyear project, the Public Dialogue Consortium provided Cupertino with guidance and facilitation for constructive communication. One goal of the dialogue project was to make it possible for stakeholders to talk openly and constructively about culture. This was accomplished by small-group discussions, interviews, community-wide forums, training and team-building sessions, and the establishment of a community organization dedicated to continuing the dialogue process.[42] Here are some of the things that the facilitators and city leaders did to develop processes to foster constructive communication.[43]

1. They involved the public early before open conflict erupted.
2. They invited participants to have a new kind of conversation, or dialogue.
3. They dealt with the most difficult issues first in small groups, not large forums.
4. They provided structure and strong facilitation to help participants feel safe.
5. Refusing to pit one group against another, they treated participants as collaborators, not competitors.
6. They put community leaders into a "listening" role rather than a "telling" role.
7. They worked through many different processes over a length of time, to build trust and community-wide collaboration.
8. They framed issues in safe ways. Rather than naming the issue "race relations," or, worse, "racial tension," they asked people to explore "cultural richness" in the community.
9. Avoiding typical public hearings or debate-oriented public meetings, they designed creative meeting formats that would be both engaging and productive.

10. They enabled participants to share ideas, make proposals, and undertake mutual planning.
11. They built capacity through participation, experience, and training, and they enabled the community to develop its own internal planning group to continue the process into the indefinite future.

HOW YOU CAN USE THIS CHAPTER

Unless you are a hermit, you can count on two truisms: (1) life in large systems will be marked by diversity and challenging differences, and (2) public policies and community issues will impact the quality of your life. This chapter can be helpful in coping with these facts of life.

1. Maintain a spirit of reflexivity by thinking actively about your interests, what is most important to you, and how your own patterns of communication enable you to integrate these with the values of others.
2. In matters of organizational life, contribute to processes that enable collaborative communication, empowerment, process management, and a safe environment.
3. Work to manage day-to-day conflicts humanely and constructively in order to avoid difficult, complex, and life-damaging disputes.
4. In communities of all kinds, including organizations, understand that many groups will have a stake in the outcome. Through various informal and formal processes, engage stakeholders in ongoing dialogue about what is important to them and how to invent solutions for mutual gain.

Interactive Case Study

CONVERSATIONAL FRAMEWORKS IN THIS CLASSROOM

Context: The focus of this case study will be designing systems for the creation of positive futures in the communities in which we live. In the exercises, the groups will focus on creating a classroom environment where differences reside in the sphere of value.

Opening exercise(s): The class will divide into three groups, corresponding to the three focus areas below. For each focus, find a table or group of chairs to be the "station" for the activities. Each group will be addressing one focus area and depicting the process and learnings they experience. Spread some butcher paper on the table and prepare the following exercises. Label each sheet with the focus. After each exercise is finished, jot down any thoughts about the exercise on the sheet, in any form. This will end up looking a bit messy. The class will rotate to each station where the group can present their results.

Focus #1: Four Characteristics

Look at the characteristics for effective work groups listed below. For each characteristic, discuss your classroom environment and how it provides each of the following. Record the insights. List ways these characteristics could be improved.

1. Collaborative Communication
2. Empowerment
3. Process Management
4. Safe Environment

Focus #2: System Design

In your small group, you will be designing a conflict management system for your classroom. You can use any methods you have found in the book so far, and especially the suggestions in this chapter. This system could address ground rules for communication, plans for tackling problems when they arrive, options for use of third parties, or contexts and processes for decision making and conflict management. Draw the design on the butcher paper. This will be a system to be used only for the students and the teachers (and possible guests) in your class.

Focus #3: Consensus Decision Making

In your small group, think of an issue that affects your class. This could be something that is also addressed in the system design group. The issue should be something internal, like the format of the final exam, rules about tardiness and class disruptions, dominating or disrespectful communication, incentives and punishments, or anything else that may require a decision in the class. Read about consensus decisions and try to make a decision in your group. You might begin by creating some ground rules for communication, followed by discussion of the issue, and finally checking to see if you have consensus. You can measure it by "thumbs up or thumbs down." If there is no consensus, have another round of discussion, followed by another vote. If someone wants to put their thumbs sideways, that could indicate they could live with the decision, even though they don't like it.

Endnotes

[1] Marshall Scott Poole and Johny T. Garner, "Perspectives on Workgroup Conflict and Communication," in *The Sage Handbook of Conflict Communication: Integrating Theory, Research, and Practice*, eds. John G. Oetzel and Stella Ting-Toomey (Thousand Oaks, CA: Sage, 2006), pp. 267–292.

[2] Anne Maydan Nicotera and Laura Kathleen Dorsey, "Individual and Interactive Processes in Organizational Conflict," in *The Sage Handbook of Conflict Communication: Integrating Theory, Research, and Practice*, eds. John G. Oetzel and Stella Ting-Toomey (Thousand Oaks, CA: Sage, 2006), pp. 293–326.

[3] Linda L. Putnam, "Formal Negotiations: The Productive Side of Organizational Conflict," in *Conflict and Organizations: Communicative Processes*, ed. Anne Maydan Nicotera (New York: SUNY Press, 1995).

[4] Lisa H. Pelled, "Demographic Diversity, Conflict, and Work Group Outcomes: An Intervening Process Theory," *Organization Science*, 7 (1996): 615–631; Lisa H. Pelled, Kathleen M. Eisenhardt, and Katherine R. Xin, "Exploring the Black Box: An Analysis of Work Group Diversity, Conflict, and Performance," *Administrative Science Quarterly*, 44 (1999): 1–28; Poole and Garner, "Perspectives on Workgroup Conflict and Communication."

[5] Barry Collins and Harold Guetzkow, *A Social Psychology of Group Processes for Decision-Making* (New York: Wiley, 1964); Kay Lovelace, Debra L. Shapiro, and Laurie R. Weingart, "Maximizing Cross-Functional New Product Teams' Innovativeness and Constraint Adherence: A Conflict Communications Perspective," *Academy of Management Journal*, 44 (2001): 779–793; Poole and Garner, "Perspectives on Workgroup Conflict and Communication."

[6] Karen A. Jehn, "Qualitative Analysis of Conflict Types and Dimensions in Organizational Groups," *Administrative Science Quarterly*, 42 (1997): 538–566; Garner and Poole, "Perspectives on Workgroup Conflict and Communication."

[7] Raymond Cattell, "Concepts and Methods in the Measurement of Group Syntality," *Psychological Review*, 55 (1948): 48–63; Robert F. Bales, *Interaction Process Analysis: A Method for the Study of Small Groups* (Reading, MA: Addison-Wesley, 1950); Dennis S. Gouran, "Communication Skills for Group Decision Making," in *Handbook of Communication and Social Interaction Skills*, eds. John O. Greene and Brant R. Burleson (Mahwah, NJ: Lawrence Erlbaum, 2003), pp. 835–871.

[8] Irving Janis, *Groupthink: Psychological Studies of Policy Decisions and Fiascoes* (Boston: Houghton Mifflin, 1982).

[9] Lawrence Susskind, "An Alternative to Robert's Rules of Order for Groups, Organizations, and Ad Hoc Assemblies that Want to Operate by Consensus," in *The Consensus Building Handbook: A Comprehensive Guide to Reaching Agreement*, eds. Lawrence Susskind, Sarah McKearnan, and Jennifer Thomas-Larmer (Thousand Oaks, CA: Sage, 1999), pp. 3–60.

[10] This map was constructed by Galisteo Consulting Group, in consultation with and under the auspices of Domenici Littlejohn, Inc.

[11] Michael J. Papa and Daniel J. Canary, "Conflict in Organizations: A Competency-Based Approach," in *Conflict and Organizations: Communicative Processes*, ed. Anne Maydan Nicotera (Albany: SUNY Press, 1995), pp. 153–182. Papa and Canary developed this model to depict interpersonal conflicts, but we find it useful for multi-stakeholder conflicts as well.

[12] Kevin Barge, "Reflexivity and Managerial Practice," *Communication Monographs*, 71 (2004): 70–96. See also, Donald A. Schon, *The Reflective Practitioner* (New York: Basic Books, 1983); Donald A. Schon, *Educating the Reflective Practitioner* (San Francisco: Jossey-Bass, 1987); Ray Holland, "Reflexivity," *Human Relations*, 52 (1999): 463–484.

[13] Barge, p. 78.

[14] Gouran, "Communication Skills for Group Decision Making."

[15] Barge, "Reflexivity and Managerial Practice."

[16] See also Sonja K. Foss and Karen A. Foss, *Inviting Transformation: Presentational Speaking for a Changing World*, 2nd ed. (Long Grove, IL: Waveland Press, 2003).

[17] Stephen W. Littlejohn and Kathy Domenici, *Engaging Communication in Conflict: Systemic Practice* (Thousand Oaks, CA: Sage, 2001).

[18] Stella Ting-Toomey and John G. Oetzel, *Managing Intercultural Conflict Effectively* (Thousand Oaks, CA: Sage, 2001).

[19] Ting-Toomey and Oetzel, p. 4.

[20] Belden Russonello and Stewart Research and Communications, "Collaborative Process: Better Outcomes for Us All," paper published on the Internet (Dillon, CO: Meridian Institute, 2001), pp. 7–8, 5 February 2007, www.merid.org/PDF/BRS_Report.pdf.

[21] Adapted from Robert A. Baruch Bush and Joseph P. Folger, *The Promise of Mediation: Responding to Conflict through Empowerment and Recognition* (San Francisco: Jossey-Bass, 1994).

[22] Dean Tjosvold, *Learning to Manage Conflict: Getting People to Work Together Productively* (New York: Lexington, 1993); Dean Tjosvold, William C. Wedley, and Richard H. G. Field, "Constructive Controversy, the Vroom-Yetton Model, and Managerial Decision Making," *Journal of Occupational Behavior*, 7 (1986): 125–138; Poole and Garner, "Perspectives on Workgroup Conflict."

[23] Gouran, "Communication Skills for Group Decision Making."

[24] Kathy Domenici and Stephen W. Littlejohn, *Facework: Bridging Theory and Practice* (Thousand Oaks, CA: Sage, 2006), p. 29.

[25] Domenici and Littlejohn, *Facework;* see also, Stephen Littlejohn and Kathy Domenici, "A Facework Frame for Mediation," in *Handbook of Mediation: Bridging Theory, Research, and Practice*, ed. Margaret S. Herrman (Malden, MA: Blackwell, 2006), pp. 228–246.

[26] Domenici and Littlejohn, *Facework.*

[27] Cathy Constantino and Christina Merchant, *Designing Conflict Management Systems: A Guide to Creating Productive and Healthy Organizations* (London: Jossey-Bass, 1996).

[28] William Ury, Jeanne Brett, and Stephen Goldberg, *Getting Disputes Resolved: Designing Systems to Cut the Costs of Conflict* (London: Jossey-Bass, 1988).

[29] Ury, Brett, and Goldberg, *Getting Disputes Resolved.*

[30] Constantino and Merchant.

[31] Steven Pyser and Cliff Figallo, "The 'Listening to the City' Online Dialogues Experience: The Impact of a Full Value Contract," *Conflict Resolution Quarterly*, Vol. 21, No. 3 (Spring 2004): 381–393.

[32] Pyser and Figallo, p. 385.

[33] Eric Brahm and Julian Ouellet, "Designing New Dispute Resolution Systems" (University of Colorado Conflict Research Consortium, 2003), 26 January 2007, http://www.beyondintractability.org/essay/designing_dispute_systems/

[34] David B. Lipsky and Ronald L. Seeber, "Managing Organizational Conflicts," in *The Sage Handbook of Conflict Communication: Integrating Theory, Research, and Practice*, eds. John G. Oetzel and Stella Ting-Toomey (Thousand Oaks, CA: Sage, 2006), pp. 359–390.

[35] James S. Coleman, *Community Conflict* (New York: The Free Press, 1957).

[36] This analysis based largely on Tarla Rai Peterson and Rebecca Royer Franks, "Environmental Conflict Communication," in *The Sage Handbook of Conflict Communication: Integrating Theory, Research, and Practice*, eds. John G. Oetzel and Stella Ting-Toomey (Thousand Oaks, CA: Sage, 2006), pp. 419–450.

[37] Terry F. Yosie and Timothy D. Herbst, *Using Stakeholder Processes in Environmental Decisionmaking: An Evaluation of Lessons Learned, Key Issues, and Future Challenges* (Washington, DC: Rudder Finn Washington and ICF Inc., 1998).

[38] Adapted from Health Canada, *Health Canada Policy Toolkit for Public Involvement in Decision Making* (Ontario: Ministry of Public Works and Government Services Canada, 2000).

[39] Jim Arthur, Christine Carlson, and Lee Moore, *A Practical Guide to Consensus* (Santa Fe, NM: Policy Consensus Initiative, 1999).

[40] See also, Lawrence Susskind, Sarah McKearnan, and Jennifer Thomas-Larmer, eds., *The Consensus Building Handbook: A Comprehensive Guide to Reaching Agreement* (Thousand Oaks, CA: Sage, 1999).

[41] Shawn Spano, *Public Dialogue and Participatory Democracy* (Cresskill, NJ: Hampton Press, 2001), p. x.

[42] Spano, *Public Dialogue.*

[43] Adapted from Littlejohn and Domenici, *Engaging Communication*, pp. 173–194.

9

Moving toward Value in Global Conflicts

In this chapter we move to conflict on the largest scale, involving ethnic, ideological, regional, and national interest. We tend to think of such conflicts as "structural," "institutional," and "impersonal," but even the grandest conflicts are personal in three important ways. First, large-scale conflicts are "made" in personal human interaction. The ideologies, prejudices, interests, values, and tensions that lie at the heart of such conflicts—even though these are based on material and historical conditions—are social and are reproduced every day in the personal interactions among people. Second, these conflicts impact the lives of human beings. How we manage national, ethnic, and ideological differences can create great harm or benefit to individual human lives. Third, people-in-interaction can create the conditions for transformation that leads to humane, even constructive, management of differences. Let's begin our discussion by looking at the personal in the global.

THE PERSONAL IN THE GLOBAL

Imagine that you became a leader in a worldwide social movement consisting of many groups and organizations brought together by a common cause. What would you face? You would see certain things happening in the world that cause you and your members tremendous concern. You would realize that where you are, both as a person and as leader of a movement, has progressed along a historical route, and in some cases this history may have involved mistreatment, injustice, domination, inequality, and war. You would see whole groups that do not share—and even resist—your cause, and you would feel that you are involved in a struggle with these groups. All of these things are part of the material and historical conditions that affect the movement and your life as a leader.

Yet, these conditions do not determine what will unfold. Even though you may perceive that you are locked into a certain course of action, you still meet, talk about the issues, analyze the history, identify options, and make decisions. You have conferences, send out e-mail newsletters, meet with attorneys, and are generally consumed by daily communication activities. You personally encounter and interact with members of other groups. Even though you face the constraints of the system, you feel a sense of agency, and you do participate in the construction of patterns that reproduce and potentially transform the emerging situation. The world is not a giant machine that grinds on in response to some levers pulled at the beginning of time. The grand affairs of communities and nations—including its conflicts—are constantly made and remade by the interactions of real people in real situations.

In these ways, then, the global is always personal. Leaders and ordinary community members act in ways that construct their social worlds. The system—which is constantly being remade—does establish constraints on individual and group action. Within those constraints, however, there is always latitude for choice—both in how we relate to one another and the decisions we make together. In other words, we have process choices and decision choices. The key question for moving large-scale conflicts from the sphere of harm to the sphere of value is always: *What can we do to contribute to the most constructive outcomes possible within the constraints in which we find ourselves?*

DEFINING INTERGROUP RELATIONS

Over time, groups define their relationships with other groups. We establish who is in the in-group and who is in the out-group, and these definitions will shift. In-group and out-group definitions may be based on nationality, ethnic or racial identification, ideological difference, moral or religious practices, or competition over limited resources. The boundaries of group affiliation do change; erstwhile enemies or competitors become allies against a newly defined enemy that threatens both groups.

Intergroup relations are constantly reconstructed and potentially transformed. How groups act toward other groups, communities, or nations is determined in large part by the nature of the relationship, be it enemies, rivals, or friends. Alexander Wendt showed how nations orient toward one another in these three orientations, and we think the analysis extends to all intergroup relations.[1]

Enemies

We treat other nations and groups as *enemies* when we imagine the world to be a dangerous kill-or-be-killed place where survival is the highest value. This is the world imagined by Thomas Hobbes in his treatise *Leviathan*, written in 1660.[2] Enemies aim to eliminate, disable, or conquer one another. Although we no longer live primarily in a Hobbesian world, nations and groups often create socially constructed worlds very much in the spirit of enmity. This was precisely the case in the Cold War. Power was viewed as the means to security—either physical or psychic—and one must act toward the enemy in a way that ultimately protects one's own nation or group. In the Hobbesian world, one of the most important ways of gaining security is through alliances, where we agree that any attack on an ally will be treated as an attack on oneself. Street gangs are an example of this kind of thinking. In international relations, the other-as-enemy model is the essence of "realpolitik," a social construction that makes enmity real. The system of allies and enemies constrains national or group leaders to think about others as enemies or allies. Behavior follows this thinking, reproducing the conflict continually.

Rivals

Rivalry—the second kind of relationship—is quite different from enmity. Wendt uses the world as imagined by John Locke in his 1690 work *Second Treatise of Government* to define rivalry.[3] In this kind of world, we admit the right of others to exist, but we also acknowledge that we must compete for the material resources of survival. We do not act toward other groups in ways designed to conquer or eliminate them, but we do vie for power. Sports provides a good analogy. You don't compete against other teams to extinguish them, only to win the game. Rivalry can be fierce, even violent, and there are rules for engaging one's rival, which comes with certain responsibilities. There are even referees who monitor and enforce the rules. The rivalry relationship is common both in economics and politics. Democrats don't try to eliminate the Republican Party; they try to prevail in a competition for votes.

Friends

Finally, the relationship of *friend* is inspired by Immanuel Kant's *Perpetual Peace*, written in 1795.[4] In this book, Kant presented a remarkable theory of peace, which is both practical and optimistic, and we will return to this work later in the chapter. Important here is the idea that international and intergroup relations based on friendship are governed by rules of nonviolence and mutual aid and are characterized by reciprocity. Groups and nations in a friendship relationship may have disagreements and differences—indeed, these are to be expected—but they agree to settle issues without violence.

We live in a world of mixed relations. On the international scale, rivalry is most common today; but enemies and friends exist as well. Where intergroup differences are difficult and frustrating, enmity and rivalry are probably most prominent. In democracies, downright enmity is hard to pull off because the political system discourages it, while at the same time promoting rivalry as a means of settling differences. Relations of enmity, rivalry, and friendship occur in a constantly changing field. Erstwhile enemies can become rivals or even friends. Just twenty years ago, the United States and the U.S.S.R. were locked in an enemy relationship, but today the United States and former Soviet nations experience rivalry and even friendship in most cases.

THE BASES OF GLOBAL CONFLICT

Interest-Based Conflict

We have talked about interest-based conflict earlier in this book, and we need only mention here that the same principles extend to international and intergroup conflict as well. Especially in an increasingly global market economy and widening democratization of the world, rivalries are mostly about competition for resources. Where national security and economic well-being is at stake, such rivalries can even involve serious sanctions and war. Interests are not always material and may involve struggles over who prevails on a political issue that has moral significance. As we will explore later in the chapter, however, morally based conflicts, while they may look like they are interest-based, typically run much deeper.

Ethnicity and Race

To some extent, all conflict has cultural implications because we learn how to orient to difference through our own cultural frames.[5] Certain conflicts, however, center on cultural difference, particularly ethnicity and race.[6] Most large-scale conflicts involving ethnicity and race emerge from a long history of inequality.[7] As one group continues to dominate the others, the dominant group's values and ideas are viewed as normal, while those of the other are marginalized. Groups closer to the norm tend to be more accepted, while those farther away may be oppressed. Apartheid in South Africa and segregation of Blacks and

Whites in the United States are two prominent examples. Others include the Tutsi and Hutu in Rwanda, the Singhalese and Tamil in Sri Lanka, the Serbs and Croats in the former Yugoslavia, and many others.

Such patterns of domination can have a profound affect on race relations, even decades after legal redress is achieved. An African-American surgeon who was recently visiting our city to do volunteer medical work was arrested and, he claimed, roughed up by two police officers, purportedly for creating problems in a bar. His first reaction was that he was treated badly because of his race. The history of race relations colors perceptions in conflicts that occur much later in time. In multiethnic regions, the patterns of domination can rarely be reduced just to two large groups—such as Black and White. Within the United States, for example, there are historical tensions between Latinos and African Americans and between African Americans and Korean immigrants.[8]

Sometimes ethnic conflicts are wrapped up with the competition for resources. For example, one of the reasons for the tension between Blacks and Hispanics in the United States is competition over work opportunities. The tension between Korean shopkeepers and Blacks results from perceived economic inequities and cultural style differences. African Americans sometimes perceive Korean shopkeepers as rude and greedy, which could be the result of limited experience with English and the employment of family members rather than people who live in the neighborhood.[9]

Korean–Black tensions also involve differences in cultural values and styles. When members of different cultural groups come together, they may find that their expectations about how people should respond and act are violated, which causes a certain amount of uncertainty and anxiety.[10] What is "verbal dueling"? To many people of European or Asian descent, it is a kind of verbal attack or abuse and considered rude. To many people of African descent, it is part of relationship building. Strong expression of feeling is considered normal and is expected among many African-American groups, while the same level of expression is often viewed as an "emotional outburst" and inappropriate by many Whites and Asians.

Groups differ too in their orientation to conflict. For individualistic cultures, differences may be attributable more to personality or interest-based differences, while the same differences might feel prejudicial, even racist, to members of more collectivist groups. Members of a dominant culture may fail to see that behavior toward a person of color evokes memories of a history of oppression. Acts that could be characterized as naive or indifferent by one group are viewed as racist or prejudicial by another.[11]

Although there is some degree of ethnic integration throughout the world, many ethnic groups live in separate neighborhoods.[12] Because of limited exposure to other groups, segregation leads to false generalizations and stereotyping, which in turn can lead to tension and conflict. While there are important general differences between groups, applying cultural generalizations to individuals is stereotyping, and it greatly limits views of variability within a cultural group. Negative stereotypes are especially damaging to groups that are working to build their place within a society. The media also exacerbate stereotypes in their portrayals of members of various ethnic groups.[13]

Metastereotyping is the kind of stereotyping that you believe other groups apply to your group.[14] As mentioned in chapter 2, our colleague, Roxanne Leppington, used videotape to help Jewish and Black members of her community overcome stereotypes. After each group viewed a tape of the other group, all parties then discussed the misconceptions that surfaced.

This exercise demonstrated that people must be careful not to attribute certain styles of communication to different cultural groups. In his cocultural theory, Mark Orbe identifies several factors that will influence how members of any cultural group will respond to other groups.[15] In addition to predominant cultural styles, people make choices about how to communicate based on their overall experience, the perceived costs and rewards of the interaction, their abilities, what they hope to achieve, and the situational context. As a result, there will be numerous and important differences in communication choices within any given cultural group.

Ideology and Moral Difference

Communities of people tend to share common ways of thinking based on certain assumptions about human experience. These are the basic ideas of life on which we rely and form our ideas about "common sense." The more we act on our beliefs, the more real they seem, and the more real they become, the more we want to act on them, sometimes establishing hardened categories of right and wrong. This core of belief forms an ideology or moral order that gives shared meaning to the experience of a group. The problem is that one group's truth is another's folly. In other words, communities of human beings—whether ethnic, political, religious, or national—often have drastically different worldviews that lead to different assumptions about what is right and good; these views often clash. These ideological differences form the basis for the most serious and intractable conflicts across the globe.[16]

Examples of persistent moral clash are all around us. Among the most prominent issues in the United States right now are stem cell research, gay marriage, and drilling for oil in the Arctic National Wildlife Refuge. On the surface, these may look like ordinary policy debates, but each is really a struggle between very different views of humanity, society, and environment. Proponents cannot make sense of one another's arguments because they do not agree on fundamental moral assumptions. Moral conflict is as fascinating as it is serious, and we return to this subject in the final chapter of this book.

GLOBAL WAR AND PEACE

Ideas Matter

If you were asked to describe the world, you would probably speak in terms of nations and international relations. Many generations have lived in a world characterized exactly this way. The most basic political unit is the nation. This idea is so strongly held that we can hardly imagine another kind of world.

Yet this was not always the case. Prior to the seventeenth century, the world was divided into loose empires, kingdoms, principalities, tribes, religious states, colonies, and small semi-independent clusters. Some regional states such as England and France approximated what we think of as a nation today, but most of the world really did not fit this mold. The political field was fluid, ambiguous, and not governed very much by geographical boundaries. People didn't think of themselves as British, French, or German. Instead, they would give an ethnic identity, a tribal affiliation, the name of their prince, or perhaps their religion. Indeed, after the Reformation, religious divisions became especially important in Europe, as people increasingly identified themselves as Protestant or Catholic.

Largely because of the Protestant–Catholic division, a devastating war broke out in Europe in the seventeenth century. The Thirty Year War was a watershed in how we think about the political organization of the world. The Peace of Westphalia, which ended the war, became a symbol for this shift in thinking. After years of negotiation about how best to organize Europe, Westphalia's contribution to political organization was the drawing of boundaries around what we today call *nation states*. Earnest diplomats, who genuinely wanted peace, socially constructed a new idea—the idea of the sovereign nation.

The idea of independent nations with geographical boundaries changed the international system dramatically. The world (as Westerners knew it) was now a set of autonomous, sovereign nations, no longer organized or governed by larger collectivities such as empires. Prior to Westphalia, an emperor, pope, or king might mediate among and even regulate the various political entities loosely affiliated under his reign. After Westphalia, each nation was on its own in an anarchic world with no central authority. Of course, empires did continue, but these were now nationally controlled empires, designed to expand the borders and the economic base of nations vis-à-vis other nations. Westphalia did not end war, but it changed the character of war.

Why is this little history lesson important in a book on communication and conflict? Our whole thinking about war and peace today is based on certain assumptions about how the world is organized. For 400 years we have thought of war primarily as a measure taken by nations to protect themselves against other nations. This is a powerful idea that, solidly reproduced for four centuries, is seemingly intractable. In this way of thinking, the system of sovereign states seems to have a life of its own.

According to classical international relations theory, nations act like individuals to protect themselves in a threatening world. Like citizens of the Old West, they do this by carrying weapons, killing others who might try to kill them, and forming gangs in which members protect one another. In a like manner, nations build arms, form alliances, capture land and resources, and fortify their borders. Most of the time, the system works, and nations live in relative peace. Nations are usually not at war. The problem is that the wars that do occur are so devastating and damaging to the human condition that they capture our hearts and minds and set the world on an eternal quest for peace.

The Kantian Ideal

How can peace be achieved in the Westphalian world? In his treatise *Perpetual Peace* written in 1795, Immanuel Kant proposed a three-pronged approach to peace among nations.[17] The pillars are (1) interdependence, (2) international organizations, and (3) democratic government. In other words, democratic nations that rely on one another and make opportunities to talk among themselves will rarely experience war. The Kantian ideal is more than a state of affairs; it is a set of ideas about how the world might be a better place. As we learned earlier in the chapter, they set the stage for a shift from seeing other nations as enemies or rivals to seeing them as friends.

These ideas have been tested over time, and they seem to hold significant promise as a basis for international peace.[18] They are like a three-legged stool, each necessary to prevent war. First, if nations are interdependent, it doesn't make sense for them to destroy one another. Second, if they join together into international organizations, they will have forums in which their representatives can talk, negotiate, and work through differences in a peaceful manner. The third leg is democracy, or representative government, in which citizens have a voice in the rules that govern them. Democracies rarely war against one another. One reason may be that democracy comes with a certain set of egalitarian values that do not accommodate war very easily. When countries share these values, they are not apt to attack one another. A more pragmatic reason is that democracy includes checks and balances that make war harder to wage.

Is International War Obsolete? The field of international relations has for many years been dominated by the idea, described above, that the world is an anarchic system of sovereign states struggling to protect their own interests; and yet, current events seem to be shaking these assumptions. Like the citizens of seventeenth-century Europe, we now face new challenges that require leaders to rethink their ideas about political organization. Ethnic wars, terrorism, and globalization, all of which defy national boundaries, are forcing us to think differently about global conflict. The breakup of fused nations such as the Soviet Union and Yugoslavia into regional ethnic states and the end of the Cold War are forcing us to create new ideas about war and peace. Actually, we can be guardedly optimistic about regional and international conflict. In the early 2000s, the number of armed conflicts reached its lowest point in 30 years. Still, some 22 countries in 2004 were engaged in violent conflict, and most of these were not international, but internal.[19]

You can still find examples of international war, but it is actually relatively uncommon these days. Instead, we see numerous civil wars, ethnic conflicts, terrorist acts, insurgencies, tribal warfare, and regional skirmishes. The real threat to peace does not seem to be international war, but strife between smaller, subnational and international groups. Many now believe that large global military capability is obsolete and must be replaced with a different kind of force, designed to keep the peace rather than win big wars.[20]

Bigger Threats. Although international war may no longer be the threat it used to be, we face other significant challenges to global security, the most important of which are the proliferation of nuclear weapons and global terrorism, a toxic combination. The end of the Cold War provided relief from the fear of mutual assured destruction in a bipolar world, but it brought with it increased dangers of the spread of nuclear materials, devices, and knowledge to nations and subnational groups. Global nuclear destruction is unlikely, but regional nuclear war is becoming an increasingly serious worry, especially with new member-ship in the international nuclear club. At the time of this writing, nine nations now have nuclear weapons (if you count Korea), and Iran seems to be working hard to get them. At the same time, however, the world at large is working to reduce this threat.

The second associated global threat today is international terror-ism, which, with the use of the suicide bomber, has changed the assumptions we make about how to make war. A generally accepted set of principles in response to the terrible combination of terrorism and weapons of mass destruction is: (1) no loose nukes; (2) no nascent nukes; and (3) no new nuclear weapons states.[21] From a communica-tion perspective, how does the world actually accomplish these goals? Implementation will be difficult and necessitate the hard work of pol-icy makers, diplomats, and technologists worldwide.

The Nuclear Non-Proliferation Treaty (NPT), now signed by 185 nations, makes three promises: (1) Nations that do not have nuclear weapons programs promise not to start them. (2) Nations that have nuclear weapons programs, but not yet weapons, promise to discon-tinue their programs. (3) Nations that have nuclear weapons promise to disarm. Actually, there has been substantial progress in the first two of these promises, and the NPT remains an important tool to mitigate the threat of nuclear war.

From Harm to Value: Peacebuilding Processes

As noted above, most war-torn areas of the world are subnational and regional, and many of the difficulties stem from years of conflict between various groups. Such conflicts are intractable and pernicious because of generations of lost trust, mutual hatred, polarization, and physical separation—all of which minimize opportunities to change fundamental relationships between warring parties.[22] At the same time, a great deal of peace work has been conducted, often with impressive results. Four processes are commonly used to help con-flicting groups move from harm toward value:[23]

1. *Preventative diplomacy*—Use of negotiation and other forms of nonviolent communication to prevent hostility, limit conflict, or keep violence from spreading.

2. *Peacemaking*—Negotiating cease-fires and peace agreements.

3. *Peacekeeping*—Use of armed forces to prevent hostilities from breaking out among conflicting groups.

4. *Peacebuilding*—Broad scale action to increase communication, reduce prejudice, and eliminate the conditions leading to vio-lent conflict.

War and conflict can be ended, but enduring peace must be built through sustained work. The peace-building metaphor, then, implies ongoing effort in many areas, not only to eliminate hostility, but to build the kind of intergroup relationships that are necessary to maintain true peace.

The term *peacebuilding* was introduce by Johan Galtung in the 1970s, and was quickly popularized through its subsequent use by the United Nations.[24] Today, peacebuilding involves institution building, political transformation, economic improvement, and reconciliation in order to create stability and prevent new violent disputes.[25] These broad elements of peace must be created in small segments of action taken by individuals and groups over time. In most cases, this means engaging potential enemies in various forms of dialogue that open channels of communication, build trust, facilitate the search for mutually acceptable solutions, and enable conflicting parties to manage their differences nonviolently.[26] Let's look at one example of the kind of interpersonal action necessary to help build peace.

Between 1999 and 2003, violent conflict erupted in the provinces of Maluku in Indonesia. For many years, Maluku was held up as a model of Christian–Muslim tolerance, but tensions lying beneath the surface worsened through the 1990s. The situation exploded in 1999, when two young men—a Muslim and a Christian—got into a fight in a bus station in the capital of Central Maluku. Within weeks, violence spread throughout the region resulting in widespread destruction, perhaps 6,000 deaths, and maybe a half million internal refugees. Through determined effort to restore order, the hostilities died down, and peacemaking activities began.

One of several international nongovernmental organizations working in the region—the International Catholic Migration Commission (ICMC)—began sponsoring village meetings to bring community members and leaders together to discuss how their communities might be rebuilt. We were invited to go to Indonesia and work with the ICMC on a dialogue institute funded by the U.S. Institute for Peace, where 40 Muslim and Christian village leaders from one of the largest islands in the region would meet to talk about their differences and their shared concerns.[27] At the institute, participants embraced dialogue as a means to identify common values, rebuild relationships, and affirm the values of religious difference. They rediscovered their historical "blood brotherhood" that could transcend other differences and make it possible to construct communities across religious lines. One event such as this will not rebuild the peace, but many processes and opportunities for positive action can contribute to what Jean Paul Lederach calls "a transformative platform," or "ongoing social and relational spaces . . . [that] generate responsive initiatives for constructive change."[28]

Although peacebuilding can consist of many kinds of action, we concentrate here on the communication dimensions of peacebuilding. As a group, these communication processes involve dialogue, and several models have been created over the years.[29]

Problem-Solving Workshops.   Created by John Burton, an Australian diplomat, problem-solving workshops invite representatives to clarify the problems causing the conflict and to explore possible solutions.[30] These workshops are often "academic" in orientation, which provides a different look and feel that may make productive dialogue possible. Participants are encouraged to think in new ways and to avoid reiterating their already often entrenched positions on the issues. Using "controlled communication," Burton and his colleagues begin by having parties identify their perceptions and misperceptions and suggest new ways of thinking about the issues. Such forums can help to create positive conditions for more formal negotiations.

Human Relations Groups.   A group of processes that rely on the emotional connection among participants have been tried in many venues. Primarily psychological in orientation, these processes bring erstwhile enemies together to explore feelings and perceptions about themselves, one another, and the situations in which they find themselves. Although several psychiatrists and psychologists have contributed to this movement, perhaps the best known is social psychologist Leonard Doob.[31] Doob and his colleagues used a sensitivity training model that emphasized constructive communication among participants.

The ARIA Process.   Developed by Jay Rothman to address particularly intractable, identity-based conflicts, ARIA stands for the four primary steps in the dialogue process: (1) antagonism, (2) resonance,

(3) invention, and (4) action.[32] During the antagonism stage, participants expose and explore their fight. This can be important for helping participants realize that they are tired of the seemingly irreversible pattern of conflict. The second stage—resonance—involves a deep exploration of the parties' basic needs and values, and the third—inventing—includes brainstorming options for working the problem through. Finally, in the fourth—action—stage, participants create actual plans for implementing solutions.

Track-Two Diplomacy. Joseph Montville, a former U.S. diplomat, coined this term to designate unofficial and informal dialogues among citizens who are members of adversary groups.[33] Unlike official, or "track-one" diplomacy, in which top-level leaders and/or negotiators work to solve conflicts, participants in track-two processes represent lower levels. Track-two work is important in peacebuilding because it can help to develop strategy, change public opinion, and build relationships.

We saw the power of track-two diplomacy when we were facilitating a peace conference in Sri Lanka, where young conference participants representing India and Pakistan, then on the verge of war, got together and wrote their own peace treaty, vowing friendship between them despite the saber rattling (or, more accurately, nuclear weapons rattling) of their respective national leaders. The idea of track-two has been expanded now to "multitrack diplomacy," involving many processes of interaction including citizen problem solving, educational exchange, and even cooperative business ventures.[34]

Sustained Dialogue. Harold H. Saunders, former Assistant Secretary of State, became convinced that peacebuilding requires "a systematic, prolonged dialogue among small groups of representative citizens committed to changing conflicted relationships, ending conflict and building peace."[35] Such dialogues consist of five phases: (1) defining the problem, (2) mapping the issues, (3) developing commitment to change, (4) building scenarios for a peaceful future, and (5) implementing agreements.

Each of these formats has been used successfully around the world in a variety of conflict situations. You can see that they overlap and share many of the same methods. In one way or another, all of them feature real citizens talking constructively across a divide to help bring peace to the region. As a group, we refer to these processes as *dialogue.* Dialogue has much potential for transforming and transcending difficult conflicts, and we devote chapter 10 to this topic.

HOW YOU CAN USE THIS CHAPTER

World conflicts have devastating effects on the lives of human beings. The human condition is marked and marred by violent conflict. Although most us will not be directly involved in resolving global conflicts, we need to understand them and to have a grasp of ways in which leaders and diplomats work to manage and contain such conflicts. If you take a stand in favor of a particular war, attempts to end war, or peace in general, you had better understand what you are talking about. This chapter can be useful toward that end.

1. Violence and attempts to stem violence are caused not by abstract nation states, international organizations, or subnational organizations, but human beings in interaction with one another. The principle remains the same whether we are experiencing conflict interpersonally or internationally: If you want to change the worlds you make, change the kinds of interaction that occurs.

2. Think about how you frame, or understand, the other. We will orient differently to other groups depending on whether we see them as enemies, rivals, or friends.

3. In international relations, adopt the Kantian ideal: interdependence, direct communication, and democracy.

4. Pay close attention to international nuclear security and follow the goals of no nascent nukes and no new nuclear states.

5. Worldwide personal dialogue across ethnic, national, and ideological lines is vital. Work to establish and maintain these kinds of efforts.

Interactive Case Study

THE GLOBAL SCALE

Context: Differences that exist on a national, ethnic, and ideological dimension have a larger order of magnitude but can still be addressed with constructive communication practices and dedication to bringing the differences into the sphere of value.

Opening Exercise(s): Students will work in small groups. A computer with access to the Internet will be needed for this exercise. Each group will find a conflict that is occurring (or has occurred) on a global scale. The group should do a Web search, using terms such as "global conflict," "international conflict," ethnic war," "moral conflict," or "religious war." When you find a suitable case for study, identify the differing "interest groups" that comprise the conflict. Divide them among the four of you. It might turn out that two of you are on one side and two on the other, or all members of the group may hold one view that is part of the conflict. Each of you should research the perspective you represent and become familiar with its interests, demands, and experiences.

Focus #1: Intergroup Relations

Each group will hold a discussion about their conflict. How would you characterize the intergroup relations? How have the relationships been defined? What has the group(s) experienced as a result of these definitions?

Focus #2: Metastereotyping

Each interest group (subgroups) should find a private place to consider the following question: *What do the other groups think of you? What stereotypes do they have of you?* After you have discussed these questions, get together and share the results with your small group. Were there any surprises? Were there any misperceptions?

Focus #3: The Kantian Ideal

Have a group discussion about the conflict you are facing. When considering the three-pronged approach to peace, discuss whether any of these prongs exists within your global conflict or within any of your interest groups.

Focus #4: Peacebuilding Processes

Your group will now do some planning to mitigate the harm that is resulting from your differences. You will work together as a group to plan a strategy to move forward together. Choose one of the processes and create the plan. You may need Internet or library research to find actual examples of steps and activities that were used. After you have chosen and researched a process, map out the strategy, complete with the time frame, the activities that will take place, the people who will be involved, and the outcome you hope will be achieved for each stage.

Focus #5: Moving the World into the Sphere of Value

The final exercise will be a full class meeting. Outside "observers" who were not involved in the research would add an interesting perspective as they listen to the strategies for ending global conflicts (perhaps the instructor and a couple of his/her colleagues). Each group will present the global conflict they have been addressing, the different interest groups represented, and the strategy for moving toward the sphere of value. After all the presentations, the observers can reflect: *What commonalities did you hear in the strategies for ending the conflict? What hope do these plans give you? What needs to happen for these strategies to be enacted?*

Endnotes

[1] Alexander Wendt, *Social Theory of International Politics* (Cambridge: Cambridge University Press, 1999).

[2] Thomas Hobbes, *Leviathan* (Oxford: Blackwell, 1946).

[3] John Locke, *Second Treatise of Government* (Indianapolis, IN: Hacket Publishing, 1980).

[4] Immanuel Kant, *Perpetual Peace: A Philosophical Sketch*, reprinted in *Kant's Political Writings*, ed. Hans Reiss (Cambridge: Cambridge University Press, 1970).

[5] Mary Jane Collier, "Conflict Competence within African, Mexican, and Anglo-American Friendships," in *Cross-cultural Interpersonal Communication*, eds. Stella Ting-Toomey and Felipe Korzenny (Newbury Park, CA: Sage, 1991), pp. 132–154.

[6] Stella Ting-Toomey and John G. Oetzel, *Managing Intercultural Conflict Effectively* (Thousand Oaks, CA: Sage, 2001); Mark P. Orbe and Tina M. Harris, *Interracial Communication: Theory into Practice* (Belmont, CA: Wadsworth, 2001); Mark P. Orbe and Melodi A. Everett, "Interracial and Interethnic Conflict and Communication in the United States," in *The Sage Handbook of Conflict Communication: Integrating Theory, Research, and Practice*, eds. John G. Oetzel and Stella Ting-Toomey (Thousand Oaks, CA: Sage, 2006), pp. 575–594.

[7] Walter G. Stephan and Cookie W. Stephan, *Improving Intergroup Relations* (Thousand Oaks, CA: Sage, 2001).

[8] Hemant Shah and Michael C. Thornton, "Racial Ideology in U.S. Mainstream News Magazine Coverage of Black-Latino Interaction, 1980–1992," *Critical Studies in Mass Communication*, 11 (1994): 141–161; Orbe and Harris, *Interracial Communication*.

[9] Moon H. Jo, "Korean Merchants in the Black Community: Prejudice among the Victims of Prejudice," *Ethnic and Racial Studies*, 15 (1992): 395–411.

[10] Stella Ting-Toomey and Jiro Takai, "Explaining Intercultural Conflict: Promising Approaches and Directions," in *The Sage Handbook of Conflict Communication: Integrating Theory, Research, and Practice*, eds. John G. Oetzel and Stella Ting-Toomey (Thousand Oaks, CA: Sage, 2006), pp. 691–724; Judee K. Burgoon and Amy Ebesu Hubbard, "Cross-cultural and Intercultural Applications of Expectancy Violations and Interaction Adaptation Theory," in *Theorizing about Intercultural Communication*, ed. W. B. Gudykunst (Thousand Oaks, CA: Sage, 2005), pp. 149–171.

[11] Harry Waters, "Race, Culture, and Interpersonal Conflict," *International Journal of Intercultural Relations*, 16 (1992): 437–454.

[12] J. Eric Oliver and Janelle Wong, "Intergroup Prejudice in Multiethnic Settings," *American Journal of Political Science*, 4 (2003): 567–582.

[13] Mark P. Orbe, Kiesha T. Warren, and Nancy C. Cornwell, "Negotiating Societal Stereotypes: Analyzing *The Real World* Discourse by and about African-American Men," in *Constituting Cultural Difference through Discourse*, ed. M. J. Collier (Thousand Oaks, CA: Sage, 2001), pp. 107–134.

[14] Lee Sigelman and Steven A. Tuch, "Metastereotypes: Blacks' Perceptions of Whites' Stereotypes of Blacks," *Public Opinion Quarterly*, 61 (1997): 87–101.

[15] Mark P. Orbe, *Constructing Co-Cultural Theory: An Explication of Culture, Power, and Communication* (Thousand Oaks, CA: Sage, 1998); Orbe and Everett, "Interracial and Interethnic."

[16] W. Barnett Pearce and Stephen W. Littlejohn, *Moral Conflict: When Social Worlds Collide* (Thousand Oaks, CA: Sage, 1997); Jayne S. Docherty, *Learning Lessons from Waco: When the Parties Bring Their Gods to the Negotiation Table* (Syracuse, NY: Syracuse University Press, 2001); Stephen W. Littlejohn, "Moral Conflict," in *The Sage Handbook of Conflict Communication: Integrating Theory, Research, and Practice*, eds. John G. Oetzel and Stella Ting-Toomey (Thousand Oaks, CA: Sage, 2006), pp. 395–418.

[17] Kant, *Perpetual Peace*.

[18] Bruce Russett and John Oneal, *Triangulating Peace: Democracy, Interdependence, and International Organizations* (New York: W. W. Norton, 2001).

[19] Benjamin J. Broome and Ann-Sofi Jakobsson Hatay, "Building Peace in Divided Societies: The Role of Intergroup Dialogue," in *The Sage Handbook of Conflict Commu-*

nication: Integrating Theory, Research, and Practice, eds. John G. Oetzel and Stella Ting-Toomey (Thousand Oaks, CA: Sage, 2006), pp. 627–664.

20 Thomas P. M. Barnett, *The Pentagon's New Map: War and Peace in the Twenty-First Century* (New York: G. P. Putnam's Sons, 2004).

21 Graham Allison, *Nuclear Terrorism: The Ultimate Preventable Catastrophe* (New York: Times Books, 2004).

22 Broome and Hatay, "Building Peace."

23 Boutros Boutros-Ghali, *Agenda for Peace* (New York: United Nations Publications, 1995).

24 Johan Galtung, "Three Approaches to Peace," in *Essays in Peace Research, Volume 1*, ed. J. Galtung (Copenhagen: Christian Eljers, 1975), pp. 282–304.

25 Eva Bertram, "Reinventing Governments: The Promise and Perils of United Nations Peace Building," *Journal of Conflict Resolution*, 39 (1995): 387–418; Ann-Sofi Jakobsson Hatay, *Peacebuilding and Reconciliation in Bosnia and Herzegovina, Kosovo and Macedonia, 1995–2004* (Uppsala, Sweden: Uppsala Department of Peace and Conflict Research, 2005); Roland Paris, *At War's End: Building Peace after Civil Conflict* (Cambridge: Cambridge University Press, 2004).

26 Broome and Hatay, "Building Peace."

27 Carmen Lowry and Stephen Littlejohn, "Dialogue and the Discourse of Peacebuilding in Maluku, Indonesia," *Conflict Resolution Quarterly*, in press.

28 Jean Paul Lederach, *The Moral Imagination: The Art and Soul of Building Peace* (Oxford: Oxford University Press, 2005), p. 47.

29 Broome and Hatay, "Building Peace."

30 John W. Burton, *Conflict and Communication: The Use of Controlled Communication in International Relations* (London: Macmillan, 1969).

31 Leonard W. Doob, *The Pursuit of Peace* (Westport, CT: Greenwood Press, 1981).

32 Jay Rothman, *Resolving Identity-Based Conflict in Nations, Organizations, and Communities* (San Francisco: Jossey-Bass, 1997).

33 Joseph V. Montville and Diane B. Bendahmane, eds., *Conflict Resolution: Track Two Diplomacy* (Washington, DC: Foreign Service Institute, Department of State, 1987).

34 Louise Diamond and John McDonald, *Multi-track Diplomacy: A Systems Approach to Peace* (Bloomfield, CT: Kumarian Press, 1996).

35 Harold H. Saunders, *A Public Peace Process: Sustained Dialogue to Transform Racial and Ethnic Conflicts* (New York: St. Martin's Press, 1999), p. 12.

PART THREE

KEEPING DIFFERENCES
AFFIRMATIVE

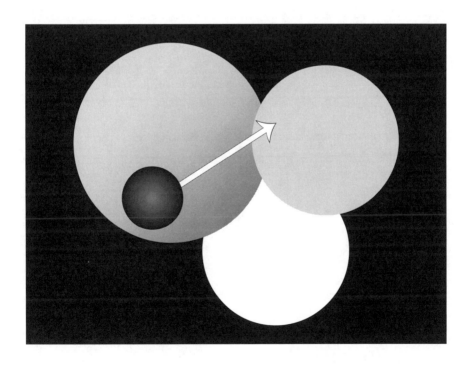

10

Transcendence
and Transformation

Over the years we've encountered innumerable intractable patterns of conflict that are seemingly impossible to manage.[1] When conflicts reach this point, they almost always reside in the sphere of harm, which makes the search for alternative forms of communication imperative. Parties engaged in difficult conflicts tend to be stuck in particular patterns of interaction that require them to rethink the ways in which they communicate with one another. New patterns of communication that can *transcend* the stuck pattern and *transform* the relationship are necessary for movement toward the sphere of value.

Most of the time people find acceptable and effective ways to manage their differences. They may use simple persuasion to influence one another. Often they negotiate solutions, and sometimes they just agree to disagree and learn to live with the conflict. Too often, however, people get enmeshed in situations that plague them for a long time and do great damage.

Such conflicts might be related to moral differences, such as that between the Branch Davidians and federal officers in Waco, Texas (chapter 5); ethnic, cultural, or religious differences, such as those that occurred in Maluku, Indonesia (chapter 9); or even historically entrenched interest clashes, such as those in the Middle East. Although many difficult conflicts do occur on the international scene, they can also occur in families, communities, and organizations. This chapter is devoted to discussing ways in which frustrating and harmful patterns can be overcome and even prevented.

TRANSCENDING CLASH

Harsh conflict makes productive communication difficult. When conversation with an adversary quickly becomes hostile, people have a hard time thinking of new ways to talk about tough issues. They fall back on old patterns of argument, repeat the same points endlessly, strike out against the other in a verbal assault, or—worse—move from words to "sticks and stones." Because direct communication is uncomfortable to many people, they opt for avoidance. If you ask people why they are not talking to the people with whom they have an unresolved issue, they will probably tell you that they have nothing to say or learn from "people like that."

Finding a Path to Productive Talk: The Learning Conversation

How do we come to a new understanding of what we are doing when we interact with enemies and rivals? Can such interactions be framed differently? Is it possible to think about these sorts of conversations in more productive ways? Many groups are dedicated to creating forms of communication that, though they may not resolve the conflict, move the discussion to a new, more productive plane. We like to think of these as "learning conversations," opportunities to learn significant new things about yourself, others, and the issue at hand. Learning conversations can accomplish a number of things.[2]

First, learning conversations open up new topics of conversation that can transcend difference. This does not mean that differences are erased or minimized. Indeed, they are often acknowledged, though they may eventually be understood differently than they were before. Second, learning conversations can change the relationship from adversarial to exploratory. Here parties come to think of one another differently and they join together, even if only temporarily, into an inquiry or quest for new ways of thinking about their differences. Finally, learning conversations create opportunities to discuss the powers and limits of a variety of perspectives on the issues they are facing. They can reveal and expose what each point of view might be able to achieve as well as what each cannot do.

William Gattis brought a number of members of the United Methodist Church together to talk about the issue of homosexuality, which is quite divisive within the Methodist community. Instead of arguing whether the church should accept homosexuality, participants were asked to do something else: "Learn all you can from others about the points of view with which you disagree . . . compare and contrast your own point of view with the viewpoint of others . . . [and] compare and contrast the strengths and weaknesses of each point of view."[3] Because the participants were willing to engage in these dialogues, they were successful in turning an otherwise contentious situation into a learning conversation.

Participants in learning conversations can also look for joining places, or common threads, they might explore to learn more, expand their awareness of options, and widen their perspective on the issues at hand. Nola Heidlebaugh says that dialogue is like weaving two very different fabrics together.[4] You don't just lay them side-by-side and sew them together; instead, you find loose spots where individual threads can be woven together to create a common place. This new common place is not the same thing as common ground or shared opinion but new possibilities for joint exploration and new knowledge. For example, you might disagree adamantly about abortion, but you could share an awareness of the impact of one's personal experience on this issue and recognition of gray areas that neither pro-life nor pro-choice advocates can explain away.

Box 10.1

Heidlebaugh uses the metaphor of weaving. Think of two or three other metaphors that could help students understand a learning conversation. What would these metaphors be like in real life?

We know that liberals and conservatives will clash on many economic, political, and social issues, but what could they talk about in a learning conversation? Could the nature of the interaction change if new common places were created for such a conversation? The key would be to reframe the issues, to think in terms of new categories on which constructive discussion might occur, including, for instance, compassion, community, reference, diversity, justice, and courage.[5] When you cut the issues in new ways, patterns of interaction will change, and transcendence can occur. This is what the creation and exploration of new common places is all about.

Two keys are needed to unlock the door between destructive interaction and productive dialogue. These are careful attention to *process* and creative management of *context*. In other words, we want to be very deliberate about *how* we talk with one another, and we want to select the subject matter that best affords an opportunity for transcendence and transformation.

Managing Process

When most people engage in a difficult conversation, they concentrate on the issues, their opinions, their goals, and what they want to be heard. These are normal and important concerns, and disputants *should* be thinking about these things. At the same time, however, process is vital, and parties to a conflict should think about *how* they want to have challenging conversations. One of the best reasons to use a mediator or facilitator when issues are contentious is that third parties can help structure the process.

When we talk to clients in our own practice about planning a meeting, a mediation, or a dialogue on issues of concern—whether conflict is present or not—we always invite them to collaborate on designing a process that is as comfortable and productive as possible under the circumstances. If we get bogged down in a moment of tension and unproductive interaction, as facilitators, we may stop the meeting and ask whether the process is working and how the tenor of the conversation might change in order to build a higher level of comfort and a more constructive tone. The whole purpose of ground rules or guidelines is to help structure the process so that it can achieve these ideals.

The Public Conversations Project (PCP), based in Cambridge, Massachusetts, is a leader in dialogue on difficult issues.[6] Among other things, the PCP has sponsored dialogue sessions on abortion, in which pro-life and pro-choice advocates come together to have a "new kind of conversation" on this issue. The group has been successful in large measure because of their careful attention to process. As family therapists, the PCP facilitators knew that people could not have a productive conversation about this issue without setting up a safe environment and constructive process. The Public Conversations Project typically does several things:

- They contact clients in advance to invite them into a new kind of conversation and discuss their concerns and ideas about how to do it.
- They negotiate ground rules that help to keep the conversation safe.
- They carefully structure the agenda so that participants are invited to address a series of questions that enable them to (1) share their personal experiences, (2) learn about the complexity of the issue, (3) discover important new things about one another, (4) abandon a polarized stance, (5) build curiosity about other people and about the issue, and (6) come to respect people who hold very different positions on the issue.
- They emphasize listening and provide opportunities for people to speak without being interrupted.
- They keep conversations private and safe in order to allow participants to take risks and to explore ideas without the threat of personal recrimination.

- They take time for participants to get to know one another as persons and to explore the issue creatively and constructively.

Good process matters whether the group is experiencing an open conflict or not. Even when a group anticipates challenging differences, they can actively think about how to structure the process to keep communication productive and to avoid open, ugly clash. Each group will be different, and each will require a somewhat different process. In general, several sensibilities can help guide process design work: affirmation, empowerment, connection, inclusion, inquiry, and creativity.[7]

Affirmation. The sensibility of affirmation is the belief in possibilities and faith that participants will have positive resources to engage in constructive communication. Affirmation tunes into opportunities to explore and make use of previous successes, visions, values, and good will. It allows participants to think about what they appreciate in themselves, others, and in the situation.[8] The spirit of affirmation does not mean that we ignore, or even minimize, problems and concerns—only that we are willing to move beyond them to look for forces that can transcend hostility, rigidity, and polarity.

Sometimes people are willing to be affirmative from the beginning—especially when an open conflict has not yet erupted. People may also be willing to express affirmation late in a conflict cycle, when they are fatigued and ready to move to a more positive place. However, disputants in hard conflicts are not usually ready to be affirmative. Participants may feel cheated if they do not have an opportunity to vent, to express strong emotion, to share their worries and anger. The process may permit or even invite this within a safe environment, but will not stop there. As soon as possible, good dialogue processes mine the positive visions lying below complaints and problems, explore stories of success, and seek out common values and interests. We like to call this the "wisdom in the whining," which means that complaints always contain a more positive vision of how things might be. If you are upset that you are not getting your mail every day, you must value prompt service; if you are tired of a coworker's radio, you must value peace and quiet; and if you wish your pastor were a better preacher, you must desire to be engaged, inspired, and spiritually awakened in worship. Each negative complaint has a "positive shadow," and an affirmative sensibility will lead process designers to think creatively about ways to bring this out.

We were once called in to work with a highly conflicted nursing department in a local hospital. When we talked to them individually, the nurses expressed extreme anger and disappointment with one another. They were unable to interact professionally and had completely lost respect for one another. We had originally intended to conduct individual mediations among these coworkers, but it was clear to us that they would be unable to talk constructively in mediation sessions. We realized that as a group, they would first need an opportunity to hear new kinds of things from one another and to begin to build a positive base for conflict resolution.

We invited the nurses to have a facilitated meeting to begin communicating in a new way. Using a strong set of ground rules, we started by asking them, one at a time, to share a story about a time in their careers in which they felt affirmed, strengthened, encouraged, and effective. During this go-round, the coworkers were able to talk about their careers in positive terms without having to worry about being interrupted, refuted, or ignored. They were free to talk about positive rather than negative stories, which was an entirely new pattern for them. In the next round, we asked them to indicate what changes would be necessary in the workplace to make it possible for them to do their jobs effectively. A rule used during this round was that they could not refer to other members of the group, but had to think of the workplace as a whole. We then asked each person to indicate how they thought the group could work together in a way that would integrate a diversity of personalities and styles. Once we gave the participants a chance to address these questions, we invited them to ask questions of curiosity to one another, to learn more and to understand their respective experiences more completely. Again, we followed a set of ground rules to make sure that people did not use their questions as a form of attack, defense, or posturing. This turned out to be an effective dialogue process for this group, and they began to build some trust. It did not solve their issues, but it did make it possible for them to move on to private mediations where they could address specific workplace issues in a safe, private environment.

Empowerment. A process that enables participants to express what is most important to them and to do so in a way that can be heard by others empowers them. Empowerment means finding the means by which individuals can use their own sources of power—their own best forms of expression—to "say" what they have experienced, what they think, how they feel, what they want, and what matters most to them. Unbridled expression may allow one person to be clear, while stomping on others' abilities to do the same. For this reason, the process must be one that permits both expression and reception—talking and listening. You are not empowered if others cannot hear or appreciate what you have to say. In process design, empowerment may require a variety of things:

- You may need to include opportunities for different forms of expression. Not everyone is empowered by speech. In fact, reticent individuals may find "talking," especially in large groups, intimidating.

- You may have to pay attention to potential problems of domination in which certain individuals will want to "set the agenda" or lead the course of the discussion, which can derail attempts to allow everyone the freedom to establish what is important to them.

- You may need to build in a variety of "venues" or structures of dialogue, including, for example, individual writing, dyads, small groups, and large groups.

- Participants may need to have opportunities to revisit and reconsider their ideas, to reality test their ideas, and to change their minds.

- The process may need to include opportunities to get information and increase knowledge.

- A detailed agenda and focus for discussion can be empowering because it enables people to think clearly about various issues and to clarify what is important.

An effective tool for empowerment that we learned from the Public Conversations Project is the "go-round." Using this technique, participants in a dialogue group each take a turn to talk about their experience or to address a question without interruption. The go-round is a listening exercise, in which the goal is to express and hear what is important to each person without formulating a response, answer, or rebuttal to what he or she has to say. All participants are asked to prepare their presentation in advance. As a result, the go-round encourages listening; you are not rehearsing or planning your comments while others are speaking. And for those who may, for whatever reason, feel they do not want to contribute, a pass rule makes it possible to remain silent without question.

We recently facilitated a meeting of about 120 teachers at a local high school who were experiencing considerable strife among themselves and with the administration. We knew going in that emotions would run high and that some teachers would not feel safe to talk about the issues involved. Safety and empowerment would be key. In order to maximize empowerment, we did a variety of things:

1. We asked the administrators to be "keynote listeners" so that they would be in a new nondominating role and could hear clearly what was important to teachers. As keynote listeners, they participated by listening rather than speaking.

2. We gave participants individual writing time to think through what they wanted to say.

3. We had both small and large group discussions.

4. We had participants build a wall mural of issues of concern.

5. We gave out a form so that participants could write their responses if they felt they had something to say that was not heard.

6. We interviewed the keynote listeners (the administrators) at the end about what they heard the teachers say, what seemed most important to the teachers, and what the next steps should be.

Connection. Dialogue processes should enable participants to think beyond their individual needs and aims and to become conscious of a system of relationships. Our conflicts are made by social interaction between people, but disputants do not always realize or recognize this. Good dialogue processes help participants become aware of communication and connection and allow them to build on the new skills collaboratively.

Connection can be established by exploring common history, shared concerns, community values, or goals that require collaboration to achieve. *Timelining* is an interesting method for initiating connection. Members of a community or organization put a large piece of butcher paper on the wall with a line running horizontally down the middle and years placed at intervals along the line. They then put their names at the appropriate period in which they joined the group and talk a bit about what was going on in the organization or community at that time. The timeline goes beyond the current date into the future, and members can talk about what they would like to see happen with the group in coming years and decades. This is an excellent technique for building a common history and beginning to generate a common vision for the future.

One of the most common and effective methods for establishing connection is to help participants move from negotiating individual demands to framing and working together to solve a problem. This approach—integrative problem solving (also discussed in the appendix)—involves framing the issue as a problem, generating options for a solution, deliberating together, and making decisions about how to proceed. Families have this kind of dialogue from time to time. Instead of arguing about whether a sixteen year old can get a car, the family could discuss ways to meet everyone's transportation needs. Several options, including a car for the teen, can be weighed and discussed jointly. The car issue cannot adequately be discussed in isolation. Because family members are connected, their needs must be looked at together, and trade-offs may be necessary. If the teenager gets the car, his need for status and transportation will be satisfied, but the parents will have to sacrifice some money and perhaps a good deal of sleep.

If two workers were having a mediation over how to organize a storage room, the mediator might ask them who uses the room, who cares most about how it is organized, and who is most impacted by decisions related to storage and the way it is organized. The sensibility of connection raises the question of who should be at the table and involved in the dialogue. Which connections are most important and which relationships are most impacted by the discussion?

Inclusion. This sensibility honors the value of difference. We want processes that include a diversity of perspectives on the issues at hand. In certain cases, this means making sure that all stakeholder groups are represented at the table. Sometimes this is not possible, so we try to be as inclusive as we can. If it is not possible to have full inclusion at one event, perhaps multiple events will add diversity to the mix.

The spirit of inclusion is more than getting many people into the room. It also means designing processes by which different points of view can be heard, respected, and used as a basis for any action that might come out of the discussion. Inclusion and empowerment complement one another; they must exist side by side. Empowerment centers on what participants can contribute, and inclusion centers on what they can gain.

An attitude of inclusion alerts us to the need for diversity, but there are practical considerations that make it challenging. Certain parties may not be willing to participate in the dialogue. Certain participants may make other participants feel unsafe, endangering their sense of empowerment. The size of the group and/or resource constraints may make full inclusion impossible. In general, we use the following guidelines to make decisions about who should be involved in a process.

1. How many people can effectively engage in the process? Sometimes space, time, and money allow a few hundred people to participate, and other times only a small number of participants is possible.

2. Who has information, important perspectives, and ideas that would enhance the discussion?

3. Who are the most important stakeholders? In other words, who has the most to gain or lose from possible outcomes?

4. Who is involved in key relationships, and what relationships may need to be transformed?

5. Who would most benefit from the kinds of learning that will occur in the dialogue?

6. Who, if left out, might try to subvert the process?

When we are creating processes for conflict management, we try to be inclusive from the beginning. In a two-party mediation, we will ask the parties to talk about their needs and how best to approach the mediation. We may check with them at several points in the mediation about whether the process is working. If a small group is involved, we may interview everyone in advance to discover their process needs and to solicit process suggestions. In a larger group, community, or organization, we will work with a design team consisting of a diversity of representatives from the system.

We once facilitated a multistakeholder engagement process to plan improvements in information technology for the American Indian Higher Education Consortium (see chapter 11). The diverse design team worked for nearly a year, before and during the process, to make decisions about how to proceed. One of the most important questions was who should be included in the processes, and we spent considerable time on this issue. We knew that it would be fruitless to limit participation to the tribal colleges, so we expanded participation to include representatives from government, funding agencies, technology companies, tribal governments, the general public, and even international representatives of indigenous education systems abroad. Over the year, we worked with various size groups ranging from 40 to 150. Since then, we have worked at several individual tribal colleges facilitating strategic planning processes. When we do this, we want to make sure that faculty, students, administration, staff, board members, and community members are involved. In the best cases, the college will sponsor several planning meetings for particular stakeholder groups, so that each voice can be heard.

Inquiry. The spirit of inquiry leads us to think about the interaction differently. Instead of arguing, debating, pressuring, or winning and losing, we see ourselves as engaged in a process of mutual discovery. We shift from, "Who will prevail?" to, "What do we have to learn?" We shift from an "all-knowing" position to a "not-knowing" one. Instead of viewing communication as an opportunity to influence, we see it as the foundation for exploration, or "collective tinkering."[9]

You can tell that change is afoot when a mediator, after hearing long series of harangues, summarizes what each person has said and then says, "Okay, it is clear that you have very different opinions on this issue and that neither of you are really persuaded. What do you want to do about this?" This question invites the parties to shift gears and to think about discovering a new path. The same kind of shift can happen after the opening statements of an environmental negotiation, when the facilitator says, "Thank you for offering your initial perspectives and hopes. In order to move forward constructively, we will need a common body of information and facts. Let's talk about how to proceed with fact finding in a way that is acceptable to all of you."

As another example, consider the case of a young man who drops out of college during his junior year. His parents are furious. After having spent thousands of dollars on his education, they feel betrayed. Their natural response is to strike out: "What?! How can you do this?" and then to demean, "You unappreciative jerk . . . after all we have done for you!" The son's reply—if there is one—will be predictable: "Get off my back. You think that you control my life. Forget it, I don't want your money." This exchange will probably make relations a bit chilly for a few months (years?), but could be transformed into a very different kind of dialogue in which the parents eventually talk openly with their son about his frustrations, goals, hopes, and fears, and he opens up to their worries, experience, and ideas. Shifting from a polarized atmosphere of hostility, this family can move into a dialogue of inquiry—to learn from each other, to ask hard questions, and to explore important issues of life.

When we facilitated public engagement events on protection against mountain lions in Arizona (chapter 5), we knew the discussions could become quite contentious and heated. Some participants, such as foothills homeowners, would strongly favor removing, even killing, the lions in order to protect the residents. We knew that other stakeholders such as conservationists would favor protecting the animal and preventing developers from building homes so close to wild lands. Transforming the conversation from a debate into a mutual inquiry would be important. Instead of having participants stand up and give a series of speeches, which would almost certainly lead to arguments, we asked instead that they systematically explore in small groups various options for how the fish and game agency should respond when there were (1) sightings, (2) interactions, (3) threats, and (4) attacks. In other words, we tried to shift the process from one of contention to one of inquiry.

Creativity. Another factor that should be taken into consideration in process design is a creative sensibility, the understanding that there are no pat formulas or formats—that dialogue processes require creative thinking and adaptability. Good mediators and facilitators are creative, even imaginative, in how they think about process. Wise parents, smart managers, effective educators, and experienced diplomats maintain the same attitude: "Hmm, this is interesting. How can we

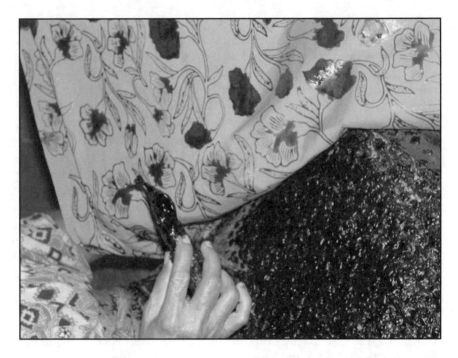

structure a process here that will be engaging, safe, constructive, and effective?" Barge says that community engagement processes require "capturing the imagination of participants, which involves creative events that inspire one's imaginative abilities."[10]

Creativity in design does not mean wild experimentation where anything goes. Participants as well as mediators and facilitators will have had experience with various processes that have worked in the past. They may need to explore new combinations or even construct new tools and techniques as needed. Design teams can be very helpful, in part because they expand the number of creative minds working to develop a process. We commonly train a design team in various standards, goals, and techniques for dialogue processes and then facilitate the team's creative discussion of how to design a particular upcoming event or events. Often this is an incremental process: The design team may put a macroprocess in place, establishing the stages or series of events to be conducted, and then after each stage more specifically design the process for the next stage.

Just thinking back on the many processes we have participated in designing, here is a list of some techniques we have used to (1) engage participants, (2) empower them, (3) bring out their best thinking, (4) use difference as a positive resource, and (5) break destructive patterns of interaction:

- Collaborative wall murals
- Fish-bowl interviews in which a small group is interviewed by the facilitator in a circle surrounded and observed by the larger group of participants.
- Participants interviewing one another
- Written forms and questionnaires
- Metaphors and stories
- Individually created posters
- Collaboratively created charts
- Creating newspaper headlines
- A dreamcatcher basket in which participants placed written hopes and dreams
- Honoring ideas on scrolls tied with ribbons
- Guided tours
- Native American dancing and prayers
- Songs and music

We could go on and on. We include this list just to illustrate how imagination can help when trying to achieve constructive communication, but we have to be careful here, because we don't want to give you the impression that dialogues are always just cute "techniques." They must be part of carefully crafted, purposeful, adapted, and effective overall processes for change in what often proves to be difficult conversations.

Process design, then, is an important element in helping parties to communicate in new ways. The second key to making such communication possible is setting the right context or focus for the discussion. What questions does the group address? How do they frame their issues, and how do they organize the topics they want to talk about? These are questions of context.

Finding the Best Context

The context is the topical frame for dialogue. It is the question that the group addresses. The context of discussion may be broad, narrow, wide-ranging, or quite focused. Constructive conversation depends in large measure on how the issue is framed. Individuals, groups, and organizations embroiled in conflict may find it unsafe to talk about allegations and hostilities, but it might be possible for them to talk about common values, goals, or future visions. It may be hard to talk about anger, hurt, and resentment, but easier to talk about personal experience. A community terrified about opening the subject of race relations may be able to explore "cultural richness." Concerns about

crime and violence may lock a group into certain ways of thinking
that are released and broadened when they shift the topic to "community safety."[11] An organization that is riddled with complaints about
unprofessional and disrespectful behavior may find it possible to
move forward by having a dialogue on how to make a productive and
comfortable work environment.

Once a topic becomes too dangerous to discuss—or too risky—it
becomes an "undiscussable issue." Issues can become undiscussable
when there is a strong history of hostility between the parties, disputants are unable to frame the issue in a way that will lead to any kind
of constructive conversation, the issue brings forth an unwanted
repetitive pattern that does damage, or the parties worry that discussing the issue will result in personal attack, misunderstanding, or loss
of face. Undiscussable issues also arise when the parties are so
entrenched in their own point of view that discussion of solutions
seems fruitless. Talking to the "other side" might even show some
level of weakness that disputants are not willing to admit. It is amazing how family, coworkers, and community members will tell you privately exactly what is bothering them but find it impossible to discuss
the problem with one another. Undiscussable issues signal a stuck
spot that must be transcended if parties are to move forward together.

Context Setting as Scoping. The metaphor of the scope, be it a
telescope or microscope, is helpful because it implies that a lens is
pointed at something. Just like a photographer looking for the right
frame, you can always "scope out" to a broader topic, "scope in" to a
narrower one, or "scope around" to different perspectives. When people were unable to talk about their views on abortion in any constructive way, the Public Conversations Project was able to help them *scope
in* to discuss the details of their experience. When community members were stuck on the issue of crime and violence, they found it helpful to *scope out* to the broader subject of community safety.

Mediators are very good at helping parties move from one context
to another. When divorcing parents are unable to get past their disagreement about sharing time with the children, the mediator will ask
them to shift topics from time demands to their children's needs.
When coworkers are attacking one another for workplace behavior,
the mediator may ask them to talk about the work environment in
general; and when one neighbor is complaining about a barking dog,
the conversation may shift to what makes a good neighborhood or
what the neighbors like about living in the area. Not only may conversation take a positive turn when the context shifts, but the parties may
find the seeds of fruitful discussion on the original issue. Spending
some time talking about their children may help the parents better

understand the children's needs and what each parent can provide. A discussion about the workplace environment may help coworkers see that problems are not personal but systemic, and discussing the qualities of a good neighborhood may bring a variety of issues to light on dog barking, including the need for peace and quiet as well as safety and security. In each of these cases, scoping to a new context can provide the basis for collaborative problem solving in each case. Notice that in each case of scoping—redirecting to a new context—the parties fundamentally shift the question they are discussing. When parties get stuck, they would be well-advised to query, "Are we even asking the right questions here?"

Context Setting Questioning. The questions a group addresses will determine in large measure the content of their discussion. If you ask participants what they want, they may engage in a struggle between competing demands. For this reason, many mediators never start with this question. If you ask participants why they think they are right, they will exchange arguments and look for you to decide who is correct. Such questions may be appropriate in legal proceedings, but they are not very productive for establishing a dialogue. Notice how each of the following sets of questions, suggested by Ferdig, focuses the discussion in a different direction.[12]

To focus on identity: Who am I? What is important to me? Who are we together? What do we both care about? What does each of us bring to this conversation based on our previous experience around the topic that brings us together?

To focus on principles: What do I stand for? What do we jointly stand for? How do our choices and actions reflect our individual and collective values? How do we want to interact with one another? What might that process look like? What can we agree on?

To focus on intentions: Where am I going? What do I want to see happen here? What are we up to in this conversation? What can we create together that brings us to where we want to be?

To focus on exploration of possibility: What are the things you value most about yourself? What are the core factors that give "life" and "energy" to the group? What are the possibilities of that which we can create together based on the best of who we are?

The Vietnam dialogues, sponsored by former Secretary of Defense Robert McNamara between 1995 and 1998, provide a magnificent example of the power of a carefully crafted question. The war, which occurred in the 1960s and early 1970s, involved North Vietnam on one side and South Vietnam and the United States on the other. Ending with the reunification of the country, the war resulted in about 50,000 American deaths and untold numbers of Vietnamese casualties, not to mention significant social and political disruption in the United States and in Southeast Asia.

About 20 years after the war, McNamara invited U.S. and Vietnamese officials and scholars to participate in six dialogue sessions on this question: "In the light of what now can be learned from the historical record, what U.S. and Vietnamese decisions might have been different and what difference would they have made in the course of the war—if each side had judged the other side's intentions and capabilities more accurately?"[13] McNamara wrote:

> I hoped to examine a hypothesis that had gradually taken shape in my mind: Both Washington and Hanoi had missed opportunities to achieve our geopolitical objectives without the terrible loss of life suffered by each of our countries. There were, I hypothesized, opportunities either to have avoided the war before it started or to have terminated it long before it had run its course. Were there such opportunities? If so, why were they missed? What lessons can we draw to avoid such tragedies in the twenty-first century?[14]

Although not all participants wanted to talk about this question immediately, they eventually did take the question seriously and embarked on a joint dialogue of inquiry in which they could see, through years of hindsight, that each side had misunderstood the other in fundamental ways and that they had missed important opportunities to change the course of the conflict. The guiding questions of the dialogue were not: "What happened? Who was right?" or "What caused the war?" Instead, the group focus created a learning conversation on missed opportunities. Productive conversation on a potentially undiscussable issue was made possible by careful context framing.

TRANSFORMING THE RELATIONSHIP

We wrote earlier that individuals and groups embroiled in difficult conflicts must find a way to transcend the patterns of communication that flummox them. As we have seen, new patterns of communication can help groups explore difficult issues in a way that can lead to insight and, in some cases, even solutions. Such conversations can do something else as well: They can help to transform relationships.

I and Thou

For Martin Buber, human relationships are of supreme importance.[15] Too often, Buber wrote, we treat other people as objects to be changed, reduced, and manipulated. This he called an *I-It* relationship: I put myself in the position of assessing, influencing, and controlling others. This kind of relationship is especially common in conflict situations, in which people move against one another as if they were objects. The key to finding new relationships is a shift toward what Buber calls the *I-Thou* relationship, in which people treat every person as a complex being who cannot be reduced and should not be treated as an object. Buber wrote that *dialogue* is a process of walking a narrow ridge between one's own experience and that of others, or, as Pearce and Pearce state it, "holding your own ground while remaining profoundly open to the other."[16]

The I-Thou relationship embodies *respect* for difference. It means that we may disagree on issues, but we respect one another because of a deep understanding that our beliefs, values, and actions are products of unique and complex life experiences. We may need to coordinate actions to make temporary solutions and resolutions, but we work out ways to do these things with respect. The dialogues of the Public Conversations Project discussed earlier in the chapter show how a shift from disrespect to respect can happen. In their sessions on abortion, no one really changed his or her mind on the issue, but nearly all participants experienced profound shifts of the second-order, from avoidance to engagement, from defensiveness to safety, and from disrespect to respect. Indeed, they often expressed amazement at the changes they felt in their attitudes toward people with different points of view after experiencing the dialogue process.

We have seen this happen many times in mediation. Participants who are initially nervous, suspicious, defensive, and polarized begin to relax a little, see the other person's point of view, and come to a new level of understanding and sometimes even respect. For us, a mediation is successful if the parties are able to achieve this kind of shift, whether they reach a negotiated agreement or not. In chapter 9, we described a dialogue process used in Indonesia among village leaders following the destructive four-year conflict in Maluku. The 40 participants repeatedly expressed their satisfaction, even pleasure, of discovering dialogue as a form of communication in which they could shift their relationship from hostility to cooperation. For example, one participant wrote: "We are required to learn about each other's knowledge and experience, and to gain understanding about the differences so that the feelings of unity and association can be reconstructed so that there will be greater reconciliation between people."[17]

This kind of transformation also happened on the other side of the globe in Catron County, New Mexico. Catron County is a vast territory in the beautiful wilderness of western New Mexico. With a population of only 2,500, the region is sustained mostly by ranching and forestry. This economic base was greatly threatened in the 1990s by federal environmental measures that sparked a conflict that not only caused considerable stress for the whole community, but threatened violence as well. At the moment when "war" seemed imminent, a small group of citizens decided to take another path and asked the New Mexico Center for Dispute Resolution to make a visit.[18]

At their first meeting, the facilitators and a small group of ranchers, loggers, environmentalists, and others agreed to air a variety of perspectives on the issue using strong ground rules. In subsequent sessions, the number of participants grew, and they began to explore their visions for the community, discovering in the process significant common values and concerns. Over time, they explored numerous topics and eventually focused specifically on five areas of concern—education, dispute resolution, land stewardship, economic development, and youth development. The dialogue expanded from the conflict that had originally brought the group together to wide-ranging discussions of quality of life in the community. Discussions took many forms, including dialogue groups, planning committees, field trips, mediations and negotiations, community visioning meetings, and youth meetings. Additionally, community members were trained as facilitators, and a local group took on the responsibility of organizing meetings in the future.

The process in Catron County did not always go smoothly. The conflicts were not always resolved, and tensions did return from time to time, but in all, a new base of respect emerged and enabled the community to begin to manage its differences constructively.

Achieving Dialogue

In this chapter we have presented a variety of thoughts and cases about how to transcend negative patterns of communication and to transform relationships among individuals and groups that experience challenging differences. Collectively, we refer to transcendent and transformative communication as *dialogue*. To summarize, dialogue:

- treats all participants as "fully formed, whole, and complex human beings."
- empowers communicators to "be assured that their stories will be heard and allow others the same privilege."
- opens "new territory where joining places may be found."
- is "multivoiced and nonpolarized."
- addresses "fresh, constructive questions that demand critical, creative thinking."
- aims to educate by allowing "participants to learn important new things."
- builds "relationships of respect."[19]

Box 10.2

Remember a time when you were fighting for something you believed in. If you saw your perspective as a "story," what was the moral of the story? Did the moral endure throughout the interaction? Did it change at all through the interaction?

HOW YOU CAN USE THIS CHAPTER

This chapter presents a variety of principles that you can use in all situations where the management of difference is challenging. We urge you to spend some time looking for insights you can use.

1. No conflict is just what it is. Every difference is socially constructed and could be constructed differently if the parties were willing and able to do so. Harm can be transcended, and relationships can be transformed.

2. Remember the I-Thou relationship: You can hold your own ground, while remaining profoundly open to others. One choice is to stay in the tension.

3. Exclusion will almost always lead toward harm; inclusion will almost always lead toward value.

4. Be conscious of face in every interaction. Destructive facework almost always leads toward harm; constructive facework almost always leads toward value.

5. Although dialogue is not always possible, it is the ideal in matters of managing difference. Aim for dialogue whenever possible.

Interactive Case Study

CONFLICTING MORAL ORDERS

Context: You are going to address some personal destructive interactions that could happen in the lives of you or your classmates.

Opening exercise(s): Think about a moral issue or point of view that is deeply rooted in your own life experience. Imagine that another person or group in a conflict situation challenged this moral stance. Perhaps this has already happened to you. How would you, or did you, feel and act? Get into small groups. Take turns telling about areas in your life in which conflict would become, or has become, a deep moral challenge. Record some notes about each of the situations, as each of your examples will be used to address one of the focuses below.

Focus #1: Managing Process: Talking and Listening

Choose one of the examples from your small-group opening exercise. For this example, go through each of the bullets for empowerment outlined earlier in this chapter and discuss how you could avoid harm and move toward value by paying attention to this type of communication.

Focus #2: Managing Process: Inquiry

Take another example from your opening exercise. What questions could you ask in the situation, either implicitly or explicitly, to stay away from harm? Instead of seeking "Who will prevail?" shift to, "What do we have to learn?" If the participants in this situation were engaged in a process of mutual discovery, what could be learned?

Focus #3: Managing Process: Creativity

Take another example from your opening exercise. Look at the sample creative processes discussed in this chapter. Use your imagination to depict this potential destructive interaction in a new way. Try to create a depiction that frames the issues in a way that opens up communication rather than closes it down. Share these depictions with the rest of the class.

Focus #4: Managing Context: Scoping

Take another example from your opening exercise. Isolate the issue that could bring this difference to the most harmful sphere. Scope out to the broader context and try to discuss the issue in your group using that frame. Now scope in to a narrower dimension of the issue and try to discuss the issue in your group using that frame. What changed as you changed the context? How might you invite people with a different moral view to change the scope?

Endnotes

[1] Stephen W. Littlejohn, "The Transcendent Communication Project: Searching for a Praxis of Dialogue," *Conflict Resolution Quarterly*, 21 (2004): 337–360.

[2] Stephen Littlejohn, "Moral Conflict," in *The Sage Handbook of Conflict Communication: Integrating Theory, Research, and Practice*, eds. John G. Oetzel and Stella Ting-Toomey (Thousand Oaks, CA: Sage, 2006), pp. 395–417.

[3] William A. Gattis, "Transcendent Discourse and Moral Conflict: The Use of Dialogue Groups to Improve Communication in Long-standing Moral Struggles" (unpublished doctoral dissertation, University of Kansas, 1985), pp. 184–185.

[4] Nola J. Heidlebaugh, *Judgment, Rhetoric, and the Problem of Incommensurability: Recalling Practical Wisdom* (Columbia: University of South Carolina Press, 2001).

[5] Jim Wallis, *The Soul of Politics* (New York: New Press, 1994).

[6] See, for example, Richard Chasin, Margaret Harzig, Laura Chasin, Corky Becker, and Robert R. Stains, "From Diatribe to Dialogue on Divisive Public Issues: Approaches Drawn from Family Therapy," *Mediation Quarterly*, 13 (1996): 323–344.

[7] Adapted from J. Kevin Barge, "Dialogue, Conflict, and Community," in *The Sage Handbook of Conflict Communication: Integrating Theory, Research, and Practice*, eds. John G. Oetzel and Stella Ting-Toomey (Thousand Oaks, CA: Sage, 2006), pp. 517–544; and Mary A. Speke Ferdig, "Exploring the Social Construction of Complex Self-Organizing Change: A Study of Emerging Change in the Regulation of Nuclear Power" (unpublished doctoral dissertation, Organizational Development, Benedictine University, Lisle, IL, 2001).

[8] David L. Cooperrider and Diana Whitney, *Appreciative Inquiry* (San Francisco: Berrett-Koehler, 1999).

[9] Ferdig, "Exploring," p. 185.

[10] Barge, "Dialogue," p. 538.

[11] Examples taken from the Cupertino Community Project. See Shawn Spano, *Public Dialogue and Participatory Democracy: The Cupertino Community Project* (Cresskill, NJ: Hampton Press, 2001).

[12] Adapted from Ferdig, "Exploring," pp. 182–183.

[13] Robert S. McNamara, James G. Blight, and Robert K. Brigham, *Argument without End: In Search of Answers to the Vietnam Tragedy* (New York: Public Affairs, 1999), p. 17.

[14] McNamara, Blight, and Brigham, p. xi.

[15] Martin Buber, *I and Thou* (New York: Scribner, 1958).

[16] W. Barnett Pearce and Kimberly A. Pearce, "Combining Passions and Abilities: Toward Dialogic Virtuosity," *Southern Communication Journal*, 65 (1999): 161–175.

[17] Carmen Lowry and Stephen W. Littlejohn, "Dialogue and the Discourse of Peacebuilding in Maluku, Indonesia," *Conflict Resolution Quarterly*, 23 (2006): 405–528.

[18] Melinda Smith, *The Catron County Citizens Group: A Case Study* (Albuquerque: New Mexico Center for Dispute Resolution, 1998).

[19] Littlejohn, "Moral Conflict," p. 409.

11

Reorienting to Difference

Mother was an excellent flower arranger. She would spend hours gathering flowers from the backyard, where a colorful garden spanned the entire property. Flower arranging is quite an art. What a pleasure it was to watch her make one beautiful arrangement in the vase and then to see her rearrange the colors and stems to construct another stunning display. Yes, there was a final display that she entered in the county fair, but that was just a moment where she chose one arrangement as the best at that time for the purposes at hand.

We have often commented that people who manage difference can be seen as *artisans*. They create and arrange materials for a practical purpose, to address a need. Artisans use a variety of media; they employ their creative *artistic* talents to develop a brick fence, a solar-powered house, a city utility system, or a pewter bowl. Where an artist can rearrange to their heart's content, an artisan drives toward choosing a final design, process, or scheme. In the field of conflict management, we have often heard that conflict practitioners are artists, those who are able by virtue of imagination and talent or skill to create works of aesthetic value, but we are inclined to think of conflict managers as artisans. The majority of the time they are craftspersons, and there is a pressing reason for their efforts: a family in distress, a workplace that is not functioning fully, a future that needs to be created, two countries that cannot decide on border policy, or two people who need a channel for clear communication. They use their skills, methods, and theory to craft a useful process that has the best possibility of generating positive change . . . though they probably will never win a blue ribbon at the county fair for flower arranging.

The previous chapter discussed how to transcend and transition seemingly intractable conflicts. In this chapter, we will discuss five orientations to challenge current thinking, stretch attitudes, and enable movement toward the sphere of value as we manage our differences through communication.

FROM STATIC CULTURE TO CULTURE-AS-PROCESS

We have had numerous requests from clients or students that ask: "How can I communicate with Native Americans?" "What are the most important principles for negotiating with white, male, CEOs?" "How can I talk to scientists?" It would be very useful if we could codify culture into a neat checklist, so people could communicate appropriately and respectfully in any given situation, but we cannot produce that checklist. In chapter 4, we discussed cultural differences as a significant consideration when addressing conflict. We concluded that by focusing on the cultural dimensions, we open our eyes to a variety of possibilities for both framing the conflict and for creative approaches to moving forward. We also concluded that a hazard of a cultural focus might be that we make assumptions too quickly about how people from other cultures think and act.

Culture and Complexity

The link between culture and conflict resolution has been explored extensively in the last decade. Kevin Avruch offers an interesting conception of culture that enables us to address cultural conflict. He begins by describing the following *inadequate* assumptions about culture.[1]

1. *Culture is homogenous.* We cannot presume that culture is free of internal paradoxes and contradictions. It is hazardous to characterize a culture in a straightforward way. ("New Mexicans love spicy food.")

2. *Culture is a thing.* Can we see individual agency in a static conception of culture? The reification of culture makes us see culture as an "it" with material or concrete existence. ("Don't invite him to join our club; his culture won't permit it.")

3. *Culture is uniformly distributed among members of a group.* Avruch offers a strong statement on this topic, noting that intracultural variation is often ignored or dismissed as "deviance." (Although she is a member of our group, she still won't play the game. She's weird.")

4. *An individual possesses but a single culture.* To the contrary, individuals possess and control several cultures. We would rarely have only one group identity. ("I grew up Hispanic so I must remain a Catholic.")

5. *Culture is custom.* Is a community's culture synonymous with its traditions or customary ways of behaving? If so, we need to ask

again where the individual agency is. ("I grew up Scandinavian, so I must eat a lot of pickled fish.") If everyone in the community is abiding by tradition or custom, what about the differences that arise? We try to imagine that people in a community compose an array of deep and wide, shallow and brief customs and traditions that evolve and change.

6. *Culture is timeless.* Culture does change throughout time. We cannot speak of the "East Coast Work Ethic" as an unchanging characteristic of the people.

Box 11.1

Think about yourself, where you come from, your family traditions and culture. Summarize these items so that someone could use the summary as they get to know you. Compare this list to the inadequate assumptions about culture.

Culture is not static, timeless, or changeless. Avruch sees it as situational, flexible, and responsive to the exigencies of the worlds that individuals confront.[2] With his view that "individuals reflect or embody multiple cultures," we are invited to look less at the pattern of culture and more at the process.[3] We can see culture-as-process as the continual process of reinvention or revalidation of who we are, how we behave, and what we value. A person's culture is responsive to situational and environmental change.

Moving Forward

One way to envision this conception of culture is to think in terms of fuzzy logic, which deals with uncertainties and with propositions that are *more or less* true or false. Avruch wants to "complexify" culture by offering that there is not a real true or false.[4] We do not need linear sets of rules for behaving when confronted with cultural differences; instead we should look at a network of possibilities or a system of cultural characteristics. With the array of options in place, we can take a *first cut* or form a *proposition* about how to move forward.

We have done some consulting in a scientific laboratory, where we were asked to assess their culture and help change it to a more business-like enterprise. This organization has a reputation for being a very efficient and productive organization. They finish their projects in a high-quality manner, meeting the deadlines and finishing under budget. In our interviews, we asked, "What is it about your organization that makes you so efficient?" Many of them answered, "We are a culture of heroes. We all rally at the last minute and perform with great courage and strength." They also told us that they had no procedures or processes in place to guide their efforts. They just "do what they have to do to get the job done, and do it right."

We were asked to help change the hero culture to a more business-oriented structure. Our first steps were to facilitate some large and small meetings to gauge the group's anticipation of change and begin to set an agenda for collaborating on the development of business processes. Some of the group asked us, "Can you help us change our 'hero culture' to a more structured system with established procedures on which we can rely? (Can you change us?)" Since our practice consists of "facilitating change" rather than "making change happen," we had to answer in the negative. We were able to help "complexify" their culture, helping them to see all the aspects of their organization that comprise their culture. They began to see that they were much more than a culture of heroes. They had other social, national, ethnic, personal, and relational groupings with which they identified, both as individuals and as a group. The following is a sample of the questions that guided them to realize their rich culture. We captured the responses on a wall chart and clustered them.

1   Tell us about your work. What is a typical day like?
2. How are you able to perform your tasks as you do?
3. What is it about yourself that leads you to work as you do?
4. What is it about the organization as a whole that leads you to work as you do?
5. What do you value most about your organization?
6. When those values are in place, what is happening in your workplace?
7. Tell us about yourself. What is your title at work? What experiences and background do you bring to this position?
8. When are you motivated to give your best effort?
9. What is your favorite part of working here?
10. If you were to tell someone (outside the organization) what you do here, what would you say?

The resulting clusters showed that this group holds a variety of different values and orientations. There were many ways to complete projects, many different things they valued, and various behaviors and personalities that did not connect to ethnic or regional stereotypes. After this realization, we were able to move forward, acknowledging the complex and changing culture as a resource for change.

> **Box 11.2**
>
> Look at the summary about yourself that you created earlier. Ask the following questions to complexify it. For each of the items, ask:
>
> 1. Has there been a time when this cultural component was not evident?
> 2. What was happening in your life to create this difference?
> 3. When you look at this part of your culture, what concerns do you have?
> 4. Which of these parts of your culture are changing?
> 5. Which parts of your culture do you want to change?
> 6. What items on this summary will be the same a year from now? Five years? Fifteen years?

> **Moving toward Value**
>
> Culture does not lend itself to checklists. A listing of nationalities does not give us a concrete idea of the culture of a group. Cultures are subject to change. If we want to value the differences inherent in the ever-changing cultures we offer, we should see culture as socially inherited. Yes, there is an aspect of tradition to how we behave, but we are also responsive to situational change and reinvent our culture often.

FROM RESOLUTION TO ENGAGEMENT

We recently met with an organization that was paralyzed because of their differences. Residing in the sphere of harm, they experienced backbiting and gossip, low productivity, palpable dissatisfaction with the workplace, and resulting physical and emotional problems. They were able to meet for eight hours to try to address the "conflict" with all twenty staff members eagerly in attendance. They were desperate for a change in the situation. "Can you fix it?" Can you fix *us*?" Early conversation at the meeting centered on stories about how one person needed to become more trustworthy and another person needed to become less dominating. The solution for them seemed to be that the bad guys needed to change so the good guys could get their work done. They were embroiled in conflict and needed help. They wanted a *resolution*. What do people really need when they are in stuck places like this? The following six needs are present when people are paralyzed by their differences.[5]

1. *Voice.* People want to be heard. They want to be heard by the people that count. In some cases, the people that count may be in the room, but in other cases, they may be those higher on the decision-making ladder. People want others to understand who they are, what they value, and what they want.

2. *Procedural justice.* People want to be given the same opportunity to manage their differences that everyone else is given. Procedures that are fair and just need to be available and consistent. If the management is given a day to retreat and work on their challenges, the entire staff would also like to be given adequate time to do the same. If some neighbors can get a hearing in court, other neighbors want similar opportunities.

3. *Vindication.* People want an outcome that shows that they are right and that their cause is just. At least they want to begin with the hope that they will prevail. We have often talked about the fantasy of "victory" in conflict management. If we can be satisfied with options that meet our interests, rather than spectacular solutions, we open a broader opportunity for forward movement past stuck places.

4. *Validation.* When experiencing conflict, feelings of hurt, anger, frustration, and victimization arise. People want these feelings to be acknowledged and validated. A teakettle metaphor may work here. Only when the water has boiled and the kettle lets off steam is it ready to make tea. People are reluctant to give up their anger, seeing it as righteous anger.

5. *Impact.* There are two levels of impact desired by those in conflict. First, they want their own personal world to get better. Second, they want a broader impact, needing connection and meaning in relation to larger issues or struggles. Sometimes these two occur hand in hand. A worker complains to the boss about unequal treatment. This worker wants to get the same benefits as others in the same job and also wants the company to improve its human resources practices to be more consistent and fair for everyone.

6. *Safety.* Conflict is a risky and scary experience. People want a safe environment to address their issues without fear of retaliation or attack.

When we find ourselves confronted by differences that are harmful, we are juggling the need for resolution (*fix us!*) along with the six items listed above. We are called to develop creative and diverse ways to address these situations.

Let's look again at a definition of conflict. Bernie Mayer defines conflict as a system rather than a thing (*that nasty old conflict keeps plaguing us*), "Conflict is a system of interaction that can involve multiple processes, the flow of energy, many different agents, different forms of communication, and many key events that can lead to a reorganization of the system."[6] With this complex definition of conflict, we can offer ways to address it that can meet the six needs above. We can use a multiplicity of interventions or processes. Mayer tells us that working within conflict requires a complicated interaction of substantive, procedural, psychological, cultural, historical, and cognitive factors. How can we organize all of those factors, and then use them when human differences block our way? We can meet the challenge by reorienting our perspective from a *resolution* focus to an *engagement* focus.

Conflict Engagement

In this new orientation, we propose to work on a variety of levels. As the needs above reveal, participants want a variety of things, which necessitates a variety of scopes. Engaging in a conflict means

> accepting the challenges of a conflict, whatever its type or stage of development may be, with courage and wisdom and without automatically assuming that resolution is an appropriate goal. Effective engagement requires finding the right level of depth at which to engage. It also means being fully aware of the many different ways we could choose to avoid conflict, including trying to resolve it prematurely.[7]

Let's work for a while with Mayer's premise of conflict engagement. In his definition, we can pull out two areas of awareness: choosing the level of depth (the conflict stage at which to engage) and knowing how to change conflict avoidance into engagement.

Conflict Stages

If we are to engage in conflict, it is important to know which particular challenge we are experiencing at a given time. If we can understand where we are most in need of assistance, we can focus there for the moment, or for the entire process. One way to describe the current conflict is to look through the lenses of developmental processes. Each of the following processes poses a challenge and a place to begin engagement.[8] We will compare each stage to the conflict at the paralyzed organization described earlier.

1. *Awareness.* Do we know we are in a conflict? Do we see that human differences have made a hurdle for us? To become aware that we are in conflict is a necessary step and sometimes

takes engagement at the awareness level. The organization in crisis became aware of their conflict when it was very late. Their differences had become harmful, and their conflict affected almost every part of the organization.

2. *Articulation.* Can we explain our conflict to someone? If we can give voice to the conflict by directly or indirectly defining and characterizing the conflict, we are aware it exists. The workplace that is able to say "fix us!" knows that something is wrong. They also could tell us the stories about "that person who lies" and "our boss who is unreliable" and "that person who never turns off the coffee pot." They did have the stories to explain the conflict to themselves or others.

3. *Mobilization.* Have we pooled our resources to bring the conflict to a level of activity where improvement or action could occur? This organization did a fine job of mobilizing. They waited too long, but they did the miraculous job of arranging a full day off for all twenty staff members to be able to attend an office mediation session. They put aside money for facilitators and meals. They made sure that all members of the administration attended, and no one was allowed to leave early or to take phone calls.

4. *Activation.* Once the parties in conflict and necessary resources have been mobilized, it is time to begin action, hoping to accomplish the goals. Unfortunately in this case, no action had occurred and no goal setting had been accomplished. They arrived at the retreat waiting to be "fixed." To make progress, we commonly utilize a variety of processes to create an environment suitable for action. We address process, safety, face needs, empowerment, and collaboration (see chapters 5 and 8).

5. *Connection.* How are we going to interact? If we are to communicate and negotiate through our differences, we should have mechanisms to connect to each other. The first method of connection at the one-day retreat was to seat 4–6 people at round tables and to invite the small group to communicate with one another. Next we asked all participants to sit at a table with others with whom they do not usually interact. Throughout the day, the group had conversation focuses and interaction tasks that enabled them to connect.

6. *Need satisfaction.* Here is where the complexity in conflict begins. The six needs discussed above (voice, justice, vindication, validation, impact, and safety) change and vacillate over the course of a conflict. A common way to discover which of the needs are at play is to ask a question such as, "For this inter-

action (session, retreat, relationship) to meet your needs, what would have to happen?"

7. *Release.* At various points in the conflict, we free up some of the pent-up energy. We may give up part of the conflict, resolve some of it, or change our stance about it. At the retreat above, we took periodic breaks, with instructions to go outside and breathe in the fresh air. We had a point in the agenda where each person was asked to do some private writing about "the most challenging thing about working for this organization." At another time, we had each person turn to the person next to him or her and discuss "something they are willing to give up in order to get the thing they desire most out of this session."

8. *Process selection.* Parties in conflict can be engaged in creating the process to address their conflict. We have stated often that "people support what they create." When people are involved in the development of the way they will move forward, more commitment and ownership can occur. In the case of the retreat, we began the day with a thorough review of the agenda. We not only walked through each step of the day but also previewed what people would be expected to do at each agenda point. We followed the agenda review with a conversation about the day, refining the agenda according to the group's comfort level. We did remove a whole segment of the agenda (visioning) as the group said they thought their organization had a pretty coherent vision already. They just needed to get past the differences that divided them so they could move forward in pursuit of the vision.

If we steer clear of the stages above, either by ignoring them, or by letting our differences obscure our vision of them, we are avoiding the conflict. If we choose to engage the conflict, we can connect at any of the above levels. Just as the stages above are not linear or concrete, engagement steps enter the system at a variety of points and can spiral or loop back and forth as the system shifts to the engagement activities. The following activities help move toward engagement.[9]

- *We can name the conflict.* Related to both awareness and articulation, people engage the conflict by naming it and identifying its nature in some way. The way the conflict is named indicates where to engage. Note the difference between, *"I am frustrated by the way you continuously shirk your duties, like turning off the coffee"* and *"Our organization needs to pay more attention to housekeeping duties, like coffee making, bathroom cleaning, and emptying the trash."* You can construct a framing that will engage participants constructively by paying careful attention to how the differences are phrased and described.

- *We can consider the costs and benefits of engagement and avoidance.* We can think through the implications of avoiding the conflict or engaging it in some way. We can also help others think in this way by asking questions like, *"If you continue to communicate by e-mail and memo, and avoid face-to-face contact, what will be the result?"* or *"If you were to take a full day off of work and address your struggles with interpersonal relations in the workplace, what could happen? What costs and benefits would you assume?"*

- *We can discuss various approaches to engagement.* We live in a time where we have access to a multitude of processes to address conflict. A few decades ago, workplace conflicts usually went like this: complain to the boss, look for the guilty party, find evidence to punish or not, and give some kind of penalty or discipline. Now we have mediation, negotiation, dialogue processes, retreats, trainings, grievance panels, and informal problem-solving processes.

- *We can rehearse engagement.* Talk through the interaction. Practice the upcoming interaction with a friend or with a professional. When we went to the organization in crisis, we gave them some pre-retreat questions to think about, so they could prepare their interaction and not be surprised.

- *We can find an appropriate forum or agent for raising issues.* It usually helps to have a clear identification of the conflict and its nature first, before choosing the most appropriate forum. When we were contacted to work with the organization, we discussed with them their needs and wondered if they could use a mediator, trainer, an organizational development expert, or a process facilitator. Even though many in the organization labeled the issue as a conflict to be resolved, the management asked us for a person to guide or facilitate the communication as the group planned for the creation of a healthy working environment.

- *We can raise the conflict directly.* Bring it up immediately, assert that there is a difference of opinion, and give attention where needed.

- *We can discuss issues of timing.* Decide when to engage in which aspect of the issue at hand. A careful sequence can help address the varied needs and complex stages of the conflict.

- *We can bring the conflicting parties together.* Whether we are the "conveners" or the "process designers" or are the parties embroiled in the conflict, we can engage the conflict by bringing the parties together to talk. Bringing people together, especially in the midst of difference, is often one of the most difficult parts of engaging. Just finding the time in our busy schedules is often the first roadblock.

- *We can provide safeguards for engagement.* We can arrange ground rules, communication guidelines, technology for distance communication, agreements for handling disruptions and unexpected problems, and conflict management tools.

The outcomes for the paralyzed organization were hopeful and creative. Plans were made for improved workplace communication. Commitments were made to develop a new attitude toward each other and to be open to new understandings of each other's perspectives. Processes and procedures were analyzed and adjusted. Lessons were learned from stories that clarified, evolved, and changed.

Moving toward Value

Differences plague us, and we know that we have a variety of options. We do not have to avoid the resulting conflict and continue to reside in the sphere of harm. We do not have to jump into a quest for resolution (one form of avoidance). We can engage the conflict, acknowledging its complexity and variableness. We can engage at any number of vantage points and challenge ourselves and others to grasp better choices with more optimism. The dynamics of human difference are a ripe foundation for productive change and healthier relationships.

FROM RESOLUTION TO TRANSFORMATION

There are not many instances in life as painful and heart wrenching as a divorce in the family. Whether it is the broken heart of the person who does not want to split up the family, or the agony of knowing that the breakup is the right thing to do in the long run, the pain is hard to bear. In divorce cases, the couple longs for the "resolution" to be final, so they can get on with life. As many of us know, even after the resolution is final, the pain still lingers, and the relationship rarely ends. The relationship usually changes into something else.

As the parties struggle to figure out how to divide stuff up, and to decide on conditions for the future, there are certain cases where the pain of divorce eases a bit. We have seen this in divorce mediation where the couple genuinely commits to focus on the children's best interests as they make decisions. The relationship has then been transformed from one of "you versus me" to "us doing what's right for the

kids." When something is transformed, its nature or form changes or
is altered, usually for the better. To transform situations where differences have become harmful into something better takes more than a
miracle. It takes energy, diligence, and a commitment to seeing differences as the opportunity to transform.

Over the past four decades we have observed the evolution of the
field of conflict management and the portrayal of mediation in several
different ways. These approaches can be offered as "four stories"—
four ways of understanding mediation.[10]

> *The Satisfaction Story:* Mediation is a conflict management process
> that is flexible, informal, and can help parties see their conflict as a
> mutual problem. The highlight of this story is that adversarial,
> win-lose negotiation can become collaborative, win-win problem
> solving. The aim is to achieve mutually satisfactory agreement.
> This type of process has been seen most consistently for years.

> *The Social Justice Story:* Mediation can support community devel-
> opment by constructing a larger context around the differences in
> groups and relationships. Those who are perceived as having less
> power can gain strength by participating in civic life, pursuing
> common interests, and ensuring greater social justice. Neighbor-
> hood mediation and environmental mediation have strengthened
> communities of interest in a variety of ways. Grassroots commu-
> nity organizers are most interested in this story, though it is not as
> prevalent in our society as the satisfaction story.

> *The Transformation Story:* Robert Baruch Bush and Joseph Folger
> have illuminated this story in the past decade, with the first edi-
> tion of *The Promise of Mediation*. They reoriented the mediation
> community by illuminating the hope that comes from conflict
> transformation. In the transformation story, "The unique promise
> of mediation lies in its capacity to transform the quality of conflict
> interaction itself, so that conflicts can actually strengthen both of
> the parties themselves and the society they are part of."[11] This
> potential of mediation is available for all types of disputes, even
> divorce. The transformation story contends that the character of
> male-female interaction can be changed generally; specifically, it
> contends that the parties can be empowered to say and hear what
> needs to be said and heard. Ultimately, the quality of social insti-
> tutions can be transformed in a positive way.

> *The Oppression Story:* We include this story last, as it is a different
> kind of story and gives us a warning. The warning is that media-
> tion can be used to consolidate the power of the strong and to
> increase the oppression of the weak. Because of its informality and

consensuality, mediation can be an easy way to bypass the legal process and to magnify power imbalances. Also, because of its confidentiality, mediation gives mediators broad strategic power, allowing potential biases free reign.

By looking at these four stories, we acknowledge the diversity in the field of mediation and conflict management. Many mediators say they utilize bits and pieces of each of the four stories in their practice. In this chapter, we hope to offer another orientation, a new arrangement for managing difference that brings us away from harm and closer to value. The transformative story has that potential. The main premise of transformation, according to Bush and Folger, is that the most important benefit is the transformation of the quality of the interaction from destructive to constructive.[12] This change in the interaction is not outcome related; it is process related—a shift from resolution to transformation. To achieve a satisfying outcome (resolution) is undoubtedly important to the parties, but this benefit rests on the assumption that individual needs can be met without changing the quality of the interaction itself. People will continue to be distressed by negative interaction, even if their separate needs are satisfied.

Transformation and the Management of Difference

Let's shift for a moment from mediation back to the management of difference. We use this focus as an invitation for continual diligence in communication, especially where human differences occur. If we are determined to manage difference constructively, we can look at conflict transformation for ideas about communication focuses. We will spotlight two dynamic processes or goals for our communication: *empowerment* and *recognition*, as defined by Bush and Folger.[13]

Empowerment is a restoration to individuals of a sense of their value and strength and their own capacity to make decisions and handle life's problems.

Recognition means the evocation in individuals of acknowledgement, understanding, or empathy for the situation and the views of the other.

For Bush and Folger, empowerment is the focus on *self* and recognition is the focus on *other*. (Note that our use of empowerment throughout the text envelops both empowerment and recognition as they are defined here.) We find out what is important to ourselves through our interaction with others. We also find out what others value.

Walking the tightrope of empowerment and recognition can transform our interaction in conflict situations from despair and adversariness to hope and possibilities. Consider the following statements:

1. *Gee, as we have been talking, I have noticed how strongly I feel about loud parties. I've always known that I like to get a good night's sleep, but I am surprised at how angry I am at being kept awake.* (empowerment)

2. *It sounds like you have a need for safety and security around your home and feel that a dog gives you exactly what you need since you are out of town so often.* (recognition)

3. *I know now that I can face the teacher and request a review of my grades. After this talk, I see how little I know about the grading procedures.* (empowerment)

4. *This situation is quite stressful for both of us. I can see that you are just as uncomfortable as I am.* (recognition)

Creating Sacred Space

As we explore the potential of transforming the conflict interaction, we are addressing more than the issue itself and more than the parties themselves. The metaphor of the umbrella may work here. An umbrella is used for a variety of purposes. When it is up, we are shaded from the sun and the rain. We can shade others if we invite then under the umbrella. In fact, the act of inviting someone under our umbrella symbolizes a move toward sharing protection, security, and safety. If we have more than three or four people who need to be shaded, we get a larger umbrella; if numbers are very large, we will need a tent big enough to shade a multitude of people. Depending on the conditions, we have an umbrella handy and can carry it with us in the closed position, or even leave it at home if we think we will not need it. In any case, we use an umbrella to create a space for shelter from the elements.

The umbrella metaphor is useful when we are confronted with a challenging communication interaction. Do we need an umbrella? How large should it be? When should we put it up? Who should be under it? Who should hold the umbrella while it is in use? Instead of putting up the umbrella, should we move to a location where the elements don't threaten us? In chapter 8 we talk about "process management" as the *how* of our communication interactions. Attending to process considerations is one part of creating the space in which to communicate.

Creating this space for our interactions is an act and an attitude. We have to own an umbrella, and we need to have the intention to use it. When we possess the ability to act and believe that we can create a secure and safe place to interact, we open up the possibility to witness the moral stories of individuals and communities. Sara Cobb sees that communication in conflict situations can illuminate *moral discussions.* Moral discussion is the reiteration of stories, elaborate plotlines, values, or character roles that reconfirm and anchor the moral of the story.[14] If these stories shift, and the moral of the story evolves, a new moral frame has developed. Cobb relates this moral framework to conflict situations.

> Parties in conflict are captured by the stories they tell about a problem, its antecedent, and the roles they played, and there is always a moral to their story, a theme that usually reconfirms, as do all other parts of the story, their description of the problem. Inevitably, the moral of the story is that the other has to change in some way, as well as offer restitution.[15]

Transformation occurs within this *sacred space*, this place under the umbrella, where we are secure enough to allow our stories and pre-conceived endings to change and evolve. We can allow interaction patterns to shift and stories to change, providing sacred spaces for transformation of relationships and communities. How do we allow stories to shift?

Owning an Umbrella. We need to own the skills and attitude that allow evolution of perspectives, understandings, and convictions. Trainings and workshops that feature constructive communication practice and facilitative conflict management are a good place to start. University courses in listening, mediation, interpersonal communication, and community building also can equip us with healthy skill sets.

Using the Umbrella. Be confident enough to put up the umbrella and to share it. Inviting others into a secure space can be comforting but it can also be scary, as you now have new responsibility and duty to interact and negotiate the space. The following statements offer some ways to practice creating the sacred space under the umbrella.

- *It seems we are about to undertake a sensitive subject. Please feel free to talk about your perspective for a while.*

- *I know that positions often change in the course of conversation, so let's not hold ourselves to any commitments until we both agree that we are finished sharing.*

- *Hey, I have an idea: let's both talk about our views on this difficult decision for ten minutes and then begin brainstorming possible solutions.*

- *It sounds like you clearly know what you would like to happen in this situation. I hope we can hold off on deciding until we discuss this a bit more, and maybe even get some other perspectives before narrowing in on the right way to go.*

Closing Down the Umbrella. Two people might use a sacred space for discussion for a finite time, even a brief time. Imagine that you want to decide where to go for spring break. You can set up a time, place, and some guiding principles. (*Let's both share some stories about the places we have ALWAYS wanted to go, and then talk a bit about other options. Let's try to decide before bed tonight.*) In other cases, you may need a sacred space that lasts for years. (*We need to build a strong foundation for our community relations. Let's create a way of communicating at these neighborhood meetings that allows us to grow and change and evolve into the strong healthy community we envision.*)

Moving toward Value

When differences present a challenging communication situation, we have the opportunity to transform the conversation from one that is positional and dogmatic (*This is what I believe and you need to accept it, as I will not change*) to one that is emergent and flexible (*For now, I have a strong opinion, and it is through our communication that I can strengthen that perspective or change it into the appropriate version*). Bush and Folger's empowerment and recognition that may occur within the interaction of the participants or within the act of creating a sacred space for the interaction both invite transformation.

FROM CYNICISM TO CIVILITY

Youth sports in the United States have gotten competitive, ugly, and deadly. Parents engage personal coaches for children as young as preschool age, resulting in amazing skill levels and intense competition to get on a team. As the competition intensifies, the behavior of parents and coaches is sometimes ratcheted to a fever pitch. Fierce verbal attacks and even physical fights occur at the games. Consider the following examples.[16]

1. *A parent body-slammed a high school referee after he ordered the man's wife out of the gym for allegedly yelling obscenities during a basketball game.*

2. *A father of a T-ball player was briefly jailed after an outburst against an umpire during a game involving 5- and 6-year-olds. The accused threatened to beat the umpire moments before walking onto the field and starting a fight. A girl who was playing in the game suffered a minor injury when she was struck in the face during the scuffle.*

3. *A youth league baseball coach was barred indefinitely from coaching his Little League teams and was criminally charged for pushing, shov-*

ing, and punching an umpire in the Little League. The umpire had disqualified two aluminum bats prior to the start of a 9- and 10-year-olds' game based on a safety rule.

This alarming trend coincides with the growing prevalence of disrespectful and cynical verbal and interpersonal communication. A London columnist sees that "cynicism is a new and dangerous 'ism.'"[17] Cynical views proclaim, *Don't get involved; nothing is going to change anyway.* People will leave a meeting and say, *Big deal, we spent four hours making plans, but I know none of them will happen. Why are we wasting our time?* The *Oxford English Dictionary* describes a cynic as a person "disposed to rail or find fault; one who shows a disposition to disbelieve in the sincerity or goodness of human motives or actions, and is wont to express this by sneers and sarcasm."[18] Our colleagues Ron Arnett and Pat Arneson have taken a close look at cynicism in their book, *Dialogic Civility in a Cynical Age.* They recount cynical communication in television, at lunch conversations, in churches, and construction firms. Here is an example of cynicism in television.

> A brief glance at television offerings reveals sitcoms that contain characters who are rude and insensitive to family and others, inviting an unthinking cynical response to important interpersonal relationships. Popular talk show formats quickly and openly discuss issues that require private deliberation inviting the audience to become communication voyeurs of an individual's personal trauma—again inviting a cynical response to another's problems. Essentially, we must ask who gets a stranger look—a person offering a cynical response to an action or idea, or a person interpreting an action or idea within a positive context?[19]

If this type of cynicism becomes routine, there may be disastrous long-term effects for society and culture.

What are the characteristics of this cynicism, other than being a negative attitude? Routine cynicism is unreflective; responses are automatic (given before one studies a situation), rejecting, disdaining, and/or not distinguishing the important from the trivial. Here are a few examples and their contexts: attending a wedding and remarking to the person next to you, "This marriage will never last"; discussing the upcoming elections, "I will not vote. Our votes don't mean anything anyway"; student at the first day of class, "No one gets an 'A' from this teacher, especially if you are a woman." These examples show that cynicism is more than an attitude. This type of language does not help us live the harsh realities of our time. We acknowledge that there is cause for frustration and confusion as we attempt to make a better world and stronger relationships. It is a long, slow process in many cases. How do we reconcile the hopelessness of the moment with a realistic and enduring sense of hope?

Cynicism and Hope

When we work to establish enduring communication that is constructive and a foundation for productive change, we cannot view cynicism and hope as the only two choices.[20] The opposite extremes can be self-correcting. We need to learn the appropriate place for cynicism, while relying on the strength of communication to open the door to hope. Being overly optimistic (marriage is forever; democracy always works; anyone can get an "A" in class) has downsides as do routinely negative reactions and comments. Communication can provide the means for finding balance between cynicism and hope. People experiencing differences can cocreate a story of respect and caring in uncertain times.

The building block for basic respect in this self-correcting communication is dialogic civility. We can keep our conversation going while we support our differences with "dialogue that embraces patience, persistence, and public discourse rooted in respect for the other."[21] Relational responsibility cannot be assumed; it is the result of hard work in forming healthy relationships at all levels. We have summarized some steps that constitute the move into civil communication, which also frames our vision of a respectful society.[22]

- Privilege *listening*. Civility is exhibited by attending to the communication of the other, especially in situations where differences are difficult.

- Privilege *additive change*. The type of change that is enduring and satisfying takes multiple steps in multiple directions. Try not to look for spectacular change.

- Privilege the *between* of relationships. Whereas cynicism is about "me," civility is about what is between "us."

- Privilege *voice and inclusion*. We must be present and attentive to our voice and the voices of others. More than listening, we must be conscientious about each moment of each interaction.

- Privilege *face saving*. If we can preserve the public image that others want or need, we can carry on our conversations with respect and dignity.

- Privilege *finding meaning in times of change*. When our lives are disrupted by views different than ours, or by life challenges that seem overwhelming, we can still find meaning in the moment. Look for it.

- Privilege *an ethic of care*. We have relational responsibilities and can carry them out by letting go of the self-focus that accompanies cynical communication.

- Privilege *a community of memory*. We participate with ideas, people, and institutions. Keeping those ties alive and functioning is enabled by communication characterized by civility.

- Privilege *a willingness to meet broken covenants*. We will let others down, and others will disappoint us. These instances can be repaired and altered. Limitations are not showstoppers; they are only temporary roadblocks.

The process of establishing a foundation of civility can become a value system that shapes our interaction with others.

Moving toward Value

When we see our differences as an opportunity to value our interactions and our actions, we can move past the harm that comes from privileging conflict and cynicism. Dialogic civility is an invitation to move in a direction where respectful communication keeps the conversation going in the midst of diversity.

FROM SOLUTIONS TO PLATFORMS

Transcending Violence: Four Capacities

Those who follow peacemaking in all its dimensions and pursue processes and skills to assist in the path to managing conflict appreciate the decades of contributions and experiences of John Paul Lederach.[23] With extensive experience as a peacebuilding practitioner, trainer, and consultant throughout Latin America, Africa, and the United States, Lederach pioneered the development of elicitive methods of conflict resolution. The key to his work is found in his definition of "elicitive." The point is to help people expand their customary ways of thinking about problems and solutions. Lederach has distilled his twenty-five years of experience to one question that must be answered if we are to redefine human affairs so we can construct positive social change. *How do we transcend the cycles of violence that bewitch our human communities while still living in them?* To answer that question, Lederach offers us a refreshing concept: *moral imagination*.

Imagine ourselves in a web of relationships that includes our enemies; the ability to sustain a paradoxical curiosity that embraces
complexity without reliance on dualistic polarity; the fundamental belief in a pursuit of the creative act; and the acceptance of the
inherent risk of stepping into the mystery of the unknown that
lies beyond the far too familiar landscape of violence.[24]

These necessary and vital capacities are in reach.

Carrie Billy is the associate director for the American Indian Higher
Education Consortium (AIHEC). This organization is the voice of the
36 tribal colleges and universities (TCU) in the United States. The TCUs
mostly exist on Indian land, and provide hope for the Indian communities in a variety of ways. Higher education offers the tribal people a
chance to learn and retain their culture, traditions, and language while
building economic development and community development. As in
any group, differences abound within the AIHEC; differences in education (*How many PhDs do you have on the reservation?*); differences in culture (*The customary way to make wild rice is this way*); historical
differences (*The Crow and Sioux are traditional enemies*); geographical differences (*Woodlands Indians understand trees, Plains Indians know buffalo*);
and even personal differences arise (*Why would we want to hire a white
person to become the CEO of our casino?*). Carrie Billy and AIHEC demonstrate moral imagination in their decisions and their work.

1. *Imagine ourselves in a web of relationships that includes our enemies.*
   In the Indian world, the centrality of relationships is crucial.
   When differences exist, it is important to imagine the web as
   something larger and more encompassing. When questions
   about federal funding changes looked like it would further
   polarize competing tribes, AIHEC convened a meeting of presi-
   dents of the TCUs and leaders of various federal agencies to *create together* some paths forward.

2. *Sustain a paradoxical curiosity that embraces complexity without
   reliance on dualistic polarity.* Ask questions that move past an
   either-or mentality to a variety of options you would genuinely
   like to know more about.

   *I have been wondering about your strong stance against bringing
   wireless technology to your reservation. What is it about this service
   that makes you so hesitant?*

   *I heard you mention your hope that your tribal college could offer a
   masters degree program someday. I am really curious about that hope. If
   it did come to pass, what would the costs and benefits be? Tell me more
   about your work with these other colleagues. How were you able to create this initiative with the Woodlands tribe over such a long distance?*

3. *Believe in the pursuit of the creative act.* People are often willing to take the time to use various mediums and environments to help them make plans and decisions. AIHEC has invited time for outdoor hikes and contemplative walks while mulling over decisions. They have offered colorful storyboarding on walls while participants are engaged in planning. One large event with TCUs had a native man situated right in the center of the room, drawing scenes from various stages of the meeting. Almost every meeting, no matter what configuration of native or nonnative people are in attendance, begins with the burning of tobacco and a prayer, centering people on the task at hand. Songs and storytelling at breaks and meals bring creative energy to a group deliberating a tough issue.

4. *Accept the inherent risk of stepping into the mystery of the unknown that lies beyond the far too familiar landscape of violence.* It is a risk to communicate respectfully with those with whom you disagree. Indian reservations have notoriously high rates of unemployment. As two competing groups discuss a finite government grant to assist with job creation, it is difficult to share hopes, plans, and resources. At one planning session where the 36 TCUs were contemplating collaboration on nationwide tribal technology infrastructure, attendees were given questions to contemplate before they returned the next day.

Think of a technology success you have accomplished in the last two years. Describe it, and list the resources (time, money, people, equipment, etc.) that were in place to enable your success. Where else in your college or community could you use these resources to improve life for your people?

The results of this discussion were then shifted from a local focus to national, asking how local resources could be used to create improvement for Indians throughout the United States. Participants accented the potential risk of sharing resources.

These capacities show us that moving past our differences requires more than just the quest for a "solution." In fact, solutions that end a conflict are hard to find. As we have explored in the previous reorientations, we are looking to change the expression of conflict and provide avenues for redefining human relationships and affairs. Lederach invites us to move away from a linear path that takes us to an agreement as a product. The conflict can be placed in a new context, a social and political space seen as an ongoing platform. The metaphor of a platform helps us envision essential building blocks for sustainable and constructive social change through the management of difference:

This strategy is not driven by the concern of how to end the immediate and most pressing symptoms of conflict, but rather focuses on
how to create and sustain a platform capable of generating adaptive change processes that address both the episodic expression of
conflict and the epicenter of the conflictive relational context.[25]

Lederach also uses the metaphors of an antacid and an immune
system. We have an upset stomach, even a lifetime of heartburn. We
can buy acid-reducing pills to take every day. We can create temporary solutions to the stuff that bothers us. Building a dynamic platform for change creates an immune system. We help our body be
prepared to fight off invaders and retain strength. Residents of Indian
country find themselves experiencing devastating social problems,
high unemployment, low high school graduation rates, and ongoing
difficult decisions about assimilation with society. An antacid solution
would be to entice a major corporation into the community to provide
jobs. Take another antacid by dumping a bunch of money into a nicer
gymnasium at the high school to entice students to stick it out in high
school. Take one more antacid and strengthen the local police force to
be tougher on drug use. Those are all admirable solutions, but if we
want to meet the challenge of genuine change, we produce a platform
that resides deeper in the web of relationships. The creation of colleges and universities on the reservations provide more of an immune

system. There are multiple processes encompassed in one support structure. The colleges work closely with high school and elementary schools to build motivation and expectation about education. The colleges offer opportunities for entrepreneurism and teach students about economic development to foster creative ideas for community vitality. The colleges also offer education on social issues that explore the most relevant and successful ways to address diabetes, addictions, violence, and depression. And as a significant piece of the immune system, the colleges provide jobs for the community.

Moving toward Value

What is required to build a platform for change in the midst of our differences? First, we must recognize that any solutions or agreements we are working on are systematically connected to a broader process of change embedded within the web of relationships. Second, we must recognize agreements and solutions for the temporary antacids that they are. If we are developing a solution that does not endure and provide long-term health, we may need to look deeper into the web of relationships.

Look at the newspaper and find a challenging situation where human differences cause deep conflict. In the related story, what solutions are proposed? Is there any talk of creation of a platform for enduring change? Scan the whole newspaper. Do you see more examples of solutions (antacid) or platforms (immune systems)?

How You Can Use This Chapter

Differences are what make us human; they can coexist; they can purposefully work and live together as relevant voices and choices. When the differences become problematic, conflict ensues. The worst conflict occurs when difference becomes harmful. This chapter has explored new orientations that may require individual, group, organizational, or system movement.

1. From static culture to culture-as-process

    Culture is not a checklist. Culture gives us a way to talk about the relationships of individuals to social groups and institutions. We can learn about the basic schemas, models, and assumptions inherent in those relationships and identify moments when they are in play and need to be attended to. Culture is a process that gives us more insights into complexity so we can hold up human differences as a valuable resource. Complexify!

2. From resolution to engagement

   It is not necessary to resolve all conflicts. Once we grasp that freeing attitude, we can move forward and engage conflict and change the way we conduct ourselves within it. Resolution will happen in many cases, but it will happen within a complex system of needs, processes, actions, pauses, timetables, rehearsals, disappointments, and hopes. Engage!

3. From resolution to transformation

   We can create sacred spaces where we transform preconceived morals that are unchanging and positional to moral frames where people can change their stories, feel empowered to know what and why they believe as they do, and recognize others for their contributions and evolving perspectives. Transform!

4. From cynicism to civility

   Interpersonal communication gives us a chance to construct a value system of civility. Based on respect for the other, we invite dialogue among persons of difference. Civility!

5. From solutions to platforms

   Conflict does not go away easily. Our differences will continue to challenge us and require us to move past quick solutions. We can create platforms of durable change by harnessing multiple responsive processes of change that are rooted in a relational context. Platforms!

Table 11.1 Moving toward Value

	Sphere of Harm	Sphere of Challenge	Sphere of Value
From static culture to culture-as-process	Republicans are so egocentric when it comes to social security.	Is there an element of the social security issue that transcends party lines?	I see that you feel strongly about this aspect of social security. What life experiences have led you to develop this perspective so strongly?
From resolution to engagement	He's such a classroom bully. Send him to the principal now so he can learn to be nice.	We should address the issue of classroom behavior.	If this classroom were running smoothly and we all felt comfortable, what would be happening? How could we create that future?
From resolution to transformation	The only way to save the owl is to prohibit logging.	Can we discuss logging techniques that might protect owl habitat?	Let's create some community dialogues about land use in the Pacific Northwest.
From cynicism to civility	Our weekly staff meetings are such a waste of time, and management is thoroughly unreliable.	These staff meetings provide an opportunity for relationship building and ensuring productivity.	We have a vision for our workplace and some goals we are striving to meet. We need to work together to achieve them. Let's take a look at the vision and goals.
From solutions to platforms	We either need marriage counseling or divorce planning.	We have a 15-year relationship that is in turmoil. What should we do?	Let's try to spend every Tuesday evening discussing our relationship and make it a high priority. Who else should be involved? What issues are most pressing? What will be the riskiest things to address? How should we conduct the discussions? Where should we conduct them? Do we need a third party to guide us? What other resources do we need?

Interactive Case Study

A COMMUNITY CONCERN

Context: This situation offers a land use and community issue that engages multiple perspectives and parties in a "conversation" about their future. A large retail giant, SuperMart, has proposed building a store in a previously rural area that is in midstages of growth. The exploration of the case will look at orientations that invite the constructive management of difference. Two role-plays will occur: one offers a glimpse of the sphere of challenge or harm; the other moves toward the sphere of value.

Opening exercise(s): There will be a community meeting where a developer will present the plans for the new SuperMart to be built in Our Town. For years, this area had been irrigated farmland. The family farmers had enjoyed selling their produce at weekend farmers' markets and in small grocery stores. Over the past decade, many of the farmers have gone out of business or retired, as larger grocery stores and other retail offerings have begun to move into the area. The proposed site has been vacant for seven years. Geese, fox, and small animals can still be seen running across the field. The local school is located one block away.

Each stakeholder group will conduct preliminary research using the Internet, interviews, media, and other discussions. Each group will build a set of interests, experiences, hopes, and goals. After each group has done its homework, the class will participate in a role-play of this case and a series of discussions focusing on a variety of issues from this chapter. After the discussion, you will have a second role-play.

Divide the class into the following sets of stakeholders:

SuperMart Representative
Developer
Neighborhood Association
Local Business Association
Environmentalist Group
Local School Board

First Role-Play

For the first role-play, have someone be a convener or facilitator. This could be the mayor, the developer, or a city council member. Take some time in this role-play to explore the positions and interests of each stakeholder group. Allow everyone a chance to speak.

Discussion

Meet with your small groups to reflect on what happened in the opening role-play and what this means for your identity as a stakeholder group. Guide the discussion along five areas of focus:

Focus #1:

Complexify Culture: Within stakeholder groups, consider your group's culture again. Describe it in more complex terms. What are the unique distinctions that people within your group hold? Are these in-process in any way? Try to describe your culture as situational, flexible, and responsive to the challenges that come your way.

Focus #2:

Engagement: Have a discussion to consider the interests of the other stakeholder groups. What may be motivating them to hold their positions so strongly? What experiences might they have had to enable this stance? Using some of the points from this chapter, consider some methods of engagement for the upcoming meeting.

Focus #3:

Transformation: Consider the story that you have hardened in your mind and in your speech. Within that story, what are the dilemmas that arise? What gray areas are there for you? What do you wonder about as you consider this story and its implications? Can you create a "sacred space" where the moral of your story may change?

Focus #4:

Civility: In planning for your interactions in the upcoming meeting, remind yourselves, "engagement does not mean agreement." How can you speak with respect and invite respect for yourself? Plan for a way to keep the conversation going.

Focus #5:

Platforms: Using the metaphor of a platform, consider moving past quick solutions to a consideration of a platform that holds processes for durable change. Consider the web of relationships as a positive resource.

Second Role-Play

Hold role-play #2 with the new ideas created from new orientations learned in the focus discussions. What has changed? What did you notice about the interactions?

Endnotes

[1] Kevin Avruch, *Culture and Conflict Resolution* (Washington, DC: United States Institute of Peace, 1998), pp. 14–16.

[2] Avruch, p. 20.

[3] Avruch, p. 5.

[4] Avruch, p. 60.

[5] Bernard S. Mayer, *Beyond Neutrality: Confronting the Crisis in Conflict Resolution* (San Francisco: Jossey-Bass, 2004), pp. 23–28.

[6] Mayer, p. 145.

[7] Mayer, p. 184.

[8] Mayer, pp. 188–190.

[9] Mayer, pp. 206–209.

[10] Robert A. Baruch Bush and Joseph P. Folger, *The Promise of Mediation: The Transformative Approach to Conflict* (San Francisco: Jossey-Bass, 2005).

[11] Bush and Folger, pp. 13–14.

[12] Bush and Folger, p. 21.

[13] Bush and Folger, pp. 22–23.

[14] Sara Cobb, "Creating Sacred Space: Toward a Second-Generation Dispute Resolution Practice," in *Bringing Peace into the Room*, eds. Daniel Bowling and David Hoffman (San Francisco: Jossey-Bass, 2003), pp. 215–233.

[15] Cobb, p. 218.

[16] 1 February 2007, http://www.naso.org/sportsmanship/badsports.html

[17] Mick Hume (January 28, 2005), "The Most Dangerous 'Ism' Now Is the New Cynicism," 2 February 2007, http://www.spiked-online.com/Articles/0000000CA8AB.hrm

[18] *Oxford English Dictionary* (Oxford: Oxford University Press, 2006).

[19] Ronald Arnett and Pat Arneson, *Dialogic Civility in a Cynical Age: Community, Hope and Interpersonal Relationships* (Albany: State University of New York Press, 1999), p. 13.

[20] Arnett and Arneson.

[21] Arnett and Arneson, p. 284.

[22] Arnett and Arneson, p. 301.

[23] John Paul Lederach, *The Moral Imagination: The Art and Soul of Building Peace* (New York: Oxford University Press, 2005).

[24] Lederach, p. 5.

[25] Lederach, p. 47.

Appendix

A Guide to Practical Skills and Methods for Conflict Management

This appendix can serve as a practical manual, giving you a starting place to look for constructive conflict-management processes. The appendix presents a variety of different methods and options in a brief and straightforward manner. It is not exhaustive, but it is a basic toolkit. The complexity of conflict and the opportunity to create unique processes to address human difference leads to many more intricate and effective processes than can be explored here. Furthermore, the methods covered in the appendix are not mutually exclusive. They overlap considerably and are often used in combination. If you are interested in some of these methods, we encourage you to investigate further.

277

SECTION 1
BASIC COMMUNICATION SKILLS FOR CONFLICT MANAGEMENT

We like to organize basic communication skills into a model we call LARC.

- Listen
- Acknowledge
- Respond
- Commit

Not only is this a handy way to organize basic skills, but it also suggests a progression with which parties in a dispute can structure their conversation. For example, when coworkers encounter a potential conflict—an area of difference that could become a problem—they take some time to reflect together on what is important and to make a joint decision about how to proceed. First, they **listen** carefully to one another. Second, they **acknowledge** what seems to be important to the other person. Third, they **respond** with their own perspectives, and, fourth, they **make a commitment** about next steps.

LISTENING

We once saw a bumper sticker that said, "Conversation is like competition, and the loser is the listener." Our world often privileges the act of speaking. In political debates and workplace presentations, the speaker is the focus. Think about whether speech is the most significant form of human communication. Communication is a transactional process jointly constructed by people in interactions, which includes listening as well as speaking.

Listening is a learned skill. We must learn to participate in communication interactions both physically and mentally and listen carefully to sustain high quality communication. Here are some principles for listening in difficult conflict situations.

DELAY judgment—Don't be too quick to criticize what the other person is saying, even in your head. Listen first to comprehend.

ATTEND to the whole meaning of the message—Try to sense everything the person is expressing. Listen for the content of the message, the importance of what is said, the implications for the relationship or the group, and the feelings being expressed.

ASK questions to clarify—Within their own experience, people have good reasons for their opinions. Try to find out as much as you can about the other person's perspective by asking good non-judgmental questions. For example,

- Ask them what happened and who was involved.
- Ask them how they were affected.
- Ask them what they hope to get for themselves and the relationship.

Active Listening

Active listeners think consciously about the meaning of messages. Consider the following four procedures for active listening:

1. *Ask yourself questions to help you anticipate material.* Suppose your roommate says, "There are lots of reasons why I don't want to go to Mexico over spring break." Ask yourself, "What are the reasons?" and listen for them. Pay attention to your roommate's answers and the reasons he or she gives. If you need more information, ask for clarification.

2. *Pay attention to nonverbal cues.* Look at the tone of voice, body actions, and facial expression to see if the verbal message is congruent with the nonverbal communication. You are listening to how something is said, as well as what is said.

3. *Silently paraphrase to help you understand.* To reach shared meaning, you can talk to yourself about the message and your understanding of it. If you hear your friend talking about all the reasons she does not want to go to Mexico for spring break, as well as a statement about all the work she needs to do for her math class, you might say to yourself, "It sounds like she is concerned with the amount of homework piling up and is torn between a trip to the beach and being responsible." If you cannot paraphrase the message, maybe you need more information.

4. *Separate the governing idea (or purpose), key points, and details to help you understand a complex message.* In each message, there will most likely be some overall message and details to support the main points. You can do a mental outline of the message by looking for the purpose of the message, "Why is she telling me about this?" for the details, "What evidence is she giving me to support her purpose?" and reasons for the communication, "What does she want me to do or know as a result of this communication?" By offering respectful active listening and attending to full messages, we are encouraged to engage in clear purposeful communication.

Asking Questions

Questions are a powerful tool to assist us in making sense of our interactions, to learn the information we need to make decisions, and to improve our relationships. One of the simplest considerations to use when considering what type of a question to ask is whether you want it "open" or "closed." Open-ended questions require an answer that is more than a one-word response.

What is it about that ruling that makes you feel so strongly about it?

How can you find the time to make such a wonderful meal when you have such a busy life?

Tell me more about your role in the project. What are your duties and tasks?

Closed questions ask for a "yes," "no," or limited response.

Do you like the new ruling?

How many hours did it take to cook this meal?

What is your job title for the project?

In general, closed questions close down a conversation and can lead to a struggle to keep the conversation going. Open questions invite responses that contain much more information and more options for moving forward with the conversation. To add depth to a conversation, follow the suggestions below.

• Ask interesting, thought-provoking, specific questions.
• Ask who, what, when, and where questions.
• Ask follow-up questions of the person who just spoke.
• Pose follow-up questions to the entire group.

Here's what these questions sound like:

What skill did you discover that you hadn't thought of before?

What accomplishment are you most proud of?

When did that happen and who was there?

What most surprised you?

Karen's story about how the bond issue for the community center failed is intriguing. I wonder if anyone has had a successful experience with bond issues and can tell us what happened.

Good questions can do many things. They elicit clear information and more detail, help people think creatively, and help discover building blocks for effective decisions. There are pitfalls; avoid questions like the following.

Leading questions are worded in a way that pressures people to answer a certain way. *Don't you think that we should expand school funding?*

Double-barreled questions ask about two distinct issues at the same time. *What do you think about city development and how do you feel about our local recycling efforts?*

Open-to-closed switch questions are another type of two questions in one. The first question is very open while the second question is very closed. An open question allows a wide of range of possible responses while a closed question allows a narrow range of possible responses. *I was wondering, what do you think about our parks department? Do they need to sponsor more activities?*

Questions that use inappropriate language cloud the communication. Be clear, avoid the use of jargon, and ask questions that are age and culturally appropriate. *If we use our block grants in this way, what will be the ROI and what kind of economic multiplier effect do we foresee for this kind of investment?*

ACKNOWLEDGING

How do we interrupt arguments that set us up for competition? The step between "listen" and "respond" helps us break the cycle of attack/defend. We acknowledge what we heard the person say before we respond. You acknowledge in order to help people see themselves, the situation, the process, the constraints, and the group's behavior. Acknowledging what you see when it occurs helps the group work more constructively together. You can acknowledge lots of different kinds of things.

- Constraints, problems, difficulties. *I see we have reached an impasse.*
- Interests, values, goals. *Many of us are interested in a pay raise.*
- Differences and issues. *It sounds like the stop signs pose the most difficult problem.*
- Hard work and positive contributions. *Wow, we sure have discussed a few tough issues.*
- Positive, respectful interaction. *I can see the two of you are respecting each other's viewpoints.*
- Recognition of others. *So, you hear his concern with your barking dog.*
- Forward movement. *It looks like our team is ready to discuss the next item.*
- Shared concerns and common ground. *Most of us want our children to be safe.*
- Consensus and agreement. *We all could live with the new zoning ordinance.*

Here we discuss four of the most useful forms of acknowledgement—restating, reflecting feelings, reframing, and summarizing.

Restating

Restating what people say helps group members to hear one another and feel understood. You can also restate as a way of checking your own understanding. You can restate:

- main points. *You want a red dress, a blue veil, and some shiny shoes.*
- significant detail. *It sounds to me like the 4:00 PM deadline is not negotiable.*
- information that may not be well-understood. *It sounds as though management has not explained the time constraints very well.*
- points that seem very important to the speaker. *I can see you feel very strongly about global warming.*

Restate when:

- members of the group seem distracted.
- the speaker seems confused or unclear.
- key values or interests are being expressed.
- requests, demands, or proposals are put forward.
- participants acknowledge one another.

Reflecting Feelings

Often emotion is an important part of what is being expressed. Sometimes the feeling is more important than the content. Reflect feelings to help check understanding, help participants feel confirmed and acknowledged, and help the group members understand the emotional dimension of what others are saying.

- You can reflect feelings when you sense that the speaker really wants the emotion to be acknowledged. *You are frustrated about the border control ruling, is that right?*
- You can reflect feelings that seem especially pertinent to the participant's position, interest, values, or perspective. *Despite all the difficulties of this proposal, you would be extremely disappointed if it is not discussed.*
- You can reflect feelings that are not being heard or sensed by others. *Your anger is very strong and you want the school board to hear it.*

Reframing

Reframing is restating something that will help give others a constructive context for understanding what they are hearing, saying, and doing. Good framing can help soften and neutralize hostile comments, save face, encourage forward movement, clarify, and introduce fresh perspectives and creative thinking.

Complaints about the past can be framed as hopes for the future.

Statement: I'm getting sick and tired of all these absences. We can't get any work done.

Reframe: So you want to see attendance improved in the future, right?

Negative statements can be framed as positive desires.

Statement: The workload here is horrendous.

Reframe: You would like a more reasonable workload.

Personal attacks can be framed as issues.

Statement: If that secretary forgets to give me my messages one more time, I'm gunna fire her!

Reframe: Messages aren't being received?

Individual concerns can be framed as community interests.

Statement: I can't check the patients as often as I should.

Reframe: So the hospital needs to work out a way for patients to be checked regularly?

Concerns can be framed as visions.

Statement: We have entirely too many meetings.

Reframe: You want a work environment in which individuals can make independent decisions.

Summarizing

Summarizing can help others see progress, identify shared concerns, define issues, and stay on track. The key is to know **when** and **what** to summarize.

- Summarize after important information has been shared.
- Summarize when focus is desired.
- Summarize when a transition is needed.
- Summarize when thought time is needed.
- Summarize as a polite way to interrupt.
- Summarize when a shared concern or common ground seems to be emerging.
- Summarize when the group needs to get clarity on its issues.
- Summarize after various interests have been expressed.
- Summarize after one or more proposals have been made.
- Summarize at natural breaking points.

Responding

We can respond with respect and civility, even when we engage diverse perspectives and our situations are painful. It is important to state our own interests, goals, values, and needs. Somewhere in the same conversation, we can look for mutual or differing goals, values, and needs. We can respond by framing the issues and options and suggesting positive resources for change.

General Principles

When responding to another person, remember the following general principles.

- Speak for yourself.
- Speak from personal experience.
- Speak directly to others.
- Identify shared concerns.
- Explore your uncertainties, gray areas, dilemmas, and doubts.
- Show curiosity, rather than posturing.
- Uncover complexities and help others become less polarized.
- Be creative rather than using standard arguments.

"I" Statements

A great rule of thumb for constructing responses is to construct an "I" statement. This statement consists of (1) a description of how you feel, (2) some indication or description of the situation, and (3) why you feel that way. You may follow this statement with an indication of what you would like to see changed. These statements show that we are taking ownership of our own feelings in connection with certain environments while offering no request for change or action for the others in the conversation. These messages usually follow a simple format, as outlined below.

I feel_____ (feeling, emotion, description) when this is happening: _____ (objective description of the situation) because _____ (why I feel this way). I would like to see the situation changed in this way: _____ (without a direct confrontation).

The simple rule of thumb is that we start these statements with "I" instead of "you." Note the differences in the following statements. Consider, in particular, the safety and comfort of the speaking environment that is being created.

"You" Statements:

You never take out the trash.

You did not grade this test fairly.

Your committee left out the most important decision!

You did not let all of your citizens vote in the election.

"I" Statements:

I am very irritated when the trash is left unattended. I would like to see a reliable system of household duties created.

When I notice inconsistency in test grading results, I feel frustrated. It would be helpful to see the protocol for grading procedures.

I am worried when it seems that all decisions were not given equal treatment. In the future, I would be pleased to see a strong decision-making process developed that includes a strong issue-identification step.

I hope that all citizens would be given equal opportunity to vote. I feel impatient when some people have to struggle to get to the voting center.

COMMITTING

The final step can be an appropriate and necessary "marker" in constructive communication. We are defining commitment not in the usual sense (a decision for a clear course of action), but rather as a step of closure—a marker in the process. This marker will indicate a deliberate next step or intended ownership of a process or decision. It may also include the decision itself or some type of final closure to the process. Have you attended meetings or conversations that existed for discussion only? In many cases, people leave these frustrated, left hanging with no clear outcome or next step. There are several productive types of commitment. The important thing is to make some sort of commitment, no matter how large or small. You can:

DECIDE on an appropriate course of action.

CREATE a constructive environment for the discussion.

EXPLORE the problem further.

SOLVE the problem collaboratively.

MEDIATE through a third party.

SECTION 2
ALTERNATIVE DISPUTE RESOLUTION

Alternative Dispute Resolution (ADR) offers a variety of methods and choices to manage conflict. Seen by many as the overall term for "alternatives to adjudication," ADR usually includes mediation, arbitration, some alternative court-related processes, and a host of new offerings for managing difference. We will address a few ADR offerings here.

ADR PROCESSES

Arbitration is a process in which private impartial parties (arbitrators) resolve a disagreement between two or more parties. It is usually less expensive and less time-consuming than settling cases in court. A person or panel will give a judgment, advice, or settlement directions to the parties based on their testimony and evidence offered. Arbitration agreements can be binding or nonbinding and are often written into the conflict-resolution clause of contracts.

Mediation is essentially facilitated negotiation. It is a process in which a neutral third party helps guide a discussion between disputants about issues between them. Because of its importance as a form of conflict management, we elaborate on this form of ADR in the following section of this appendix.

Ombuds is a function provided by an independent office or person in an organization who supplements the existing administrative or formal grievance procedures. Ombudspersons assist people with interpersonal misunderstandings or disputes and, where appropriate, make recommendations for improvement in the working relationships of the entities they serve. They are often able to identify and track systemic problems and suggest ways of dealing with those problems.

Early Neutral Evaluation (ENE) gives parties a frank, confidential evaluation of the legal merits of their dispute. Usually performed by a judge, the independent research is performed before the case goes to court.

Minitrials is a process where each party presents a legal summary of its case before a third party before the case goes to trial. The third party is usually a judge and makes an advisory ruling regarding the settlement range, rather than giving specific solutions for the parties to consider.

Negotiated rule-making (reg-neg) brings together a group of representatives or stakeholders with a federal agency to negotiate the text of a proposed rule. If this group reaches consensus on the rule, then the federal agency can use this as a basis for its proposed rule in the Federal Register.

Partnering is a process used in a variety of ways, but most commonly between the federal government and contractors. Partnering workshops try to prevent disputes after the contract is awarded and before the work begins, creating a team approach to the project.

ONLINE PROCESSES

Online Dispute Resolution (ODR) takes place either entirely or partly online and addresses disputes that arise in cyberspace as well as those that occur in face-to-face interactions. ODR methods range from negotiation and mediation to arbitration and modified jury proceedings. As use of the Internet increases across the world, conflict management was quick to grasp the opportunities it provides. From its inception to address Internet disputes, ODR has expanded to aid communities and large systems in using online methods for discussing their problems. Some of the Web sites that offer ODR are automated and require little human intervention; others involve a neutral third party as a facilitator. Can online processes help parties bring value to their disagreements? A healthy commitment to process, proper organization, and an experienced mediator or conveners are the characteristics of online processes that can bring mutually satisfactory outcomes. The following is a sample of some of the tasks that might be employed using ODR.

- *Blind bidding.* This is a simple tool that can be used when there is a sticking point, perhaps something quantifiable like money or resources. The parties can be moved closer together or brought to resolution about that one point.

- *Enhanced negotiation.* There are sophisticated types of software that help people look at alternative solutions and consider what trade-offs they are willing to make.

- *Interest identification.* Sometimes people are not clear about their priorities and the interests behind their strongly held positions. Through assessments and sets of questions, parties can identify and explore their interests, hopes, goals, and needs concerning the issue at hand.

- *Polling.* Surveys and polls can be used to gather information between face-to-face meetings and can display results in ways that are framed with face-saving communication. These displays can prevent defensiveness or frustration with polarized interests.

- *Drafting.* Drafting a document online is often challenging at best and conflictual at worst. Reaching agreement on language and changes is cumbersome when done by e-mail. Software for online drafting enables participants to collaborate on changes and sometimes work by video conferencing to see each other and the document at the same time.

- *Monitoring enforcement.* If an agreement is reached that asks a stakeholder group to do something, checklists and other monitoring communications can alert the rest of the stakeholders when certain goals have been set. Of course, the challenge here is not to offer a "legal watchman" who polices the next steps and angers the parties.

NONVIOLENT COMMUNICATION

Nonviolent communication, or compassionate communication, as it is sometimes called, is not usually included in the set of ADR options, but it is gaining such rapid acceptance that we offer it here among alternative methods. The communication skills associated with nonviolent communication are very much in line with the skills covered in section 1 above. By focusing consciously on what we are observing, feeling, needing, and requesting, we can inspire compassion from others and respond compassionately to others and ourselves.

SECTION 3
NEGOTIATION AND MEDIATION

NEGOTIATION

Negotiation is a conversation where two or more parties attempt to reach an agreement. When people are experiencing differences as challenging or harmful, they negotiate to find a path, allowing the differences to be valued and serve as the basis for creation of positive steps forward.

When Do I Use It?

You will probably negotiate for something every day. Whether you are consulting with your boss, hoping for a raise, or are discussing your proposal for border control, you are managing your differences through a back-and-forth communication aimed to resolve the issue at hand. More formal negotiations occur in business and professional environments where parties meet at a bargaining table and use communication skills to try to get what they want. The essential ingredient in effective negotiation is the ability to communicate well amidst the human differences at hand. In ordinary negotiation, you do not use an intermediary, but you do experience control over the process and the outcome of the discussion. In more elaborate forms, negotiation can be done by parties' representatives, as in management-labor relations, lawsuits, and international relations.

How Do I Do It?

There are basically three forms of negotiation. The first, and perhaps most common, is *positional bargaining*. Here the parties just keep compromising until they meet in the middle. Negotiating the price of a house or a car is a good example. Negotiating a teenager's curfew is another. The second kind of negotiation is *quid pro quo—something for something else*. In other words, the negotiators trade favors: If you give me something I want, I'll give you something you want. If you let me stay out until midnight, I'll do extra chores this week. The third approach is *interest-based negotiation*.

Roger Fisher and William Ury introduced interest-based negotiation as a means of working toward mutual gains, or "win-win" solutions. Compared to positional bargaining that focuses on competing wants and demands, interest-based or *principled* negotiation is based on the interests or the needs *behind* what people say they want. Consider the case of two siblings fighting over an orange. Both children want the orange, and the parent has to decide what to do. Treated as a zero-sum game (the resources are finite), the parent might see that the only choice is to cut the orange in half, or perhaps the parent will say, "I will give the orange to the child whose room is the cleanest," or "I will give the orange to the child who asked me first." It turns out that one child wanted the orange for the juice, while the other child needed to grate the peel to bake a cake. Both *wanted* the orange (their positions) but each *needed* the orange for a different reason (their interests). The key question would have been, "What is it about that orange that makes you want it?" Successful interest-based negotiation is based on four principles.

1. *Separate the people from the problem.* In the negotiation, address the problems and the issues, not the personalities and the relationships. If one person feels threatened, it is more difficult to address the issue at hand.
2. *Focus on interests, not positions.* As the story of the orange illustrates, win-win solutions are based on meeting parties' goals and interests, not necessarily granting what they demand.

3. *Invent options for mutual gains.* Many people in conflict see the "fixed pie" as a certain amount of time, resources, staff, assets, and even personal attention. Constructive negotiations assume a larger pie. By expanding the pie before dividing it, a larger range of options can be considered.

4. *Use objective standards if possible.* Base the decisions on principles that both parties agree can be used to evaluate criteria. These criteria may include standards like market value, precedent, agreed upon standards, and institution policies. Keep emotions and personal feelings out of the conversation as much as possible.

To prepare for a negotiation, keep these points in mind:

1. *Consider what a good outcome would be for both of you.* These outcomes might be discussed at the negotiation table, or they can be determined individually in preparation for the negotiation. You probably already know your "position." It is most likely the first thing that comes to your mind when you ask yourself, "What do I want?" To determine your interests (number 2 above) you can ask yourself, "What is it about this position that makes me want it so much?" For example, you may know that you want $5000 for the damage done to your gate when one of your guests accidentally backed into it. That one position may have a variety of interests behind it.

- You may want to preserve (or end) the relationship with that person.
- You want the gate repaired for safety reasons.
- You think that your friend was too flippant about the damage, and $5000 would help her realize how important your house and belongings are to you.
- You may be concerned about your friend's drinking problem and see that a large monetary payment would scare him into thinking carefully before drinking and driving.

2. *Identify your BATNA.* BATNA is the acronym for the *best alternative to a negotiated agreement.* It is the course of action you will pursue if you don't reach an agreement in the negotiation. If you know your BATNA when you enter the negotiation, you will know whether any deal you are discussing makes sense or when you should walk away from the negotiation table. If your position is that you want $5000 for the damaged gate, ask yourself, "Am I willing to go to court if I don't get the full $5000?" What can you fall back on if you don't get the $5000? Maybe you are willing to accept less money. Maybe you are willing to have the other side repair the fence. Maybe you are interested in seeing your friend attend a course on alcoholism. Or maybe

you are willing to have your friend guarantee that he will never come to your house again. Knowing these alternatives and feeling confident that you would be satisfied with them is a sign of a strong BATNA.

3. *Try to determine the other side's positions, interests, and BATNA.* Doing some research or just reasoning about the other person's perspective can be helpful. In the case of the damaged fence, the other person's position may be a refusal to pay any money. Her interests might be:

- Financial preservation. I am so broke that I need to fight hard to preserve any money I have.
- Reputation. I will look so foolish to everyone if I give in. I want to be seen as a strong negotiator. I don't want anyone to know I had been drinking that night.
- Principle. I am not sure that I damaged the fence. I should not have to pay for something I didn't do.
- Friendship. I would like our friendship to continue but not in the same power structure.

The Harvard Negotiation Project has a worksheet to help identify and explore ways of improving the BATNA (see resource list at end of appendix).

What Outcomes Can I Expect?

When participating in a negotiation, you can expect to know better what you want, understand what you are willing to settle for, and have a better understanding of the other side's needs and goals. You will have a much better grasp of the issue at stake and the alternative solutions available.

MEDIATION

In mediation, a third party facilitates a negotiation process between parties who are experiencing conflict. It is an attempt to help parties whose differences are residing in the spheres of challenge or harm move to the sphere of value.

Sometimes called an intervener, a neutral, a third party, or a settlement facilitator, a mediator is a person who guides the communication between parties in conflict. Sometimes a co-mediator team conducts the session. Responsibilities of a mediator are:

1. Introduce the process.
2. Create trust in the process and in the mediator.

292 Appendix

3. Guide the parties in an exploration of their "stories" (what brings them to the mediation table).

4. Help the parties identify and focus on their interests, rather than their positions.

5. Lead the parties in a process of issue identification, option generation, and option evaluation.

6. Assist the parties as they narrow options and craft an agreement.

7. Ask questions to reality test the agreement.

8. Serve as a "recorder" and write the agreement that the parties create, if necessary.

9. Protect confidentiality of the proceedings.

When Do I Use It?

Mediation should flow naturally from negotiation. If you are in the midst of, or want to attempt, a negotiation and feel that assistance is needed to guide the process, you can use a mediation process. When human differences are making your relationship challenging or harmful in some way, direct negotiation may not be the most accessible option. Mediation offers a safe and effective way to address differences and gives hope that the differences can eventually coexist as valuable resources.

For some of the issues, you will have complete control over deciding what process will provide the most satisfactory approach. If you are trying to figure out a major life decision, such as adopting a child, you may choose to have the conversation with the help of a mediator. In other cases, you might not have as much control. If you are involved in a case that has found its way to the courts, such as a car accident, financial problem, or divorce or custody suit, you might use the court-connected mediation service, where mediator(s) will be assigned to your case, and the court sets up the logistics. Many contractual relationships, whether they are employment, consumer relations, construction issues, health-care relations, or other relationships where you are tied by a contract, have agreed upon methods of mediation to manage any potential conflicts that may occur.

You can look in the yellow pages of the phone book, check with your regional or state mediation association, or do a Web search to find mediators of all kinds to assist you with your issues. In large-scale cases, the American Arbitration Association can provide neutrals. When you choose a mediator, you are choosing to become more familiar with your motivations, your interests, and your goals, while exploring the motivations, interests, and goals of the other. Surprising outcomes often result, as parties are able to move away from positional bargaining to create interest-based solutions.

How Do I Do It?

The mediation flows generally through stages, but it can be as organic and creative as the parties desire. The stages described below are the commonly accepted ones and provide a reliable structure for mediation.

1. **Opening.** The introduction to a mediation sets the stage for the process and begins to build trust in both the mediator and the process. During this opening, the parties gain understanding about what they can expect during their interactions. The introduction usually includes:

   a. Welcome and thanks. It is important to reinforce that the parties voluntarily chose to come to mediation and that this effort alone constitutes a good faith effort to manage their conflict.

   b. Introductions. The mediator and the parties need to be introduced. During this segment, the mediator may check to see if parties agree to be addressed on a first name basis (versus more formal labels, like "Mr. Smith" or "Dr. Jones").

   c. Definition of mediation. Mediators often like to personalize their definition of mediation. In general, they will emphasize the process and the helpfulness of a neutral third party.

   d. Role of mediator. It is important to clarify the role of the mediator immediately. Mediators give communication guidance and facilitate the negotiation process; they do not serve as any type of judge or jury, do not make recommendations, and do not advise (other than process advice). The mediator is impartial, which means that the mediator has no stake in the outcome of the process.

   e. Confidentiality. One strength of the mediation process is its confidentiality. What is said within the mediation process can be kept confidential, especially by the mediator. Parties often sign a confidentiality agreement before the session begins. If all parties agree to disregard confidentiality, then the parties and the mediator are free to discuss the case.

   f. Caucus. Occasionally, the parties and/or the mediator may see that it would be beneficial to ask for a series of private meetings with the parties. Each party would meet for a short time with the mediator. The discussions in that session could be confidential or the information could be shared with the other party, either in a private session or when both parties meet together again. Caucuses are most effective when emotions are high, parties seem hesitant to speak or share information, and when the session seems especially stuck.

2. **Storytelling.** This phase of the mediation process is a time for the parties to share their interests, hopes, concerns, and stories. After the introduction, the mediator can open with a question, such as, "Let's begin this process by hearing about what brought you to mediation. Which one of you would like to begin? What brings you here today?" As the parties tell their stories, the mediator uses communication tools to summarize, reframe, clarify, and begin focusing on interests. By the end of this phase, it would be helpful to have both parties understanding each other's interests, as well as realizing their own interests. Important information will be out in the open, and the basis for doing some problem-solving talk has been created.

3. **Issue framing.** Before any discussion about possible solutions, paths forward, or agreements, it is necessary to frame the issue(s). This phase entails the identification of the questions that the parties want to work out. In simple mediations, there may be only one glaring issue. In more complex cases, it may be necessary to list the issues that divide the parties and to prioritize them. An agenda may be set, which could be accomplished in one setting. Depending on the number and complexity of issues, multiple meetings may be scheduled. This discussion is a significant one, as the parties gain ownership of the issues they will be discussing, which will help to build commitment to eventual outcomes.

4. **Option generation.** This phase can be addressed either in an informal and flowing manner or in a more formal problem-solving format. Informally, the mediator may ask a general question, "What can we do about (issue) that meets your need for (interest of party A) and your need for (interest of party B)?" As the session moves forward, the mediator can help steer the options that are generated toward those that meet the interests of both parties. In a more formal option generation stage, the mediator may take some time to discuss process concerns with the parties. Together, they may determine a way of working with which they can all agree. They may decide to set a time limit and begin with a brainstorm session. Still using the question posed above, the parties would list all the possible solutions, without any evaluation of them. Once a full list has been created, they can move to the next stage.

5. **Option evaluation.** Once a set of options has been identified, the parties can assess each of them from the perspective of their interests. The mediator can ask, "Let's look at each option, one at a time. How does this meet your need for (interest of party A) and your need for (interest of party B)?" The list of options will narrow down, hopefully to a workable few. As they narrow down, choices for agreement may become clearer.

6. **Reality testing.** At this point, parties may be beginning to feel optimistic, sensing that agreement may be possible. Mediators now will ask the tough questions that will determine the workability of the options for agreement. Several examples follow.

   • When you get back to the workplace, how will this new arrangement be put in place?

   • How will you be able to finance this agreement?

   • What will you do if one of you does not keep up their end of the agreement?

   • Can you do this?

   • Can you afford this?

   • Will there be time to make this happen?

   • What will be the biggest challenge in putting this agreement into action?

7. **Agreement.** This phase could entail a variety of things. If the mediation does not find options that meet the interests of both parties, they could "agree to disagree." If that type of agreement results, it is important that the mediator not display any disappointment or dissatisfaction. The parties participated in a high-quality process and crafted a way of moving forward, and they will live with the consequences. An agreement is not the only way for that future to be created. If mediation does reach an agreement, it is usually written up, sometimes handwritten, and sometimes typed into a computer. In either case, the parties and the mediator sign the agreement; copies are made and distributed at the session. Often the mediator serves as a recorder, writing down the language that the parties want to use in describing their agreement. If the mediator sees or hears something different or contrary to what has been discussed or decided, the mediator may ask, "I see in this part of the agreement you are wanting to do X, and I just want to check this out with you a bit more thoroughly. Earlier, you had stated that you wanted to do Y. Can you help clarify that before we write it into the agreement?" Most importantly, any agreement needs to be

clearly written, be specific, and use the words and phrases that
the parties specify.

What Outcomes Can I Expect?

There are a multitude of mediation programs in the world today.
You may experience mediation results in many different contexts.
Whatever the situation, you will learn significant things about yourself and others, while addressing an issue in contention. Here are a
few examples.

- If your neighbors complain that your tree is dropping pollen-
  laden blossoms in their yard, a mediation could give you new
  understanding of what it means to be a good neighbor and help
  you become aware of your own and your neighbor's interests,
  goals, life struggles, values, and perspectives. You might decide
  collaboratively to chop down the tree, or you may end up rak-
  ing the blossoms out of their yard.

- You may end up in a court-related situation because of a law-
  suit, a consumer complaint, a family struggle with divorce or
  custody, or maybe even a criminal issue. If mediation is encouraged before the case goes to trial, you may be able to take care of
  the issue so going to court is no longer necessary. If your case
  does not settle in mediation, you will have a deeper knowledge
  of the other side's perspective and still might be able to settle
  out of court. A high number of cases leave mediation and settle
  "on the courthouse steps."

- In school settings, whether elementary, middle school, high
  school, or higher education, you may find yourself in a conflict
  with a student, staff, or faculty member. Mediation can give you
  a path forward that could affect your grades, your career at that
  school, or your interpersonal relations. Schools that are lucky
  enough to have mediation programs experience efficient and
  effective use of resources and are able to diffuse tense situations
  earlier than lengthier traditional administrative processes.

- You may face a difficult conflict in your workplace with a fellow employee, a boss, or even a customer. Organizational mediation can level the playing field so workplace issues can be
  discussed and decided, increasing productivity and decreasing
  stress and dissatisfaction.

- As a member of a community or region, you may encounter the
  need to make difficult choices about land use and environmental
  issues. These types of mediations usually address policy and
  community choices, allowing groups of people to have a hand in

crafting workable decisions. Often very complex and lengthy, these processes can engage multiple stakeholders in a process that protects a multitude of interests in preserving the environment.

International mediation can occur within or between countries and could be sanctioned by the government(s), or it could be an informal process conducted by experienced peacekeepers. Mediated global outcomes can affect border control, human rights, trade policies, and a host of other difficult international issues.

If you want to be a mediator . . .

Students in courses on communication and conflict often look into becoming a mediator. The first step is to take a basic 40-hour mediation training course. This will provide basic knowledge and a good foundation, but you will need additional practice and experience. You can volunteer in a community mediation program or as an intern with a mediation department or organization. We also recommend additional training in advanced mediation, family mediation, workplace mediation, or any number of other specialties.

SECTION 4
SMALL- AND LARGE-GROUP PROCESSES

FACILITATION

Many small- and large-group processes benefit from the services of a facilitator. Facilitators are neutral third parties, like a mediator, who help the group establish and maintain a productive process. Here are some of the things facilitators do.

- Help organize the group's work.
- Maintain impartiality.
- Let the group decide what it wants to accomplish and help them get there.
- Help create a safe feeling in the group.
- Help clarify group goals.
- Assist in selecting participants.
- Help set ground rules and guidelines.
- Encourage members to be committed to the group.

- Help group members work together.
- Set up the room and equipment.
- Keep the discussion within the time limits.
- Guide the discussion.
- Ask helpful questions.
- Make sure everyone has a chance to participate.
- Help the members feel they are contributing.
- Provide focus.
- Manage behavior.
- Help participants communicate.
- Summarize what has been said.
- Keep notes.
- Provide encouragement.
- Manage disagreements.
- Help the group make progress.

When Do I Use It?

Facilitators are beneficial when you want a group process that has clear communication, an effective agenda that leads to productive outcomes, a way for conflict to be managed, and an opportunity for inclusive and constructive communication in the midst of diverse views.

How Do I Do It?

As a process manager, the facilitator is more concerned with process and group dynamics than with content. A facilitator does not impose judgment or give solutions to the group. To effectively manage the process, a facilitator needs to remember the following.

1. What is the goal or desired outcome of the session?
2. In what direction is the group actually heading? Is it toward the outlined goal or desired outcome?
3. Is there a difference between numbers 1 and 2 above?
4. If there is a difference, the facilitator may need to intervene to redirect the group's focus toward the outlined goal or desired outcome.

To keep a group focused and directed on task, a facilitator can rely on tools such as ground rules, a clear agenda, and a safe environment. A design committee, the facilitator, or the group itself can set *ground rules*. The most effective ground rules usually focus on common courtesy and civility, such as "one person speaks at a time, no personal attacks, keep comments concise and brief." Facilitators must ensure that there is a *clear agenda*. A clear agenda creates a common set of assumptions for all participants involved. Remember that group members come together with different sets of perceptions, ideas, beliefs, and values. It is important for a facilitator to display, discuss, and refer to the agenda. Most sessions have an agenda for the day and a smaller "mini-agenda" for each portion of the session. A *safe environment* allows participants a place to freely share points-of-view, negotiate issues, and discuss options. Facilitators acknowledge the voices of participants, directing and redirecting comments in the appropriate direction. People want to be heard and recognized.

What Outcomes Can I Expect?

Usually a facilitator can help you establish and achieve a clear set of goals, keep the meeting orderly and organized, allow everyone to speak, help resolve conflict, and provide a useful written report of results.

COLLABORATION AND CONSENSUS BUILDING

Collaboration occurs when two or more people interact in pursuit of a shared goal. This means choosing to work as a group instead of working individually toward shared goals that might move you from the sphere of challenge or harm to the sphere of value. Collaboration essentially means using interest-based negotiation. In small and large groups, it expands this concept to encompass problem solving.

In collaboration, the situation is defined as a problem to be solved, not a disagreement to be settled: "How can we lower our workload, get projects completed faster, and increase expertise and creative input without increasing costs?" In collaborative problem solving (as in negotiation), we . . .

1. ask people to identify their interests.
2. discover shared interests and separate interests.
3. carefully frame the issue so that the parties can creatively explore options.
4. identify the criteria by which options can be kept or eliminated.
5. deliberate consciously about the trade-offs for each option.
6. isolate the options that will meet the interests in a way that is acceptable to everyone.

Collaborative group decisions are most often made by consensus. Consensus does not mean that everyone is equally enthusiastic about the outcome. It *does mean* that:

- everyone believes that this is the best decision that could be made at this time, with this group, under these circumstances;
- everyone agrees that at this time and under these circumstances, consensus is preferable to nonconsensus;
- no one who could block or obstruct the decision will exercise that power; and
- everyone needed to implement the decision is willing to do so.

Although individuals may not agree with every aspect of the decision, all agree to support it *as a package*.

When Do I Use It?

Consensus-based decision making is important under the following circumstances.

- The solution is not clear, or there is disagreement about the solution.
- Parties are willing to negotiate.
- Time is sufficient, and the process is feasible.
- Various stakeholders have important interests that must be taken into account.
- Certain stakeholders would move to block the decision if they were left out of the decision-making process.

How Do I Do It?

Consensus decisions are best accomplished in small groups, preferably less than ten people. If the decision is significant and affects a large number of people, it is important to include as many representatives in the process as necessary. If large numbers of people are involved, stakeholder *representatives* can come together in a collaborative, consensus-based process. The group must have adequate time, as consensus decision making takes much more time than voting or assigning the decision to one person or a subgroup. Consensus processes typically follow a process such as this.

1. Convening: This means getting ready to talk. It involves several steps:
   - Assessing the situation and issues.
   - Mapping the stakeholder system and establishing what interest groups should be included.

- Inviting participants.
- Setting up logistics and arrangements, including time and place.

2. Process Design: This involves working with stakeholder representatives to accomplish the following:
- Designing a process.
- Clarifying roles and responsibilities.
- Setting the agenda.
- Writing a process agreement, ground rules, or guidelines.

3. Deliberating: Here participants engage in dialogues to explore their respective interests, positions, and goals. Several things can be accomplished at this stage:
- Framing the issues.
- Identifying options.
- Discovering common ground, shared interests, and key differences.
- Weighing the gains and losses of each option.

4. Deciding: Here the group comes together in a set of consensus decisions. They may:
- Write a single-text agreement.
- Make consensual decisions.
- Identify issues that remain unresolved.
- Determine next steps.

Participants can respond to a consensus decision in any of the following ways:

1. Support consensus entirely. (*I support it.*)
2. Support consensus with a reservation and rationale. (*I think this may be a mistake, but I can live with it if my concerns are noted.*)
3. Nonsupport. (*I don't see the need for this, but I won't object vocally.*)
4. Stand outside of consensus. (*I personally can't support this, but I won't block others from supporting it.*)
5. Withdraw from the group. (*I can't support it, so I'll withdraw from the group so that I don't interfere.*)
6. Block consensus. (*As a member of this group, I stand against this and will not permit consensus to happen.*)

Consensus can be declared in all of the above situations, except the final one. If there is even one objection blocking the group, this must be worked out before the proposal can be adopted. The group can amend the decision or reconsider the decision. The group continues until they reach an outcome that will not be blocked.

Obviously, then, consensus is something that must be built. To do it well, the process takes time and deliberation. Here are some things to keep in mind.

1. Consensus building is more a process of creativity than persuasion.

2. Consensus requires an attitude of collaboration with an emphasis on what participants can do together as a community. Consensus works when the participants see themselves as partners rather than adversaries.

3. Participants in a consensus process should work together to establish a way of working, define the problem, frame the issues, and gather information, all of which creates a common context for understanding the work. Early context-setting is necessary for fruitful discovery of values, interests, and goals; creation of integrative options; careful deliberation; and decision making.

4. Premature identification with positions can reduce the effectiveness of necessary context-setting work, making consensus building difficult or impossible.

5. Consensus relies on identifying common concerns and visions and jointly creating action plans.

6. In a good consensus process, differences are explored and expressed openly in a respectful and safe environment.

7. Empowerment and recognition are keys. Participants should be able to identify what is most important to them and express this in a way that others can appreciate and respect. Participants should also be able to hear and understand the perspectives of others, even those with which they disagree.

8. Consensus communication aims more to understand the perspectives of others than to persuade others they are wrong.

9. In a consensus process, genuine differences are acknowledged and allowed to stand on their own merit. Agreeing to disagree is itself a form of consensus. We can achieve consensus on the idea that certain disagreements are necessary and healthy.

10. Differences are not viewed as a problem but as a valuable resource that can make values and interests clear, identify the centers of passion, stimulate creative thinking, and provide a basis for continued dialogue.

11. Consensus building thrives in communities that appreciate a multivalued world. When communication begins to resemble a debate between two options, consensus will probably break down.

12. Consensus building is an ongoing process that is never complete.

13. The product of consensus should be viewed as partial, organic, and changeable.

What Outcomes Can I Expect?

A final decision will be made. Often this decision is a better one than a single person or subgroup could have reached.

• Many people understand the decision and the process by which it was reached.

• Commitment and ownership of the decision will exist among the participants.

• Participants will be informed about many aspects of a complex issue.

• A rich exchange of ideas will provide resources for future decisions.

• Communication skills will be enhanced.

Public Engagement

Public dispute management is the range of processes and methods for managing conflicts and developing policies involving public issues that engage citizens and governments collaboratively. Public engagement methods can help you decide if and when and how to get involved.

When Do I Use It?

As a member of the public, you are often called on to at least consider decisions that need to be made, policy that needs to be set, issues that need attention, and concerns that need to be resolved in your neighborhood, community, or region of whatever size. You can do an informal or formal assessment of your status in this conflict and decide how and when you could get involved. This assessment could include looking at the causes of the conflict, the people who are substantively affected by the conflict's outcome (including yourself), the interests of those people (stakeholders), the feasibility of using a collaborative process to address these issues, and the resources you have to enable you to get involved.

How Do I Do It?

Some type of assessment and convening function, as described in the previous section, needs to be completed. The convening efforts would identify the issue in question, establish the network of stakeholders who should be involved in the initiative, create a process design (a way of working together), and generate process options for managing the public issue at hand.

Many processes are available, depending on what you want to do. Here is a partial inventory of public engagement processes:

Public Opinion Processes.   Public opinion processes are designed to discover public attitudes. Although useful in initial stages of public engagement, they do little to engage stakeholders in the issues at hand.

Surveys—Best done by polling experts, this kind of research can be valuable in ascertaining the range of opinion on particular issues.

Focus groups—Focus groups are an excellent method for getting in-depth information about feelings, values, concerns, and ideas. These must be done systematically and with careful observation and record keeping. Although harder to codify than surveys, focus group responses are usually more thoughtful and complete.

Deliberative polling—This method seeks public opinion, but only after participants have had a chance to participate in a town-hall type meeting on the issue, in which they can learn more about and explore the options with others. It seeks an opinion informed by social interaction rather than an uninformed, individualistic opinion.

Public Education Processes.   Educational processes aim to build understanding of technical and policy issues among stakeholder groups. They can be helpful, and even necessary, but do little to mine the wisdom of members of the public. The public is skeptical of public education campaigns that are perceived as one-sided.

Forums and presentations—These can be helpful in disseminating information, but they can also lead to a lack of trust because, by themselves, they do not involve the public in discussion.

Interactive Web sites—These are a good way of educating the public, but they are limited to those who own the necessary equipment and who are inclined to participate in online work. The advantage of Web sites over forums is that they record threaded discussions in which stakeholders can learn from one another.

Study circles—Stakeholders spend up to several weeks reading material and discussing issues while also sharing concerns and ideas. Study circles are an excellent means for informed public input.

Dialogue groups—Dialogue groups are especially helpful in situations where stakeholder groups are in conflict with one another over an issue. Here they can explore their differences and common ground in a safe, productive setting. Dialogue groups are especially helpful to build respect and trust prior to participating in actual planning or deliberation processes. (See next section.)

Public Input Processes. Public input is very common in policy development. It is even required in the United States in many areas. Several approaches vary in their levels of actual public participation.

Public hearings—Probably the worst form of public input, hearings can be polarized and combative. As part of a larger set of processes, however, they do allow some public input, and if the sponsors show that they are taking this input seriously, hearings can help to build trust. Follow-up is essential.

Issue-framing workshops—Especially designed to elicit ownership of an issue, these processes engage stakeholders in collaborative issue identification. They are useful for grounding issues in terms that stakeholders appreciate and understand, eliciting policy options and reality testing.

Consensus planning workshops—If well-designed and facilitated, these meetings provide an excellent collaborative approach to stakeholder involvement and trust building. Unlike public hearings, consensus processes involve stakeholders in the actual planning process. Many creative and effective communication processes can be used and are developed in these workshops.

Multistakeholder road mapping—This kind of event involves a multistakeholder group of manageable size to work through the ideas produced in other, larger workshops to create a refined action plan.

Formuls for e-democracy—Internet-based processes of collaboration, discussion, and deliberation.

Public Deliberation Processes. Similar to the planning processes described above, these types of events allow participants to discuss policy problems in some detail with particular emphasis on the pros and cons of various options without having to achieve consensus. These processes are most helpful where there is a diversity of perspectives on an issue and where participants will probably not be able to reach consensus. Public deliberation and dialogue processes build mutual understanding—if not agreement—and are especially helpful to policy makers, who can listen for shared and separate values, creative ideas, deep concerns, and public judgments of policy options.

Citizen conferences—This is an expanded focus-group format in which a diverse group of citizens, carefully selected to represent stakeholder groups, conduct a Q&A of experts to learn more about an issue and then deliberate about specific policy options, discussing the pros and cons of each option. The group then gives a report to policy makers.

Deliberation forums—Unlike a pro-con debate, participants at a deliberation forum systematically address a set of policy options on an issue, openly exploring the gains and losses of each option along with its underlying values. Policy makers listen and learn from the public wisdom expressed.

Study circles—In addition to allowing groups to explore an issue over time, they may also deliberate over an extended period on policy options.

Other Public Engagement Processes. The above list is just a sampling of the many processes available for public engagement. Here are some other common formats.

Open Space Technology was developed by Harrison Owen with the purpose to gather an entire organization or interested parties in one place and enable them to talk about topics together. This provides the experience of the "whole system" being in the room to discuss and form actions around decisions. One unique aspect about this event design is the ground rule, "be prepared to be surprised." This intervention allows people to temporarily restructure the organization around their interests, passions, and concerns and makes visible the underlying energy patterns of the organization. According to Owen, outcomes based on the passions and interests of participants are more likely to become reality.

This process is one of the ultimate forms of participatory action, as the group creates the agenda and runs the meeting for the entire time, addressing issues they really care about. Four simple principles guide the Open Space activity.

1. Whoever comes are the right people.
2. Whatever happens is the only thing that could have happened.
3. Whenever it starts is the right time.
4. When it is over, it is over.

Future Search Conference is a three-day large group, organization, or community-wide intervention developed by Marvin Weisbord and Sandra Janoff. A Future Search Conference enables the participants to discuss their past and present and to focus on their desired future as an organization. The outcome of the conference is a specific future vision with concrete action steps.

Gaming methodologies—Methods such as Prosperity Games™ and scenario gaming can be used to engage stakeholder teams in a realistic systemic interaction to create and test various futures. This use of gaming methodology employs a stakeholder engagement process occurring in a live, interactive setting. A useful tool for large-scale strategic planning, games provide an exciting and productive step toward a road map to the future. Representing a wide range of interests and diversity of views on key issues, players representing numerous stakeholder groups propel their collective intelligence into a working consensus.

Public dialogue—See the next section.

What Outcomes Can I Expect?

The best results of public engagement processes are the opportunities for shared power among citizens and elected officials. Trust and respect can be established and encouraged to grow. The public knows that it has been heard, and the elected officials have been heard. Since they worked together to frame the issues, to deliberate on the tough options for addressing the issues, and on the final decision, all participants should be able to experience ownership and commitment to the action steps required by the decision. A social world will have been created where multiple voices and perspectives are honored and explored.

SECTION 5
DIALOGUE

We wrote extensively about dialogue in chapter 10 of this book. Here we provide additional, more practical information about how dialogue can be done. Dialogue is not really a method per se but an attitude or approach to any communication in which important differences must be addressed. Dialogue is a spirit that can infuse any of the methods outlined in the previous sections of this appendix.

The Public Dialogue Consortium characterizes dialogue as a process in which participants remain in the tension between *holding their ground* and *being profoundly open to the other*. When you are *holding your ground*, you express ideas, values, beliefs, and feelings passionately.

- *I would like to share with you my strongly held beliefs, but I recognize that this is only my perspective and it is one of many.*

- *Today it will be interesting to begin to understand the good reasons we all have for the perspectives we hold.*

- *Could I take a moment to tell you a couple examples from my life that have led me to hold this perspective?*

Being profoundly open to the other shows readiness to listen and to understand, if not agree to, the good reasons that all participants in the conversation have for holding their positions.

- *What is it about that issue that makes you believe it so strongly?*

- *What are some examples from your life that allowed you to form that perspective?*

- *What is at the heart of the perspective you hold? What do you believe most strongly?*

- *Let me make sure I am hearing you correctly. I understand that you believe this (perspective), and want to make sure that (outcome) happens. Do I have that right?*

WHEN DO I USE IT?

When you are truly interested in the differences that exist between and among you and others, you are ready for dialogue. When you are experiencing conflict with others and want it resolved in a way that salvages and strengthens your relationship, you are ready for dialogue. When you are just as concerned about the process of communication as you are about the outcome of communication, you are ready for dialogue.

HOW DO I DO IT?

Dialogue has the best results when accomplished in small groups. These small groups could be free standing, such as five neighborhood groups set up to discuss community safety at a day-long meeting. The groups could rotate members, such as in a large multistakeholder meeting where participants sit in one dialogue group for a part of the day, switch to another group with new stakeholders, and switch again to gain multiple perspectives. Or you could establish a dialogue group informally with one small group to discuss an issue, such as homeland security or diversity on campus.

The circular nature of dialogue stems from an attitude that we *manage our differences* rather than *resolve our differences*. Using methods and processes that offer an ongoing conversation about managing difference in the spheres of challenge and harm and the potential to move the differences to the sphere of value reinforces the circular nature of dialogue.

The Public Dialogue Consortium created the *CVA method*, which asks participants in a dialogue to explore an issue from three perspectives. Careful attention to context can help a conflicted, or potentially conflicted, group experience a movement of mind, or shift of consciousness, from the stuck spot to a place of constructive conversation. CVA stands for (1) *concerns*, (2) *visions*, and (3) *actions*. Essentially a tool of scoping or context shifting, CVA invites participants to move their minds around a circle that connects problems, solutions, and plans.

In a CVA process, the group will discuss concerns, visions, and actions in turn. We normally start where the group's energy is. If, as is commonly the case, the group is stuck on problems, or concerns, we start there and facilitate a discussion about their worries. We then ask the question, "If these problems could be solved, how would things be different? What would result?" The group then explores outcomes, which is their vision for how they would like things to be. Let's say, for instance, that a work-group is very concerned about a new peer evaluation system, saying that it would hurt coworker relationships and add to their workload. The group would—under visions—discuss how a system might work if these concerns were solved. Next, the group will move to actions, or what needs to be done to mitigate the concerns and build the vision.

Sometimes you encounter a group with a lot of energy for visions: "We need to get along better and have a workplace where everyone is comfortable. We need a supervisor who provides good leadership and allows everyone the freedom to do their job well." In this kind of scenario, we would start by leading a dialogue on vision. Let the group dream a little and build the vision of the kind of outcome they hope for. Then move to actions, "What would need to happen to make this vision possible?" And then to concerns, "What concerns do you have about this plan and this vision?

Sometimes groups start out with much energy for action: "We should do this and we should do that." They are full of ideas about what could be done. Fine. Let's start there and let them brainstorm. However, we would not recommend stopping there. Help the group move from its list of actions to visions: "How will things change if these actions are implemented?" And then to concerns: "What are some of the problems you foresee in achieving this vision or implementing these actions?" You may even go around the circle—concerns-visions-actions—several times while the group reality tests and refines their ideas.

CVA can also be helpful when a group is stuck on problems, visions, or actions. If there is a lot of argument about the problem (concerns), intentions, goals (vision), or courses of action, it may be helpful to move temporarily from one to another. So, for example, if the group can't stop arguing about what the problem is, it might set that topic aside for a little while to concentrate on goals or visions. The same would be true with conflicts of action; productive conversation in these cases might be achieved by returning to concerns and/or visions.

CVA Method

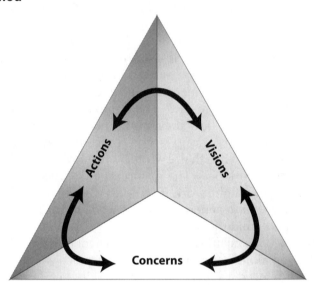

WHAT OUTCOMES CAN I EXPECT?

At a minimum, you can expect the satisfaction of experiencing a process that illuminates healthy, respectful communication. You may use a model that is emergent, giving you the utmost process control. In this model, a community organization holds a series of focus groups or establishes a design team to explore an issue and frame various ways in which it might be discussed. A unique series of dialogue meetings is designed based on the outcomes of the focus groups. The Public Dialogue Consortium is a leader in using this model.

You may use a model that is more private. This model consists of a series of private dialogues to explore personal feelings, ideas, and perspectives on a controversial issue. Representatives with opposing points of view are included, and the session is highly structured and facilitated to assure a safe environment and prevent destructive debate. The leader in this method is the Public Conversations Project.

You may have focused discussions that result in policy implications. In a series of meetings, participants deliberate about an already-framed issue. Sessions follow a standard format. Educational materials are distributed in advance, and the discussions focus on policy options and community action. Leaders in this model are the National Issues Forums and the Study Circle Resource Center.

You may reach a vision of the future or a set of actions to guide your future steps. Vision to action workshops offer a flexible approach for communities in large- and small-group formats to explore concerns, visions, and actions. Accomplished in a single- or multiple-session design, these events invite participants to move from a discussion of concerns to visions and then to create action plans.

Practical Guidelines for Dialogue

Goals	Guidelines
Create the right conditions.	1. Don't wait until conflict breaks out. Engage stakeholders in conversations early on.
	2. If open conflict has already happened, look for the right moment, often when participants are tired of fighting or become desperate for new solutions.
	3. Work initially in small, private groups.
	4. Be careful about the role of leaders and other powerful persons. Allow all of the voices to be heard from the start.
	5. Build on prior success. Avoid single-shot interventions; use a grow-as-it-goes process.
	6. Be creative about process. Think about what will work best now under the conditions currently experienced.
Manage safety.	1. Think consciously about time and place.
	2. Provide appropriate structure.
	3. Solicit agreements on process.
	4. Promote good facework.
	5. Respond to willingness and felt need.
	6. Find a shared level of comfort.
	7. Leave an out.
	8. Use an impartial facilitator.

(continued)

Practical Guidelines for Dialogue *(continued)*

Goals	Guidelines
Provide a process that encourages constructive conversation.	1. Take sufficient time to explore. 2. Encourage listening; build listening into the process. 3. Help participants to listen beyond mere content. Listen deeply to lived experience, stories told, values, shared concerns, and differences. 4. Ask good questions designed to open the conversation, not close it down. 5. Frame issues carefully to capture a context that will create a joining place. 6. Be appreciative. Look for positive resources, and look for the reasons behind negative comments. 7. When speaking, aim to be understood rather than to prevail in a contest. 8. Base positions in personal experience, and help others to understand your life's experiences. 9. Maintain a multivalued rather than bipolar viewpoint. Listen for all the voices.
Maintain ends-in-view and think about possibilities for outcomes of the conversation.	1. Discover the heart of the matter, or learn what is most important to all participants. 2. Build respect by looking for the ways in which others are experienced, complex, concerned, intelligent, healthy, and rational. 3. Learn about complexity; develop a healthy suspicion of a two-valued framing of any issue.

SECTION 6
PRACTICAL RESOURCES

Bush, R. A. B., and J. P. Folger. *The Promise of Mediation: Responding to Conflict through Empowerment and Recognition.* San Francisco: Jossey-Bass, 1994.

Daniels, S. E., and G. B. Walker. *Working through Environmental Conflict: The Collaborative Learning Approach.* Westport, CT: Praeger, 2001.

Domenici, K., and S. W. Littlejohn. *Mediation: Empowerment in Conflict Resolution.* 2nd ed. Long Grove, IL: Waveland, 2001.

Fisher, R., and D. Shapiro. *Beyond Reason: Using Emotions As You Negotiate.* New York: Viking, 2005.

Fisher, R., and W. Ury. *Getting to Yes: Negotiating Agreement without Giving In.* New York: Penguin, 1991.

Gastil, J. *By Popular Demand: Revitalizing Representative Democracy through Deliberative Elections.* Berkeley: University of California Press, 2000.

Harvard Business School. *Negotiation.* Boston: Harvard Business School Publishing, 2003.

Kayser, T. A. *Building Team Power: How to Unleash the Collaborative Genius of Work Teams.* New York: Irwin, 1994.

Keltner, J. W. *The Management of Struggle: Elements of Dispute Resolution through Negotiation, Mediation, and Arbitration.* Cresskill, NJ: Hampton, 1994.

Littlejohn, S. W., and K. Domenici. *Engaging Communication in Conflict: Systemic Practice.* Thousand Oaks, CA: Sage, 2001.

Mayer, B. *The Dynamics of Conflict Resolution: A Practitioner's Guide.* San Francisco: Jossey-Bass, 2000.

Owen, H. *Open Space Technology.* 2nd ed. San Francisco: Berrett-Koehler Publishers, 1997.

Pearce, W. B., and S. W. Littlejohn. *Moral Conflict: When Social Worlds Collide.* Thousand Oaks, CA: Sage, 1997.

Pearce, W. B., and K. A. Pearce. "Combining Passions and Abilities: Toward Dialogic Virtuosity." *Southern Communication Journal* 65 (2000): 161–175.

Public Conversations Project. *Constructive Conversations about Challenging Times: A Guide to Community Dialogue.* Cambridge, MA: Public Conversations Project, 2003.

Spano, S. *Public Dialogue and Participatory Democracy: The Cupertino Community Project.* Cresskill, NJ: Hampton, 2001.

Verderber, R. F., and K. S. Verderber. *Inter-Act: Using Interpersonal Communication Skills.* Belmont, CA: Wadsworth, 1992.

Weisbord, M., and S. Janoff. *Future Search.* San Francisco: Berrett Koehler, 1995.

Winslade, J., and G. Monk. *Narrative Mediation: A New Approach to Conflict Resolution.* San Francisco: Jossey-Bass, 2000.

Yankelovich, D. *The Magic of Dialogue: Transforming Conflict into Cooperation.* New York: Simon and Schuster, 1999.

Web Sites

National Issues Forum: www.nifi.org

Public Conversations Project: www.publicconversations.org

Public Dialogue Consortium: www.publicdialogue.org

Bibliography

Allison, Graham. *Nuclear Terrorism: The Ultimate Preventable Catastrophe.* New York: Times Books, 2004.

Altman, Irwin. "Dialectics, Physical Environments, and Personal Relationships." *Communication Monographs* 60 (1993): 26–34.

Altman, Irwin, A. Vinsel, and B. Brown. "Dialectic Conceptions in Social Psychology: An Application to Social Penetration and Privacy Regulation." *Advances in Experimental Social Psychology.* Ed. L. Berkowitz. Vol. 14. New York: Academic, 1981. 76–100.

Amato, P. R. "Explaining the Intergenerational Transmission of Divorce." *Journal of Marriage and the Family* 58 (1996): 628–40.

Amato P. R., and B. Keith. "Parental Divorce and the Well-Being of Children: A Meta-Analysis." *Psychological Bulletin* 110 (1991): 26–46.

Anderson, Kristin L., Debra Umberson, and Sinikka Elliott. "Violence and Abuse in Families." *Handbook of Family Communication.* Ed. Anita L. Vangelisti. Mahwah, NJ: Lawrence Erlbaum, 2004. 629–46.

Arnett, Ronald C., and Pat Arneson. *Dialogic Civility in a Cynical Age: Community, Hope and Interpersonal Relationships.* Albany: SUNY Press, 1999.

Arthur, Jim, Christine Carlson, and Lee Moore. *A Practical Guide to Consensus.* Santa Fe, NM: Policy Consensus Initiative, 1999.

Ascher, W. "The Moralism of Attitudes Supporting Intergroup Violence." *Political Psychology* 7 (1986): 403–25.

Averill, James. "A Constructivist View of Emotion." *Theories of Emotion.* Ed. K. Plutchik and H. Kellerman. New York: Academic, 1980. 305–39.

Avruch, K. *Culture and Conflict Resolution.* Washington, DC: U.S. Institute of Peace, 1988.

Babrow, Austin. "Uncertainty Value, Communication, and Problematic Integration." *Journal of Communication* 51 (2001): 553–73.

Bachman, G. F., and L. K. Guerrero. "An Expectancy Violations Analysis of Factors Affecting Relational Outcomes and Communicative Responses to Hurtful Events in Dating Relationships." *Journal of Social and Personal Relationships,* in press.

Bales, Robert F. *Interaction Process Analysis: A Method for the Study of Small Groups.* Reading, MA: Addison-Wesley, 1950.

Banks, Stephen P. Banks, and Patricia Riley. "Structuration Theory as an Ontology for Communication Research." *Communication Yearbook 16*. Ed. Stanley Deetz. Newbury Park, CA: Sage, 1993. 167–96.

Barber, B. K., and J. A. Olsen. "Socialization in Context: Connection, Regulation, and Autonomy in the Family, School, and Neighborhood, and with Peers." *Journal of Adolescent Research* 12 (1997): 286–315.

Barge, J. Kevin. "Reflexivity and Managerial Practice." *Communication Monographs* 71 (2004): 70–96.

Barge, J. Kevin. "Dialogue, Conflict, and Community." *The Sage Handbook of Conflict Communication: Integrating Theory, Research, and Practice*. Ed. John G. Oetzel and Stella Ting-Toomey. Thousand Oaks, CA: Sage, 2006. 517–44.

Barge, J. Kevin, and Martin Little. "Dialogical Wisdom, Communicative Practice, and Organizational Life." *Communication Theory* 12 (2002): 375–97.

Barnett, Thomas P. M. *The Pentagon's New Map: War and Peace in the Twenty-First Century*. New York: G. P. Putnam's Sons, 2004.

Barrett, K. C. "A Functionalist Approach to Shame and Guilt." *Self-Conscious Emotions: The Psychology of Same, Guilt, Embarrassment, and Pride*. Ed. J. P. Tangney and K. W. Fischer. New York: Guildford, 1995. 25–63.

Baxter, Leslie A., and Barbara M. Montgomery. "A Guide to Dialectical Approaches to Studying Personal Relationships." *Dialectical Approaches to Studying Personal Relationships*. Ed. B. Montgomery and L Baxter. Mahwah, NJ: Lawrence Erlbaum, 1998. 1–15.

Beatty, Michael J., and James C. McCroskey. *The Biology of Communication: A Communibiological Perspective*. Cresskill, NJ: Hampton Press, 2001.

Bell, R. A., and J. A. Daly. "The Affinity-Seeking Function in Communication." *Communication Monographs* 51 (1984): 91–115.

Bell R. A., J. A. Daly, and C. Gonzalez. "Affinity-Maintenance in Marriage and Its Relationship to Women's Marital Satisfactions." *Journal of Marriage and the Family* 49 (1987): 445–54.

Berger, Charles R. *Planning Strategic Interaction: Attaining Goals Through Communicative Action*. Mahwah, NJ: Lawrence Erlbaum, 1997.

Berman, B., and G. Margolin. "Observed Patterns of Conflict in Violent, Nonviolent, and Non-distressed Couples." *Behavioral Assessment* 14 (1992): 15–37.

Berns, S. B., N. S. Jacobson, and J. M. Gottman. "Demand-withdraw Interaction Patterns between Different Types of Batterers and their Spouses." *Journal of Marital and Family Therapy* 25 (1999): 337–48.

Bertram, E. "Reinventing Governments: The Promise and Perils of United Nations Peace Building." *Journal of Conflict Resolution* 39 (1995): 387–418.

Booth, A., and P. R. Amato. "Parental Predivorce Relations and Offspring Postdivorce Well-Being." *Journal of Marriage and Family* 63 (2001): 197–212.

Boutros-Ghali, Boutros. *Agenda for Peace*. New York: United Nations Publications, 1995.

Brahm, Eric, and Julian Ouellet. "Designing New Dispute Resolution Systems." *Beyond Intractability*. Ed. Guy Burgess and Heidi Burgess. Boulder: University of Colorado Conflict Research Consortium, 2003. http://www.beyondintractability.org/essay/designing_dispute_systems/

Brazerman, M. H., A. E. Tenbrunsel, and K. A. Wade-Benzoni. "Negotiating with Yourself and Losing: Making Decisions with Competing Internal Preferences." *Academy of Management Review* 23 (1998): 225–41.

Brock, Timothy C., and Melanie C. Green, eds. *Persuasion: Psychological Insights and Perspectives.* Thousand Oaks, CA: Sage, 2005.

Broome, Benjamin J., and Ann-Sofi Jakobsson Hatay. "Building Peace in Divided Societies: The Role of Intergroup Dialogue." *The Sage Handbook of Conflict Communication: Integrating Theory, Research, and Practice.* Ed. John G. Oetzel and Stella Ting-Toomey. Thousand Oaks, CA: Sage. 627–64.

Buber, Martin. *I and Thou.* New York: Scribner, 1958.

Burgoon, J. K., and J. L. Hale. "Nonverbal Expectancy Violations: Model Elaboration and Application to Immediacy Behaviors." *Communication Monographs* 55 (1988): 58–79.

Burgoon, J. K., and A. Ebesu Hubbard. "Cross-cultural and Intercultural Applications of Expectancy Violations and Interaction Adaptation Theory." *Theorizing about Intercultural Communication.* Ed. W. B. Gudykunst. Thousand Oaks, CA: Sage, 2005. 149–71.

Burrell, Nancy A., Cindy S. Zirbel, and Mike Allen. "Evaluating Peer Mediation Outcomes in Educational Settings: A Meta-Analytic Review." *Conflict Resolution Quarterly* 21 (2003): 7–26.

Burton, John W. *Conflict and Communication: The Use of Controlled Communication in International Relations.* London: Macmillan, 1969.

Bush, Robert A. Baruch, and Joseph P. Folger. *The Promise of Mediation: Responding to Conflict through Empowerment and Recognition.* San Francisco: Jossey-Bass, 1994.

Bush, Robert A. Baruch, and Joseph P. Folger. *The Promise of Mediation: The Transformative Approach to Conflict.* San Francisco: Jossey-Bass, 2005.

Canary, Daniel J. "Managing Interpersonal Conflict: A Model of Events Related to Strategic Choices." *Handbook of Communication and Social Interaction Skills.* Ed. John O. Greene and Brant R. Burleson. Mahwah, NJ: Lawrence Erlbaum, 2003. 515–50.

Canary, Daniel J., William R. Cupach, and S. J. Messman. *Relationship Conflict.* Thousand Oaks, CA: Sage, 1995.

Canary Daniel J., Brian H. Spitzberg, and B. A. Semic. "The Experience and Expression of Anger in Interpersonal Settings." *Handbook of Communication and Emotion: Research, Theory, Applications, and Contexts.* Ed. P. A. Andersen and L. I. Guerrero. San Diego: Academic Press, 1998. 189–213.

Cattell, Raymond. "Concepts and Methods in the Measurement of Group Syntality." *Psychological Review* 55 (1948): 48–63.

Caughlin, John P., and Anita L. Vangelisti. "Conflict in Dating and Marital Relationships." *The Sage Handbook of Conflict Communication: Integrating Theory, Research, and Practice.* Ed. John G. Oetzel and Stella Ting-Toomey. Thousand Oaks, CA: Sage, 2006. 129–57.

Chasin, Richard, Margaret Harzig, Laura Chasin, Corky Becker, and Robert R. Stains. "From Diatribe to Dialogue on Divisive Public Issues: Approaches Drawn from Family Therapy." *Mediation Quarterly* 13 (1996): 323–44.

Chen, Guo-Ming, and William J. Starosta. *Foundations of Intercultural Communication*. Boston: Allyn & Bacon, 1998.

Christensen, A. "Dysfunctional Interaction Patterns in Couples." *Perspectives on Marital Interaction*. Ed. P. Noller and M. A. Fitzpatrick. Clevedon, England: Multilingual Matters, 1988. 31–52.

Clore, G. L., A. Ortony, B. Dienes, and F. Fujita. "Where Does Anger Dwell?" *Perspectives on Anger and Emotion: Advances in Social Cognition*. Ed. R. S Wyer, Jr. and T. K. Srull. Hillsdale, NJ: Lawrence Erlbaum, 1993. 57–87.

Cobb, Sara. "Creating Sacred Space: Toward a Second-Generation Dispute Resolution Practice." *Bringing Peace into the Room*. Ed. Daniel Bowling and David Hoffman. San Francisco: Jossey-Bass, 2003. 215–33.

Coleman, James S. *Community Conflict*. New York: The Free Press, 1957.

Collier, Mary Jane. "Conflict Competence within African, Mexican, and Anglo American Friendships." *Cross-cultural Interpersonal Communication*. Ed. S. Ting-Toomey and F. Korzenny. Newbury Park, CA: Sage, 1991. 132–54.

Collins, Barry, and Harold Guetzkow. *A Social Psychology of Group Processes for Decision-Making*. New York: Wiley, 1964.

Constantino, Cathy, and Christina Merchant. *Designing Conflict Management Systems: A Guide to Creating Productive and Healthy Organizations*. London: Jossey-Bass, 1996.

Cooperrider, David L., and Diana Whitney. *Appreciative Inquiry*. San Francisco: Berrett-Koehler, 1999.

Cronen, Vernon E., Kenneth M. Johnson, and John W. Lannamann. "Paradoxes, Double Binds, and Reflexive Loops: An Alternative Theoretical Perspective." *Family Process* 20 (1982): 91–112.

Cronen, Vernon E., W. Barnett Pearce, and Lonna Snavely. "A Theory of Rule-Structure and Types of Episodes, and a Study of Perceived Enmeshment in Undesired Repetitive Patterns (URPs)." *Communication Yearbook 3*. Ed. Dan Nimmo. New Brunswick, NJ: Transaction Press, 1979. 225–40.

Daniels, S. E., and G. B. Walker. *Working through Environmental Conflict: The Collaborative Learning Approach*. Westport, CT: Praeger, 2001.

Davitz, J. R. *The Language of Emotion*. New York: Academic Press, 1969.

Devine, Patricia G., David L. Hamilton, and Thomas M. Ostrom. *Social Cognition: Impact on Social Psychology*. San Diego: Academic, 1994.

Diamond, L., and J. McDonald. *Multi-track Diplomacy: A Systems Approach to Peace*. West Hartford, CT: Kumarian Press, 1996.

Dindia, Kathryn, and Leslie Baxter. "Strategies for Maintaining and Repairing Marital Relationships." *Journal of Social and Personal Relationships* 4 (1987): 143–58.

Dindia, Kathryn, and Lindsay Timmerman. "Accomplishing Romantic Relationships." *Handbook of Communication and Social Interaction Skills*. Ed. J. O. Greene and B. R. Burleson. Mahwah, NJ: Lawrence Erlbaum, 2003. 685–721.

Docherty, Jayne S. *Learning Lessons from Waco: When the Parties Bring their Gods to the Negotiation Table*. Syracuse: Syracuse University Press, 2001.

Doherty, William J. "Cognitive Processes in Intimate Conflict: II. Efficacy and Learned Helplessness." *American Journal of Family Therapy* 9 (1981): 35–44.

Doherty, William J., and John M. Beaton. "Mothers and Fathers Parenting Together." *Handbook of Family Communication*. Ed. Anita L. Vangelisti. Mahwah, NJ: Lawrence Erlbaum, 2004. 269–86.

Domenici, Kathy, and Stephen Littlejohn. *Mediation: Empowerment in Conflict Management*. 2nd ed. Long Grove, IL: Waveland Press, 2001.

Domenici, Kathy, and Stephen Littlejohn. *Communication and the Management of Face: Theory to Practice*. Thousand Oaks, CA: Sage, 2006.

Doob, Leonard W. *The Pursuit of Peace*. Westport, CT: Greenwood Press, 1981.

Druckman, Daniel, and Kathleen Zechmeister. "Conflict of Interest and Value Disensus: Propositions in the Sociology of Conflict." *Human Relations* 26 (1973): 449–66.

Ellis, C., and E. Weinstein. "Jealousy and the Social Psychology of Emotional Experience." *Journal of Social and Personal Relationships* 3 (1986): 337–57.

Emery, R. E. "Interparental Conflict and the Children of Discord and Divorce." *Psychological Bulletin* 92 (1982): 310–30.

Eysenck, H. J. "Biological Dimensions of Personality." *Handbook of Personality*. Ed. L. A. Pervin. New York: Guildford, 1991. 244–76.

Ferdig, Mary A. Speke. "Exploring the Social Construction of Complex Self-Organizing Change: A Study of Emerging Change in the Regulation of Nuclear Power." Diss. Benedictine University, 2001.

Festinger, Leon. *A Theory of Cognitive Dissonance*. Stanford, CA: Stanford University Press, 1957.

Fincham, Frank D. "Communication in Marriage." *Handbook of Family Communication*. Ed. Anita L. Vangelisti. Mahwah, NJ: Lawrence Erlbaum, 2004. 83–103.

Fincham, Frank D., and T. N. Bradbury. "Cognition in Marriage: A Program of Research on Attributions." *Advances in Personal Relationships*. Vol. 2. Ed. W. H. Jones and D. Perlman. London: Kingsley, 1991. 159–203.

Fine, Marlene G. *Building Successful Multicultural Organizations: Challenges and Opportunities*. Westport, CT: Quorum Books, 1995.

Fink, Clinton F. "Some Conceptual Difficulties in the Theory of Social Conflict." *Conflict Resolution* 12 (1968): 412–60.

Fisher, Roger, and D. Shapiro. *Beyond Reason: Using Emotions as You Negotiate*. New York: Viking, 2005.

Fisher, Roger, and William Ury. *Getting to Yes: Negotiating Agreement without Giving In*. New York: Penguin Books, 1991.

Fitness, Julie, and Jill Duffield. "Emotion and Communication in Families." *Handbook of Family Communication*. Ed. Anita L. Vangelisti. Mahwah, NJ: Lawrence Erlbaum, 2004. 473–94.

Fitzpatrick, Mary Anne. *Between Husbands and Wives: Communication in Marriage*. Newbury Park, CA: Sage, 1988.

Foerster, Heinz von. *Observing Systems: Selected Papers of Heinz von Foerster*. Seaside, CA: Intersystems Publications, 1981.

Foss, Karen A., and Kathy L. Domenici. "Haunting Argentina: Synecdoche in the Protests of the Mothers of the Plaza de Mayo." *Quarterly Journal of Speech* 87 (2001): 237–58.

Furstenberg, F. F. "Divorce and the American Family." *Annual Review of Sociology* 16 (1990): 379–403.

Galtung, Johann, ed. *Essays in Peace Research.* Vol. 1. Copenhagen: Christian Ejlers, 1975.

Galtung, Johann. "Three Approaches to Peace." *Essays in Peace Research.* Vol. 1. Ed. J. Galtung. Copenhagen: Christian Ejlers, 1975. 282–304.

Gastil, John. *By Popular Demand: Revitalizing Representative Democracy through Deliberative Elections.* Berkeley: University of California Press, 2000.

Gattis, William A. "Transcendent Discourse and Moral Conflict: The Use of Dialogue Groups to Improve Communication in Long-standing Moral Struggles." Diss. University of Kansas, 1985.

Geertz, Clifford. *The Interpretation of Cultures.* New York: Basic Books, 1973.

Gibb, Jack. "Defensive Communication." *Journal of Communication* 11 (1961): 141–48.

Giddens, Anthony. *Profiles and Critiques in Social Theory.* Berkeley: University of California Press, 1982.

Gottman, J. M. *What Predicts Divorce? The Relationship between Marital Processes and Marital Outcomes.* Hillsdale, NJ: Lawrence Erlbaum, 1994.

Gottman, J. M., and R. W. Levenson. "Marital Processes Predictive of Later Dissolution: Behavior, Physiology, and Health." *Journal of Personality and Social Psychology* 63 (1992): 221–33.

Gouran, Dennis S. "Communication Skills for Group Decision Making." *Handbook of Communication and Social Interaction Skills.* Ed. John O. Greene and Brant R. Burleson. Mahwah, NJ: Lawrence Erlbaum, 2003. 835–71.

Gray, M. R., and I. Steinberg. "Unpacking Authoritative Parenting: Reassessing a Multidimensional Construct." *Journal of Marriage and Family* 61 (1999): 574–87.

Gudykunst, William. "The Uncertainty Reduction and Anxiety-Uncertainty Reduction Theories of Berger, Gudykunst, and Associates." *Watershed Research Traditions in Human Communication Theory.* Ed. Donald P. Cushman and Branislav Kovačić. Albany: SUNY Press, 1995. 67–100.

Guerrero, Laura K. "'I'm So Mad I Could Scream': The Effects of Anger Expression on Relational Satisfaction and Communication Competence." *Southern Communication Journal* 59 (1994): 125–41.

Guerrero, Laura K., and Peter A. Anderson. "The Dark Side of Jealousy and Envy: Desire, Delusion, Desperation, and Destructive Communication." *The Dark Side of Close Relationships.* Ed. B. H. Spitzberg and W. R. Cupach. Mahwah, NJ: Lawrence Erlbaum, 1998. 33–70.

Guerrero, Laura K., and Angela G. La Valley. "Conflict, Emotion, and Communication." *The Sage Handbook of Conflict Communication: Integrating Theory, Research, and Practice.* Ed. John G. Oetzel and Stella Ting-Toomey. Thousand Oaks, CA: Sage, 2006. 69–96.

Guerrero, Laura K., M. L. Trost, and S. M. Yoshimura. "Emotion and Communication in the Context of Romantic Jealousy." *Personal Relationships* 12 (2005): 233–52.

Halford, W. K., M. R. Sanders, and B. C. Behrens. "Self-Regulation in Behavioral Couples Therapy." *Behavior Therapy* 25 (1994): 431–52.

Hall, Edward T. *Beyond Culture.* Garden City, NY: Anchor, 1976.

Harré, Rom. *Personal Being: A Theory for Individual Psychology.* Cambridge, MA: Harvard University Press, 1984.

Harré, Rom. "An Outline of the Social Constructionist Viewpoint." *The Social Construction of Emotions.* Ed. R. Harré. New York: Blackwell, 1986. 2–14.

Harrison, Tyler R. "Victims, Targets, Protectors, and Destroyers: Using Disputant Accounts to Develop a Grounded Taxonomy of Disputant Orientations." *Conflict Resolution Quarterly* 20 (2003): 307–29.

Hart, Craig H., Lloyd D. Newell, and Susanne Frost Olsen. "Parenting Skills and Social-Communicative Competence in Childhood." *Handbook of Communication and Social Interaction Skills.* Ed. John O. Greene and Brant R. Burleson. Mahwah, NJ: Lawrence Erlbaum, 2003. 753–97.

Harvard Business School. *Negotiation.* Boston: Harvard Business School Publishing, 2003.

Hatay, Sofi Jakobsson. *Peacebuilding and Reconciliation in Bosnia and Herzegovina, Kosovo and Macedonia, 1995–2004.* Uppsala: Uppsala Department of Peace and Conflict Research, 2005.

Health Canada. *Health Canada Policy Toolkit for Public Involvement in Decision Making.* Ontario: Ministry of Public Works and Government Services Canada, 2000.

Heider, Fritz. *The Psychology of Interpersonal Relations.* New York: Wiley, 1958.

Heidlebaugh, Nola J. *Judgment, Rhetoric, and the Problem of Incommensurability: Recalling Practical Wisdom.* Columbia: University of South Carolina Press, 2001.

Herrman, Margaret S., ed. *The Blackwell Handbook of Mediation: Bridging Theory, Research, and Practice.* Malden, MA: Blackwell, 2006.

Hetherington, E. M., and M. M. Stanley-Hagan. "The Adjustment of Children with Divorced Parents: A Risk and Resiliency Perspective." *Journal of Child Psychology and Psychiatry* 40 (1999): 129–40.

Hobbes, Thomas. *Leviathan.* Oxford: Blackwell, 1946.

Hofstede, G. *Culture's Consequences.* Beverly Hills, CA: Sage, 1984.

Holland, R. "Reflexivity." *Human Relations* 52 (1999): 463–84.

Hymes, Dell. *Foundations in Sociolinguistics: An Ethnographic Approach.* Philadelphia: University of Pennsylvania Press, 1974.

Jabusch, David M., and Stephen W. Littlejohn. *Elements of Speech Communication.* San Diego: Collegiate Press, 1995.

Jacobson, N. S. "Behavioral Couple Therapy: A New Beginning." *Behavior Therapy* 23 (1992): 493–506.

Jacobson, N. S., and A. Christensen. *Integrative Couple Therapy: Promoting Acceptance and Change.* New York: Norton, 1996.

Janis, Irving. *Groupthink: Psychological Studies of Policy Decisions and Fiascoes.* Boston: Houghton Mifflin, 1982.

Jehn, K. A. "Qualitative Analysis of Conflict Types and Dimensions in Organizational Groups." *Administrative Science Quarterly* 42 (1997): 538–66.

Jo, M. H. "Korean Merchants in the Black Community: Prejudice among the Victims of Prejudice." *Ethnic and Racial Studies* 15 (1992): 395–411.

Johnson, Fern L. *Speaking Culturally: Language Diversity in the United States.* Thousand Oaks, CA: Sage, 2000.

Jung, Eura, and Michael L. Hecht. "Elaborating the Communication Theory of Identity: Identity Gaps and Communication Outcomes." *Communication Quarterly* 52 (2004): 265–83.

Kant, Immanuel. *Perpetual Peace: A Philosophical Sketch.* 1795. Ed. Hans Reiss. *Kant's Political Writings.* Cambridge: Cambridge University Press, 1970.

Kaplan, R. E. "Maintaining Interpersonal Relationships: A Bipolar Theory." *Interpersonal Development* 6 (1975/1976): 106–19.

Karoly, P. "Mechanisms of Self-Regulation: A Systems View." *Annual Review of Psychology* 44 (1993): 23–52.

Katsh, Ethan, and Janet Rifkin. *Online Dispute Resolution: Resolving Conflicts in Cyberspace.* San Francisco: Jossey-Bass, 2001.

Kayser, T. A. *Building Team Power: How to Unleash the Collaborative Genius of Work Teams.* New York: Irwin, 1994.

Kelly, Adrian B., Frank D. Fincham, and Steven R. H. Beach. "Communication Skills in Couples: A Review and Discussion of Emerging Perspectives." *Handbook of Communication and Social Interaction Skills.* Ed. John O. Greene and Brant R. Burleson. Mahwah, NJ: Lawrence Erlbaum, 2003. 723–52.

Keltner, John W. *The Management of Struggle: Elements of Dispute Resolution through Negotiation, Mediation, and Arbitration.* Cresskill, NJ: Hampton Press, 1994.

Kilmann, Ralph, and Kenneth Thomas. "Interpersonal Conflict-Handling Behavior as Reflections of Jungian Personality Dimensions." *Psychological Reports* 37 (1975): 971–80.

Knight, Jack. *Institutions and Social Conflict.* Cambridge, England: Cambridge University Press, 1993.

Koerner, Ascan F., and Mary Anne Fitzpatrick. "Toward a Theory of Family Communication." *Communication Theory* 12 (2002): 70–91.

Koerner, Ascan F., and Mary Anne Fitzpatrick. "Understanding Family Communication Patterns and Family Functioning: The Roles of Conversation Orientation and Conformity Orientation." *Communication Yearbook 26.* Ed. William B. Gudykunst. Mahwah, NJ: Lawrence Erlbaum, 2002. 36–68.

Koerner, Ascan, and Mary Anne Fitzpatrick. "Communication in Intact Families." *Handbook of Family Communication.* Ed. Anita L. Vangelisti. Mahwah, NJ: Lawrence Erlbaum, 2004. 177–96.

Kriteck, Phyllis. *Negotiating at an Uneven Table.* San Francisco: Jossey-Bass, 1994.

Laing, R. D., H. Phillipson, and A. R. Lee. *Interpersonal Perception: A Theory and Method of Research.* New York: Harper and Row, 1972.

Laursen, Brett, and W. Andrew Collins. "Parent-Child Communication during Adolescence." *Handbook of Family Communication.* Ed. Anita L. Vangelisti. Mahwah, NJ: Lawrence Erlbaum, 2004. 333–48.

Lazarus, R. S. *Emotion and Adaptation.* New York: Oxford University Press, 1991.

Lederach, Jean Paul. *The Moral Imagination: The Art and Soul of Building Peace.* New York: Oxford University Press, 2005.

Leeds-Hurwitz, Wendy, ed. *Social Approaches to Communication.* New York: Guilford Press, 1995.

Lewin, Kurt. *A Dynamic Theory of Personality.* New York: McGraw-Hill, 1935.

Lewis, Julia M., Judith S. Wallerstein, and Linda Johnson-Reitz. "Communication in Divorced and Single-Parent Families." *Handbook of Family Communication.* Ed. Anita L. Vangelisti. Mahwah, NJ: Lawrence Erlbaum, 2004. 197–214.

Lim, T. S., and J. W. Bowers. "Facework: Solidarity, Approbation, and Tact." *Human Communication Research* 17 (1991): 415–50.

Linker, J., A. Stolberg, and R. Green. "Family Communication as a Mediator of Child Adjustment to Divorce." *Journal of Divorce and Remarriage* 30 (1999): 83–97.

Lipsky, David B., and Ronald L. Seeber. "Managing Organizational Conflicts." *The Sage Handbook of Conflict Communication: Integrating Theory, Research, and Practice.* Ed. John G. Oetzel and Stella Ting-Toomey. Thousand Oaks, CA: Sage, 2006. 359–90.

Littlejohn, Stephen W. *Theories of Human Communication.* Belmont, CA: Wadsworth, 2002.

Littlejohn, Stephen W. "The Transcendent Communication Project." *Conflict Resolution Quarterly* 21 (2004): 337–60.

Littlejohn, Stephen W. "Moral Conflict." *The Sage Handbook of Conflict Communication: Integrating Theory, Research, and Practice.* Ed. John G. Oetzel and Stella Ting-Toomey. Thousand Oaks, CA: Sage, 2006. 395–418.

Littlejohn, Stephen W., and Kathy Domenici. *Engaging Communication in Conflict: Systemic Practice.* Thousand Oaks, CA: Sage, 2001.

Littlejohn, Stephen, and Kathy Domenici. "A Facework Frame for Mediation." *The Blackwell Handbook of Mediation: Bridging Theory, Research, and Practice.* Ed. M. S. Herrman. Malden, MA: Blackwell, 2006. 228–46.

Littlejohn, Stephen W., and Karen A. Foss. *Theories of Human Communication.* Belmont, CA: Wadsworth, 2005.

Lock, John. *Second Treatise of Government.* Indianapolis: Hacket Publishing, 1980.

Lovelace, K., D. L. Shapiro, and L. R. Weingart. "Maximizing Cross-Functional New Product Teams' Innovativeness and Constraint Adherence: A Conflict Communications Perspective." *Academy of Management Journal* 44 (2001): 779–93.

Lowry, Carmen, and Stephen Littlejohn. "Dialogue and the Discourse of Peacebuilding in Maluku, Indonesia." *Conflict Resolution Quarterly* 23 (2006): 409–26.

Lulofs, Roxane. *Conflict: From Theory to Action.* Scottsdale, AZ: Gorsuch Scarisbrick, 1994.

Lumsden, Gay, and Donald Lumsden. *Communicating in Groups and Teams: Sharing Leadership.* Belmont, CA: Wadsworth, 2000.

Markman, H. J., and C. I. Notarius. "Coding Marital and Family Interaction: Current Status." *Family Interaction and Psychopathology: Theories, Methods, and Findings.* Ed. T. Jacob. New York: Plenum, 1987. 329–90.

Mattelart, Armand, and Michele Mattelart. *Theories of Communication: A Short Introduction.* London: Sage, 1998.

Mayer, Bernard S. *The Dynamics of Conflict Resolution: A Practitioner's Guide.* San Francisco: Jossey-Bass, 2000.

Mayer, Bernard S. *Beyond Neutrality: Confronting the Crisis in Conflict Resolution.* San Francisco: Jossey-Bass, 2004.

McNamara, Robert S., James G. Blight, Robert K. Brigham, Thomas Biersteker, and Herbert Schandler. *Argument without End: In Search of Answers to the Vietnam Tragedy.* New York: Public Affairs, 1999.

Metts, Sandra. "Relational Transgressions." *The Dark Side of Interpersonal Communication.* Ed. W. R. Cupach and B. H. Spitzberg. Hillsdale, NJ: Lawrence Erlbaum, 1994. 217–39.

Metts, Sandra, and William R. Cupach. "Postdivorce Relations." *Explaining Family Interactions.* Ed. M. A. Fitzpatrick and A. L. Vangelisti. Thousand Oaks, CA: Sage, 1995. 232–51.

Metts, Sandra, and Erica Grohskopf. "Impression Management: Goals, Strategies, and Skills." *Handbook of Communication and Social Interaction Skills.* Ed. J. O. Greene and B. R. Burleson. Mahwah, NJ: Lawrence Erlbaum, 2003. 357–402.

Millar, Frank E., and L. Edna Rogers. "Relational Dimensions of Interpersonal Dynamics." *Interpersonal Processes: New Directions in Communication Research.* Ed. Michael E. Roloff and Gerald R. Miller. Newbury Park, CA: Sage, 1987. 117–39.

Montgomery, Barbara M., and Leslie A. Baxter, eds. *Dialectical Approaches to Studying Personal Relationship Processes.* Mahwah, NJ: Lawrence Erlbaum, 1998.

Montgomery, Barbara M., and Leslie A. Baxter. "Dialogism and Relational Dialectics." *Dialectical Approaches to Studying Personal Relationships.* Ed. Barbara Montgomery and Leslie Baxter. Mahwah, NJ: Lawrence Erlbaum, 1998. 155–83.

Montville, Joseph V., and D. B. Bendahmane, eds. *Conflict Resolution: Track Two Diplomacy.* Washington, DC: Foreign Service Institute, Department of State, 1987.

Moore, Christopher W. *The Mediation Process: Practical Strategies for Resolving Conflict.* San Francisco: Jossey-Bass, 1996.

Morson, Gary Saul, and Caryl Emerson. *Mikhail Bakhtin: Creation of a Prosaics.* Stanford, CA: Stanford University Press, 1990.

Newcomb, Theodore M. "An Approach to the Study of Communicative Acts." *Psychological Review* 60 (1953): 393–404.

Nicotera, Anne Maydan. "The Constructivist Theory of Delia, Clark, and Associates." *Watershed Research Traditions in Human Communication Theory.* Ed. Donald P. Cushman and Branislav Kovačić. Albany: SUNY Press, 1995. 45–66.

Nicotera, Anne Maydan, and Laura Kathleen Dorsey. "Individual and Interactive Processes in Organizational Conflict." *The Sage Handbook of Conflict Communication: Integrating Theory, Research, and Practice.* Ed. John G. Oetzel and Stella Ting-Toomey. Thousand Oaks, CA: Sage, 2006. 293–326.

Notarius, C. I., and N. A. Vanzetti. "The Marital Agendas Protocol." *Marriage and Family Assessment: A Sourcebook for Family Therapy.* Ed. E. Filsinger. Beverly Hills, CA: Sage, 1983. 209–27.

Nudler, Oscar. "In Replace of a Theory for Conflict Resolution: Taking a New Look at World Views Analysis." *Institute for Conflict Analysis and Resolution Newsletter* (summer) 1 (1993): 4–5.

O'Keefe, Barbara J. "The Logic of Message Design: Individual Differences in Reasoning about Communication." *Communication Monographs* 55 (1988): 80–103.

Oliver, J. E., and J. Wong. "Intergroup Prejudice in Multiethnic Settings." *American Journal of Political Science* 4 (2003): 567–82.

Orbe, Mark P. *Constructing Co-Cultural Theory: An Explication of Culture, Power, and Communication.* Thousand Oaks, CA: Sage, 1998.

Orbe, Mark P., and Melodi A. Everett. "Interracial and Interethnic Conflict and Communication in the United States." *The Sage Handbook of Conflict Communication: Integrating Theory, Research, and Practice.* Ed. John G. Oetzel and Stella Ting-Toomey. Thousand Oaks, CA: Sage, 2006. 575–94.

Orbe, Mark P., and T. M. Harris. *Interracial Communication: Theory into Practice.* Belmont, CA: Wadsworth, 2001.

Orbe, Mark. P., K. T. Warren, and N. C. Cornwell. "Negotiating Societal Stereotypes: Analyzing *The Real World* Discourse by and about African American Men." *Constituting Cultural Difference through Discourse.* Ed. Mary Jane Collier. Thousand Oaks, CA: Sage, 2001. 107–34.

Owen, Harrison. *Open Space Technology.* Potomac, MD: Abbott Press, 1993.

Papa, Michael J., and Daniel J. Canary. "Conflict in Organizations: A Competency-Based Approach." *Conflict and Organizations: Communicative Processes.* Ed. Anne Maydan Nicotera. Albany: SUNY Press, 1995. 153–82.

Paris, R. *At War's End: Building Peace after Civil Conflict.* Cambridge: Cambridge University Press, 2004.

Parkinson, B. *Ideas and Realities of Emotion.* New York: Routledge, 1995.

Pearce, W. Barnett. *Communication and the Human Condition.* Carbondale: Southern Illinois University Press, 1989.

Pearce, W. Barnett. *Interpersonal Communication: Making Social Worlds.* New York: Harper Collins, 1994.

Pearce, W. Barnett, and Vernon Cronen. *Communication, Action, and Meaning.* New York: Praeger, 1980.

Pearce, W. Barnett, and Stephen W. Littlejohn. *Moral Conflict: When Social Worlds Collide.* Thousand Oaks, CA: Sage, 1997.

Pearce, W. Barnett, and Kimberly A. Pearce. "Combining Passions and Abilities: Toward Dialogic Virtuosity." *Southern Communication Journal* 65 (1999): 161–75.

Pelled, L. H. "Demographic Diversity, Conflict, and Work Group Outcomes: An Intervening Process Theory." *Organization Science* 7 (1996): 615–31.

Pelled, L. H., K. M. Eisenhardt, and K. R. Xin. "Exploring the Black Box: An Analysis of Work Group Diversity, Conflict, and Performance." *Administrative Science Quarterly* 44 (1999): 1–28.

Peterson, Tarla Rai, and Rebecca Royer Franks. "Environmental Conflict Communication." *The Sage Handbook of Conflict Communication: Integrating Theory, Research, and Practice.* Ed. John G. Oetzel and Stella Ting-Toomey. Thousand Oaks, CA: Sage, 2006. 419–50.

Petronio, Sandra. *Balancing the Secrets of Private Disclosures.* Mahwah, NJ: Lawrence Erlbaum, 2000.

Petronio, Sandra. *Boundaries of Privacy: Dialectics of Disclosure.* Albany: SUNY Press, 2002.

Planalp, Sally. *Communicating Emotion: Social, Moral, and Cultural Processes.* Cambridge: Cambridge University Press, 1999.

Poole, Marshall Scott, and Johny T. Garner. "Perspectives on Workgroup Conflict and Communication." *The Sage Handbook of Conflict Communication: Integrating Theory, Research, and Practice.* Ed. John G. Oetzel and Stella Ting-Toomey. Thousand Oaks, CA: Sage, 2006. 267–92.

Public Conversations Project. *Constructive Conversations about Challenging Times: A Guide to Community Dialogue.* Cambridge, MA: Public Conversations Project, 2003.

Putnam, Linda L. "Formal Negotiations: The Productive Side of Organizational Conflict." *Conflict and Organizations: Communicative Processes.* Ed. Anne Maydan Nicotera. New York: SUNY Press, 1995. 183–200.

Pyser, Steven, and Cliff Figallo. "The 'Listening to the City' Online Dialogues Experience: The Impact of a Full Value Contract." *Conflict Resolution Quarterly* 21 (2004): 381–93.

Rifkin, Janet. "Online Dispute Resolution: Theory and Practice of the Fourth Party." *Conflict Resolution Quarterly* 19 (2001): 117–24.

Rogers, L. Edna, and Valentin Escudero. *Relational Communication: An Interactional Perspective to the Study of Process and Form.* Mahwah, NJ: Lawrence Erlbaum, 2004.

Roloff, Michael E., Linda L. Putnam, and Lefki Anastasiou. "Negotiation Skills." *Handbook of Communication and Social Interaction Skills.* Ed. John O. Greene and Brant R. Burleson. Mahwah, NJ: Lawrence Erlbaum, 2003. 801–34.

Roseman, I. J., C. Wiest, and T. S. Swartz. "Phenomenology, Behaviors, and Goals Differentiate Discrete Emotions." *Journal of Personality and Social Psychology* 67 (1994): 206–21.

Rothman, Jay. *Resolving Identity-Based Conflict in Nations, Organizations, and Communities.* San Francisco: Jossey-Bass, 1997.

Russett, Bruce, and John Oneal. *Triangulating Peace: Democracy, Interdependence, and International Organizations.* New York: W. W. Norton, 2001.

Saunders, Harold H. *A Public Peace Process: Sustained Dialogue to Transform Racial and Ethnic Conflicts.* New York: St. Martin's Press, 1999.

Saussure, Ferdinand de. *Course in General Linguistics.* London: Peter Own, 1960.

Schellenberg, James A. *Conflict Resolution: Theory, Research, and Practice.* Albany: SUNY Press, 1996.

Schelling, T. C. *Choice and Consequence.* Cambridge, MA: Harvard University Press, 1984.

Schon, Donald A. *The Reflective Practitioner.* New York: Basic Books, 1983.

Schon, Donald A. *Educating the Reflective Practitioner.* San Francisco: Jossey-Bass, 1987.

Shah, H., and M. C. Thornton. "Racial Ideology in U.S. Mainstream News Magazine Coverage of Black-Latino Interaction, 1980–1992." *Critical Studies in Mass Communication* 11 (1994): 141–61.

Shapiro, Daniel L. "Negotiating Emotions." *Conflict Resolution Quarterly* 20 (2002): 67–82.

Shaver, P. R., J. Schwartz, D. Kirson, and C. O'Connor. "Emotion Knowledge: Further Explorations of a Prototype Approach." *Journal of Personality and Social Psychology* 52 (1987): 1061–86.

Shimanoff, Susan. *Communication Rules: Theory and Research.* Newbury Park, CA: Sage, 1980.

Sigelman, L., and S. A. Tuch. "Metastereotypes: Blacks' Perceptions of Whites' Stereotypes of Blacks." *Public Opinion Quarterly* 61 (1997): 87–101.

Sillars, Alan L. "Attributions and Communication in Roommate Conflicts." *Communication Monographs* 47 (1980): 180–200.

Sillars, Alan L. "The Sequential and Distributional Structure of Conflict Interaction as a Function of Attributions Concerning the Locus of Responsibility and Stability of Conflict." *Communication Yearbook 4.* Ed. Dan Nimmo. New Brunswick, NJ: Transaction, 1980. 217–36.

Sillars, Alan L., Daniel J. Canary, and Melissa Tafoya. "Communication, Conflict, and the Quality of Family Relationships." *Handbook of Family Communication.* Ed. Anita L. Vangelisti. Mahwah, NJ: Lawrence Erlbaum, 2004. 413–46.

Sillars, Alan L., Gary R. Pike, Tricia S. Jones, and Kathleen Redmon. "Communication and Conflict in Marriage." *Communication Yearbook 7.* Ed. Robert Bostrom. Beverly Hills, CA: Sage 1983. 414–29.

Smith, Eliot R. "Social Cognition Contributions to Attribution Theory and Research." *Social Cognition: Impact on Social Psychology.* Ed. Patricia G. Devine, David L. Hamilton, and Thomas M. Ostrom. San Diego: Academic Press, 1994. 77–108.

Smith, Melinda. *The Catron County Citizens Group: A Case Study.* Albuquerque: New Mexico Center for Dispute Resolution, 1998.

Spano, Shawn. *Public Dialogue and Participatory Democracy: The Cupertino Community Project.* Cresskill, NJ: Hampton Press, 2001.

Stafford, Laura, and Daniel J. Canary. "Maintenance Strategies and Romantic Relationship Type, Gender, and Relational Characteristics." *Journal of Social and Personal Relationships* 8 (1991): 217–42.

Stephan, W. G., and C. W. Stephan. *Improving Intergroup Relations.* Thousand Oaks, CA: Sage, 2001.

Stiff, James B. *Persuasive Communication.* New York: Guilford, 1994.

Sugarman, D. B., and G. T. Hotaling. "Dating Violence: Prevalence, Context, and Risk Markers." *Violence in Dating Relationships: Emerging Social Issues.* Ed. M. A. Pirog-Good and J. E. Stets. New York: Praeger, 1989. 3–32.

Susskind, Lawrence. "An Alternative to Robert's Rules of Order for Groups, Organizations, and Ad Hoc Assemblies that Want to Operate by Consensus." *The Consensus Building Handbook: A Comprehensive Guide to Reaching Agreement.* Ed. Lawrence Susskind, Sarah McKearnan, and Jennifer Thomas-Larmer. Thousand Oaks, CA: Sage, 1999. 3–60.

Susskind, Lawrence, Sarah McKearnan, and Jennifer Thomas-Larmer, eds. *The Consensus Building Handbook: A Comprehensive Guide to Reaching Agreement.* Thousand Oaks, CA: Sage, 1999.

Thio, Alex. *Sociology.* Needham Heights, MA: Allyn & Bacon, 2000.

Ting-Toomey, Stella, and John G. Oetzel. *Managing Intercultural Conflict Effectively.* Thousand Oaks, CA: Sage, 2001.

Ting-Toomey, Stella, and Jiro Takai. "Explaining Intercultural Conflict: Promising Approaches and Directions." *The Sage Handbook of Conflict Communication: Integrating Theory, Research, and Practice.* Ed. John G. Oetzel and Stella Ting-Toomey. Thousand Oaks, CA: Sage, 2006. 691–724.

Ting-Toomey, Stella, K. Yee-Jung, R. Shapiro, W. Garcia, T. Wright, and John G. Oetzel. "Cultural/Ethnic Identity Salience and Conflict Styles in Four U.S. Ethnic Groups." *International Journal of Intercultural Relations* 24 (2000): 47–81.

Tjosvold, D. *Learning to Manage Conflict: Getting People to Work Together Productively.* New York: Lexington, 1993.

Tjosvold D., W. C. Wedley, and R. H. G. Field. "Constructive Controversy, the Vroom-Yetton Model, and Managerial Decision Making." *Journal of Occupational Behavior* 7 (1986): 125–38.

Tomm, Karl. "Interventive Interviewing Part 3: Intending to Ask Lineal, Circular, Strategic, or Reflexive Questions." *Family Process* 27 (1988): 1–15.

Tracy, Karen. *Everyday Talk: Building and Reflecting Identities.* New York: Guilford, 2002.

Ury, William. *The Third Side: Why We Fight and How We Can Stop.* New York: Penguin Books, 1999.

Ury, William. *Getting Past No.* New York: Penguin Books, 2000.

Ury, William, ed. *Must We Fight?: From the Battlefield to the Schoolyard—A New Perspective on Violent Conflict and Its Prevention.* San Francisco: Jossey-Bass, 2001.

Ury, William, Jeanne Brett, and Stephen Goldberg. *Getting Disputes Resolved: Designing Systems to Cut the Costs of Conflict.* London: Jossey-Bass, 1988.

Van de Vliert, E., and M. C. Euwema. "Agreeableness and Activeness as Components of Conflict Behaviors." *Journal of Personality and Social Psychology* 66 (1994): 674–87.

Van Lear, C. Arthur. "Testing a Cyclical Model of Communicative Openness in Relationship Development: Two Longitudinal Studies." *Communication Monographs* 58 (1991): 337–61.

Vangelisti, Anita L. "Messages that Hurt." *The Dark Side of Interpersonal Communication.* Ed. W. R. Cupach and B. H. Spitzberg. Hillsdale, NJ: Lawrence Erlbaum, 1994. 53–82.

Vangelisti, Anita L., and L. P. Crumley. "Reactions to Messages that Hurt: The Influence of Relational Contexts." *Communication Monographs* 65 (1998): 173–96.

Vangelisti, Anita L., J. A. Daly, and J. R. Rudnick. "Making People Feel Guilty in Conversations: Techniques and Correlates." *Human Communication Research* 18 (1991): 3–39.

Vangelisti, Anita L., and R. J. Sprague. "Guilt and Hurt: Similarities, Distinctions, and Conversational Strategies." *Handbook of Communication and Emotion: Research, Theory, Applications, and Contexts.* Ed. P. A. Andersen and L. K. Guerrero. San Diego: Academic Press, 1998. 123–54.

Verderber, R. F., and K. S. Verderber. *Inter-Act: Using Interpersonal Communication Skills.* Belmont, CA: Wadsworth, 1992.

Waller, W. W., and R. Hill. *The Family, A Dynamic Interpretation.* New York: Warner Books, 1951.

Wallis, Jim. *The Soul of Politics.* New York: New Press, 1994.

Waters, H. "Race, Culture, and Interpersonal Conflict." *International Journal of Intercultural Relations* 16 (1992): 437–54.

Watzlawick, Paul, Janet Beavin, and Don Jackson. *Pragmatics of Human Communication: A Study of Interactional Patterns, Pathologies, and Paradoxes.* New York: Norton, 1967.

Weisbord, M., and S. Janoff. *Future Search.* San Francisco: Berrett Koehler, 1995.

Wendt, Alexander. *Social Theory of International Politics.* Cambridge: Cambridge University Press, 1999.

Werner, Carol M., and Leslie A. Baxter. "Temporal Qualities of Relationships: Organismic, Transactional, and Dialectical Views." *Handbook of Interpersonal Communication.* Ed. Mark L. Knapp and Gerald R. Miller. Thousand Oaks, CA: Sage, 1994. 323–79.

Wheeless, Lawrence R., Robert Barraclough, and Robert Stewart. "Compliance-Gaining and Power in Persuasion." *Communication Yearbook 7.* Ed. R. N. Bostrom. Beverly Hills, CA: Sage, 1983. 105–45.

Whisman, M. A., and N. S. Jacobson. "Power, Marital Satisfaction, and Response to Marital Therapy." *Journal of Family Psychology* 4 (1990): 202–12.

Wilmot, William W., and Joyce L. Hocker. *Interpersonal Conflict.* New York: McGraw-Hill, 2000.

Winslade, J., and G. Monk. *Narrative Mediation: A New Approach to Conflict Resolution.* San Francisco: Jossey-Bass, 2000.

Yankelovich, D. *The Magic of Dialogue: Transforming Conflict into Cooperation.* New York: Simon and Schuster, 1999.

Yosie T. F., and T. D. Herbst. *Using Stakeholder Processes in Environmental Decisionmaking: An Evaluation of Lessons Learned, Key Issues, and Future Challenges.* Washington, DC: Rudder Finn Washington and ICF Inc., 1998.

Index